An Untenable Fragrance of Violets

A Trilogy

❧

Lynne Heffner Ferrante

BOOK I
INNOCENCE LOST

An Untenable Fragrance of Violets
A Trilogy

Book I – Loss of Innocence

...and coming soon:

Book II - Unintended Circumstances

Book III – Once More Unto the Breach

Book IV – A Walk in the Woods
(The Rest of the Story)

...also

The Art of Lynne Heffner Ferrante

ISBN: 1453804439

ISBN-13: 9781453804438

Dedicated to my dear husband Joe Ferrante who has stood by me, supported me in all my endeavors, to whom I owe my very life; to my beloved mother, Sarah Appleman Addelston, to whom I owe more than my life; to my dear friend, teacher and mentor Hope Franzese, Dorothy Walmsley; to my children, Bruce David Heffner, Wendi Arlene Heffner, Caryn Jill Heffner Malchman, Andrew Todd Heffner, Kevin Seth Heffner, Tracy Beth Heffner Jones, Lynne Elise Cortes Calabrese whose story this also is, and to all my adored grandchildren, Joshua, Daniel, Noah, Matthew, Amanda, T.J., Sara, Christopher, Kaeli, and Chloe.

Thanks to my editor Christine Giordano, Linda Coleman, Eileen Moskowitz, Patra Apatovsky, Madeline Toor, Tina Curran...and especially to Erika Duncan and HerStory who coaxed, prodded, guided and encouraged me relentlessly and who are directly responsible for me completing this monumental task.

"Forgiveness is the fragrance the violet leaves on the heel that crushed it." ...*Mark Twain*

"So many of the conscious and unconscious ways men and women treat each other have to do with romantic and sexual fantasies that are deeply engrained not just in society but in literature. The women's movement may manage to clean up the mess in society, but I don't know if it can ever clean up the mess in our minds." ...*Nora Ephron, born May 19, 1942*

Introduction

The Ungraspable, Uncomfortable, Inconceivable, Unacceptable, Ineffable, *Untenable Fragrance of Violets*...the big question is, what are the nature and demands of forgiveness, and how do you know who must forgive whom, and when, and how?

...If you're going to write your memoirs, or a novel based on your life, my advice to you is to get going, write it, and finish this thing as quickly as you are able. If you let the thing drag on year by year, you will run into the same conundrum that has been haunting me forever, a collection of cartons filled with manuscripts and rewrites and inconceivably a final story containing thousands of pages that ultimately becomes a series of books.

I keep on writing as the world moves onward, replete with meteorological, economic, political, societal changes creating a background noise, a magnetic force that envelopes, encompasses, consumes the rest. My Taurean spirit makes me strong and stubborn; my Gemini rising star infuses me with creative flow. No one can do battle with these two forces, together, they can master the universe. The problem is that I am a veritable chrysalis. Every moment I live is a learning growing experience; a chrysalis is "anything in the process of growing or changing...". I once named an art gallery "Chrysalis".

I am told that I need to choose a theme to focus on. Less is more, everyone says, a mantra I have avoided all of my adult life. I am a more is more kind of person, there is no escaping this truth. It is evident in my art, in my home, in my garden. In my family. In the entirety of my life.

My art, my studio, my gallery, even my home have been critiqued by some as worthless, untenable, because they are so filled, so encrusted with stuff. And yet, I have been successful. I have persevered, continued with art forms that give me great pleasure, and fought the mighty dragon of minimalism, and managed to survive in the art world. I continue to ask myself, did Jackson Pollack limit his drips and splatters to create a painting with 'less'. Did de Kooning put just a few forms, colors, slashes or lines less in his complex and evocative paintings? Was Kandinsky ever asked to remove just a few items, shapes, squiggles? My East Hampton mentor Alfonso Ossorio, did he limit the encrustation of assorted flotsam and jetsam, jewels, eyeballs etcetera, etcetera in his rich assemblages? And haven't I been compared to Ossorio in at least three periodical critiques (and once to Louise Nevelson's compilations of wood scraps and spindles)?

So here's the thing. I have this vision of my story as it is; my last and most important work of art that is comprised of all the details of my life, colored, textured cross threads woven into the woof and warp of a carefully constructed rich complex tapestry. I have been rereading my favorite authors, and note that their vocabularies are rich with hyperbole. What do I do? Yeah, I know, show it, don't tell it. Where indeed does that leave that age old story telling technique called "narrative". Storytellers sat around fires since the beginning of mankind *telling* stories. I'm sure they added detail, and some were probably better than other in spinning evocative simile and metaphor, but the stories were told none the less. This is just me, bitching, because if they are right, I will have to completely rewrite that huge accumulation of forty years' endeavor.

I don't have one simple story, a memory of a period in time, a problem solved. I cannot write a simple memoir; what I have is a saga. The very fact of the interaction, the conflict between all of these disparate elements is the heart and soul of the story, its life force. What it really appears to be is an anthology of interwoven novellas, essays, thoughts, memories... Maybe it will eventually be unreadable, a tree in a forest that fell, sound and motion that no one was there to experience; a huge, deep infinite, tangled forest, too many trees, a situation that makes exploration impossible, a lengthy and cumbersome tome. Does this matter? As long as it is recorded, I can rest easy. One friend has told me I must decide whether I want to write an all encompassing story for my own personal satisfaction or a more marketable endeavor for popular consumption. I ask myself if these are mutually exclusive.

So where *do* I begin? With love, faith, marriage, children, art, law, loss, recovery? Therein lies the rub. Begin at the beginning, a little voice whispers in my head. It's only logical.

But the entire chronicle is written, already, has become so lengthy that it has been divided into three separate books.

Now, having reached the entrance to my eighth decade, it seems as good a place as any to finally end the tale, for chances are, I won't be here to update those last few chapters, and all that is going to be resolved, already is, and that which won't be, will not change. Ultimately I begin today, in 2009, introduce myself at this moment in time without giving away the story, and then continue with the source of all adversity, the first domino that falls against all the others, one by one, until they are all knocked down, lying on the ground, motionless.

Lynne Heffner Ferrante

Prelude

As I slip in and out of the warm fuzz, barely able to identify the odd shapes and colors that slide back and forth in front of my eyes, I whisper faintly, please, let me have my baby, bring my baby to me... and fade out again.

I hold the tiny blanket swathed creature naturally in the crook of my arm, as though he has always been here in this custom fitted cradle. I kiss the fuzzy top of his pungent infant head, noting the slight point resulting from the force of the expulsion of his birth. I inhale deeply, the ineffable musky clean baby odor of his skin. I sigh. I have waited so long; all of my life. I reach with one hand for the pastels and sketch pad on the bedside table always within my reach; it is second nature to me. I balance the soft, warm fragrant package and begin a drawing of that darling face. I give the process, the impulse, no conscious thought. Within a few years more, I have piles of them, sketches of the different children at different phases, starting with each one mere moments after birth. I adjust the blankets; shift the position of the precious bundle, somehow instinctively aware of just what to do. I am so comfortable with this mama baby thing, I think to myself, as I feel myself drifting again...

Now, I sit in the soft damp sweetly smelling grass, the little ones sprawled across the thick woven plaid blanket that my mother brought back from her last European voyage during her summer vacation, this one to Scotland. The children are still carefully dressed against the early spring weather, but the sun presses warmly on their chubby bodies, heating their skin and their soft hair. They will turn platinum blond, again, this summer, I think, as I arrange their picnic lunch, pb&j and bologna, American cheese...bananas and chocolate chip cookies; all of the gourmet necessities of the day. Apple slices and carrot sticks in a plastic container; piled haphazardly on the blanket, a small collection of library books to read to them. In the distance, other children play on the playground equipment. I watch them cavort on monkey bars and envision painting a portrait of them in this setting, climbing and clamoring; hanging upside down arms akimbo, laughing and screaming. I promise them that they will have the chance to swing before they leave, although swings have never been my personal favorite. I breathe deeply again of the fresh spring air, and feel a great joy. What more can anyone want in life, I think, but my eyes are beginning to feel sticky and dry, and I am having trouble keeping them open, and I drift off...

The older ones dig and dig like crazy, in the hot sand, until they have a large crater-like area. The little ones play with brightly colored plastic shovels and assorted sand toys, *occasionally returning from a short jaunt to the nearby surf with a shell or pail full of salty water, to pour over the sifting sand, and carefully sculpt their creations. I watch them with a great happiness, my eyes coveting their lithe browned bodies and adoring their flyaway white blonde hair. Ready, Mom, the oldest says softly, a glow of adoration cloaking his serious face, beaming at me as he helps me fit my belly, huge with child again, into the big sand pit. Now you can lie on your stomach, he laughs infectiously, and the others join him. It is a big joke, this clumsy and immobile whale-like mommy, usually slender and perpetually active. I feel so comfortable that I wish I could stay here for whatever short time I have left till the birth, a giant turtle protecting its eggs in the hot sand. I place my chin on my folded hands, and watch my beloved children do their summer beach things, racing in and out of the surf, digging and building. I adore their serious faces that can in a moment open into wide laughter and raucous giggles. I adore their perfect limbs and bodies, toasted now to a golden tan. I am indeed, blessed. I feel myself drifting as the heat of the sun beats down on my motionless body, lulling me. I must keep watching them, I think, I cannot fall asleep...*

They run through the drifts of brilliantly colored leaves, whooping and hollering with joy. What a marvelous day! The sun beats strongly, but without the great heat of summer, and the air is sweet with fall aromas, dying leaves, fading flowers, cooking, barbecuing meat. Everywhere, there is color, magenta, red, orange, yellow, azure blue of sky and golden green of grass. All of us, mother and children come together in the midst of a clearing in the wooded park, and our bodies crush one another in a great giggling hug. Love you Mommy, they all scream, and love you babies, I answer smiling widely, wanting to say more, but choking on the emotion of my love for them, and needing to wipe away the crushed leaf dust and fine sand that whirls into my face with the autumn breeze, making me blink, encrusting and closing my eyes. Everything swirls with the breeze, and I wonder where I am.

Soon, I feel myself lying down, and think that I must have fallen in the midst of our raucous celebration of life and love, but moving my fingers tentatively in the area around my body, I feel the tight slick crispness of hospital sheets, smell the clean antiseptic odor of hospital, and realize that I must have just had my baby. I can sense the painful hardness of full breasts. I feel myself grinning from ear to ear, and once again, ask the moving room shadows for my child.

No, answers the nurse gently, her crisp whiteness beginning to come into focus, I cannot bring you your baby. There is no baby, she sighs apologetically. You are mistaken about that.

But you don't understand, I say, I need to see my baby, I want my baby. Hot tears are forming behind my eyes, and suddenly begin flowing profusely, uncontrollably cascading down my face, and I feel my chest and intestines constrict, and my heart begins that familiar pounding, and I feel once again that incredible pain of incomprehensible never-ending loss.

My babies, I sob. I want my babies. Please, I plead from the depths of my soul, someone, get me my babies.

The Present Day

CHAPTER 1

Gears mesh, wheels turn. This roller coaster ride that is my life is accelerating, hurtling mindlessly through time and space. Time *itself* is escalating more and more rapidly in every area of my existence; minutes, hours, days, weeks, months, march increasingly more quickly to the tick tick ticking clock. Seasons, too, arrive and end with rapid fire speed.

In the remarkable year of 2009 winter which *always* seems eternal draws to a close before I can get my usual proper rant against it into full throttle. Spring is born yet again kicking and screaming, dripping wet. Storms, wind, and rain; *après moi le deluge,* says Winter grinning sardonically, fading into the distance. I breathe deeply and prepare to brave this season as I have survived the turmoil that is my entire life, but I am stunningly aware that a landmark birthday is drawing rapidly closer.

I awaken on this momentous morning feeling no different from any other day. Seventy I guess is the new thirty-nine. But for the creeping decay and degeneration of bone and muscle, non-responsive body parts and the inevitable, inescapable slowing down, I am the same person that I have always been. True, I have this faintly emerging sense that I am wiser, but I am still essentially alone, still driven, still defensive. How can I have lost six children, be repeatedly compelled to defend myself against outrageous allegations, without becoming defensive? I refuse to think about all that on this day...

The thing is, it's impossible to accept. I cannot be seventy years old. I must be caught between blips in the time/space continuum; it's obviously just one more grand conspiracy to deal with. My clearly skewed internal messaging unit tells me that I am thirty-five or thereabouts. My bathroom mirror tells me that my face is the same, hazel eyes, even features, surrounded by curly auburn-brown hair. I am not *that* decrepit, not *that* fat. I still look normal, almost, if I squint at my image. No. I refuse to accept it. I am obliged to make another one of my legendary dreaded signature declarations. If anyone believes, I proclaim to myself loudly, hopes that I will go gentle into that good night they are gravely mistaken.

The morning sun streams through my wide triple bedroom window, siphoned through highlighted squares of stacks and rows of mullions as I stretch my body luxuriously preparing to arise; get ready for an entire day as it slowly begins to unfold hopefully before me. My mind meanders lazily as cascading representations of dreams and fantasies emulsified in gathering dust motes drift by in continuous recombinant images on sliding shafts of sunlight. They glide over the vari-colored flowers that cover every chair, pillow, and bedcover, bounce off my art that covers every wall; flowers, combinations of multiples of design and pigment are my trademarks. Everything in my life is dictated by the irrepressible artist that dwells inside me. It is who I am, a magnetic life force that pulls imagery to it, demands to be surrounded by, enveloped in pattern and texture and color.

Usually I kind of run or almost skip. I never just walk but today I feel a peculiar disconnect and pace around the house. I am dressed now in my usual jeans and sweatshirt, socks and sneakers, not the couture of an old lady (not wearing purple yet) ready for another fruitful day in my studio. I glance around me as I progress, feeling my surroundings, enveloped by them, one with them; their creation, their very existence is part and parcel of my art, is intrinsic to my being. I relish all the color and texture, the expanse of terra cotta tiles that make up most of the floor as background, the remaining floor dark walnut planks; I am always explicitly aware of the rest of the rich colorful tile work and art, the cedar covered walls and heavy distressed cedar beams, the view through banks of French doors of wide gardens, pool, pond, and haphazard blue stone of the patio. I am consumed with that which is visual; the entire thrust of my being revolves around the filling of that eternal blank canvas that is my reality. I am the artisan who is responsible for the actual plan and labor for all of this; the design of the house itself, the creation and installation of tile and grout, the laying of wood planks, the digging of ponds, the planting of trees and bushes and flowers.

But I am studiously preoccupied, avoiding that elephant in the middle of the room, ignoring that-which-I-am-forbidden-to-think-about, thoughtlessly, compulsively picking objects up and putting them down; pieces of collections, ceramic frogs and turtles, tea pots and cookie jar lids, candlesticks, plates and vases, multiples of family photographs showing laughing children in a wild variety of small disparate frames. A faint tinkle of that laughter follows as I walk around the room in a kind of daze, switch on every single one of my abundant Tiffany lamps one by one. Illuminated colored glass is for me one of the necessities of life that attempts to satisfy that persistent uncontrollable need for color and pattern; another dimension is created to an elaborate stage set for the melodrama that is my life. Appraisal of the abundance of exotic patterns and glowing hues, a thrilling enough activity in ordinary times is at this moment merely a mindless pursuit that aspires merely to camouflage an unfathomable void. From the corner of one eye I am able to see the waterfall and stream flowing to the pond itself, hear the soft soothing burbling of the water, carefully and deliberately designed to disguise the assault of the outside world.

The studio sings its siren song, calling me to work, but round and round, concentrating on avoiding conscious thought I circle the dining room obsessively staring with no deliberation at all at the table, which is set as usual, for company. Maybe one of the children will suddenly arrive for a surprise visit. You never know. My eyes fondly caress a polyglot collection of damask floral cloth and round hemp placemats, teal ceramic chargers from the household exchange, so-called (the town dump), and handcrafted one of-a-kind dishes from that exalted mercantile establishment Home Goods, purchased in a moment of madness, absurdly placed next to hand painted stemware reclaimed also during dumpster diving. The bulk of my rich bounty and collections are foundlings. I am ready, hopeful for any visit, prepared to serve dinner on a moment's notice, to anyone whom I love, indeed to any visitor. Come, eat, says my mother, smiling. *Essen, essen*, repeats my grandmother. *Ven a comer, Mange, mange*, echo other voices floating enticingly, invisibly in the wide airy expanse of my familiar inner sanctum. In my complex multi-layered world, the offering of sustenance is the ultimate commemoration of love. There is a coat of dust on everything.

So where is my celebration? Where are my seven children? They are still children to me, although my oldest son, Bruce, will be fifty years old, himself, this year. Lynnie, my youngest, will be thirty-eight. We used to be so close. I don't know where it all went; time, and love, and life.

There has been no word of any visit planned, not even the faintest hint of the surprise party I am shamelessly craving. I catch my breath, inhale deeply, and doggedly assume control. I refuse to think about it, whine about it, waste time on self-pity. A magnetic force draws me slowly though my long galley kitchen to its end, following the warm cadences of terra cotta, surrounded by all that jazz, color and the carefully displayed collections, my art, to the French door between the laundry room and cellar door and I wander finally into my studio. I lose myself in busy work, dusting and gluing and priming and varnishing, which gently, inevitably, morphs into creation; placing curious pieces of flotsam, beads, odds and ends of evocative remnants and tiny figurines, rusty metal scraps on weathered boards, restlessly changing course, suddenly adding color to flowers and landscapes, glazing, scrumbling color over almost completed surfaces. I am marching to the strains of an unheard symphony. I can see my hands, so like my mother's, slender, still smooth and supple, dexterous, decrying the threats of age and arthritis, as they deftly obey the commands of my mind. This is my tried and true modus operandi.

... I reach with one hand for the pastels and sketch pad on the bedside table always within my reach; it is second nature to me. I balance the soft, warm fragrant package that is my infant son and begin a drawing of that darling face...

My art; this is, has always been, my miracle balm, solace for every major or minor failure or disappointment. Of late, I fill any vacuum of time or space with my writing. This is a natural evolution because I am eternally obsessive about producing art, something to look at, to hold in my hand, to read; vessels to contain angst and transform it into meaningful substance, something tangible, something that will outlive me, proof of life.

... I hold the tiny blanket-swathed creature naturally in the crook of my arm, as though he has always been here in this custom-fitted cradle. I kiss the fuzzy top of his sweet head ...

All at once I feel the angry rush of blood to my head, burning my cheeks. *Why should I need to prove anything at all?* I ask the world at large. I am who I am, my own validation should prevail. I am, woman, wife, mother, artist, sculptor, homemaker, lover, friend, gardener, cook, nurturer, sister, advocate, activist, fighter, writer; Mother. And I am of course, an integral part of a family. Yeah!

I forget for a moment, that everything in my family, my life, is different from the norm. I neglect for an instant to recall this family's history, our ultimate destination, arrived at with so little ease, and so much pain. That is why I awoke this morning with normal feelings in an abnormal world. Why would I at this late date expect anything at all from my children? Why do I still expend time and energy on this subject? And yet I think somehow that they must remember, at least this time. This year as I complete my seventh decade of life I wonder if I am unreasonable to believe this to be a landmark, a reason for festivity; an occasion to convene, to create a new memory to add to the collection. There are *so* many *good* memories, lost in the overwhelming deluge of the perfect storm. I sometimes wonder if these adult strangers have any recollections of our lives together, of their mother...at all.

... I sit in the soft damp sweetly smelling grass; the little ones sprawled across the thick woven plaid blanket that my mother brought back from her last European voyage. The children are still zealously dressed against the early spring weather, but the sun presses warmly on their chubby bodies, heating their skin and their soft hair ...

I have begun to apply gesso to a series of canvases reclaimed from the landfill, planning my next project, series of paintings, dipping my brush into the thick viscous white mixture, brushing back and forth, covering exposed areas of someone else's truth and invention methodically, mindlessly, as thoughts continue to invade my consciousness... In the beginning, it wasn't like this. Marginalization happens slowly and stealthily; alienation is a gradual thing. For my part there is no screaming and banging of fists and household items, no ranting and raving, no tears or recriminations, mostly. This is not an absence of emotion, an inability to feel. How many of my loving, sincere and abject invitations and pleas have ended in rejection over time? After all these years there is no mourning; that has all been done already. Acceptance is a necessary element of survival, life continues in its familiar vacuum. I move through it with accustomed obedience, an automaton...*Mostly*.

I strive to pretend that it doesn't matter. I laugh about it, make light of it but secretly crave the whole deal, the entire enchilada. I want the party, the presents, the cards, the flowers, the attention; the expressions of love. For a moment, having finally arrived, in my head at least, at a new and acclaimed destination called normalcy in this journey that is my life, I try to convince myself that I deserve the same rewards that everyone else receives, but I am that fallen tree that no one has heard fall.

... They run through the drifts of brilliantly colored leaves, whooping and hollering with joy. What a marvelous day! The sun beats strongly, and the air is sweet with fall aromas. Everywhere, there is color. We come together in the midst of a clearing in the wooded park, and our bodies crush one another in a great giggling hug. Love you mommy, they all scream, and, love you babies ...

What would my mother say about the state of affairs between me and the kids, today, if she were here? I feel her sitting next to me, touching my warm hand with her cool one. See her lovely serene aged face, her short gray curls, her small compact well dressed and always well assembled and accessorized body. Call them, be the bigger person, she says, stroking the back of my hand gently. But I am always the bigger person; I am tired of being the bigger person. I want to be the loved person, the wanted person. You are wanted, she insists, I am always here for you. But I know that, and the truth is it is the children that I am wanting. Still, I am aware peripherally of a figure sitting there by my side, I can feel her presence, but when I turn my head, there is no one there. I am alone. I want *my* mother back; I whine, petulantly, a question mark in there somewhere, feeling a great dark hollow in my chest and stomach. Why do my children dismiss theirs? How has this happened?

A huge wicker basket painted white is overflowing with purple irises, assorted gladioli, red and pink and orange roses, white daisies, sunflowers, chrysanthemums and delphiniums, yellow and blue, and much more, all my mother's favorites. Tucked into the arrangement are giant wooden and stainless steel kitchen implements, spoons and spatulas and forks and oddities. Mom, Grandma, who loves anything to do with cooking, will be pleased. I hope. As ever, I want to please her. Expectation is a tangible essence, hanging thickly in the air. Although all seven kids are along on this Mother's Day voyage to Kew Gardens Hills, in the borough of Queens, only three are visible in the wide rear seat, since the basket sits across their laps, the three middle ones, Wendi, Caryn and Andrew, whose small heads barely clear the masses of flowers. Their foreheads and hair are all that can be seen. Bruce sits in the front, with me, holding baby Lynnie on his lap, and Tracy squeezes between Andrew and the car door. She holds a giant fudge frosted chocolate cake that we baked this morning, on her lap, in a round Tupperware container with a green bottom, resting her small chin on the top, her face framed by masses of ringlets, her dark eyes wide and glowing. Kevin sits directly behind me, one thumb in his mouth, index finger curled around his nose the other holding my long wavy auburn hair; twirling, twirling. He removes the thumb from his mouth for the moment. Are we here yet, asks Kevin, and we all laugh; it is an old familiar family joke. Here is exactly where we are, is the answering chorus. The thumb goes back to its warm moist home; a faint glimmer of a self-satisfied grin can be discerned behind Kevin's fist.

We are bringing everything except the actual food. On this occasion, although she is the guest of honor, Grandma insists on providing the important cuisine, she will not take no for an answer, she will not be done out of her joy of cooking, her obsession with the preparation of life-sustaining nourishment, the profound and solemn application of love. We can look forward to all our favorites, noodle soup, pot roast, roasted chicken, roast potatoes, sweet potatoes, mashed potatoes and rice, chopped liver, gefilte fish, salad, three kinds of vegetable, rye bread, crescent rolls, and muffins, and heaven only knows what else. Grandma doesn't skimp. You never know, she always says, you wouldn't want to run out of food. Better there should be a little extra, than not enough. So she makes something else, again, maybe some fried chicken, it shouldn't be a total loss; leftovers will go into sandwiches and packages for the road, with some fruit for digestion, for us to eat on the long way home, we shouldn't starve during the long drive. We are all at least I am, salivating in expectation. The word skimp does not exist in her lexicon, is anathema to her world.

There is a tiny silent moment. Only a moment and small voices intrude on the silence. Grandma is going to love this, whispers one of the kids, softly. I love Mother's Day, says Caryn, and I love Grandma. And I love you too, Mom. Me too, says a small voice from somewhere under the basket, followed by a chorus of echoes. In these days I am very loved, very wanted.

CHAPTER 2

It is normal to need to be the wanted person. I recall that for as long as I can remember, I have wanted to be wanted. Maybe that is the problem. That is why I fall back into work. Wanted is not what I am feeling, right now. But I know the cure for this malady, not-wanted-ness.

Busy work will help to build that protective wall that thwarts the assault of discontent. I have manically gessoed everything in sight, including some reclaimed frames for some future use or other, but all is not lost, there is always some other labor to attend to. I know that in addition to prep-work for different art forms, organization of this madness that is my home and studio is an integral part of the process.

I begin as usual with a thorough studio housecleaning, mindless involvement with the detritus of the resources of creation that leads inevitably to new focus, new themes, art forms, and projects. There is plenty to rummage through; I never reach the bottom. The studio is crammed full of my art, of work in progress, of piles and receptacles full of supplies and tools; cartons of papers and memorabilia, pages and pages of manuscript. Jars filled with tiny fragments of multi-patterned dish shards called *tesserae* have taken over of late, necessities for my latest art form of choice, mosaics. The walls are covered, every square inch, with art, paintings, etchings, assemblages, and dangerously overloaded shelves. Rifling through this amalgam of stuff in the name of organization touches creative nerves, opens doorways to innovation and inspiration. Interesting things are wont to happen. New works are spawned. Problems disappear and nightmares, dreams and wishes are forgotten. My old mentor sublimation is the desired and easily achieved consequence.

I blink back tears that threaten to overflow my eyelids, sense face muscles tightening into that constant mask of sadness, struggle to swallow past the accustomed lump growing in my throat. My skinny twelve-year-old body is folded tightly, protectively around itself, a defenseless crumpled mound. The echoes of shouts and screams originating in the kitchen inhabited by my battling parents are monumental, indeed, this time. My only thought is to escape them, hide from the current Donnybrook assaulting my ears and my awareness. Some day, I think, I will have children and no matter what happens they will never have to experience this pain and terror. I disappear into my room and paint and paint and paint and paint, blocking out the fear and pain from my entire being. As if I can lose myself completely in this other world, this world of mindless creation, apart and safe from

11

the unacceptable and agonizing real one; slowly, ultimately, my escape world becomes my reality.

Everything in my life is filtered through a narrowly constructed context of art. Everything is a potential painting. I recall with a stab of chagrin that I have frequently been told pejoratively by those who are not particularly fans of mine, with no lack of derision, that I have linseed oil and Dammar varnish running through my veins where others have blood, that I am unable to see past my easel, although it has served me so well for so many years as metaphorical crutch and makeshift shelter. It is as necessary to my existence as milk to an infant. All I need for salvation is a board or a canvas, sitting on my easel, tubes of paint, a basket of papers and stuff to collage and glue.

I can hide behind a canvas. I can forget about not being wanted, when I am immersed in the filling of a pristine white surface. I am thrilled in retrospect that I constructed so many canvases at the end of last season, because now they, along with the newly prepared foundling ones, are ready to be covered with interpretations of sketches and notes recorded in my journal in the depths of winter dreariness while I hide under deep soft cushioning quilts listening to music, Singers and Swing, ... *that old black magic has me in its spell, if that's not enough, it will have to do, until the real thing comes along, sometimes I wonder how I spend the lonely night, dreaming;* watching old movies...

I am safe in this familiar place. Just last November as the last leaves fell and the cold began creeping into the days, limiting my ability to work outside at my giant summer easel, a jumble of crossed two by fours and hinges, a rain gutter and pail attached to the bottom on a slight angle to catch the extra paint and save it, I completed a series of six foot square paintings, poured color, like Paul Jenkins or Morris Lewis. I have left my signature impressionist floral landscape and its natural progeny and moved on. Now, I am driven to try a new approach, thick color, smeared and globbed and troweled and glazed and scrumbled, generous intensely tinted pigment dragged over more chunky hue. And I am bombarded continually with other new ideas. A series of giant rock and canyon semi abstracts, huge heavily textured collages of multicolored patterned fabric scraps, strongly stylized portraits of children and grandchildren. And I hear a faint melodious whisper, *I'll be seeing you in all the old familiar places that this heart of mine embraces, all night through...*

My day dreams are full of them. I am hoping that they will be shocking and sensual. I am busy with it all. Maybe, I will dig out that old series of paintings I started so many years ago, the ones that illustrate the story of my life, executed in my trademark impressionist expressionist approach, each reminiscent of one of my favorite masters, Bonnard, Renoir, Cezanne, VanGogh, Gauguin, Matisse,

Chagall. They have lain unfinished for too long now. It would be a good thing to complete them. Maybe I will finally finish writing the story, also.

Busy, busy, busy.

That thought that is forbidden, sublimated, avoided; that fearful joyous momentous thought, carefully eluded for a piece of time, finally emerges from the depths of me, takes a deep breath, gathers up a huge bunch of courage, and tiptoes on tiny cat feet across my mind:

Will anyone call to say Happy Birthday, Mom?

CHAPTER 3

I wander again to the backyard worktable to sort bits of colored glass and *tesserae*, jars of pigment, pieces of patterned paper and exotic foreign language newsprint, odds and ends of strangely shaped wood scraps, rescued orphan knick knacks, canvases and frames, planning even more new projects, keeping busy refusing to think about anything, pretending again, still, to forget what day it is. I need to lose myself in my work.

I have set up a large worktable under a cantilevered umbrella in that small corner tucked between my barn and the studio, bordered by a hedgerow of privet to hide the mess from neighbors and approaching visitors, where I can smash crockery that I have been accumulating all winter. Smashing dishes is truly therapeutic when demons descend and memories attack. Could that be why I have so extensive a collection? There are enough packed jars and other receptacles to fill a decently sized library. I'm talking about large rooms with wall to wall, floor to ceiling shelves. The sheer volume of *tesserae*-filled jars is bizarre, frightening. If I live to be three hundred and seventy years old, I think, I will never use up all this stuff. But I continue collecting and smashing anyway. Why do I do this? Why is everything I do always couched in groups, series, multiples, and masses?

We make our way over to the huge superstructure that is the earsplittingly noisy and frightening elevated train system, the 177th Street Elevated, climb the high, deep, concrete and steel stairs to the elevated platform, and wait for our train. I shrink in terror from the platform edge, and cringe when I hear the loud, raucous train approaching. Once aboard, we sway from side to side as we race across the borough of the Bronx, and glide finally downward into the stifling black tunnel that is New York City at its best. Manhattan, Downtown; we live Uptown, in the Bronx. We swerve and rock and bump our way across the Bronx until we enter the underground system somewhere approaching Manhattan where we now bounce and roll some more until with damp and shaken marrow, we arrive at our destination. I sit on the highly varnished woven wicker seats, my legs dangling, feet barely above the floor, picking the perpetually regenerating scabs on my knees, and wish myself anywhere but here. My natural clumsy tomboy self dreads the tutu-ed humiliation that awaits me in ballet class; my soul dreads the discordant errors that seem impossible to avoid when my banana bunch hands refuse to find the proper mellifluous sequence of piano keys. To my ears, I butcher Prelude, Concerto, and Symphony alike with equal opportunity destruction, and yet my mother glistens and glows with pride when I can be cajoled and sometimes bullied to play the piano for company or in concert. There is an endlessly present pressure for me to excel, to compete with the extraordinariness that surrounds me.

My mother is, in our family circle, known as a mensch, *a* balabusta, *a prodigious woman of many talents, amazing energy. Today, she takes her educator persona and her sad-faced offspring on an expedition of higher learning. In the early 1940s, as war still rages in the European theater where my father is stationed, my mother dresses me in what I recall as my Saturday trip-to-the-city uniform. A red felt roller hat covers my once curly now suddenly stick straight permed and overdressed, for a five-year-old child, hair, matches my red chinchilla coat purchased at Russeks of 39th Street on sale; my hand-tailored by Mom coral, orchid and teal plaid, copied from something she has seen at Saks Fifth Avenue, taffeta and velvet dress, crisp white knee socks that refuse to cling to my narrow calves, and my treasured black patent leather shoes, in whose surfaces I can clearly see my reflection.*

I am easily reconstructed but it takes some time for Mom to put herself together into that perfect bandbox state of being, and she is nothing if not efficient. I always watch her ministrations to face and fashion with awe. To this day I have never been able to duplicate or come close to that elegant Vogue *look, no matter how I try. She is the quintessential stylish lady of the world, as presented by the most highly revered woman's fashion magazines,* Vogue, Harper's Bazaar, *which she voraciously devours. Beneath her perfectly fitted two-piece suit, basis for the entire svelte look, is—what is called in these days—a* garment; *a rigid elastic and rubber concoction of underwear that smoothes and constrains flesh that is not on board with the agenda of the day. Gone is the bra-less mini-skirted free and easy flapper of a few short years ago, pre-Great Depression, pre-war. No longer is her lovely face framed by that helmet of wild curls, every hair of her blond pompadoured upsweep is in place. She sports another of her many matched suites of bejeweled costume necklace, earrings. The ever present color-coordinated patterned silk scarf twirls softly around her neck and drapes across her collar and over her shoulder, secured as usual by a pin from the suite. My Mom is not only beautiful, stunning, she is perfect. She is a movie star. This is, I know, the gold standard. I feel shabby and worthless next to her. And although I adore her, I would rather be anywhere else than with her on this despised and very familiar voyage.*

We leave as early as possible in the morning, after a suitably nourishing breakfast of pancakes fashioned into cartoon images, Donald Duck, Mickey Mouse, Dumbo, bunnies,

14

cats and dogs, to please me, or French toast cut with cookie cutters, drenched in jelly and syrup, creativity in everything she touches, an elaborate gesture of her love, in continuing family tradition of food as love, a reminder that to be creative is a way of, an intricate part of, the meaning of life.

I lope along picking at my recalcitrant socks which aspire to locate under my arches deep in my shiny shoes trying to keep up with her, skipping and hopping, roller hat bouncing, straining the elastic that is tucked under my chin. She always has our itinerary planned right down to the last detail, and every moment is carefully articulated and scheduled. I know this because she explains it all to me when we are spending intimate mother-daughter time together sewing, styling hair and painting nails, cooking and baking. Saturday is the only time she has to accomplish her ambitious goals, because she needs Sunday to grade the increasingly regenerating piles of papers for her English classes. Although I loathe all this organizing, I fall automatically into her habit, and it persists throughout my own life.

Every morning she travels cross Bronx by crowded noxious bus, hanging onto leather straps to keep from falling against her fellow commuters although there is little chance of that given the sardine like packing together of passengers. She struggles gamely to reach the East Bronx school where she teaches. She is a dedicated teacher, who loves her work, but who suffers through an ongoing love/hate relationship with the complicated policies, relationships and political atmosphere of the New York City school system until the day she retires. She is as poor a politician as my father is genius. He is the one with the practiced poker face, the attorney's silver tongue, I have heard.

But at this time, my father has still not returned from his stint in the European theater during the horrific sequel to the war to end all wars. We girls are on our own. And Mom, the quintessential educator, will not be stopped from doing her thing. Her only child, that would be me, will have access to the best and most extensive of cultural education, access to every possible opportunity that an educated cultural life can provide. I am not convinced of this, of the reason or value of it, and I resist gamely. In my mind, I am roller skating up and down the macadam pathways of our apartment house development, avoiding the heavy chained fence that protects the forbidden green lawn; I am pushing doll carriages with my friend Ruthie, playing the proud mama, tending to my carefully appointed baby dolls, practicing for a later day; and other Saturday occupations of childhood that are left there in the real world, left behind tantalizing, just out of my reach.

What do I understand of first generation American thinking and goals, educate your children, give them every opportunity to succeed? Provide them with everything that you do not have, and want with all your heart and soul and are powerless to obtain for you? My mother has the education, I will acquire that plus all of the embellishment, fulfill all of her dreams. In her perfect world, I will obtain the security she prizes by becoming a teacher, just like her, in addition to those dreams. She has it all planned. My head spins; I am assailed by a moment of pure terror.

15

When I am small and still have those fat golden sausage curls, she tells me longingly it seems that I am the next Shirley Temple. Later, there is a new chant. You look just like Margaret O'Brien, she qvells, pulling at my skirt, patting my hair, you're going to be such a star. There is a strange sense of yearning in her voice. Part of our itinerary as far back as I can remember is the compulsory attendance at every child star movie that graces the silver screen. It gets so that the sight of America's little darlings and the sounds of their perky tinkling voices sends chills through me, embryonic feelings of inadequacy do battle in my chest and stomach. Envy and despair follow.

The more my parents praise me, the more they expect from me, the more I shrink into myself, until there is nothing left but an unheard cry for help.

You look just like a movie star, she says once more as though repetition will make it so as we march rapidly down Fifth Avenue. I struggle to keep up. I twist to look in the carefully designed and elaborately appointed Sacks window or Bests or some other, as we pass at a rapid clip, trying to keep up with Mom's determined sprint. The windows fly by. It is like looking at a landscape through a train window. What I see in disjointed spots of reflection separated by a succession of window frames is a plain faced, freckled, knobby-kneed straight-haired, despite Mom's frenzied attempts to the contrary, child, with big sad eyes, a rather desperate look, staring back at me.

At Christmas time she takes me on a grand tour of department store windows, the entire gamut fifty ninth street to fourteenth covering Fifth Avenue across to Second and I gaze with wonder at animated mannequins in splendid dazzling holiday attire involved with cherubs, elves, Santas and reindeer pulled sleds filled with toys and gaily wrapped sparkling packages and masses of darling animals; trains careening over intricate tracks and plethora of stars and moons in deep navy skies, everything covered with glitter and magic. On some frigid Saturday mornings she brings me to ice skate at Rockefeller Center in that small enclave deep down in this city canyon surrounded by immense office buildings, guarded over by the annual sixty or so foot glowing Christmas tree. I stumble gamely on bending ankles to make the obligatory rounds, a frigid smile pasted on my face, wiping my forever slowly dripping nose with clumsy mittened fingers and I am rewarded afterward for my efforts with a steaming cup of hot chocolate.

On Thanksgiving Day 1945 we charge through the massive roiling throngs to attend the Macy's Day Parade which has been cancelled for the war years and has finally returned and I delight at the giant inflated balloons, Mickey Mouse, Harold the Clown, Felix the Cat, and my favorite, the entire family, Mama, Papa and Baby; for moments I can even see beyond the crowds, become accustomed to the smell of damp overcoats and the rapidly intensifying lack of sensation in frozen limbs and nose.

On our other customary itinerary, once we arrive downtown, we begin the ritual dance. Her menu for the activities of the day reads like a Gilbert and Sullivan operatic anthology program. My focused and creative mother is the very model of a modern major general; she's got a little list, and they'll none of them be missed. It is the period of my life when I am being prepared for the cultural life; the day consists of long stunning tedious sessions listening to the Young People's Concerts, at Carnegie Hall, on 57th Street.

We lunch, my especially best part of the day at the Hamburger Train on 57th Street or Schraft's, on 5th Avenue and 46th Street or my real favorite, the Automat where I get to put nickels into a slot and spin a glass cage around to access my choice, and share a table with strangers. Schraft's milk served in long thick glassware bulbous at the top (the direct opposite of my grandmother's jelly jars to which I have grown accustomed) always seems to be lukish warm and thickish, with little floating bits of cream, which makes my stomach rebel. And the place itself is dark and crowded and filled with some other sort of unfamiliar people whose noses appear pinched tightly by invisible clothespins. Mom always cranes her neck this way and that, looking, looking, what is she looking for? The answer is celebrities, who frequent this place. Mom is enchanted by celebrity. At the Hamburger Train, I am excited as our lunch arrives at our place at the counter on a tiny railroad car following the tracks that edge the perimeter of the countertop. The day continues with my piano lessons, piano theory and creative composing in Julliard and in the Carnegie Hall building. Then my ballet and interpretative dance lessons at Dalcroze School of Music. I hold my breath as the brass accordion gate of the elevator closes us in followed by the slamming steel door and the clanking swaying of the stifling confining box. I feel my stomach plummet to my feet as the sudden motion leaves part of me behind, for a horrible moment, and my ears pop.

Friday afternoons after school I am brought to art classes at the MOMA (the Museum of Modern Art) for drawing and painting lessons. On alternate weeks when the Saturday morning concerts are not scheduled, I am ensconced in classes at the Art Students' League, also on 57th Street taught and surrounded by renowned artists of the day, Adoph Gottlieb, Hans Hofman, George Grosz, Franz Kline, Morris Lewis, figure drawing and water color. I will be educated in the varied tenets of the arts, damn it, if it is the last thing my mother does. With a helpless stoicism, I follow gamely along. I like this a bit better than the music stuff, or the marathon shopping tours that fill the Saturdays that are without lessons and concerts.

⤎⤏

Each shopping forage is a ritual unto itself; it rarely varies. Mom and I get off the train early enough to stop for our new ritual breakfast and by the time the first doors are open, we are right there at the head of the surging line. We begin with Bloomingdale's at 59th and Third, moving briskly through from the awesome top floor to the delicious first, systematically going up one aisle and down the other, missing nothing. Then adjusting our outer clothing for the weather in the real world outside fantasyland, march even more briskly pausing only to glance covetously into the occasionally super elegant side street emporium or clothing and accessory establishment. Onward troops to Fifth Avenue

17

and Saks, Bests; down the length of Fifth Avenue, zigging and zagging, back and forth across to catch the various cherished storefronts careful not to let the tiniest detail escape our collective devining eye. Picking up tempo, we cycle back across to Russeks at 39th Street where we search the bargain tables for treasures and Mommy is called Dahling and M'am. There, Mommy rests her feet while seated on a period piece probably Victorian or Queen Anne loveseat in the dress or coat or suit department playing a part of wealth and sophistication while the mute elegantly coiffed and coutured salesgirl brings out item after item for Mommy's approval, undeceived, a little taciturn and tightlipped but aware of her responsibilities. Mommy, haughty and affecting a pinched nose that tilts toward the ceiling is Katherine Hepburn preparing for an assignation with Clark Gable. I am barely a participant, serve as audience; I merely move along carried by Mommy's momentum, feeling sometimes as if I am an airborne accessory kite sort of creature, a mini-parade balloon flying gaily if unwillingly behind her on a whimsical breeze as she continues onward.

This game bores and embarrasses me, especially when Mommy reverts to cultural form and tries to get a price lowered for some minor imperfection. She may look the part of a high society matron, but her roots in the lower New York ghetto cannot help but surface. For some reason this makes me feel funny, makes me look down at my shiny patent leather Mary Janes and wish I were anywhere else, as a hot sensation creeps through my cheeks. My spirits lift when I see Mommy begin to look rested for I then know that the next stop is either the Automat or Chock Full of Nuts where a mere lunch becomes yet another adventure, another fantasy game. Food is always there to console. Then we charge again down Madison and across 34th where we brave the madding crowd at Orbach's, and from here on, things began to get more and more hectic. Saks 34th, Macy's, downtown to Fourteenth Street and Lane's, and finally, strength beginning to fade, the famous – da, tada dah, tada dah - S. Klein's on the Square where we two adventurers discover bargains and goodies of mind boggling magnitude. Mommy is in her glory, and even I bored and exhausted as I am get drawn into the excitement.

That the bargain hunt aspect of our activities resembles a brawl, is terribly demeaning, reaches a place of almost frantic frenzy is never fully reasonable to me; I join in the fracas because it is a part of a sacred bonding ritual, and after all, one of the few rites to become a major part of my life. I still pay homage to similar shrines because unwittingly I am programmed blindly to do so. Ultimately, I continue the ritual in translation, in an Odyssey through mélanges of garage and yard sales, and the quintessential bargain place for assemblage artists and others addicted to obsessive acquisition and short of pocket book, the village dump.

Finally, clutching great bags and boxes, spoils and plunder of wondrous delight and unheralded bargain, we stagger toward the subway praying for seats in a companionship created by our great mutual pain of well worn foot and cramped arm and hand. Inevitably, we sink gratefully onto the lacquered cane woven seats of the Subway car, happy to be finally heading homeward. Paralyzed with agony and exhaustion, we somehow arrive home, where with relief we begin to feel life returning to our extremities, prepare intimate gastronomic delights together. We bake awesome elaborate confections from Mommy's huge collection of newspaper or magazine recipe clippings. After checking and rechecking our purchases gleefully, now and then with disappointment, we withdraw to some sewing project or beauty regime. There is always so much to do. We are so close. There is so much time.

When we exhaust every ritual and activity on our usual itinerary, we retire to our shared bedroom for the night. I have a supply of storybooks, Bobbsey Twins, Pollyanna, Nancy Drew, The Secret Garden and The Little Princess, all of Louisa May Alcott, neatly hidden, awaiting escape into fantasyland. And when all else fails and sleep will not come, for the passageway into it is guarded by the goblins of ineffable fears, I fantasize my way into a never never land of imagined reality that slides me past the sentries of my subconscious. I am aided and abetted by my fevered imagination instigated first of feature cartoons and then movies, and later of actual theater productions.

Gradually Mom introduces me to real theater, off and on Broadway, beginning with musicals, Annie Get Your Gun, Brigadoon, Oklahoma, and of course South Pacific. She is obsessed with viewing everything that is brought to the stage. For now, the concerts take center stage.

ॐ

Mom is focused. She is always on a mission. Shopping trips, concerts and lessons, music and art; my mother marches along to a pounding determined rhythm that only she herself hears, pulling me along hopping and skipping frantically in her wake. Actually, the art thing is good; it touches something deep inside me.

*But the music of those Saturday morning Young Peoples' Concerts at Carnegie Hall plays inside my head, also, and make no mistake, I am beguiled by, drawn to the music. The wolf stalks Peter, bombom **bomp**, bombom **bomp, da, da, da, da, da, da DAH!** I am enchanted by* Peter and the Wolf. *Flutes delicately evoke dawn in the forest, and eyes closed, I am right there, lured into* The Hall of the Mountain King. *We the audience of kids, willing and unwilling, arrive at the huge ornate concert hall en masse, captive of our parents' dreams and plans, of enforced culturization; small children, restless disinterested; but our attention is seized in a moment and we catch our collective breath as a huge screen descends slowly from the curtained valance across the stage and the music begins, swiftly illustrated by a cartoon. It is* The Sorcerer's Apprentice *and it captivates me, enchants me, becomes a part of me; accompanies me for the rest of time. There it is again, I always cry out with joy; they have the Sorcerer's Apprentice, today.*

The music still sounds in my ears, that relentless marching cadence as the clever brooms carry their pails of water from the sorcerer's flooded lair. Again and again, faster and faster; I am mesmerized, there is something about the imagery, the frantic stick figure brooms with their bouncing flailing and hellishly splashing water pails, the race against time set to the strong compelling music of Tchaikovsky that becomes a part of me; This is a significant lesson for me to learn; it is the lure of the visual that reaches me. A tiny invisible creature bursts into being within me, smiling and wielding a baton, or is it a long paint brush? Follow me, it says, and skips and floats above me beckoning

I become aware of a subtle implicit promise, a reinforcement of that notion tickling my senses and hopes that there surely is some higher albeit momentarily unseen power to whom one may look for strength in what I am beginning to see as an overwhelmingly overbearing world.

Soon it becomes evident that I am never really alone. The call of my muse is as insistent as the relentless march of those maniacal ramrod brooms. The more the ideas come, the faster and more feverishly I work...the more and longer I work, the more the ideas come. Ultimately, my art becomes more real to me than my world. My world itself is always repugnant enough to send me rushing back to my work, until the work itself becomes the reality.

Years later, my babies arrive, it seems, as if planned and delivered by the sorcerer's apprentices, rapidly, one after the other; a series of stepping stones. There is nothing I won't do for them; my love for them overwhelms me. I look at them, one at a time or all in tandem, and an indescribable surge of emotion rises up from my soles until it reaches my throat where it sticks, choking me. Yet, I resist all pressure to follow with my mother's program. I offer my children, instead, the peace of mind and free will to seek their own goals, joys, and satisfactions. Maybe they feel deprived, who knows? But my mother is not deterred. That generation later, my mom takes my own children to see the classic Disney production, Fantasia, which contains the same Sorcerer's Apprentice imagery in one part of it. She happily applies her program seamlessly to the next generation, taking up the gap that I have created in my attempts to free my own children from what, in my own mind, I see as enforced tedium. With typical tunnel vision and selective blindness, I fail to see how it has all influenced me.

Sunrise, sunset, sunrise, sunset; swiftly go the years...I made a choice to avoid competition out of fear of failure. There were paths to take, and I chose the easy one, fell into the welcoming arms of a fantasy which had been programmed into my head and mind since as far back as I am able to remember...

Life continues, things change; my need becomes desperate as I struggle alone to fulfill my responsibilities. And struggle it is. Finally, a mother of six then seven, absent support or aid, I earn the money needed to cover their daily needs with my art, producing paintings like those relentless, focused brooms, one after the other, again and again. The canvases lean one upon the other in my bedroom turned studio, like a construction of playing cards, or dominoes.

I develop methods of mass production to satisfy my quota and keep the coffers filled, keep my babies safe and sound. I practice intense mental exercises to promote inventive thinking so that I will always have new ideas, in order to keep the mercurial market interested, the paintings moving and selling, my bank account solvent, and the larder stocked. I work like this for so many years, so intensely, that my method becomes a part of me and of my art itself. The medium becomes the message. While I agonize over lost time, lost direction, my lost art career trapped in the ongoing battle for survival I produce my work prodigiously, and develop many individual and combined media and methods, and accumulate a mammoth collection of works; experiments, and leftovers that have not sold; new ideas never implemented. There is an entire other world out there, a world of art operating on a different plane of existence, as I bathe babies, find and lose love, seek security, drown in the loss of days and years, sink further and further into depression, lose more and more of the tiny remaining fragments of myself. I am drowning in art, stuff, forever moving here and there. Perpetual motion; inevitably I actually morph into a Sorcerer's Apprentice.

CHAPTER 4

I still work that way, I am an amalgam of mixed metaphors, a sorcerer's apprentice in a runaway train that cannot stop producing art, flying across the tracks, diving into a tunnel, to fill a hunger that never abates, on a quest that never ends. Even my memoir, begun as a journal during difficult times, has burgeoned into an overwhelming collection of disorganized and uncontrollable masses and masses of pages; history, anecdote, essay in desperate need of structure.

It is normal for me to lose myself in thought of art and writing, hiding from reality. But in moments I feel myself snap abruptly back into the present. I am studiously refusing to address the silent phone. Where are my children, today?

They may not be in my life right now, at least not all of them, but my husband is right here beside me. I feel that familiar leap in my chest as I watch him walk toward the car this morning, with that controlled athlete's stride, wearing the predictable plaid flannel shirt over his T-shirt, neat khaki pants, baseball cap, as he leaves on his mission to corral my traditional birthday lobster. He ducks as he walks under my jasmine and honeysuckle-covered front gate trellis, mumbling softly though good naturedly under his breath about the excesses of my garden, and opens the giant wooden driveway gates designed to protect it from voracious deer, so that he can leave. Soon, he and our new red car have been swallowed in the maw of the deserted pine and oak enveloped road, and I am left contentedly studying the varied details of my carefully created Shangri-La. Why a red car? It makes a loud statement, **I am someone.** This is something that I need, crave; to actually be someone. I have not yet figured out why I am driven by this need. I stand at the open front door, French again, more glass and mullions which I have all over the place, because for no identifiable reason I adore them, all but hypnotized by the panorama of my front yard garden oasis, brick walkways and oval flower bed vignettes, camellia, knockout roses and peonies, in front of spreading mature backgrounds of evergreens and flowering trees, another tiny pond and waterfall. We have forsworn lawns this time; miss them only rarely mostly when the smell of newly mown lawn reaches nasal passages...

... I sit in the soft, damp, sweetly smelling grass the little ones sprawled across the thick woven plaid blanket the sun pressed warmly on their chubby bodies, heating their skin and their soft hair ...

I shut off all thought processes with studied deliberation, and wait. He returns proudly several hours later with a carefully packed foil pan in a white plastic bag; already steamed and ready to eat, just store it in the fridge and heat it for ten minutes in a 350° oven. He repeats the instructions he has been given, beaming, smiling broadly. This is just one of the myriad things that he does to make me happy, to express his deep feelings for me. Happy Birthday, he says with repressed excitement and we tuck my lobster away until later. We have figured out a way to enjoy the flavor of these delectable crustaceans without experiencing their actual murder. We are sitting on floral brocade upholstered reproduction French Provincial bar stools of pickled oak at the ceramic covered island that is our kitchen table, hanging out, talking. I am looking at him, and thinking about how lucky I am, counting my blessings as I have been told to so many times. I think about my waiting birthday lobster. You have to adore a man who will acknowledge a secret passion, and make certain it is satisfied, year after year. That would almost be sufficient for me, even if he had not rescued me from more than one disaster in the beginning, cushioned me from loss, healed my deep and substantial wounds, taken care of me with such sweetness and solicitude over these many years, supported me through this journey. I have witnessed him so many times wring his hands metaphorically because he cannot, no matter how he tries, bring the children back to me. But he and I together, we are my life today, in the absence of my children...

They dig in the hot sand, and play with brightly colored shovels and sand implements, pouring shells or pails full of salty water over their creations in the sifting sand. I watch them with great happiness, my eyes coveting their lithe browned bodies, adoring their flyaway white blonde hair. I feel so comfortable that I wish I could stay here forever. I place my chin on my folded hands, and watch my beloved children do their summer beach things, racing in and out of the surf, digging and building. I adore their serious faces that can in a moment open into wide laughter and raucous giggles, their perfect limbs and bodies ...

Any calls while I was out, he ventures tentatively, daring to breach the safety of my tightly closed veneer. I am somewhere else, in another time and place. No, none, my held breath explodes, as I allow the pent up disappointment out into the light of day; not one call. Did you bring in the mail? He hands me the bundle of envelopes that he has placed in the slightly chipped foundling ceramic bowl with its hand-painted flowers on every surface which sits in the middle of the dining room table, right now. Its flaw does not negate its beauty. I leaf through them, expecting nothing, disdain and feigned ennui attempting to hide the very lively fact that I am still hopeful for at least one birthday card.

I swallow my disappointment with great deliberation and I look at him, and think once again about how truly blessed I am. We have been together through thick and thin for so many years. After so long, we treasure each and every moment, and neither of us can conceive of life without the other. We are at our ages very aware of coming inevitabilities.

After all these years, his elegant craggy features, his light hazel eyes, his thick curly silver hair still make me catch my breath. Although he is years my senior, we both still feel that profound connection when our eyes meet, we still share our lives with comfortable intimacy. We each do those small things necessary to please, to ensure the other's happiness. We avoid confronting issues that would upset each other. We protect each other from any possible emotional discomfort, in particular the ghosts of the past. He would do anything to remedy my family breach. Although he can fix just about anything, he cannot make my children contact me, make them care.

I am so lucky to have you, I say, crestfallen at the failure of my children to appear is some form, disappointed, changing the subject, my focus. My husband is my life in these days. An overwhelming wave of joy traverses my body like an electric current. The day I met you, I say, was the best, the most fortuitous and most important day of my life. Yeah, he says, permitting a burst of emotion to slip from his usually staid countenance, in mine, also, and he stands up and comes over to me, puts his arms around me, and squeezes. I revel in the fleeting warmth of his body against mine, envelop him with my own arms, and hug him back. You are my life, I say, this time out loud. *You* are all I need. Damn them, anyway.

CHAPTER 5

It is still galloping onward, time, and the weather soon changes for the better. I feel the sun roasting my shoulders, see solid ground where puddles rippled, seemingly forever, just yesterday. On this special day, I change hats and now I work in the garden, my other escape and joy, perfecting another artwork, this grand immense sculpture that is my land, one ear pealed for the sound of the telephone ring. I have left the phone inside, in a grand cavalier gesture, to show that I'm not anxious. I wander inside when my gurgling stomach notifies me that it is time for lunch. We watch the talking heads do battle on cable news about healthcare and Iraq and racism, observe the mad rantings of Tea Baggers, and join in the battle for a brief moment, hollering and cursing, and withdraw to eat BLTs, and talk about the weather and politics, and he says, that's some lobster, isn't it? And I agree, with solemn acquiescence, yeah, some lobster, I can't wait. And I really mean it. Our conversation is notable for the absence of reference to the children and the vacuum caused by the silent telephone.

The minutes and hours are passing, the afternoon and expectation along with it, is slowly being eaten away, and I am still looking for ways to fill the time, make the day disappear, the tension disperse along with it. Suddenly, old tears are streaming down my face. Stop, I scream in my head. I clasp my hands over my ears, as if to stave off outspoken thought. I will not play this game.

I take deep cleansing breaths, clench my teeth, steel myself, return to my safe havens, my saving graces, my art, my garden, bouncing back and forth as usual, one process feeding off the other, checking accomplishments off my mental list. I am studiously refusing to address either teeming thought or the silent phone.

CHAPTER 6

But then I relent, allow myself to think about them one by one, focus for a moment on recollections, allow thoughts of them to slip into my consciousness; count their names out loud, using my fingers as arithmetic aids. Yes that's all seven accounted for. For seven kids, they are very silent. The silence is deafening.

Later, Kevin phones, I think that night or is it the next. Hi, Mom, he sings out this bright cadence, Happy Birthday. We cover for a brief moment all the trivia of health and family news; in mere seconds it is, gotta go. Kevin is number five, my son the doctor, my rocket scientist. He lives with his family in Montreal. I see him every two or three years if I am lucky, and he does phone a couple of times a year. Strangely enough, Lynnie and Wendi, who both live close by, forget. Wendi, number two, is a linguist and language teacher, French and Spanish. She is so busy with her complex life that I am rarely able to see her or her three children although she passes my home daily on her way to and from work, lives less than a half hour away. Lynnie, number 7, who lives just down the road from me is the quintessential mother to her two extraordinary children. She is incredibly busy with their care and nurture, their busy complicated schedule.

Caryn, number three, who lives in New Jersey and whom I no longer know anything about save for a rare trickle of stray sibling gossip, and probably Tracy, six, who has become an elementary school teacher there in Las Vegas and deals with her own issues, also, will not call. Between them, there are three more grandchildren whom I will not see. That is a given. Bruce now also living in Vegas who like me has that entrepreneurial gene, dabbles as a day trader, buys and renovates homes, and runs a successful auto body shop, either. He is divorced, no children. I haven't seen him in nearly ten years, and every year or two I get a phone call from him. Just last week Andrew, four, living in Albany, New York my math, creative and general all around genius, who usually calls or sends a card, informed me by email that he is looking forward to a possible visit in September with his wife and daughter. I need to be content with that news. They do all live out of town. But it is only May, and it is still my birthday, my *seventieth* birthday.

I am unable to understand it. Strong feelings of indeterminate origin and rationale continue to immerse me with their intensity, despite my efforts to contain them, banish them. I am unwillingly filled with disappointment and not a little rage. I'm not certain, I inform myself tentatively, if this is forgivable.

But here is a birthday gift for me, tiny violets, purple and white, that appear each spring with abandon, never in the same place twice. One day there is nothing there, and it rains, and suddenly bunches and masses of the invasive little darlings are all over. If I pull them out in frustration for their indiscriminate choice of location and their joyful abandon and disregard for garden planning and personal space, they will return with their adorable smiles, and pick up where they left off, marshaling their collective forces in more and more progressive numbers, thumbing their precious yellow noses at me as they invade the entire garden.

Preoccupied, I stumble absentmindedly over a length of garden hose, my aging coordination sabotaging me yet again, and I am stepping accidentally on violets growing in between the worn bricks of my garden walk. Their fragrance rises and tickles °my nose, overwhelming me with their joyous aroma. I look down, and see the crushed blossoms. I'm so sorry, I cry mutely to the powers that be feeling hot liquid welling up in my eyes and nasal passages, and the fragrance rises and overwhelms me again.

I am so sorry, I cry out silently again, this time for my errors of judgment and faulty decisions, for feeding the gaping maw of the monster that is unintended circumstances, for whatever I have done that has caused this massive breach, dissolved and fragmented this family. I wish to be forgiven, to glue the shards of my family, my life, back together as easily as I am able to create an image with tesserae.

But in the reality show that is life, I am not exonerated despite loud and numerous declarations of forgiving and forgetting. I am marginalized, cast out of the family, treated like the horse that also ran in the race. My sins are of commission, not of omission. In that sense, it is the way I always planned it, but not like this, *not like this*. I have always grabbed the bull by the horns, made bold decisions, taken chances, gone for the gusto. *All those tired metaphors.* I had prided myself in being a problem solver. Solve *this*, I tell myself impotently.

෫෯

My lobster is reduced to a sad pile of jagged crimson shells. The tiramisu is gone, and my husband sitting upright jaw agape is snoozing on the sofa, the strains of NCIS murmuring in the background. This day has ended. Night has fallen, and I am surrounded by darkness, unable to sleep, tossing and turning. I am treated to a recurring revolving regenerating internal videotape of my life. Patterns emerge and combine like mating amoebas, grow and reproduce and split apart. Life and art imitate themselves in an endless loop of non-sortable ungraspable film. This is my story to write. Thoughts and phrases, entire pages and chapters, flow through my mind, with interminable speed. Get up and write I tell myself, but my limbs refuse to obey ... I don't wish to leave the warmth and luxury of bedclothes, soft embracing pillows and comforter, that which is not capriciously named. Comforted, I feel myself drifting.

You'll lose it by morning an internal voice chides me sternly, startling me awake. You'll never remember, never get it back. Midnight thoughts are ephemeral, as unable to be grasped as wisps of frosted winter breath. Move now. Get up.

A sigh and then, familiar with this truth, enamored of my fluency when somnambulant, dismayed at my aphasia when awake, I force myself somehow to obey. Once up seated naked on the bed's edge in the darkness, clutching pen and notebook with icy-tipped fingers, I begin to scribble, haphazardly, in no order. Order will find itself, later. I plumb my awakening memory for recently imagined phrases, brilliantly formed sentences, jewels of wisdom, diffusing in puffs of mist, nearly gone, grabbing dissolving words from the air. Then, somehow enveloped now in bathrobe and slippers, I tip toe through the silent black house, plod upstairs to my little attic office, boot up the old HP, and try to find that hazy alpha zone, begin typing whatever comes to mind.

There is no getting around it, the damage that has been done, the destruction that has been wrought, is deep and thorough. I need to understand everything that has happened. As the beginning of the eighth decade of my life looms before me, it is time for me to find a meaning for my existence, which feels as though it is lost in paradox and contradiction, blame and accusation and misinterpretation. Although I have always tried to do the right thing, many of my life's choices have been wrong ones, and have been compounded exponentially into major catastrophes.

But the sins for which I am being castigated are not real. To me, at least, they are not real. Where has all of this misunderstanding come from? How in the name of all that is holy can I make clear to them all what truly took place? There must be something that will exonerate me. In a world filled with inexplicable events, here is the penultimate mystery to be solved. All I need is valid evidence to prove my innocence, although it has always been considered an impossibility to prove a negative, manifest in my own situation. In the meanwhile, what I need to do is continue to immerse myself in my writing, in disentangling memories and history, examining and interpreting journals and records that I have uncovered long hidden in cartons and closets. There is a lot going on.

Immersed in all of this, floating in the greater scheme of things, I am bouncing back and forth from despair and hopelessness to acceptance and joy. I am a hummingbird who never lights on any surface it would seem, but hovers before each reality, not knowing which to attend to. Wherever I am in my life, there are always a chaotic assortment of pointed questions and polarizing emotions awaiting analysis and response. It is time to have a conversation with someone wiser and more spiritually connected than I am. My favorite rabbi, Marc-with-a-"c" Gelman, is always available; all I need to do is read his weekly column in *Newsday*, Part II.

And it is another summer day. I have survived once again the angst of yesterday. I wake up this morning, rays of sun pouring through the window once again, the sweetly unrelenting fragrance of Privet wafting intoxicatingly through the window. I feel a sense of calm, a lessening of anger, of pain. Have I somehow in the night, forgiven, been forgiven by some higher force without even realizing it? Has Rabbi Gelman's column this week connected with raw nerve endings and battered psyche? He has quoted Mark Twain. *Forgiveness*, he recites, *is the fragrance the violet sheds on the heel that has crushed it.* I don't even know what that means. Just thinking about it makes my brain ache.

There is however an actual presence in the room; forgiveness and the specter of love. Maybe he knows something I don't. I breathe deeply, enveloped suddenly by that familiar all-encompassing aroma of the privet growing outside my bedroom window. The fragrance of privet makes no demands, asks for no explanation, it merely envelopes with an essence of love. Let the violets forgive, I will continue my journey to remember, to survive and to understand. Forgiveness is a complicated and difficult matter for another day. Love is a strange and enigmatic essence, burdened with guilt, difficult to grasp.

27

CHAPTER 7

1943

Look what the postman brought you, says my mother, holding out a worn manila envelope, covered with the familiar strong black smartly angled slashes of alphabet letters that create names and addresses. I recognize my name, and our address. My mother, the consummate educator, has already taught me to read, to write both cursive and script. I recognize his sloping scrawl. Do you want to open it? I shake my head, no, looking downward.

I sit at a miniature replica dining room table placed in the corner of the bedroom that I share with my mother in our tiny wartime construction apartment. I am aware that she is watching me. I look with some awe at her familiar bronze chestnut hair swept up from the back, and twirled around to form a pompadour in front, then fastened in that familiar '40s do. I can sense her sky blue eyes gazing tenderly at me, watching me at play. The table is set with tiny flower-patterned porcelain dishes and elaborately pattern stamped tin tableware; an assortment of porcelain-faced dolls in delicately hand-tailored ruffled dresses sit around the table as if waiting for refreshments. I am the mommy in this scenario, waiting to feed my babies. I may play at being mommy, but carefully wrought bronze sausage curls brought up to the rear of my head and held by a large taffeta bow, of pink, yellow, apple green and forget-me-not blue plaid, clearly define me as the child. One of my dolls wears the exact replica of my own outfit, an organdy pinafore, of pale yellow, embroidered with tiny rosettes and miniature pale green leaves, over a soft cotton dress with Peter Pan collar and short puffed sleeves. My mother has carried on the tradition of the old country, where you were a scholar, a teacher, a farmer, or a tailor. Her father and his father were farmers and furriers, tailors, her mother a seamstress. Although she is a teacher, atavistic memory, or just plain DNA has persevered, and her exquisite needlework does her ancestors proud.

My mother carefully rips the package open, removing a small round black disc. Daddy has sent you another song, she says, feigning delight, when it is easy to see that she is feeling only loneliness and despair. Do you want to hear it? Yes, I nod, obediently, and she pulls a shabby and faded nearly colorless square suitcase from beneath the bed, and opens the simple latch, producing a small phonograph. She takes the tatty electrical cord and plugs it into the wall. She places the black disc on the spindle, in the center of the turntable, and turns a black knob to a mark stamped on in tiny white letters against the faded brown faux leather. Meanwhile, I patently ignore both my mother and the phonograph, as with intense deliberation, I go through the elaborate charade of feeding each of the dolls tiny spoonfuls of air moving the spoon from miniature china cup to pursed porcelain lip.

28

There is a sudden burst of noise, a scraping, scratching sound, and a rough disarming static, and we both jump, startled, looking at each other. I giggle, and my mother smiles softly, indulgently, as our eyes lock. I can literally feel the current of love that passes between us. All at once we hear that familiar deep rich baritone, strictly a capella, *from the halls of Mon-te-zu-u-ma to the shores of Trip-o-li, we will fight our country's ba-at-tles, on the land and on the sea ...*

My mother wipes at a tear that trickles across her cheek, threatening to land on her only silk blouse, which she wears with each of her carefully tailored suits when she teaches her classes at P.S. 76, across the Bronx. In a corner next to an ancient Singer sewing machine, and an assortment of colored threads and sewing implements, there is an entire library of patterns: McCalls, Butterick, Vogue. *She cannot pass a fabric store without entering, and despite vows of abstinence, never leaves without some fresh pattern or woven treasure tucked resolutely under her arm to add to her growing collection, visions of completed sewing projects dancing in her mind, creating a momentary respite from thought and daily stress. Some intense inner force has directed her to carefully choose the particular fabric she has used to create her smashing suit, from the vast stash of worsteds, wools, gabardines and more, that are carefully stored in dresser drawers, closet shelves, in an assortment of bags and cardboard boxes. My mother's collections are everywhere.*

I go back to feeding my dolls as if nothing has occurred, my face a tight mask. There has been no package, no record, no song; I have not heard the voice of my father, whose face I would not even remember if I did not have photos placed all around me; a dumb black plastic record is not my father. I force all thoughts of Daddy and records and songs from my mind. I am totally engrossed in my occupation, being the momma, and a great feeling of tenderness flows through me. But an instant later, a strange heat unexpectedly begins to seep through my body, up into my face. I am aware that I am clenching my eyes and cheeks. I cannot identify or control the emotions that rush up in me, but suddenly I am grabbing the disc from the twirling turntable, the needle is scraping across it, the grating, irritating sound is meshed with that of my fingernails skittering over the disc and I have knocked it to the floor, where it shatters, splitting into several jagged sections. There is a moment of absolute silence.

My mother carefully picks up the pieces. Daddy will send you another record; don't worry, she says, with tense studied patience. It's okay. I understand, she says. She puts one hand on her chest the other encompasses the cracked pieces of the record. Her face says that she feels as though a similar crack has begun to travel across her chest. She takes a deep breath, and continues blindly with her efforts to clean up the broken plastic pieces. Life goes on, she murmurs. There is a war on. She shoves the suitcase with its phonograph back under the bed. She leaves the room, overcome with emotion. I can feel that she does not want me to see her upset. I hug my own chest, needing to feel her arms around me, needing to absorb her warmth, to feel her consolation, but I am alone. Except I have my babies.

∾∾

After my mother leaves the room I take a deep breath and purse my lips, sticking out my chin. I continue resolutely to pursue my favorite and customary occupation. I slip into the kitchen, push a chair over to the cupboard, and scan the assortment of foodstuffs in colorful cardboard boxes, finally choosing one. It will be baby food, anyway, no matter what its actual purpose was meant to be. Somewhere in another room I can hear the soft desperate sounds of my mother's sobs. Ignoring them with quiet deliberation, I climb down, and carefully open the top of the box, spooning out two tablespoons of flakes, and then reverse my steps to return the box to its home. I add a few drops of water, fetched from the bathroom tap, to the flakes, mixing the mess until it has a creamy consistency. I proceed to feed my babies, for real, stuffing the truly nasty stuff into their delicate porcelain faces, between their tiny teeth, and down into their stuffed cloth bodies. I murmur customary little words of love and endearment, encouragement, and consolation so familiar to me, as I perform my maternal chore. I am so engrossed in my activity that I fail to hear my mother return.

*What are you doing, asks my mother with a sharp edge to her voice, those dolls will be ruined. Already, a dark stain is spreading across their muslin chests. The actual value of material things appears to have a most serious importance. They're not dolls, Mommy, I answer scathingly shaking my curls; they are babies, **my** babies. I kneel and put my arms around the bunch of them, drawing them together, pulling them out of their seats onto the table, upsetting the carefully arranged dishes, and sob into their collective meticulously fabricated artificial hairdos. And I will spoil them if I want to. And babies need real food, not just air, I think silently. Babies don't need packages, and songs on records, babies need both a mommy and daddy. And babies need lots of hugs. Fat choking tears are welling up in a giant bubble in my chest; threatening to flood my cheeks. I don't want any more presents, says the tiny voice in my head, I just want my daddy. I am unable to express these feelings out loud; they stick in my throat in a great loathsome lump.*

I watch as my mother steels herself against the advent of my great sobs and sluices of tears that refuse to appear. I imagine that this is how she feels, missing Daddy, emotion welling up inside of her threatening to split her face, to explode from her mouth, her nose, her eyes, because this is how I feel. But I am as still and rigid and cold as one of my porcelain dolls, my face frozen into its familiar mask of sadness. I gulp silently and take a huge breath.

When I grow up, I say in my tiny singsong telling a story voice, mimicking my favorite storyteller, my mother, I'm going to have lots of babies; real babies. And they will have a mommy, me, and a daddy. And they will all be together, always, and they will love each other, and take good care of each other, and never be apart. The end, I say firmly.

My mother pulls me onto her lap, wraps her arms around me, her cheeks damp, her eyes dreamy and soft, her voice crooning love. When Daddy comes home, she says tenderly, we will buy a great big house in the country. Her eyes are somewhere far away as she reaches out to a side table piled high with papers and pulls out a huge familiar stack of magazines and pages neatly ripped from some of them, and we start looking through them. This is a familiar and comforting ritual to me, and I am very willing to play this game, sitting close to my mother, the warmth of her seeping into me through the fabric of our clothes, included in her world. Look at this, and this, and this. We dream about rooms, colors and patterns and fabrics, collections and accessories, French doors, furniture and patios, ponds and streams and waterfalls and gardens.

What about my baby sister, I ask her getting excited, joining her dream with mine, my brother. Can we get babies, too, real babies, for our new house?

My freckled pigtailed skinny little friend Linda who lives down at the end of the long institutional hallway in her family's apartment behind the last door has come running toward me excitement pouring from every pore, eyes wide and bright, arms waving and askew, a huge smile splitting her lightly freckled face; guess what, she calls, my mother just came home, and we have a new baby sister. Come and see her, she cries out joyfully, and I follow silently sensing an immutable excitement rising in my chest. So I stand at the head of this white lace covered bassinette with its pink ribbons, its tiny lace trimmed pillow embroidered with a minute lamb and a pink and blue rose on one corner and stare at this tiny perfection that is Linda's new baby sister, and miniscule seed is planted deep inside of me. I can feel it down there, a tiny tingling kernel of need and longing that begins to grow, has its own voice, demands to be heard. Baby dolls will no longer suffice.

❧☙

My father's record and my family of baby dolls fade into the distance with time. It is not the end of the story. It is a new beginning. One short year later, throbbing with longing, excitement and a not a little dread, I await a very special occasion. I clutch a large doll, dressed in a replica of my own outfit, under one arm. This is of course, a letter perfect WAC uniform, the cap sitting jauntily on my carefully newly bobbed hair. My brown oxfords are polished to perfection. My mother has created and sewn these outfits, mine and my doll's. The occasion is the return of my father, from his five-year stint in Europe and France as an Army JAG officer, Judge Advocate General. My last memory of him, at one year of age, is watching him walk away from us, down the street in his captain's regalia, on his way to serve. My only other recollections of him are faded and dog-eared photographs showing his compelling presence, his steady gaze, his thinly elegant Clark Gable mustache and his quirky devil-may-care Errol Flynn grin. Soon I will have the real thing not merely symbols of his existence.

Over the five long years of my father's absence, mementos I hoard, guard with my tiny life, include a small white box containing two cotton bolls, purchased while he is in training in Georgia, a brown striped and polka dotted conch shell with my name engraved on it that roars like the ocean when you hold it to your ear, a tiny replica of a Swiss chalet music box, assorted postcards in his scrawling illegible handwriting, and the most memorable, those tiny plastic recordings of his deep baritone of the Battle Hymn of the Republic, *and the Marine Anthem, worn wafer thin.*

31

We stand there, frozen in a family snapshot, my mother, her sister Etta, my uncle Herman, my grandma and grandpa, various family friends, and watch as Daddy strides down the sidewalk near our apartment complex in 1945 Bronx, New York, just after the glorious occasion of VE Day; Victory in Europe. We stand in front of the tall brick buildings that seem to go on forever, in this immense apartment house development spawned by the end of the war. I am overjoyed that my daddy whom I idolize is finally home, the image of him walking away has haunted me for so long. ... I have no idea what lies ahead. At this moment, I cautiously keep my feelings to myself, as I have been taught. Parkchester, built and owned by Metropolitan Life Insurance, sports row after row of six-story red brick prison-like institutional buildings, kind of a bad Holocaust joke, and wide green lawns, surrounded by knee high steel posts swung with heavy chains, to delineate the macadam areas of traversal, and pristine lawn. The message is clear. Keep off the grass. We are now post war, but everything in our lives is military, mimics the military. Daddy's military presence manifests itself in his posture, his bearing, and would have been sufficient to identify him as a returning armed forces personage, without the uniform, the crisply rimmed captain's cap; his brisk six-foot stride bespeaks his military *identity. I watch him approach, a mixture of pride and terror choking me. We wait, the entire family, as his figure, tiny in the distance, grows larger and larger as he grows nearer. And then there he is, standing right in front of us. I want to shrink into the forest of warm sturdy legs behind me, but I am my father's daughter, and thus also a soldier, am I not? And soldiers are brave. As he draws near, I step forward, offer him my gift, a well practiced crisp salute; as I salute my daddy smartly my spaniel eyes are mirroring all the woes of the world. He salutes back, sharply, his emotions well hidden, and his visage stern. The photo of us together on that day, shows me, huge sad eyes and tight lips, and becomes the poster to my life from that day forward. Is he touched, amused, happy? No one knows. At least, I don't.*

Part I

Steve

CHAPTER 8

The present day—2009

The minutes and hours of my special day have passed, the afternoon, evening, hope and expectation along with them, were slowly eaten away as I sought ways to fill the time, make the day disappear, the tension to disperse along with it. On this new day, I continue my keep-busy work, even though the big day, itself, is gone. Soon enough I have hit a proverbial wall. Nothing is coming out right. It is one of those times when it is necessary to leave the studio, take a cleansing break; give creativity a rest.

I wander outside to investigate the coming signs of spring. If I can successfully nurture my garden, my family substitute, maybe I can find a way to nurture my children, bring them home. In late winter I cut branches of forsythia, a tradition, to force indoors, and aware that soon inside and out they will be screaming their yellow song. Now I fear for my border of hostas, which last year were dragged underground by unseen creatures, and gratuitously replanted helter skelter in strange places, where they dutifully appeared, finally, to gamely wave their mauve and orchid flags. This year, there are no signs of them at all. It is a lethal frosting on top of a toxic cake. Anger and frustration come over me, as I realize that once again the moles and voles have decimated my tulips and crocuses. Anger and frustration have become my most loyal companions.

Swallowing surging lament before it chokes off my air supply I look around, and notice that with an absence of rain, infant leaves are drooping, quickly, it seems, the earth is looking dry and crumbly. It is generally evident that plants need water to live and to grow, but it appears lately that there is always either feast or famine. So I move onward. Once again I change hats, putting my art on a convenient shelf, safe and sound for later, compensate for loss. I water the flower beds, and some of my new shrubs and perennials, finding this to be as mind numbingly satisfying, as healing as it ever has been. Just standing there, hose in hand, pointing and spraying. I am giving life.

I am a life giver, I reassure myself, hoping to convince myself that this is true. Anyone can be a mother, birthing and raising babies; I rebuke myself as if unconvinced, that kind of life giver. I fill my empty nest in different ways; in addition to my intense involvement with my art, I nurture plants, propagate plants from cuttings; make flowers bloom, instead of merely putting brush to canvas. My garden is overcrowded with my infant plants. I can stand for hours and water, in a kind of daze, an alpha state, with thoughts tumbling around one after the other, wondering offhandedly just how and when I began this pursuit. Sometimes I am rewarded for my efforts with a solution to a dilemma, personal or artistic. Sometimes it is merely another activity of more mindless sublimation.

I do know this: plants do not challenge the conditionality of love. They offer their beauty and bounty asking nothing in return. I note that each plant, like every one of my actual children, has its own identifying quality. All at once the children have reinserted themselves into my reality, despite intense concentration, concerted measures taken. I blink such thoughts away. Identifying qualities of my plants, I remind myself. That is what I am addressing. Those tiny red leaves that are appearing on my rose bushes, the climbing hydrangeas who have those fat sensuous buds, who promise to reach new heights, this year. I am thinking faster and faster, to forestall incoming thoughts. Day lilies and irises who are already showing substantial foliage, a thickening where flowers, purple and white and yellow, might be beginning their voyages upward to suddenly burst free of the verdant restraint of foliage, to bloom.

I pointedly, repeatedly, and constantly avoid thinking about the attributes and failings of my children. Methinks the lady doth protest too much, says Mom quoting the bard as usual, invisible, but here, anyway. I ignore her, and use my love of art and garden unabashedly to escape, to protect myself when life is intolerable. This is no metaphor for life, I remind her when prodded by her gentle disapproving jab; it is all merely a tool for survival. So, I focus on the promise of life and color, which is everywhere. It is still, however, I remind myself, merely a promise, and I have learned from life, over and over again, that promises are easily broken.

☙❧

It was only one day, and my birthday vanished swiftly. Even though this time, it was a biggie, I am aware that there is no longer reason to hope or dream of mother and child reunions. I feel myself sinking into that familiar black murky bottomless pit of depression that haunts me, from time to time. That faint voice deep in the core of me is crying out for help.

A strange dreamlike drive through winding curving oak and stunted pine, on a road to nowhere called Daniel's Hole, past the East Hampton airport with its forbidding fence dividing real life from waving grain in a golden field-like area passing for runway. Concentrating carefully on barely noticeable indentations that signify turns, Industrial Road which unsurprisingly houses varieties of industry as well as a plant nursery and a nursery school and LTV, the local cable network, bouncing over rutted railroad tracks on Wainscott Harbor Road, automatically obeying signs, my thoughts meander, a benevolent lump rises in my throat; *Deaf Children Playing,* a sign asserts loudly, and finally I slip into a parking space left just for me in the tiny busy country strip mall. I wince at the reminders generated of nurseries and children. Distracted, I wander into the office of the wondrous Dr. Blake Kerr, who spent six years in Tibet trying to save this special little country with its rich culture from the horrors, abuses, and vagaries of its Chinese rulers; Blake Kerr along with his friend John Ackerly were arrested on October 1, 1987 in the midst of demonstrations and revolution for being squatters, his book about his exploits has a forward by the Dali Lama himself. Who will write *my* forward if I ever finish my story? I am investigating the mystery of my latest debilitating depression and that magical medication I was given the last time, should I take it again, can he renew my prescription? Can he save *me*? I can barely muster a smile, a greeting for the receptionists; barely explain why I am here. They have vague information about my malaise, look at me quizzically; scour my face with their eyes for hints and revelations perhaps of danger. Just how profound is my melancholy? I don't have an appointment and controlled substances may not be prescribed without a physical exam, so while I am waiting for the generally overbooked doctor to appear, a nurse carefully keeps me tentative company, makes casual conversation. What do you do? I'm an artist. Oh, I'm a writer. Yeah? I write, too. She tells me about a writing workshop that meets on Thursday evenings at a location so memorable to me. A sudden sensation begins to come to tingling life in my of late insensate body, akin to that faint flutter signifying the unforgettable awakening quiver denoting life in early pregnancy; something in me has been touched, I am coming back alive. Why don't you join us tomorrow night? Obediently, I follow the vaguely apparent landmarks to a place of further revival propelled perhaps by the magical Lyrica.

Happenstance once again presents me with opportunity. Depression is bearded in its lair, once again blocked by creativity. This is something else; I leave my unfinished art projects on a shelf for later, I am on a new quest. Now, hopefully, I can find a way to organize and clarify the multiple facets of my story, another art form in my life. For too long I have been held hostage to my inability to attack this overwhelming job, at least with any permanent success.

A profound revelation occurs; with this new inspiration. I finally rewrite numerous pages of hyperbole and narrative, produce another twenty *first pages* in a new learning system that encourages the creation of first pages to add to my story that is comprised of first pages, prologues and prefaces and leading chapters. I am back immersed in the process. I struggle with my latest *bête noire*, structure, but I am told that will come. I pointedly put aside thoughts of guilt and evidence, of proving my innocence; of the bad acts of others.

My muse is gone, replaced by my writing group. Art isn't easy, like the song says. The entire premise is based on reading new work out loud, and the response of the listener who is the ersatz reader. No more rambling narratives. Show it, don't tell it. Think about the listener/reader. Get into the moment, create a container; fill it with flashbacks and backstitches. Time to get down to work; get it all together. Tighten it up, make the edges raggedy. Say more, say less. I have read the first samples of my writing before the group. I am gently instructed that I need to: get into the moment, put my feet on the ground, focus on that moment, explore and recount my feelings, stick to one narrow concise element of my life. I don't need to tell it all, every moment, they say with an aura of great wisdom, and they have been here for a while, they are the success stories. Yes, I do, I say silently. Choose one, they continue; it's a Sophie's Choice. Delete extraneous paragraphs and pages. Murder my favorite words, my *little darlings;* this is the mantra of my co-conspirators.

There is a potluck feasts of green tea, with ginger and lemon, hummus and fresh bread and crackers; salad and rice dishes and pasta, chicken wings and an assortment of cookies and cakes. The act of creation demands sustenance beyond the spiritual. I can relate to this, because it is a familiar part of my life. Soft light barely illuminates the assembly, as chairs and tables, dark polished pine are moved to accommodate the slowly growing group, in this uncomfortable borrowed place. Stiff wooden chairs, Americana; heavy round dark gleaming tables rearranged, pulled into a rudimentary three-leaf-clover grouping. It is awkward, we are in someone else's space, like borrowing a stranger's underwear, certain that even if it has been carefully laundered, it has already been worn, is of another; has that strange essence. The light is dim, making it difficult to read, more so for these aging eyes. There is a bar, mirrored, glass shelves, strangely empty of bottles and glasses, and glass cases disconcertingly displaying guns as well as an effusive collection of awards. Neither is of any interest to me; indeed even thoughts of guns make me shudder. I'm not much on second amendment rights. This is created to simulate the cozy intimacy of someone's den; what it actually is is a game room in what is known as the Veteran's Hall in our local cultural center in Southampton with which by this time I am quite familiar. We come together, a motley assortment of would be authors, women from disparate lives with assorted histories, reading our various contributions to this potluck literary feast, each in her own right hungry for approval, thrilled to hear one another's contribution. Everything we hear is inspiration, directly or indirectly. Memories are triggered; buttons to secret emotional treasure troves are pressed. Hidden vaults of awareness are revealed. Intimate voices appear. Old secrets and painful memories are exposed. Skills are honed. Growth can be measured in words and smiles and head shakes of my sisters in crime, week to week. Gradually, a womblike sense of safety and nurture is created. There is so much to tell, I just don't know where to begin, I lament wringing my hands metaphorically. What is your story really about, they ask, what is the trigger the thing that set it all in motion? I don't need really to think that hard, there has already been so much contemplation, so much intense analysis; I venture timidly into that part of my story which has given impetus to all the rest, where I have decided after much thought and scrutiny and discussion regarding the main thrust of the story with my peers, it actually begins.

CHAPTER 9

1956

Adelaide who is really Vivian Blaine tosses back her bleached blonde head takes a great slurping snort through her nose, is singing that a *poyss-ssin* could develop a cold; Marlon Brando is Sky Masterson, mumbling his words and barely singing, and someone hollers that, it's good old reliable Nathan ... Frank Sinatra is Nathan Detroit, singing about placing bets and being a bad boy, luck be a lady tonight, you got the horse right here, his name is Paul Revere, sue me sue me shoot bullets through me, and sit down, you're rockin' the boat. Innocent and lovely Salvation Army lady, Sarah Brown, Jean Simmons, is warbling something about bells and falling in love, if she were a bell she'd be ringing, and I am sitting in the balcony with Steve on our first date trying not to focus on our entwined hands, palm to palm, fingers meshing, hot and sweaty. I can think of nothing else, the only thing I can focus on is the state of our hands. The message about falling in love, good girls and bad girls, good boys and bad boys, is lost. He offers me a Raisinette or a Goober or something from the tiny box he purchased before the movie at the twinkling gaily lit fluorescent refreshment stand, you don't want popcorn, do you, he asks me hopefully, nervous, look how much they want for *that stuff*? I don't care about popcorn, and I never notice that slight tilt he has towards parsimony. I cannot reach for a Raisonette with my other, my outer hand, without contortion, so I say, no thank you, and smile brightly, not really meaning it, really craving this chocolate confection, my favorite snack. Still, our hands are attached in moist misery, each of us fearful of letting go. Will that signify rejection? Will it be an irretrievable act, signifying the end to any future connection? All I can think about is that warm wet dismal spot in the universe that is where our palms are joined it would seem in enforced misery, into perpetuity. I am able to focus on nothing else; the movie meanders by in the background.

We are at the Midway Theater on Continental Avenue in Forest Hills, on the cusp of quaint old Forest Hills Gardens, very familiar to me. I walked the twenty blocks on Saturday afternoons, en masse, keystone kids, when I was in Stephen A. Halsey Junior High, for the ritual afternoon movie matinee. My hand shared that same problem with Jaime Gonzales and John Huntington and Michael Hamburg, Richard Spivak, in those days, at different times, with lots less threat and intensity. Later, I watched myriad movies with my girlfriends, Shelly Saltiel, Letty Taboh, Rochelle Rolnick, Joyce Keller, Jane Sterinbach, at the same theater; the Midway is a neighborhood tradition. Now, I move onward, into the fearful world of adult connection. Although the venue is the same, the goals and rules are oh so different.

The movie has ended, and we move shivering slightly bundled in our winter wear, walking briskly along, past the well stocked, well after hour tightly gusseted shops of this usually bustling avenue. I am aware of the excesses of shoe and handbag, stationary and pottery, lingerie, evening wear in these store fronts, the obscure and secretive seeming apartments above, but they are mere backdrop to this moment. I am enjoying the somehow comforting smell of his grey wool tweed overcoat, his starched shirt, in the crisp late winter night, like the idea of being seen with this apparently made to order tall, dark, good-looking young man. Would you like something to eat, he asks, and I answer pizza with a question mark, looking at my shoes, and he admits self-consciously that he has never had it, pizza, reminds me that he received his high school education in a Brooklyn Yeshiva, that he isn't certain about the status of pizza in reference to the rules of *Kashris*, Jewish kosher law, finally relents after some prodding, tomato sauce and cheese and bread dough sound reasonable, no meat appears to be involved. So we are on our way to the Pizza Palace by the park near the corner of Queens and Yellowstone Boulevards, right next door to that baby furniture emporium that contains all of that tantalizing infant paraphernalia that I covet, see playing such an important part in my near future. I am ambiguous about the Yeshiva thing. It means on one hand that he fills my parents' criteria for romantic candidates of being Jewish, along with that all important pre-law or pre-med requirement. He will be a lawyer. So, all appears to be in order, at least in the standards department. I am also comforted by his obvious orthodoxy, not only does it place me back in the most secure place of my childhood, my grandfather's solid embrace, but it separates him by miles and massive moral barricades from the rest of the college boy candidates that abound. He rises automatically head and shoulders above the competition.

So now we are sitting at this tiny table, our pizza between us, and still our hands are connected, still sweaty and uncomfortable. I have no recollection of how we manage to remove our outerwear, under the circumstances. We smile at each other uncomfortably, and I can feel that we are each seeking to give and to receive excessive and intimate beams of approval, and failing. I am examining his face, seeking thunder bolts of awareness, signs signifying that we are *beshert*, meant for each other, that he is the one I have been waiting for. It is a pleasant face, strong even features, well placed, wide even mouth, straight prominent nose, long lashed greenish hazel eyes, nice complexion. He will make good looking babies, I think, smiling inwardly. This is of monumental importance, the baby making part, not the good looking part, I think to myself piously, although... The pizza is growing cold, it is difficult to attack with one hand, the pieces are not cut through, remain attached to each other also. My stomach is gurgling and my mouth watering. My lesser angels dictate, and I shrug and disconnect, pat the top of his hand awkwardly, and guiltily grab a slice, trailing strings of mozzarella, ignorant of his wince. He follows, but watches me carefully, then eyes his knife and fork, uncertain about protocol, the rules of pizza eating, not entirely convinced that this strange new food, the very act of touching it, will not send him to perdition.

Saturday night, date night, of the following week, it is Kim Novak and William Holden in *Picnic* and something magical is happening. All at once, although it is not *a Sunday morning, without a warning*, through forces beyond our control, we are a couple. All of a sudden, almost automatically, the theme from the movie becomes *our song...and moon glow brought me you*, we sing in unison looking deeply into each other's eyes. Moonglow and the Theme from Picnic, is its full title, and when we hear it, our eyes meet and we grin at each other with our brand new secret and an intimate awareness. And we are back in the palm-to-palm mode, dealing once again with sweat and discomfort and newness. After a few more dates, some close dancing at fraternity parties, we begin to relax, to feel comfortable in each other's presence. He is beginning to look at me in a new way, a kind of intimacy and affection. Our eyes are meeting more and more frequently with inside knowledge, connecting, communicating; he is showing me a sweet soft side, loosening up, telling jokes; making amusing quips, making me laugh. It appears that there is nothing we cannot talk about. He tells me about growing up Jewish in Brooklyn with his sister Elaine and I tell him about being an only child and my obsession with having babies. I am in tune with his suddenly emerging really wacky sense of humor. I am experiencing something that I have never had in my life before. I am feeling connected and yes, happy.

When Steve finally gets up the courage to kiss me, I am ready, await this moment with caught breath, and I am surprised at how sweet and gentle it is, this first kiss and at my own warmly enthusiastic response. This is not spin the bottle kissing, it is something more profound. *You must remember this, a kiss is just a kiss a sigh is just a sigh...* I notice that we fit together, rather well, that I enjoy the feel of his body close to mine, the sense of warmth and intimacy, the distinct scent that emanates from him, his maleness. His face contains a strange expression, warm and intimate, approval. I feel good and cared for and adored, and something more. It feels great. He calls me Lynnie; no one has ever called me Lynnie. Mom and Daddy are adamant about diminutives, nicknames or rather the shunning of them. His eyes go over me with intensity and joy, meet mine and I feel that I am finally someone; Stevie's girl. *His* family is big on diminutives which somehow gives them a special aura in my mind.

Spring comes and goes, I have finally graduated from high school, and then summer arrives, and now we are at the beach, Rockaway, where his parents have a summer cottage; a bit of seaside delight here in Queens, on the edge of the city. We are old friends, an established couple. The cottages are built close together, it is possible to see into the neighbor's house through any window, you can stand at the sink or toilet looking out the window, doing your business and see someone across the alley standing at a toilet looking out the window right back at you, privacy or rather the lack thereof is more a running joke than a reality; the cottages are ancient and barely holding together, their state of quaint disrepair is their main charm. We cross the cracked and rutted bumpy squares of sparkling sunlit city concrete walkway as we trudge in unlaced sneakers from the tiny screened porch to the boardwalk, climb the wide splintery aged stairs, remove our shoes and slog barefoot through the hot drifting dunes. Usually, we can't wait to get out there on the scalding sand, on our blanket under the sun, hearing the ocean crashing in the background, smelling the pungent briny air. We settle our belongings in the sand, join hands and run helter skelter down to the water, and dive through the frigid waves for what feels like hours like little kids, and retreat to the blanket, pulling half of it over us, beyond excitement to be close together with so little clothing on, icy skin touching more icy skin on hot blankets, no guilt, we are at the beach, aren't we, and bathing suits are the dress of protocol. Protocol is always the true decider in our 1950s world.

For a number of idyllic June weeks in 1956, we are in our own personal Shangri-La. We exist in a maelstrom of cherry cheese knishes on the boardwalk, rides at the Playland amusement park, the cyclone; lots and lots of pizza, lots of kissing and groping and pressing innocently together under blankets in the sand.

He nicknames me Long Tall Sally, after the song that plays incessantly on the radio, and I call him Zshu Zshu, which is what his little niece Amy calls him, unable to say Stevie. Everyone in the family calls him Stevie. We are so close that it seems impossible to figure out where one of us ends and the other begins. When we fall asleep in his sister Elaine's Chevy one night after the movies, he changes my name to Suzie, wake up little Suzie, he grins, the song is playing softly as I blink awake. Steve is big on nicknames, in true family tradition, large also on humorous commentary of anything and everything. I find this endearing and entertaining, and find myself laughing a lot. It suggests an openness and family expansiveness that is alien to my experience. It feeds my imagination, enhances the fantasy picture I have formed of his family, oh so different from mine; feeds into fantasies of the future. We play tennis, miniature golf and bowl, and attend Giant-Dodger games, rooting for opposite sides; visit his old childhood friends Sandy and Alice in the Bronx. I am amused and a little dismayed when he drives around and around the block seeking the perfect parking place close to the front door in an area where there are none at all, passing up those rarities that are a block or somewhat away. He has shortcuts to everywhere that take longer and are not shortcuts at all, and he will not consider any other way, won't even discuss the matter. I find this quirky and endearing. He makes me laugh, tickles my intellect. We finish each other's sentences, read each other's minds; cannot bear to be apart for one moment, spend time apart on the telephone talking about nothing, merely being as close as any such electronic connection can make us, in time and space. There are more long silences than talk, yet, we are connected, over distance. *My prayer is to linger with you, at the end of the day, in a dream that's divine ...*

I am feverishly creating greeting cards that are entire books, illustrated in water color and India ink, held together with gaily colored ribbons, telling stories about us, tickling his fancy, showing him who I am, how I feel, desperate to impress him with my creativity, my intelligence, my love. He is entranced, enthused, thrilled by my art, my ingenuity, my brilliance, can't stop bragging about me to everyone and anyone. I am confiding my deepest thoughts, and desires, letting him know how important my art is to me, telling him again and again about the significance to me of children, wanting babies. I am determined to capture this applicant for the job of my future husband, certain that there are no others, unconvinced of the possibility of choice. Yes, he says, yes; whatever you want, I just want to make you happy. Always at the back of my mind is escape from the turmoil of my parents' home. He wants me, will anyone else? *My prayer and the answer you give may they still be the same for as long as we live...*

Suddenly the Fourth of July approaches and before I know what has happened I am a counselor at Camp Paradise, which my father, putting his army experience to work, is directing this year. Every year it is a different camp, as he charms new employers into hiring him, slams old doors behind him in furious huffs. I am in charge of five small girls in Bunk 2, and I am responsible for the scenery for all camp theatrical productions.

I have sent a letter to the Broadway theater where this show is appearing, and at my request, Steve and I have seen *My Fair Lady* gratis, and been invited backstage so that I may examine the scenery firsthand for the camp's upcoming production; I will have to fly by the seat of my pants for the second production, *The King and I*, but I have seen it with Mom, twice. Mom has a great hunger for theater, on and off Broadway, and we are frequent attendees. I follow after her, mimicking her taste, attempting to be like her, to be her, although I know that a career in either theater or public school education is the very last thing I will ever attempt, shudder at the mere thought of such a thing. Daddy comes by his love of theater honestly, following in the family tradition; rumor has it that his mother Julia (who had been born in Riga, in Russia) refused to become betrothed to his father William Mordecai (whom she met in Philadelphia) until he had a real profession, so he left his acting career behind him, and became a dentist. (One of William's brothers founded the United Parcel Service in San Francisco, the other retired early to Florida and his sister Rachel had two children.) Albert's brother Harold followed in his father's footsteps, and his other brother, Aaron, became a pharmacist, but Daddy, like Steve, faced with the choice of medicine or law and hating the sight of blood went to law school.

Steve, in between his first and second year at Queens College, has his own summer job at a local day camp at Forest Park. Mom and Daddy breathe a sigh of relief, hoping that separation will cool down what has become a hot and heavy romance. Already, I am wearing Steve's small gold TAU fraternity pin, which means that we are engaged to be engaged, and we are talking about marriage. We have already planned our itinerary; pinned this year, engaged next year, married the next. Our parents are rigid with terror that this will really happen; I am seventeen, he is nineteen. We believe that we are adults, our parents see two children.

We are battling what we see as adult discrimination against our inalienable rights as the adults we know ourselves to be, to love and happiness, and vow to keep our connection alive. Hormones are doing battle with 1950s mores and restraints. Our method of choice has become letter writing, and missives fly back and forth with nerve-wracking speed, filled with incredibly cheesy corn and romantic hyperbole, and lofty melodrama. It is all *sealed with a kiss...*

I love you, my dearest Lynnie. So far my summer has been miserable because I'm not with you. I long to hold you and tell you how much I miss you and love you. I can't stand being in Rockaway. I miss you so much and am so lonely that my life is miserable. Last night I was out with the fellows, trying to forget my loneliness. Today I counted the days until we can see each other again. It's not fair that we should be both having miserable summers separated from each other when we love each other so much. I will call you on Wednesday between 9 and 9:30 P.M. to find out about next weekend, and to tell you that I love you so very very much.

MMmmmphfff.* With all my love, Steve.

*(Secret code—The sound that is made when two people kiss and talk at the same time, as observed in the comics!)

I am going through the motions of caring for my charges, attending to activities of camping, counting the moments to Mail Call, salivating and day dreaming of my next letter.

My dearest Lynnie, I love you. The first thing I did after work was to rush home to see if a letter had come from you. Today I was elated discover you had not neglected your Stevie...It's hard to find words to express how lonely I am or how much I miss you, my dearest babe. I'm sure you understand how much I love you and need you, Lynnie. Please write often...write about anything, spilt milk, dirty bunks, bad chow mein, whatever, but write....

Goodbye for now, my Lynnie. With all my love, Steve.

From time to time, I am called to the main office for a phone call, tingling with expectation; I am going to hear his voice. I fly over the rutted grass tufted pathway my chest tight, my stomach leaping, my attempts at speed hindered by the terrain and the confinements of time itself.

My dearest Lynnie. I am writing this letter right after talking to you on the phone. I don't know why, but I always feel terrible after talking to you on the phone. Maybe it's because you're so near and yet so very far away. Hearing your voice makes me want to hold you so badly I could scream. I'm going to see you this week even if I have to walk to (camp) Paradise.

Goodbye for now. I love you...mmphfff.

Whenever possible, to the chagrin of my parents who keep their upper lips stiff, their faces tightly grimly happy, and their hopes high, Steve comes for the weekend to visit. He is hitching rides with other visitors, wherever they can be found, the boyfriends of other employees, taking trains and buses, getting here any way he can. When he arrives, the emotional intensity of our reunion overcomes us, enhancing the intensity of our erstwhile bond. When I have off time, especially at night, we take thick rough woolen camp blankets to the woods, follow that winding path, find ourselves a private spot under the wide expanse of black sky and an entire galaxy of gleaming stars, and cling together in the cool damp summer Catskill Mountain night wrapped in our scratchy covers, reveling in the tastes of each other's mouths, which have become the center of this vast universe we are sharing. We are further tantalized by the amazing and frightening tingling sensations that are invading our bodies, assaulting the balance of our consciousness. *My world is a rapture in blue with the world far away and your lips close to mine...*

My dearest Lynnie, I love you. Don and I got home by 2:00 A.M. Monday. I wish I could have stayed until curfew time Sunday, but I guess I have no right to complain since I'm getting transportation to Paradise pretty conveniently and inexpensively. But I hate to leave you when we have a chance to be alone together. I'm glad you gave me your picture, since now I have a chance to look at you often. Today I took my kids on another hike through Cunningham and we bumped into another couple on a blanket (what again?). The place is jumping with lovers. I may be coming up late this weekend because of the visiting day traffic, and because I don't know how I'm getting up yet. But I'll be up to see you for sure, my Lynnie, come hell or high water. I love you. Mmmmphfff! and Mmmmphfff! With all my love, Stevie

It becomes inevitable that this summer separation will bring us closer together. I sanctimoniously repulse the advances of bevies of handsome male counselors who flirt with me with intense adolescent anticipation during every waking hour that Steve is not there, disappear into the background frustrated when he is.

My dearest Lynnie. We got home about midnight. First we dropped Joanie's aunt and the camp mother's husband in New York. I was at my sister's house by one thirty. The trip was miserable. I had to sit in the back, and boy was it ever cramped. I had no place to put my left arm so I resorted to wrapping it around my head (what?). Sarell and Don ribbed me about my frugality (damned cheap) and called me a cheapskate. I received two of your letters, and a giant (boy was it ever) postcard. I don't know why you called your second letter 'silly'. It was beautiful. I get such a glow inside of me when you tell me how much you love me. It is such a wonderful feeling to have the one you love tell you how much she loves you. It made me feel secure and wanted. You're the most wonderful thing that ever happened to me, my Lynnie, and I love you so much. Before I loved you, my life had no real meaning or significance. Now I have something that makes my life worthwhile...you, my dearest Lynnie. So don't tell me ever that telling me how much you love me is 'silly'. All the way home I kept thinking how lucky I am to have such a wonderful person like you loving me. I love you, I love you, I love you...Today while taking my boys on a hike through the woods (what again?) I discovered a feather on the path. It had such a beautiful shade of blue that I was intrigued by it. After all, how often do you come across a feather of a bluebird or blue jay (I think it must be one or the other)? I showed the feather to a few people, but nobody seemed interested ('so what'... 'good for you'). It just goes to show how the truly fine things in life like nature fail to arouse most people, while some theatrical garbage termed 'spectacular' attracts millions. I'm sending the feather to you, my Lynnie, hoping you'll get as much a kick out of it as I did when I found it. I hope you won't think I'm being over sentimental and absurd. It's just my way of sharing a wonderful experience with you and telling you how much I love you. I don't know yet if I'm coming up this Friday. I love you. Mmphfff. Stevie.

This has become the best most fulfilling period of my lifetime; I feel that I have come home. A day without a letter plunges me into the deepest recesses of an elevator shaft; a letter received is the most exotic aphrodisiac.

My dearest Lynnie...Now I know how you feel when I don't write to you. The first thing I do when I get home from work is see if a letter has come. Today there was no letter for the second straight day (even though I got three on Monday). I'm not complaining, though; you're probably busy working on the set of "The King and I". I'm hoping you don't think my 'feather letter' was silly and childish I also received a new one year deferment from my draft board. I love you. I'm still not sure whether I'm coming up Friday. I'll call Don tomorrow to find out if he's coming. Please write, even though I may see you before I get your letters. I'm used to your wonderful letters in which you tell me how much you love me. It gives me such a warm feeling when I read your letters. It helps me forget a little how lonely I am without you near me. I love you so much, so very much, my Lynnie. W.A.M.L, S.

A weekend without a visit is as agonizing as a long prison sentence without parole; then there is the thing that we are getting closer and closer, more and more solid. I feel the promises for the future coming alive.

My dearest Lynnie...I just got through talking to me friend, Sandy, on the phone. He chewed me out for not calling sooner (he's right), he sold his car (remember the '53 Dodge) so he and Alice can get married September or so. She's working downtown and makes $40 a week (not bad?). Next Saturday, Alice is going to Gloria's shower...remember Joe and Gloria are getting married Sept. 15. I'm getting kind of envious hearing those wedding bells ringing for everyone else. But my day will come soon, (I hope). I've got my bride all picked out, too. She's the most wonderful girl in the whole world and the only girl for me. Her name is Lynnie, and I love her so much. Sandy and Alice are crazy about you, and Sandy told me we'd get together when you get back. He told me he never thought I could love someone as much as I love you, but he doesn't know the half of it. I'm calling Thursday night. I love you, my Lynnie, Mmphfff. WAML, S

My dearest Lynnie, I love you. Today was a miserable rainy day. I really don't mind rain, except when it ruins a planned day. Rain always makes the air cleaner and seems to absolve man from his sins (I'll bet you didn't know I could be so philosophical). Tonight I'm calling Sandy to see if we can get together Saturday. Only five more days and my girl will be home (I hope) OBOYOBOYOBOY! Friday I think I'll go to the beach party with the counselors of my camp. They're going to have beer, so I can get soused and dream you are with me. Don't forget to pack my bathing suit, which is on the line outside the Pixie house. I forgot to tell you in yesterday's letter to say goodbye to everyone for me, and thank them for everything. I love you, my Lynnie, and can't wait till you're home again with me. The summer went pretty fast, but the next five days can't go fast enough for me. With all my love, Steve.

My dearest Lynnie, This will probably be my last letter of the summer since you'll be home (I hope) before any later letters could reach you at Paradise. From now on, I'll be telling you how much I love you in person (for about sixty years). I was very surprised when I got home just now to find a letter from you. The one you wrote Monday I received today. Last night Dave and Lenny barged into my room and woke me up to tell me they were back from their camping trip. It rained again today. I don't care how much it rains as long as it doesn't spoil any of our plans. I called Sandy last night to find out if we're getting together Saturday, but he's taking Alice to Gloria's shower. I told him that we may drive up to see them the weekend after you're home. Only two more days of work, and only four days until I can see my baby all the time again and tell her how much I love her. I'll call you tomorrow night MMmphff.

I have come to the conclusion that Steve loves me, really and I am all aglow with hope and expectation for our future. *My prayer and the answer you give may they still be the same for as long as we live that you'll always be there at the end of my prayer...*

When camp is over, I gratefully return to the real world, and prepare to begin my college career at the same college, Queens, as Steve, so that we can remain together as much as possible. Steve's mother and father sit with mine at my high school graduation and there is great exultation when I am awarded a St Gauden's award for my art. I walk up to the podium to receive my diploma and medal with my head held high. Starry eyed and decked out in resplendent formal attire we celebrate this momentous occasion at my elegantly planned prom and then later in private. I am taking my academic credits all together, now, since this may be the last time we have together before charging headlong into the world of adult responsibility. We are joined at the hip, or whatever. Next year, he will begin law school, at night, and I will be transferring to Pratt Institute to resume my art studies, without the stress of academia, but we will be engaged by then. There will only be the stress of separation on weekdays, as we await our wedding the following spring.

We have our itinerary, Steve always plans every detail, and true to design, Steve presents me with my diamond engagement ring which we had purchased together at that discount jewelry shop under the el in the gray dreary aging west Bronx some months ago, that early spring of '57; for some strange reason, I am unable to recall the moment although I can sense the damp frigid winter air threatening snow, the rank and stagnant odor of rot and corrosion and petroleum fumes that encompasses inner city streets in areas that have endured long life and inherent decay. The store is nestled in the middle of a nondescript gray street everything existing beneath a coat of gloomy industrial residue, its faint incandescent glow and suggestion of warmth and promise emanating barely from its tightly protected outer skin. So consumed with a cautious ecstasy of promise and newness we tentatively choose my ring, a one carat emerald cut diamond with matching baguettes on either side and proceed homeward tingling with a grave satisfaction and slightly desperate hope. A week later, his mother has died.

CHAPTER 10

June, 1958

I am watching them from the kitchen. Steve's discomfort seems tinged with the certain knowledge that tomorrow at this very time he will be in the process of deflowering my father's only daughter. His face begins to flush; I can just figure what he is thinking. He attempts to find a location for his size twelve shoes. His tanned young nicely proportioned face is strained. I study his familiar features, hungrily, admiring and proud, straight chiseled nose, just a hint of Judaic curve, firm even nicely shaped lips, gold flecked gray-green almond eyes, and high Slavic cheekbones. He stops himself time after time from nervously running slim fingers through his carefully combed dark hair. It contrasts with the white fringe that circles Daddy's bald dome, barely disguised by his slight graceful albeit sparse comb over, his proverbial sardonic smile nearly obscured by that familiar sharp thin mustache. My father's tall solid body sporting the start of a slight bay window is ensconced in his position before the blaring television, immersed in a ball-game. I imagine the one thought going through his mind over and over again. I just know that he wants intensely to remove his shoes, pants, shirt, and spread out in shorts and T-shirt, as he always does.

Steve barely graduated from gangly adolescence at twenty-one, sits gingerly, awkwardly on the edge of a really uncomfortable seat, watching distractedly, his mind obviously on other things. His own six-foot frame vies with my father's for space. The two men, the young and the middle aged, seem to usurp every inch of air in this room. He glances at my father, and drops his eyes quickly, and I know that he is praying that he will not be drawn into conversation with his future father-in-law. He has not yet developed lawyer

48

skills sufficient to joust with the prodigious Albert. He has also chosen to study law rather than medicine to avoid contact with blood. There is nowhere to escape to in this tiny four-room apartment in a two-family home in Flushing, Queens. There is precious little area to share.

Anxiety and expectation are hanging tensely in the air, pervading everything. We have eclipsed Mom's grand pre-wedding dinner, and there seems nothing left to do but wait as time passes, and the ecstatically awaited moment arrives. There are no common grounds for conversation, wedding business having been long completed. Mom's special *gedempte,* pot roast, swimming in rich gravy, has disappeared, along with all the trimmings, biscuits, salad, floating potatoes and carrots, stewed plums and apricots, and the obligatory giant devil's food cake with thick fudge frosting. Daddy and I have managed to decimate that. Aaron, father of the groom, has left. Not a large man, and given to silence rather than conversation, his absent wife having been the conversationalist in the family, he is barely missed.

What has Aaron thought about our home, I wonder; it is so different from his own. No presumptuous imitation period furniture protected by layers of slipcover and plastic, here. I wonder if he thinks I am good enough for his precious only son, his son the future lawyer. I have become well acquainted with Steve's family in the last few years since we met. Although my parents are head and shoulders beyond in education, and possibly intellect, we are not in the same financial strata as Steve's family. His father has become wealthy in the *schmotta,* the dress business. This, and the remuneration it brings, is his badge of honor.

But Aaron is an administrator, although he started many years ago as a newly arrived eight-year-old immigrant from Poland, by pushing a broom, as he is fond of reminding anyone who will listen and our life is filled with creativity. We may not be wealthy, but we can do things with fabric, too. Mom has wrestled with yards and yards of it, to sew a complete and massive wall of fully lined drapes in the style vernacular of the day, cream butcher linen covered with huge hunter green, chartreuse and teal elephants ear leaves in a kind of new age art deco pattern, tailored with pinch pleats and installed with an elaborate series of draw strings. It is a part of a stage set for the production of *The Perfect Home* as she would like to perceive it. The sofa that Steve and Daddy sit on is a contemporary sectional, sporting vertical stripes in the same greens as the drapes, lightweight and simple of line, and in this brave new world of contemporary design most shocking to all who have seen it, no arms. It wraps startlingly around the corner of the room, going where no honorable sofa should dare to go. truly uncomfortable, but very up to date, taken detail by detail from *Better Homes and Gardens*, or one of the piles of descriptive pages Mom has clipped and saved for future reference. It lives on a wide swath of tightly woven intricately knotted persimmon wall-to-wall carpeting. It is all very *avante garde*, almost succeeds in convincing the viewer that life here is normal.

Mom is very proud of her room. She may not own her own home, but her apartment is the epitome of Metropolitan Design. There are oak and glass cabinets filled with well read books, old and new, classical and contemporary. Her precious blond oak Hardman console piano, my nemesis, is pushed up against the wall amongst the bookcases. Every available leftover space is filled with her collections of bric-a-brac, miniature brass statuary, hand-painted clay figurines, mementos of Daddy's tour in France and other little things that I have been required to dust and polish each week of my life for as far back as I can remember. A grouping of charming gouache paintings on a soft blue gray paper depicting French peasant life that Daddy brought home from the war, framed in light oak to match the furniture, are arranged over the sofa. The immense well mullioned picture window, drapes pulled open, is filled with plants, as is every window sill in the apartment. This is the closest Mom has ever come to having a yard and garden. The ever burgeoning Collieresque mounds of magazine clippings delineate her as yet unrequited dreams for her future, which is rapidly diminishing, in her fifty second year.

I brush my mother's hair with quick tender strokes, relishing that ritual so much a part of the strange long nights occasioned by the continuing war. Mommy and I have our girl's night in, identified by this hair styling, face creaming thing, which follows the intimate mother/daughter business of discovering new recipes together, and sharing the joyful tasting during a cozy dinner for two. Daddy, of course, is still in Europe, waiting out the end of the war. I barely remember him, but I have my growing collection of airmail letters and postcards, and photos piled haphazardly in a shoe box. I am six years old when he returns, ending the intimate relationship Mommy and I have developed during the separation occasioned by the war, limiting future mother/ daughter access. There is no longer any time for those private moments between us, although Daddy, lost in his post-war angst, is rarely home anyway. In these times, the specter of his always imminent arrival haunts attempts at recreating those precious moments.

I take after Mom, they all say, we both have that small pointy chin, stuck resolutely out, we each are immovable once committed to a project or direction. Mom travels daily to perform her duties as an English teacher on the other side of the city in a less desirable area, and returns to our tiny apartment in time to greet her latch key child, perform her household chores, and keep her appointment with her small confidante and buddy. It is not just hair dressing and cooking in which the two conspirators take part, but the sewing of clothes, for ourselves and for my many dolls, and the creation of myriad craft projects. One begins a project and finishes it. This is responsibility, as is Mom's dedication to her own chores and the lip stiffening business of keeping home fires burning during an intolerable and lonely period in world and personal history.

The sad thing is that few of the dreams described by Mom to me ever see fruition. These dreams are delineated with such yearning, in such detail that I can feel Mom's hunger in my own bones. House, garden... War times as well as post-war dynamics are responsible for the murder of many dreams. These are hard times, all around. But I watch my mother do all those necessary things with that stiff upper lip, that jutting chin, that steely determination, and wonder at her resoluteness. As I get older and more aware of such things, I ask Mom, awed, how she does it, go on day after day, year after year, with no pot of gold, and not even a rainbow, save for in her dreams This is when I make that resolution about letting all of my sins be of commission rather than omission. I resolve to take risks; once you can identify a risk, you can determine how to handle it.

She prods and encourages me to read, and I follow her lead. I read the Pollyanna, Anne of Green Gables, and The Bobbsey Twins first and Kipling's Just So Stories, all of Louisa May Alcott's series about the March girls, and then Frances Hodgson Burnett's Little Princess and The Secret Garden. I have my own dreams, my head whirrs with myriad fantasies and plans for my future. As I lie in my twin bed, enveloped in a pool of apple green and dusty rose quilted chintz coverlet and pillow sham, lovingly crafted by Mom and her ancient well worn Singer, I spin my glorious future adventures in the dark, my eyes tightly shut, and so drift off to sleep, to the softly modulated poignant sounds of sobbing that accompany my mom's tears of frustration and disappointment. The home she knows she will never own, the yard, the garden, the eat in kitchen, formal dining room, sun porch ... sweeping front lawn and elegant entrance, the compassionate and tender husband, loving and sweet and calm and supportive. Always, she delineates pitifully some plan, some hope, and despairing, finally surrender to the certain knowledge that it will never, can never be. She cannot get past the dream. Dreams are realized by taking chances, leaps of faith, and Mom is no risk taker, she is a child of the '20s, the Great Depression.

Fight, I think, willing Mom to go beyond her hopelessness, but Mom does not have the resolve to do so. She has determination, the stubborn desire, but not the resolve, not the focus to see it to fruition. Perhaps she merely dissolves in that negativity that pervades her family, their European refugee ancestors. The Kinahurra Kurse, is what I call it. There is nothing you can do, failure is predetermined. To tempt fate by rejoicing on success is to embrace failure; years and years of pogrom and endemic societal abuse have become part and parcel of collective cultural memory. Every dream Mom has is extracted from the reality of her life. She is indeed a woman of valor, right out of Talmudic pages, but her sins are of omission. She is paralyzed by risk, unable to get beyond the fear of it. I repeat what has become my mantra, clenching my teeth, sticking out my chin in that old familiar way.

Years later when she is in her seventies I finally convince her to build next door to me, and I supervise the construction, the completion and décor, actually do the landscaping myself, trying to include what I recall from those old magazines and clippings. Ultimately, I go all out in a later renovation in yet a different location, finish her space nearly exactly idea for idea of what she has always wanted, it is her dream home.

I have retained all the lessons I learned in these intimate times with Mom, including several vital lessons of survival. I will not hesitate, I think, I will breathe deeply and move. All important are creativity and duty, and above all, let my sins be of commission rather than omission, this has become an insistent mantra. Creativity is a given, its demands and rewards are indelibly engraved on my DNA and have been coerced into my existence over time. The matter of making decisions in the direction of positive realization is a matter of self-discipline, and of creating a series of actions that become a pattern, a habit. The issue of duty is another thing ... this is tricky, and not a simple matter. The honing of one's ability to perceive duty, to identify responsibility is a question of experience, a skill earned by trial and error, a decision-making ability that requires delicate balance and profound reasoning powers. A risk reasonably to be perceived defines a duty to be obeyed, a concept embedded in an infamous legal premise that I do not discover until much later.

Mom her eyes clouded and her face blank is washing the last of the dinner dishes, and I am wiping absentmindedly, my mind also on other things. Some of them are the same as those things predictably on Steve's mind, some are not. I give a somewhat hostile swipe at the dark gray Formica countertop, its austerity enhanced by pink and aqua boomerangs, trimmed with striated aluminum. I drape the soggy frayed towel with its coordinated chartreuse, aqua and green stripes that I know so well, over the back of the red aluminum barstool, that I remember all the way back to our apartment in the Bronx during the war. Tomorrow, I will leave all this behind for new things of my own choosing. A new life will be starting. There is a huge lump in my throat. Mom's antenna is extended into full momma mode, and she turns her head sharply, *what*, she asks cryptically? Startled out of my reverie, I jump, what? Nothing, I answer, lying. Come on, she says matter-of-factly, I know something's wrong. Spit it out. What's going on? Nothing, Mom, really, nothing, I lie.

The dishes done, Steve and I retire to the privacy of my tiny bedroom that I have painted a bright orange over the old ice blue, creating an eerily glowing color reversal. Too late, I learned about color reversals, in my art studies at Pratt Institute in Brooklyn this past year, after the damage was done. We move awkwardly in this tiny space amongst my collections, books, art supplies, paintings and assorted clutter, and fling ourselves onto the daybed. Feet are on the ground according to the rules as delineated by Ann Landers and her sister Abby, leaning against the pillows. A giant shroud-like six-foot long at least rose-colored plastic bag, stuffed with my wedding dress, hangs from the closet doors, slightly ajar, truly the pink elephant in the middle of the room. I turn on the radio, and the Beatles harmonize mellifluously and pleasantly at us. *I want to hold your haaaaannnnnnnd,* then *all you need is love, da, ta da ta da*.....and Al Hibbler moans, *oh my love my darling I've hungered for your touch.* We reach automatically for each other, and fall into our familiar well practiced embrace. We are so close, that we are practically one person, our lips are so connected and involved that we may not be able to disconnect. I have felt nothing better in my entire life than his arms around me, his warm body pressing against mine. I know that this must be love. What else can it be? It fills all of the criteria delineated in our repertoire of popular songs, has been reinforced by Steve in his own words.

...I love you, my dearest Lynnie. So far my summer has been miserable because I'm not with you. I long to hold you and tell you how much I miss you and love you...

Things are warming up, I reach back, unhook my bra, and attempt to get Steve to move his hand under my shirt, but he draws it back. I try to position us so that our bodies are closer together daringly removing my feet from the floor, tentatively moving my leg over his. I am being directed by forces stronger than my own. We have been in similar situations before, but never so tantalizingly close to permission, and actual success. Always, there has been that insurmountable barrier of what is not to be done, but I am sensing the end of old ways, the beginning of new. Now, a subtle unspoken, un-addressed wrestling match ensues. I am feeling that omnipresent sense of intense yearning. What's wrong with that, I ask myself, tomorrow at this time we will be man and wife. He pushes me away. What kind of girl are you, anyway, he banters, a slight smile around his lips, but his hazel-green almond eyes are icy cold. Who is this that I am marrying? A joke, but maybe not; Steve's attitude and treatment toward me lately, since his mother's death, in fact, have changed. He has an edge, now. He has lost that sweetness, and has become harshly critical, almost cruel. He is not only hypercritical, he is snide, punishing. I have been telling myself that he is still mourning his beloved mother, and has some feelings of guilt about the time he has not spent with her during the last year of her life. He has been with me. In my Pollyanna world, this will pass. *Hey there, you with the stars in your eyes, love never made a fool of you, you used to be so wise...*Rosemary Clooney whimpers about lessons learned but it is all lost on me.

Stubbornly, I try to seduce him again, giving it all I've got and he pushes me sharply away. We can wait, he says, and abruptly gets up to leave. We have a busy day tomorrow, let's get some sleep, he says.

... I hate to leave you when we have a chance to be alone together...

I walk him to the door of the apartment, feeling empty, disappointed, dismayed, an ineffable sense of warning tickles my consciousness. I wave gaily, good bye, with my best and most loving smile, as he descends the stairs, looking up and waving also. See you tomorrow, his words float eerily upward through the stairwell as the door shuts behind him, and I go back inside.

Mom waylays me in the narrow hallway. Now, are you going to tell me what's wrong, she asks? She pushes me into my room, and sits us both down on the bed. Now, she demands. Spill.

Oh, Mommy, I begin, tears spilling from my eyes, sluicing down my cheeks, we have to call off the wedding. I can't marry Steve. Something is very wrong. What can be wrong at this late date she demands softly, a *Yeshiva bucha*, a good Jewish boy, a Lawyer, for goodness sake. His family has money. He will be a good husband. You will be his wife. He will take good care of you. You will be a mother. I've changed my mind, I don't want to be a wife or a mother any more, I say. I am only nineteen years old, I whine. I can continue my art studies, I can be an artist. But you always wanted children … she breaks off and I don't allow her to finish, I don't really need a husband, I say cavalierly. I can take care of myself. He's different since Ida died. He's mean to me. He's not the same Stevie I fell in love with. I'm scared. Words float in my subconscious. *Mean to me, why must you be mean to me ...* which are soon eclipsed by different more recent words...

... Before I loved you, my life had no real meaning or significance. Now I have something that makes my life worthwhile... you, my dearest Lynnie...

Brides always have last minute jitters, she tells me. It's perfectly normal. NO, no, I whisper, not like this. But Lynne, she moans, how can we cancel? The hall and the flowers are already paid for and 200 dinners. Aaron has provided all sorts of liquor and wine. Champagne. This is your wedding, Mom, I want to say. Who needs all these flowers, all this food and booze, all these people? I know her answer, it's not me, and, it's Aaron; all of his business connections to *shmooze*, all those people to impress. And what would I tell my friends, she asks plaintively. Oh boy, I think, everything is always about social mores and status, how things look, what people will say. What about how I feel, I ask myself with a growing sense of futility. Yeah, okay, I say out loud with resignation, surrendering as usual, you're probably right. You've caved again haven't you I murmur silently inside my head to no one at all.

She leaves me, then, and I prepare for bed, my last night as a single girl, and my final moments as a virgin. That at least is something to rejoice in. I will be free. I will have my own home. I will do as I wish. I can have babies. And, of course, finally, sex, and that, I *know*, means, love.

> *... It's funny the way we both think of the same things at the same time. I keep thinking how wonderful it will be when some day soon, we'll be together always. I just don't want to be away from you for more than two seconds at a time. I love you so much...*

After tossing and turning, unable to sleep for a long while, dinner and terror combining forces in my stomach, I slip into the kitchen, where Mom stands looking out of the kitchen window, obviously thinking deep thoughts. Can you fix me some Alka-Seltzer, I ask her. Yeah, she says, wait one moment. I can do that. She turns on the tap, and reaches for one of those small shrimp cocktail glasses that fill the cabinet to overflowing, stacked precariously one into the other.

He's not the same since Ida died last year, I mumble under my breath as I head back to my bed for the last time.

1957

I am standing in Mom's familiar kitchen in our garden apartment in Forest Hills, next to the old red stepladder where I have thrown my handbag when I returned from my new summer job in the city as a girl Friday. I have braved the suffocating July heat and repeated assaults of fellow subway companions, felt yet again another hard body pressing against my thin summer dress and carefully inserted the point of my French heel onto the tender portion of his foot just above the toes and ground, gratefully triumphant when he slipped faceless into the crowd. I am munching on a huge slab of Mom's seemingly ever regenerating chocolate cake, a glass of milk on the red Formica counter; Pat Boone is singing in the background.. School is out. Did you hear, I ask him brimming with excitement, Camus has won the Nobel prize for literature; I have been studying French philosophy this year, in French, and have fallen in love also with Camus, Sartre, too. He grins at me, with condescension, something akin to disdain or maybe even scorn. The courts aren't protecting obscene matter under the first amendment, he says, brimming with self importance, showing his involvement in the study of law, pre law as it were. I don't even notice, I am completely involved in my plans for the future and the present. I think it's cute the way he is moving on into the adult world, although a little scary. Steve has just arrived at my door at the end of his first work day as an insurance underwriter, his summer job, and our plans are to join friends for dinner, and then continue to a movie. This of course is followed by our mutually much anticipated infant tradition of heavy necking in the car. We begin that weekend in July as we plan every other, in each other's company. He grabs the piece of cake that I have cut for him in advance.

We stand together comfortably in the kitchen in the bubble of our safe happy private little world, all of life before us, smiling contentedly at each other, when the sudden shrill shriek of the telephone breaks the mood, the strident voice on the other end of the call draws Steve away, he leaves quickly, barely a word except for his destination, heads anxiously to the hospital. I am not invited to join him, no, he says when I ask, you stay here. Despite the one carat emerald cut diamond on my left hand, I am not yet a part of his family, so he rushes off without me. This, at least, is what he tells me, admonishing me to stay out of it, it is not my business. I am left confused, stunned, my face burning for some arcane reason, but Daddy leaves his office moments after my own call to him, Daddy, I think that Ida is really ill, races home, and drives me to the hospital. I am taken aback, dismayed, but too worried about Steve and his mother to notice that something is awry. Steve is thrust into the midst, unprepared and stunned, of the catastrophic and untenable last moments of life of this person, his beloved, revered and adored parent, unable to grasp even the barest of comprehension, of the ramifications of this situation. I am a helpless observer of this life and death drama, feeling like a useless appendage, though willing to understand that we are in the midst of heartache. I cannot even imagine what it could be like to be about to lose your mother, am unable to even wrap my mind around the thought. I am in time to watch the last act, from backstage, as the final curtain falls on what seems to be a most grotesque and hideous fantasy ...

She won't die, she won't. Steve repeats this over and over again burying his face in his arms as though the mere act of repeating it will influence fate. He refuses to accept anything that is being said, explained to him by family and healthcare persons who surround him mouthing explanations and platitudes. He will not even acknowledge my existence, as I try again and again, his future wife, to comfort him; he thrusts me away. I hover guiltily in the shadows, more and more confused.

Aaron wrings his hands and tries in his anguish of final defeat to foment some last minute miracle and his sister Elaine tries to tell Steve why they haven't told him of the impending end. It is suddenly painfully obvious that Aaron is sadly misguided by his desire to save his beloved son any unnecessary pain, as has been Ida, herself; Elaine's motives may have been partially at least a final vengeance directed toward the prodigal son, the favored sibling, an ultimate grab for the precious last days of her mother's life, her preoccupation with her inheritance.

*Ida's clear caustic voice rises above the tumult, characteristically forceful, though weak. So Aaron, all of these people that you know; all your **connections**; what are they doing for me now? And the poor man twists his hands some more, and reassures her, or tries to, insisting that he has someone coming in, a specialist of stupendous repute and ability, who will affect a last minute cure. And the dying woman throws her last sarcastic barb at the man with whom she has shared the past thirty years. Perhaps she is unaware that her beloved only son stands within earshot. She is able to voice her fury with the world and the* *powers that be at this last moment only by directing her anger at the one person upon whom she can focus at this moment, who is so close to her that it will not matter, her husband. And your friend, President Eisenhower, of whom you always brag, what can you do now, Aaron, call your friend IKE? Get Ike to help, Aaron; all of your special connections that you prize so highly. Maybe your connections can save me, she snarls. She gasps, takes a last breath, and she passes away.*

She's gone, cries Aaron. She's NOT, sobs her heartbroken son, she can't be. Her daughter wails and cries and lapses into hysterics, thinking all the while, I know, about the safe deposit box where the jewelry lies, and of the best items of furniture, sorting and cataloguing in her mind, and what she will do with them, growing stronger than she has ever been during her mother's tenure.

I have known, we both have known, that Ida was ill, but in our preoccupation with each other, neither Steve nor I have been aware of the gravity, to say nothing of the terminal state of her disease. We have not been informed because of the importance of this final year of Steve's college, preparatory to Law School. The family has decided that Steve need not be faced with the trauma of his mother's impending demise at this crucial time in his infant law career. I realize too late that I should have been more observant, more aware, and less possessive. And there is a totally unfamiliar and entirely distinctive family dynamic here with which I am unfamiliar.

❧❦

1947, Rego Park, N.Y.

Stevie hides in the heady perfumed depths of his older sister's closet, in the new house nestled elegantly on a pretty residential street in Rego Park, waiting gleefully to scare her. He stays still as a mouse, for fear of being found out before having a chance to put his plan into action. Soon his patience is rewarded when he hears Elaine enter and with a great sigh, heave her school books on the bed. She throws herself down beside them, dials a well memorized phone number, and begins a conversation with her friend, Florence, so intimate in aspect and so delicious in detail as to make Stevie catch his breath with fear of discovery, although he doesn't begin to understand what they are talking about.

Finally growing bored with the repetition of breathless fact after breathless fact, he decides that the momentous time has arrived, and filled with that familiar ineffable titillating adrenalin high pops out instantly before he can change his mind shouting a jolting BOO. And chortling shrilly wriggles and slips through her furious grasp and out of the room before she can lay a hand on him and possibly break his miserable little neck like she has threatened so many times, her heart pumping a mile a minute. A book crashes against the slamming door in accentuation of her shrieking threat.

Elaine says a quick goodbye to her wondering friend and rushes right down the stairs to make sure that her mother is with whining clarity made aware of this latest infraction of the prodigal son.

57

Elaine is a plump and not unpretty girl, in fact bears a slight resemblance to Elizabeth Taylor which her parents fail to see immersed as they are in their other preoccupations, but unattractive in her habits, her posture, and very aware of an over blossoming bosom, walks with a slouch to hide the self-consciousness that she feels. Her clumsiness and insecurity are due at least in part to the feeling that she has of being a second rate person. Stephen being a boy and the heir, as well as pride and joy of the two doting parents, is the one who is being groomed for familial success as potential professional man...Doctor, lawyer, whatever. It doesn't even matter to them, she thinks with an amazing lack of loyalty, that she actually is the one with the brains in the family. She is always being put down, while that numbskull of a brother of hers is treated like a princeling; the oversight and promulgation of his future and all that it held is their main occupation.

To make matters worse, Steve is always tormenting her, an activity for which he is never punished. Somehow, his behavior is considered to be adorable and normal. She thinks that he is a little weird, enjoying hurting her like this. She should not have even bothered to tell her mother, for as always, her supposed true recital of abuse comes out sounding like the petty and trivial picking of a jealous and vicious carping sister.

When Elaine has returned stomping angrily to her room, and their mother has finished crooning over the triumphantly glowing boy, and stuffed him with goodies, his mother suddenly changes her manner, and proceeds to lambaste him for his dirty fingernails, unfinished homework, and muddy shoes. She sends him off to his room with orders, shrilly issued, to clean up that very instant. She rewashes the shiny ashtray that holds one flicked ash in its gleaming palm, and straightens the plastic covers over the fabric slipcovers on the sofa and chairs. She puts the half read newspaper neatly and precisely on the stack of its brothers on the kitchen stepladder on its merry way to the trashcan outside in the alley.

Ida follows the same routine that she began at the time of her marriage, twenty years previously, a profound and meticulous attention to thorough whether necessary or not housecleaning. Her furniture is covered with a series of coats, fabric, plastic, and antimacassar. Her ash trays although rarely to never used are buffed to a glazed reflective surface, wood tables and floors both gleam with their layers of polish; all else is organized and stored or displayed with impeccable precision. Newspapers are relegated to the stepladder in the kitchen immediately after a most perfunctory glance, mostly of supermarket advertising, there to await nearly immediate disposal. She would then commence her daily attention to the purchase of foodstuffs and household necessities, visiting every different market commensurate with the special sales of the day, thereby saving pennies and nickels and dimes, sometimes quarters, until she has amassed in secret a goodly fortune, which she keeps divided in every different bank in the area. She considers these savings to be her own money, earned by her, saved for that proverbial rainy day or the division of her two children, whichever comes first. Her children, of course, are her priority in all that she seeks to attain in this life.

Steve goes upstairs to his room oblivious to the usual machine gun rat-a-tat of his mother's criticism, and glowing with satisfaction over his coup, throws a nasty face and wiggly finger ear at Elaine as he passes her open door, and retreats quickly to his own room slamming the door quickly and sitting down quietly at his desk. Gone are the naughty sibling, the outrageous gadfly, and here is the student, the Yeshiva boy, their son, the doctor...or maybe, the lawyer...he never could stand the sight of blood...

He senses that he doesn't have much imagination but he intends to compensate for this lack by a combination of focus and hard work. He puts long hours into the studying and memorizing of facts, and by dint of this concentration, manages to keep a consistently above average grade. His collection of facts is memorable, but it never occurs to him to channel any of them into original thought.

Steve's cultural capacity is as limited as that of both his parents. His father is a first generation immigrant from the ghettos of Jewish Poland, who had worked his way through sheer diligence and strength of spirit to a position of responsibility and monetary reward with a garment district concern where he had begun forty years before by sweeping floors. As a matter of fact, Aaron Heffner had never even learned to read or write, and signed his name on his checks with an 'X'.

He isn't the dominant parent in that family, for Ida, the mother, wears the cloak of power there and directs every action that exists with her iron arm and her sharp tongue. Her children are unable to function at all without her pointed directive, and fear to disobey her with a terror that forbids even the slightest infraction. They pay homage to her as though she were a goddess of power and magnitude unequaled in both song and story.

Steve revels in their Jewishness, and in his own loyalty to ritual, though he never takes the slightest trouble beyond memorization to comprehend the grave and time honored meanings of the ancient words and customs. He remains staunchly true to his beginnings even as his acquaintances and cohorts are beginning to question them.

He never learns how to love, because he is never shown love. Adulation, expectation, pride, perfunctory hugs and kisses, but love? He doesn't even begin to have any frame of reference upon which to base a thought. He never reads anything that isn't nonfiction, and relegates to the realm of fantasy anything that he trips over at the movies or wherever it is implied that something of that capacity could exist. He cultivates what he thinks to be a fine tuned sense of humor that never leaves the arena of childish teasing and sibling or peer type ridicule, frequently confusing funny for cruel. He moves through his childhood with few friends, and into adolescence in solitary studiousness, beginning to emerge into clumsy and naive gregariousness tinged with shyness only in his college years, when a surfeit of earlier baby fat suddenly falls away to reveal an unexpectedly handsome young man.

*Elaine passes by me in the white antiseptic hallway of the hospital the atmosphere heavy with grief and whispers to me surreptitiously, **soto voce**, that her mother's four carat diamond ring is now hers, despite what Ida may have said about giving it to me, hers, she repeats with some glee. I am horror stricken. I don't care about the stupid ring, I have my own, purchased for me by my beloved. Her mother has just died! What I am concerned with is the suffering of my adored fiance. Steve, deaf and blind to anyone, anything, grits his teeth and swallows the threatening tears, allowing merely a token few to slide through, and by keeping his grief tucked firmly and tightly inside himself, manages to lock away with it all of his potential feelings for a lifetime. Now he needs to reaffirm that common wisdom that has been his constant mantra since forever, about it not being what you know, but whom you know.*

It would seem, a full year later, that life has moved on, and at least by Jewish law, nuptials are permitted to proceed.

CHAPTER 11

I awaken to a cold chill, on a hot muggy June morning, and prepare in quivering silence for my wedding. I can hear the rise and fall of voices, Mom and Daddy talking, a cadence that suggests disagreement, as usual, maybe, nothing new, but I know there is the sound of intense movement going on, of preparation. I feel that tightening in my lower extremities. Why do they always have to do this? What are they fighting about today, of all days? It adds another layer to the sense of unease, the intense fear that I am feeling, still thinking about last night, still having second thoughts about the entire marriage thing. I have no clue at all what it entails, except being together finally. I am craving that warmth and physical connection. I am still wondering if I know Steve at all.

Platters of bagels are untouched, cream cheese and lox are ignored, for once. Always there is food; it is the necessary accompaniment of every function of life. I am about to commit myself to a frightening new existence in a brave new world and all these people can think about is food. It is surreal. Everything is surreal. Our nerves are strung tightly, no one can eat much now; but not to worry, in true family tradition there will be plenty to eat later. This time, this smorgasbord will be my mother's to offer, rather than assault. Mom is nothing if not a rabid and efficient buffet aficionado. Mom sports a new elegance in a fitted *peau de soie* tightly fitted ice blue to match her eyes concoction, long sleeves and high neck, and with a big bustle that starts at the sides and goes around to the back, where it is lifted and tucked and swirled, a blue silk rose planted at her waist. Sartorial details fill my mind, in an attempt to ward off untenable emotions. She has lost over fifty pounds with the help of some nut-burger diet doctor precisely for this occasion, and she is flaunting her taut new self on her big day. She has been planning for this for many years. My wedding is only one of so many of her dreams that actually will come true.

Daddy's white tuxedo jacket is casually opened to reveal a pink cummerbund that celebrates his stately bay window, he will wear a blue and white yarmulke, the colors of Israel, crocheted by Julia, his mother. He is keeping it carefully folded in his breast pocket until the big moment, when he arrives at the synagogue. The rest of his life, I am well aware, is comfortably agnostic and irreverent, at least on the surface. Who knows what Albert really believes? He is inscrutable. Steve and his father, I know, will have matching outfits, but only the ordinary white satin yarmulkes. They are already wearing theirs. Their faith is traditional, tangible and true, their understanding of it as deep as the worn soles of their shoes. It is all nothing more than rote in the greater scheme of things.

We pile carefully into my father's latest well worn Oldsmobile, Daddy and Mom in the front, Jane my Maid of Honor in the rear with me and the rose plastic encased pouf of my many tiered and ruffled eyelet, wedding dress, which is draped across our laps. I carry a cardboard box holding my white silk shoes, white that can be dyed a color after the wedding so it shouldn't be a total loss, and a tiny white beaded purse, created by Grandma Julia. A light summer dress covers me for the short trip to the site of the festivities. I have my makeup on, and my hair is carefully arranged, by a hairdresser friend of a friend who has graciously agreed to visit the house this Sunday morning, in a taut French twist, the way that Steve likes it; I am wearing everything but my white eyelet wedding dress.

We pull up and disembark mere moments later at the Kew Gardens Jewish Center, a synagogue that I have never even seen before, although it is located just blocks away from our house. I am acquainted neither with this temple nor its rabbi. We are here because it has been impossible to find space for us in the Rego Park Jewish Center where Steve and his family are members, in this coveted June time span. A religious ceremony is imperative. All of Aaron's business and political clout could not make that happen. The debilitating trauma of this momentous glitch has finally abated. A virtual stranger will administer this most intimate of ceremonies, by attrition. What does this portend for its emotional validity or for our future? A shiver runs through me.

We are ushered to a private dressing room, as cold and uninviting as a public restroom. My attendants clumsily and lovingly help me wriggle into a floating hoop slip, carefully fastening it, and the dress is carefully, worshipfully removed from its pink plastic casing, its many tiers and ruffles springing free, and slipped over my head. At least a hundred tiny fabric ensconced buttons are carefully connected to their individual minuscule cotton loops by my mom and Jane. The dress is a gift from Aaron, by way of one of his Thirty-Fourth Street Dress manufacturer buddies as he is wont to repeat with intense pride to anyone who will listen. I have my garter, encrusted in blue rosettes, my something blue. My mother's pearl and diamond earrings are my something old. My something new is a string of freshwater pearls that Daddy and Mommy have bought for me, for this occasion. The blue garter is borrowed from Steve's sister Elaine. I have fantasized that this union will benefit me in addition to the obvious, with the addition to my family of what I have craved for so long, a sister.

I am finally ready. You look just like Elizabeth Taylor, Mom *qvells*, her highest form of compliment, tears forming in her eyes. I am presented with a huge white and pink bouquet of Stephanotis, lilies, and roses. The other ladies in the party have pink rose corsages on their wrists or pinned to their dresses. Janie has crammed her still tomboy body into a fitted ruffled pink dress and pink dyed silk shoes, and looks about as thrilled and as comfortable as if she were being held captive, bound and gagged, in the trunk of a car.

I am ready to proceed. Except that now, I suddenly have to pee. Only you, says Janie, *Gut in Himmel,* God in Heaven, says Mom, what do we do now? Mom is anxious, she has retreated to Yiddish. I shrug, in mock helplessness. It is my one glaring feature of pure reliability. The actual restroom is divided into three by five foot cubicles, and the dress with its hoop is at least six feet wide. Janie gets an idea, and she and Mom each go into an adjacent cubicle, me in the center, holding the skirt above my head as I go blindly about my business. I am chagrined and horrified that I must forego paper, because my arms are tucked in above my head, in the middle of the skirt. My worst fear, aside that someone will come in and see us in this ridiculous situation, is that I will get lipstick on the skirt that surrounds my upper torso, upside down. I repeat over and over again, please don't let me get lipstick on the skirt. That should be the least of your worries, drones Mom, with that heavy Jewish intonation that surfaces in times of stress.

It is the first act in a comedy of errors, a nineteenth-century drawing room comedy, Theater of Life that masks the truth, which is my ongoing terror, my certain knowledge and ever escalating awareness that I am making a huge mistake. And yet, contradictorily, I cannot deny that I love this bright, handsome boy to whom I am betrothed. What does this all mean? Damned if I know. And so we continue with the farce, the elegant festive farce that covers the deep dread and agony that permeate my being.

The felony is compounded. Everywhere we go we are stalked by a photographer, even in our most private moments, click, click, and click. Somehow, he has missed the bathroom, thank God. Everything about this wondrous day will be recorded into perpetuity for all to see and remember. Albums of memories will be created, slides will be filed in white leather gold encrusted cases. Snapshots will be handed around for wallets, and the *crème de la crème* will be framed and will adorn table tops into perpetuity. I am posed with Mom in front of a mirror, Mom's arm around me, looking as serious as this moment requires, and a little frightened, and our faces are caught by the camera in the mirror, the backs of our heads as a frame for this sentimental moment. Then, I am seated in the middle of a carpeted room, the full extent of my long dress and train spread all around me, so that I appear to be the pistil of a huge white flower. Later, I will be photographed with the bridegroom, the stamen, arms around each other, smiling into each other's eyes, blushingly thinking about the possible conjunction of stamen and pistil.

We will be recorded standing between our three living grandmothers, in their long black and rose, silk and crepe dresses and their matching wide brimmed straw summer hats, their sturdy practical laced up shoes, my two and Nany, Steve's mother's mother. We will be immortalized standing under the *Chupah,* as we say our vows. The moment we each stuff a piece of wedding cake into each other's mouth will be, according to popular tradition, the act that clinches our pact. It is now recorded in the annals of time, chiseled in stone.

The chapel is filled with large arrangements of pink roses, the *Chupah* is covered with them, and there are the same vase arrangements at points every twenty feet up and down the audience, on both sides, and, at the podium where the rabbi waits. Steve's rabbi from Rego Park, a last moment surprise and a testament ultimately to Aaron's power, is sharing this solemn occasion, a joint effort. Aaron's connections have paid off this time. Success is especially guaranteed by the multiple representatives of God. It couldn't hurt, say the grandmothers in automatic unison. Mom and Daddy escort me down the aisle to the usual strains, their arms supporting my elbows, practically dragging me along. Terror sits like a huge ice egg in the pit of my stomach. It is probably the child of those immense sculptured ice swans that adorn the over-laden buffet table that is being obscenely decimated even as we have been preparing with great seriousness for the big moment. Suddenly, I am wishing for some chopped liver. Here it is, my own wedding, and I can't even manage to taste the chopped liver. There is something intrinsically unjust about this. I am being buffeted around in a world of non sequiturs and inconsistencies.

What if I trip on my train on the way down the aisle? What if I cannot repeat the vows properly and everyone laughs at me? What if Steve changes his mind at the last minute, and leaves me standing there, alone and mortified? What if it is I who run desperately from the Chupah? I look at Steve, and he is as pale as Casper. He attempts a stiff wink at me, I glimpse a tiny piece of my Stevie, and I relax a bit.

We stand through the interminable prayers and incantations, as my heart keeps repeating, hurry up, before I cut and run. I clench my teeth to keep from blurting out some awful thing, fearful of my uncontrollable mouth, praying for speed, and finally it is our turn to speak, to agree to love, honor, cherish, for as long as we both shall live. We both know that this is a mere formality, for we have already signed the *Ketubah,* the Hebrew marriage contract, in the rabbi's study, and even that has been recorded for posterity by the camera.

Okay. Here we are, surrounded by love, immersed in love, radiating love, and we are truly feeling love at that moment, at least I believe we are. No one knows, however, just what this thing called love, is, really. There is already a song reiterating that thought, at least, one. There are no definitions or guidelines, save for the love ballads of the day which have at least in part formed my ideas and beliefs, to date. But a mellifluous voice sings softly in the back of my head. *You must remember this, a kiss is just a kiss a sigh is just a sigh, the fundamental things apply as time goes by...* and I shudder for a brief moment, seeking desperately some imminent truth that eludes me... *moonlight and love songs, never out of date...no matter what the future brings, as time goes by.*

❧

So finally, we are married. We have each sipped the holy wine, and all that remains is for Steve to stamp on the wrapped wine glass and break it, a tradition that marks the precise moment of the union. Except for that long awaited momentous occasion to come, later when the food is consumed the musicians packed up and gone, the guests long gone, and we retire alone to The Honeymoon Suite. Steve stamps down with passion and joy and feeling, and the glass does not break. A sigh ripples through the onlookers. Steve rolls his eyes and attempts a feeble smile, and slams his foot once again onto the recalcitrant glass, which fails yet again to cooperate. Finally, the third time being the charm, Steve smashes the silly glass, there is a communal release of breath, and our relieved family and friends moan with joy, and clap their hands with abandon. You can barely hear the rabbi intone the magic words; you are now man and wife. We kiss awkwardly in front of the mob of relatives and strangers, and think about our new freedoms and permissions. At least I am, and I assume Steve is. The only feeling I have is the tremendous desire to get away from this aura of celebration by mostly strangers, from all the noise and bustle, conviviality and good will, as soon as possible. I do not like being the center of attention.

Soon, we find ourselves in the ballroom, twenty tables, and each holding ten people, divided by the polished oak dance floor. The flower arrangements have been moved to decorate this room, now. The wedding party sits at a dais, up front, where all can see them. We will be that *center of attention*, for the duration of the festivities, not my favorite thing. Let the festivities begin. In moments there is a great banging on glasses with spoons or forks; the guests are demanding for the bride and groom to kiss. Every time they do this, the bride blushes a deep crimson. And the shy groom defers, mostly, because he prefers privacy, prefers to avoid intimacy.

Steve and I reluctantly parade to the center of the dance floor to the strains of our song, *Moonglow and the Theme from Picnic*, and perform the first dance, gliding around the room in an awkward rendition of the waltz into which the music has subtly morphed, conscious of the many eyes on us. Love is in the air, and celebration. It is impossible not to feel good, optimistic. We are settling into this marriage thing. He squeezes my hand, holds me closer and closer in the spirit of the moment, and feeling warm and secure, my fears begin to lessen. Mom was right, it was just jitters. Everything will be all right. We love each other, we will be fine. And I feel a snap, a swishing sound, and I am waltzing better than earlier, encumbered as I am by my flounced dress. I am lighter and more graceful for some strange reason, and I am feeling fine until I spot the ruffles of my white hoop lying on the dance floor, sad and rejected, twenty feet away. I feel the blush creeping up my neck, and attempt a nonchalant shrug of shoulders, and mince off to the ladies room with Janie, who has recovered the errant hoop, and is prepared to fulfill her duties as Maid of Honor, and come to my aid in my moment of distress. This should be the worst of your worries, drearily intones someone's aunt with the same mournful voice as my mother, patting my arm as we go by. *Kinnehora;* this is the classic Jewish cry against the potential of malevolence, the old evil eye.

When we return, I dance with Daddy hiding my flushed face in his tuxedo lapel; he clenches me comfortably to his firm round bay window, as usual, my feet barely touching the floor, and that crazy grin on his face, swoops and swirls and glides across and around the floor, entrancing his audience with his fancy footwork staring into my eyes with that glimmer of twinkle, that teasing unknowable challenge. It feels good. This doesn't happen often, and moments like this are rare and to be treasured. Steve dances with Mom, and with his sister, Elaine, stiff and reserved. Nervous. Still. And then everyone joins in, and the floor fills up. And it is time to eat. This is the way it always goes. Food is brought in and dispersed by the silent army of white-clad bow-tied waiters that suddenly appear huge round trays held easily aloft.

I am surrounded by the accoutrements of celebration, yet I inhabit my own world gripped by terrors of different evolution; the specter of looming forever, of the unknown, of the vague promises and implicit threats of love, old memories. I recall the details of the menu, first, because I cannot, still, face the ignominy of more significant dread and memory. Stern-faced waiters bring around tiny portions of chicken or fish, trios of tiny roasted potatoes, a teenchy salad. There are baskets with rolls, one for each guest. Champagne glasses are kept filled from Aaron's abundant and seemingly unending stash, finally, dessert, wedding cake and coffee with non dairy cream or tea. We cannot finish quickly enough, we need to get out of here and get down to business. We continue to smile at each other, conspiratorially. We play the lead parts in this drama, called, *The Wedding*. Later, his look says. Oh, yeah, mine answers. He does love me, I dare to think, remembering, craving the warmth of his arms. And, when we have completed the required walk around the room to thank our guests for coming to this solemn and wondrous event, and Steve has, like magic, deftly secreted envelope after envelope into his tuxedo pockets, we change out of our celebratory outfits into travel wear. We glide stealthily outside to a waiting taxi that takes us to the International Motel, at Idlewild Airport, for our wedding night. We will catch a plane for Bermuda, in the morning. I picture everyone that we have left behind chanting gaily in unison, sing-song, *I know what you're doing* ... I cannot escape what appears to be a permanent state of blush. Maybe that is because there is one thing on my mind.

Efficiency is the name of the game. Steve is in his true element when he is planning. We must be ready to board our plane to Bermuda early in the morning. We arrive by taxi at the International Hotel, which is right there at the airport. We are both anxious; this is a long awaited moment, finally. Steve is grinding teeth that are clenched, and I am very quiet. No further need to search for darkened empty streets and vast sheltering leafy trees to hide under in Aaron's Cadillac, for hasty, sweaty, frustrating forbidden embraces. Now, we have rights, as legal spouses, and we are drunk not with the excesses of flowing champagne, but with the freedoms and permissions we have long awaited.

CHAPTER 12

The motel room points an accusatory finger at us, you know what my purpose is, it says. Naughty, naughty, you are having naughty thoughts and desires. Tsk, tsk. The huge bed screams out an invitation, and laughs at our uncomfortable reticence. Window shades titter as Steve approaches to lower them. There is nothing outside but field and runway. I am experiencing a weird combination of sensations, expectation, fear, unease, regret, hope. Steve is his usual calm self, on the surface, and yet I sense some turmoil, maybe even fear.

We stand in the middle of the room, flushed with expectation and awkwardness. Really, anticipation is almost a living creature, making us a threesome, voicing silent demands. A need seems to arise to address minutia, to cover our discomfort. Finally, someone moves. Who is it? It is not at all clear. We begin to bustle around, looking for places to store our things. Busy work. The room begins to be less forbidding, feels more like home, if a temporary home once our belongings are spread around. We claim the space, make it our own. I kick off my shoes, and leave them on my side of the bed, at least the side that I have claimed as my own. Steve stares at them, lying there, akimbo, as though they have committed some grave crime. I pretend I don't see his look (oh that Stevie, I grin to myself) open my small accessory suitcase, and remove my comb and brush, my toothbrush. I carry the toothbrush into the bathroom. Steve waits for me to leave the bathroom, and we pass each other sideways in the narrow doorway so as not to accidentally brush against each other, to touch, as he brings in his razor and his other toiletries. We avoid each other's eyes, until we can no longer play this game of self conscious do-si-do.

My bed is narrow and covered with soft quilts, and I have my favorite baby doll tucked into my tight protective embrace. I awaken suddenly, strange sounds filtering through my dreams, and there are the shadows, shadows, the ones out there in the open that often frighten me, and the fluttering curtains and the click clack of the gently rocking blinds. Mommy turns on the light and there is nothing there, and I fall back to sleep. Then late in the night, sometimes, I hear strange noises issuing from the huge bed across the room that Mommy and Daddy now share, since his return, and funny kind of struggling, a clumsy kind of muffled dance. I hear Mommy saying, no or stop, maybe, stop the baby will hear, or hear her cry out in some sort of pain, and I sense a feeling of incipient violence, underlying power struggle, terrified, unable to comprehend what lies before me. I am too frightened to say anything, knowing that I am supposed to be asleep, fearing my father's wrath discovering that I am not.

That was a long time ago. Throwing caution to the winds, I slip off my dress, and fling it cavalierly across the arm chair near the bed, and as Steve watches, it slides to the floor. Steve winces. A place for everything and everything in its place is his credo. He goes into the bathroom and when I hear the door lock, I begin to giggle. Steve is a very private person, even at a time like this. I find my *pegnoir* set, white and virginal and fluffy with chiffon and lace, and slip into it, and creep into the bed, pulling the covers up to my chin, think twice, and fold them down. Steve comes out of the bathroom dressed in a brand new pair of striped pajamas, carefully buttoned top to bottom, and shiny new leather slippers. He sits down on the bed, and removes the slippers, placing them carefully side by side next to his side of the bed, and throws me a look, note this lesson I am giving you about neatness and order, the look says and I choke back a defiant retort. He also slides under the covers. There is a space between us large enough to accommodate three more people.

He reaches up and turns off the light. Now, in the darkened room, freed from self consciousness by obscurity, unable to postpone the inevitable, he finally turns to kiss me, pulls me toward him. We are together in bed for the first time, accompanied by the icy and forbidding presence of awkwardness personified. Soon, nature overcomes discomfort, and we are up to our old Cadillac and Chevy activities, everything else forgotten. Optimism joins forces with hormones. In no time at all, *pegnoir* and pajamas have disappeared; *pegnoir* tossed to the far corners of the room, pajamas folded almost neatly on the bedside chair, and for the very first time except for the beach and that was with bathing suits, we are skin to skin. It is almost too much to bear, this new sensuality, the pressure of our new permissions. Steve tries to recall the adult movies that his buddy Sandy, the married man, has shown him, adept at the first stages of this dance, but the next moves, not so much. Virginity, it appears, is overrated.

We flounder around, hit and miss, not really getting it, hampered even more in our objectives by the necessity for protection. I had always believed that this long awaited activity was instinctive. The biggest problem always was or had seemed to be in avoiding this act, not in trying to get it right. You never heard of it not happening, merely the regrets of it happening at the wrong time or place, or with the wrong person with tragically untenable results. There is a lot of grabbing and straining and scraping and bending and folding, and no penetration. All instincts be damned, it just isn't working. Just as we are about to achieve some level of success, at least at a rudimentary level, the giant bed begins to slide, each of the two twin beds that form this King size monster, moving in different directions. Steve and I land on the floor. Although he has landed directly on top of me, no connection has been made. We arise again and again and persevere, but each and every attempt ends the same way. Steve gets up and redresses in his pajamas, and sits on the edge of the bed. His face is contorted with his distress, he is crying. I am a failure, he sobs, I am not a man. I have failed in my responsibilities. I could not even break the damned glass. It was a premonition. It was *beshert*. I have this secret feeling that it is my fault, not his, that maybe it would have been better if we had practiced a little beforehand. My own virginity is not an advantage, here.

I try to console him, to tell him that we just need some practice, that we are just tired and stressed, I love you, I say sincerely, but he pushes me away, his face like granite, his tight body signaling rejection. Rejection; my worst fear and nightmare; that which has the overriding influence on everything I feel or do. Now, I don't know what else to do, so I do nothing. Don't worry, I murmur, we'll figure it out, an idea surfaces, a light bulb moment. Could you just hold me? And reluctantly, he does, and I don't feel as rejected, and we fall into a restless sleep.

In the morning, we arise and prepare for our honeymoon trip. We both avoid the elephant in the center of the room. I look at him, raising one eyebrow quizzically. He feels my gaze. I don't want to talk about it, says Steve petulantly. I feel helpless. I feel that essence of rejection surrounding me, clutching me with its icy talons. What can I answer to that?

❧◦❧

Browning remnants of corsages, plucked from centers of bridal bouquets, are carefully pinned to left hand lapels of traveling suits. It is the morning following one of the most popular wedding days of the year in the middle of June. We are joined by equally self-conscious, exhausted couples; a sea of lemmings, we board the B.O.A.C. flight for Bermuda, *en masse*. I have never felt so alone, even in a crowd. They are all married, loved, loving; I am not any of those except married, I am thinking.

I take my seat in the stifling plane, but I am going through the motions, with no other apparent choices. My mind is numb, my body aches from repeated falls between the two sliding beds. Love has turned out to be less than I have expected. There is no exit from this dream. Do what Pollyanna would do, I command myself. This will pass, I am a woman, now, and I must be compassionate. Men may have all the power, call all the shots, but woman is the nurturer, woman has strength. I am now owned like a piece of property, a silent partner stuck in this marriage, what is there to do about it, now? Why didn't I stick to my guns before it was a *fait accomplit*? But here I am. I must move on. There is only one direction.

Now, there is a more immediate problem to face. I grit my teeth and clench the arms of my seat, certain that here having reached this apex of life, the balance of it is about to be dashed to the earth below in a broken assemblage of twisted steel. I am experiencing total fear of flying, I find out later, according to the thesis of my cousin Erica Jong, the author of *Fear of Flying*, whom I have actually never met. Her maiden name is Mann, shortened from Weismann. My mother's mother's name was Weismann. Now my thoughts are a frantic babbling mess. At this moment, I am not certain that I care, about anything. Steve is checking his list, pushes my hand away when I reach for him. He is busy, and I am suddenly an appendage; a less than vital ornament. I am becoming chillingly aware that I will need to recognize my place in this union.

Three hours later we can see the brilliant aqua waters and the white beaches as the plane angles and turns into the airport. The sun is blazing, and sunlight sparkles on the water. In the distance are pink stucco houses, and masses of fecund vegetation. These hours have passed, in unfettered silence. The knuckles of my clenched fists are white with the intensity with which I grasp the arms of my seat. Fasten your seat belts; we are now landing in Bermuda. The pilot makes his customary speech, and we anxiously await the big moment. My grasp only loosens when we have finally landed on the ground, and I expel the breath that I have been holding, in my absolute and lonely terror.

When we leave the plane, along with the joyful membership of impatient newlyweds, we can smell the ripe Caribbean air, mixed with sunlight and flowers. We are escorted from the airport through the town to our hotel in a strange open bus with a striped canvas roof. The musical accompaniment is a combination of the usual assorted traffic noises, car horns, and bursts of a police whistle. Traffic cops abound in their shorts and short-sleeved shirts, and uniform caps, British Caribbean style; Bermuda shorts. I experience a light-bulb moment. This is where that phenomenon comes from, I murmur; this is a new fashion statement, which I have never connected to a geographical location. What? Steve asks me; nothing, I reply. It is of no consequence. What is the difference what I think? No one ever cares what I think, I say with petulance, inaudibly. I am not sure where this emotion is coming from, it just rises up from my chest into my throat after years of my being ignored, dismissed, unheard as I become aware of my true status. The town is bustling, traffic moving and jamming every street. Cops blow their whistles, and wave their arms, and people obey. There is order. Everything is neat and clean and orderly, even the burgeoning plants and tropical vines are trained and orderly. Shops and boutiques beckon, music whispers from windows. Wide lawns welcome us to the Castle Harbor Hotel, and we can see golfers swinging and moving in the distance, the sparkling ocean a background to their play. Sunlight glistens on and reflects from every surface. Everything is in *order*, and Steve is in his glory. He informs me that he is anxious to organize our belongings in our room, and settle in, *then* we can see what the organized activities are. I am longing to see the countryside, lush and free and mysterious.

We have landed, though, in the lap of luxury, and the tropical breezes lull me into complacency. Honeymoon, honeymoon, whispers the breeze, enjoy your special time, this may be all there is. What does it matter that we have differences of personality, of interest? We have love, and a marriage certificate.

&

High ceilings, stone floors, tawny stucco, carved mahogany pillars and trim; classical British plantation style, the hotel is old and lovely. Low cushioned dark stained cane furniture, and marble tables join together on hemp carpets. Huge flower arrangements abound. We repeat the settling in process of the night before, in our new room, far more elegant, much warmer than the icily transient airport motel. I am feeling like royalty, engulfed in this grand sense of wonderful, and anxious to begin the activity of the night. Tonight will be better; we were just exhausted last night, and pressured beyond imagination. I feel this strange sense of yearning; my body is supple and vibrating in the sultry tropical heat. Tonight will be better. Tonight, all my dreams will come true. I just know it. I have the effervescence and immortality of youth, the faulty memory of hopeless optimism. We love each other. Love will solve everything. Every song I have ever heard says so.

I wait in the huge king size bed in this elaborate hotel room, all decked out in white lace nightgown and *pegnoir* once again, very bridal. I take what I believe to be a seductive pose, and wait. I try another more elaborate pose, and wait again. I wait for my groom, my lover, my beloved. Then I try something more subtle, less deliberate, and not so brazen. Do I really need to be alluring? Isn't my mere presence sufficient, by now? At least the management has assured us that the bed is secure.

By some accident of happenstance, today is the anniversary of Steve's mother's death, last year, right after we became engaged. I hope that since the year of mourning is over, and the stress of the wedding itself, Steve will once again become as if by magic, the same old Stevie that I fell so in love with three years ago. Just call me Pollyanna. The only experience I have with mourning is my grandfather, and I have this memory so tightly tucked away that I cannot even recall the sensation of loss, never mind a period of mourning, but I was just a child, then. Steve is an adult, and now, a married man.

...Today I counted the days until we can see each other again...
It's hard to find words to express how lonely I am or how much I
miss you, my dearest babe. I'm sure you understand how much I
love you and need you...

I wait. And I wait. Still, Steve does not appear. Something very strange is happening. He has disappeared into the huge walk-in closet, and he is missing and presumed lost. I begin slowly to realize that something is very wrong. This is too bizarre. Where is my eager groom? I tiptoe awkwardly in my elegant though less than comfortable French heeled satin slippers into the closet, and see a flickering light, that casts a strange glow over our belongings and the closet walls. I creep further into the room, past the angled entrance with its cream colored stucco walls, and finally locate a small glowing wax-filled glass on a high shelf in the somber privacy of the tiny roomlet. I watch it for a moment, flicker and glow, wondering what to say. This is a *Yourtzeit*, memorial candle; Steve has brought it on his honeymoon to say *Kaddish* for his mother, the prayer for the dead. Now, I can hear him.

Yis Kaddash v'yis kadol …

I am moved by the expression on his tear-stained face, grief and yearning and desperation, shimmering and glowing in the candlelight, the intensity of his obvious pain; I have no idea what it feels like to lose a parent, but I can still imagine, and care. I touch his shoulder tenderly with my hand, wishing to expiate his agony somewhat, heal this awful anguish, but he is lost in a world of his own heartache in which I have no place. He jumps, startled. What are you doing in here he demands. It's only a closet, I return tentatively and a bit anxiously, shaken at his tone, I was looking for you, I was worried.

Just leave me alone. … He turns away from me.

Stevie, I know you miss your mother … I begin, helplessly, but stop abruptly as he turns to me, a look of intense loathing on his handsome face, viciously, grabbing my shoulders tightly with his hands.

Listen to me, he spits between clenched teeth. Don't you ever mention my mother again; it's all your fault … his voice fades off. Don't even say her name, he bursts, suddenly, you are a Delilah, a temptress, you're not good enough to speak her name, his voice wanders off and he clenches his teeth again to keep the tears that loiter dangerously in the corners of his eyes from flooding his face.

I am stunned to paralysis by this sudden transformation, and these are the last words I have expected to hear. I slip out of his grasp and run from the stifling closet, throwing myself onto the huge bed, too shocked even to cry, and think to myself that maybe what he needs is more time to cure his great pain. I vow that I will try to understand, be a compassionate wife. I cannot be childish about this, cannot be so selfish and self-occupied that I fail to comprehend his feelings. Wouldn't I want him to be the same towards me, in the same circumstances? I will try to intuit his feelings, and I will try my best not to do anything to displease him. I want, need so much to be loved. I fear so much that he will not continue to love me; that he will stop, that I will lose him, too, that no one else will ever want me. Really, how could I expect anyone to ever love me? And it is true. I did keep Steve from seeing his mother in her dying days when we were spending all our time together, mostly following blindly after those always demanding hormones that kept us clinging to each other. Not intentionally, but just the same … is that what this is really about? What is really happening in that closet?

When I was small I have this thing about closets. I share my bedroom with my mother, in that snug three room apartment in Parkchester in the endlessly sprawling post WWII development. The thing is, I hate to be alone at night because of the closet. Sometimes the door is carefully closed, but frequently either it is forgotten, or gently swings open on silent hinges to varying degrees of openness with the natural air currents of the room. Depending upon the size of the opening, and the intensity of the confluence of its space, the manner in which things have been hung or thrown, the shapes that the shadows take on become more or less threatening.

A small child, for instance, can imagine sets of eyes in brass or paste diamond buttons gleaming evilly from the depths. Sleeves and shoes can almost be seen to move in the shadows if I concentrate hard enough. I stare fearfully unable to remove my own eyes from them, frightened that the mere act of removing my eyes from that spot will animate the figure lurking in the darkness at which time it would pounce and do unspeakable things to a little person lying still and almost unseen beneath the coverlets. These creatures are never permitted to bare vulnerable flesh to threatening forces without; are kept in place by tensely clenched fingers clutching the soft cloth tightly to my slight quivering body. I keep my attention riveted on the moving shadows, paralyzed with fear but unable to stop the escalating terror although, I realize that should the light be turned on there would no longer be anything of danger. I ultimately begin to repeat over and over again in my head a plea to some all powerful being whose identity I cannot discern but know is there. I plead urgently with invisible unknown magical powers that Mommy will unexpectedly fancy something from the offending space, or anywhere in the room for that matter and come in to get it, and then I can ask her to shut the disobedient door. Mommy, there are people in there, ghosts and monsters. Don't be silly, see? The light goes on and I am safe. Mommy is there. But what really lives in that closet, in the dark?

Sometimes, I manage to gather up unimaginable forces of courage from deep down inside, hating to lose yet another night's sleep to terror. I quickly scurry across the room and slam the horrible thing shut, hoping that I have made it in time before some unspeakable force is able to escape its murky constraints and leap into the room to further menace me or worse. Finally I slide quickly beneath the tight and protecting covers to slip with a great sigh off to sleep. Sometimes I dream about that open closet door, from which ineffably horrid things emanate as from some Pandora's Box, and I wake up then in a cold sweat, panting and whimpering as though it is real.

As I get a little older, I make it a habit to shut the door securely before getting into bed, and double check before turning out the light, in case something beyond my control allows it to pop open again.

I glance up but the closet door is closed.

Much later, he rejoins me silently in the huge bed. This time, I am not his partner, his beloved; I am an object, an object for something besides pleasure. It feels like uncontrollable anger, unmitigated anguish, and retribution. He takes over this business of love, machinelike, holding my arms down at my sides, stabbing me again and again with rhythmic fury. Instead of the long awaited tender expressions of love, sensations of delight, I am treated to intense unremitting grinding pain, accompanied by the sluicing torrent of his silent tears, which I can feel as his face presses against mine. Suddenly, he has got the mechanics of this undertaking figured out. Why has it taken anger, or even grief, to inspire him? I lay awake, eyes wide and glassy, staring at the cracked and ancient ceiling for long hours afterward, following the patterns of the cracks with my eyes. This is not his fault, I tell myself, my body rigid, this is my own fault. I have kept him from his dying mother. I am the guilty one. I should never have gone into that closet.

CHAPTER 13

Steve lies on his side, his back to me, snoring gently, in the deep sleep of satiation. I sidle silently, soundlessly across the icy sheets and spoon him, seeking some comfort in the absorption of at least some meager warmth. I slip my arm around his middle, and tentatively, carefully place my hand on his warm chest, entangling it in that familiar sparse nest. He didn't mean to hurt me, I know, I tell myself. He is the one who is hurting, and anyway, I am to blame. This doesn't mean he doesn't love me.

We awaken the next morning in a luxurious suite of the excellent Castle Harbor Hotel in beautiful Bermuda. Steve has forgotten last night, or decided to pretend that he has. He is full of smiles and enthusiasm for the activities of the day; tennis, beach, pool. He is at his best when following a plan, competing in an activity. Do I think it is strange that he appears to have no memory of the previous night's event? I don't even allow myself to think about it, unwilling to give it even that much reality, quite willing to store it away somewhere dark and inaccessible for eternity. Nothing further is said about that night. Ever. He never, ever mentions his mother, and I am afraid to. Life continues. I am willing to forget everything, if only he loves me, if only our life is normal. Normal in my family is hiding problems in a closet. So I tuck away all bad thoughts in some distant subconscious file cabinet, make my mind a blank. We continue with the business of learning the mechanics of marriage, with dedication and vengeance. Think positive, Pollyanna, I say to myself again sadly. Do I have a choice?

We have decided that practice is the only method for achieving success in this long awaited exotic newly available sport. I have filed the memory of that first night away forever. It never happened. Hormones and wishful thinking have succeeded in coloring my sense of reason, camouflaging my memories, tinting them with the rose of colored glasses. Neither Steve's selective memory of nor his singular personal triumph of our first night at the Castle Harbor has guaranteed any manner of future success, but I am willing to continue, for the cause. Ultimately, practice has made me so sore that I can barely walk, yet, we cannot seem to figure out the momentum, the rhythm of this thing. Without his now somewhat dissipated fury, Steve has issues of rhythm, and I, it seems, have subliminal at least issues of trust. We murmur words of love between us, gaze into each other's eyes with deep emotion, and dance provocatively closely, body parts warm and touching. Yet, always in the back of my mind are three questions: How can he have hurt me so badly, like he did that first night? What does it all mean? And, how can I keep from losing him? The memory returns, despite my attempts at blocking it out, and I am unable to fully trust him, unable to let myself go. I am unaware of inconsistency in my feelings and thoughts, which only serves to confuse me more. I want to forget everything except being a beloved bride. I begin a habit of long term, keeping all my feelings inside. I have no one to confide in.

But we gamely play the parts assigned to us. We weather that first few nights in Bermuda, confiding in a few young couples with whom we have become acquainted, who have earnestly confided similar procedural concerns during meals at the communal dining table. We find that we are not alone in our mechanical distress. We sigh huge mutual sighs of relief, compare notes, and armed with a new set of happily shared guidelines from our new best buddies, get down to the serious business of perfecting at least our mechanical skills in this new and greatly touted, long awaited sport. We love each other, I tell myself. Mistakes happen. Memory fades, and rationalization colors facts. Everything will be all right.

We make our entrance to the dining room the next morning; Steve wears his success like a badge of honor, proudly festooned across his face. Practice does make perfect. Barely able to walk but smiling with triumph we join the world of the initiate, married adults with ugly well hidden secrets. Why do I feel so empty, now, in the face of success? Where is all that joy that insistently promised happiness?

All other things being equal, Bermuda is still Bermuda. Everything is golden, glorious weather, exquisite scenery, charming people and sights galore. How can you not be happy in a Caribbean paradise such as this, especially if you are accustomed to tucking emotions deeply away? I am becoming accustomed to that heavy burning rock in the pit of my stomach.

The rest of the week appears to be everything a honeymoon should be. Moonlit walks, dancing till dawn, pink sand, sailboats, golden sun and rolling surf, dressing up and practicing new names … except that our new status, new roles, seem to have brought with them a whole new set of rules in our formerly lighthearted relationship, pre-marriage. I didn't know about this, no one warned me in advance.

What are you having for dinner, make sure you order on the dinner menu, instructs my new husband. But Steve, I'd like a shrimp cocktail, I plead. Why do I need to plead? No, you can't have it, its fifty cents extra, he intones. Here, I retort, rummaging around the bottom of my tiny purse for loose change, here's the fifty cents. My husband is irate, no, are you crazy? I pay for my own wife. Then pay for it, I whisper. No shrimp cocktail, says my beloved. Case closed. A one man court of law has decided my fate. A new family tradition is born. *E pluribus Unim*. Of many, one…One of many.

Then, dessert; those tempting little fruit tarts, apple and raspberry, are verboten because there is an extra charge for them. I feel so helpless. I think of the special Lindzer tarts of my childhood, shortbread and raspberry jam. What is going on? I think I want my Mommy. While we await our order, he carefully, with stone face, places the basket of bread on the adjacent table, so that I will not fill up on bread and thereby lose my appetite for the expensive meal that follows, he says, barely moving one facial muscle. A slow terrible paralysis is creeping over my entire body, making me feel even more helpless. Its first casualty is my ability to express my thoughts, a well established response for me, for so long now, in any case.

Later, as the soft warm romantic evening breezes caress my bare arms, we stroll around the quaint village, my new husband, me, and a third party, the personification of dread and despair that sits on my chest. I eye a lady delicately licking an ice cream cone, and look beseechingly at my bridegroom, the man with whom I will spend the rest of my life. Don't even think about it, he murmurs, catching my glance. I am a small child again, and my parent has forbidden me an ice cream cone. I look at the ground, miserably, struggling to swallow the hot lump in my throat, wondering where our lives will go from here, the need for ice cream becoming a grotesque living creature growing in size with each passing moment. Where is the gentle caring support assured by love and marriage? Where is that freedom that marriage promised; is supposed to insure? I appear to be right back to where I have always been, a child controlled by a parent. If I had any real mad money, I would buy the ice cream myself.

I have to catch up with him, when I stop to look in a shop window; his stroll is more of a stride, a lope, like Daddy's. But he is on a mission, walking. We are taking a walk. Walk is the operative word. That means, no stopping. Defiantly, I slip my arm from his and slide away, wander into a boutique, and stroke the renowned sweaters and gloves being displayed, hungrily. When he notices I have disappeared, he backtracks, discovers me in the little shop. I ask, I plead, but he refuses to let me buy white kid gloves or a cashmere sweater; I am a little surprised … everyone who visits Bermuda buys kid gloves and cashmere sweaters, at least. And this is our honeymoon. Everyone I know has reminded me not to forget to buy gloves and sweaters, almost as if this might well be the sole reason for such a trip.

Where are all those envelopes filled with money that are our wedding gifts? Isn't half of that mine? No. The money is going into a savings account, I am told. Whose decision is this, I inquire, don't I have anything to say about it? I am astounded and furious given my new adult status and rank at being left out of plans and decisions. No, you don't. I am your husband (he assumes a countenance of superiority) it is my job to make important decisions. I am the boss (he purses his lips, juts out his chin). You don't know anything about money, you're just a woman, he states with great condescension. This is something I never expected, never even thought about. I just thought it would be me, and Stevie, forever. Swell, okay, I tell myself. We can deal with this, later. But … isn't just a little bit of honeymoon indulgence part of the picture? I am sensing with rising dread a portent of an entire lifetime to come. This is not the realization of childhood fantasies of family and love. I only wanted a shrimp cocktail, a tart or some ice cream. And I am denied the quintessential embodiments of love including, it seems, the gastronomical ones.

You must remember this, a kiss is just a kiss a sigh is just a sigh; the fundamental things apply as time goes by, no matter what the future brings, as time goes by. Moonlight and love songs, never out of date…

1943

My mother dresses me in overalls, a T-shirt, unembellished business socks, no ruffles, and polished oxfords; my Mary Janes and ruffled socks are not for school, just for special occasions. I watch her tug on her undergarment, and wonder anew at its purpose, Mommy's naked body is neatly put together, and not unpleasant, familiar and comforting to gaze at. I run my hands down my own slight frame as I watch transfixed. It is not all that different from mine, except for a few bulges that I do not possess, nor wish to. She deftly drops a simple rayon slip over her head, and I stare, fascinated as it floats into place as if it knows the way. Next, a cream colored blouse with slight delicate floral embroidery across the chest, and a collar that is strangely long, looking remotely like floppy rabbit ears hanging there, until it turns into a bow under my mother's deft touch.

Nylon stockings, carefully applied because I am told, of the war, and high heeled pumps, the ones I step gingerly into on evenings and weekends, when I am permitted to play dress-up with my mother's things, when I lose myself in the aroma of my mother, in her clothing; the war, again. Strangely enough, she keeps these stockings in the tiny freezer part of the refrigerator, at the top, having been told that this keeps them from getting those sudden and devastating ladders, crawling up, or down, slowly and fatefully leaving their nasty track that renders them useless. They should be called tracks, I muse, not ladders. I have watched fascinated, holding my breath, as they inch along on their magical journey to nowhere. Stockings are difficult to obtain now, another of those wartime rationed commodities.

Last, the neatly fitting tailored suit jacket. She finishes with the proverbial paisley or flower-patterned silk scarf, deftly wound and curled and tied, and pinned to her suit collar with the usual bejeweled pin, part of a set, e pluribus unim *that sports earrings and necklace. Sapphire to match her eyes, gold to echo her hair, pearls to complement her porcelain skin. Now, a touch of lipstick, and a bit of scent, and the metamorphosis is complete. I stare up at her in awe, breathing in the exotic aroma so that I can remember it until I see her again. That familiar feeling of approaching abandonment is creeping into my chest, in direct proportion to her degree of readiness. Soon, I will be devastatingly alone, again. It must be because of the war, I think. I have to work, you see, because Daddy is away, because of the war. The only thing I know of war is that everyone talks about it continually, Daddy is missing, and Mommy is unhappy. Otherwise, I have no idea of what this thing is, this miasma that envelops all of our lives with its ineffable sense of gloom and terror.*

All at once her demeanor changes; she has donned her day persona, pulled out of the air, from the secrets of the murky closet or the unyielding chest of drawers. She is suddenly an elegant woman of the world, esteemed teacher, and she is off to her own wars, off to teach her hoards of to me faceless students who take her from me each day. She has put on her workday self, along with her outfit. I feel my stomach sinking, my eyes tear. I hastily wipe at them, and swallow to get control. It seems for some reason to be imperative that I do not allow her to see my discomfort, know my feelings. The elegance is her cover, her superficial coating of a confidence I can sense she does not feel. She glances at herself in the big round mirror above the mahogany art deco dresser in the bedroom, turning and preening, and she whispers, I wish Daddy could see me. I see you, I whisper back invisibly, but she is already walking toward the door, her huge handbag over her shoulder, her bulging briefcase under her arm. I follow obediently, grabbing onto the corner of her jacket.

❧❦

A faint memory of Daddy flits across my mind, and then it is gone.

At first, I can't quite recall it all, but it presses at my consciousness, an instant replay; a little blurry. The scene has repeated again and again until it is indelibly etched onto my brain. I have seen it frequently over the years, and never know when once again unsummoned and unwanted, it will appear once again.

There I am in my new Red Riding Hood raincoat that gives me delicious shivers as I think about Grandma and that wolf and I somehow summon up vague simultaneous thoughts of terror and goodies which survive in a confusing non sequitur of hovering memories. My mother's enthusiasm leads me to believe that it is undoubtedly a possession to be cherished. Just like the one in the story.

From that day to the present, try as I may, I cannot recall the rest of the apartment on Holland Avenue in the Bronx where we lived for my first year. Neither can I recall any part of our time there; except for the repetitious iron bars of the fire escape, its pattern and cadences appearing as I look from the window. I am, of course, only one year old. I remembered quite clearly, however, my mother lifting me up and unaccustomedly holding me very tightly, so that I know something is different, maybe even amiss, and carrying me to the window. The sash is raised and we look out on the fire escape, the orange and rust and black iron slats and ladders rising endlessly out of and beneath each other. Beyond them, three stories below, the ancient concrete sidewalk slopes steeply away from us. On that sidewalk, sparkling and dapper in his crisp newly issued army uniform, his narrow sculpted Errol Flynn mustache lifting quixotically to one side over that familiar rakish grin, his captain's cap doffed cavalierly in mock salute, his overcoat casually over his arm stands my father. He blows a kiss, waves, turns on his heel, and jauntily strides down the hill and out of our lives for five long years. The little I am able to recall of Holland Avenue is a faint image of the streets lined with stores of all kinds, walking up and down the cracked paved concrete hills with my mother, the stone walls, paths and hills and trees of Bronx Park West across the street, and the clatter of the elevated trains.

❧◦❧

But now a few short years later my mother on her way to work drops me off to be cared for this day after an obnoxious bus ride across the Bronx and rushes off. Hansel and Gretel Nursery School, says the whitewashed wood plank sign propped up in front of the sparse yard, littered with toys. It has dark blue trim, and a rudimentary painted image of a boy and a girl holding hands. I have barely recovered from the noxious fumes of the traffic, and the pungent crush of strange bodies, when I am made to sit at a long low table on miniature chair, like and so unlike the one at home where I play with my dolls, and forced to eat icy cold runny soft-boiled eggs and congealed cream of wheat, although my stomach rebels, and my internal core is reduced to stone. There is a war on. Think of all the poor starving children in Europe.

Then, according to regimen, all of the other parentless-for-the-day children sit on small potties, placed randomly around the classroom, pants and panties around our ankles, until we perform. This is our morning activity. Those who do not, are left to contemplate their failures, until they persevere. It is a great time to exercise the imagination, disappearing into other more interesting inner worlds of the mind. Our caretakers are away in their usual covert place somewhere else, but I can see them past the half open doorway of the adjoining kitchen, clutching coffee cups and pastries, conversing and laughing, a world removed from their charges, who obediently follow a rigid and controlled schedule with very little care involved, waiting for the day to pass. It passes very slowly. Finally, they feign great critical sighs for our inadequacy, and we are released from this particular activity, stiff from the lengthy time in that forced position, red circles engraved by pressure on our collective bottoms.

Later, our clothing resettled in its proper position and recovering quickly as children do, at least on the surface, we all wander out to play on the grounds, where most of the other children obediently swing or slide. I am the renegade, subservient to my imagination, disinterested in mindless play, finding assorted treasures in the dirt, in the sparse brown grass, buttons and pieces of rotted wood, bottle caps, shiny, flaking mica rocks, and a sort of Bronx *beach glass, really weathered broken bottle shards, dreaming up new scenarios and art forms from sand and stick and stone. Whatever are you doing? Stop that immediately, wash your hands, find a toy, and join the other children. Nice little girls don't do that. Let me push you on the swings. No, no, just the thought of swings makes me queasy.*

Be good, now, I am warned; whatever is wrong with you? Why can't you play nicely like all the other children? What is this pressure, this necessity to be like everyone else?

Sometimes they do force me to swing, and I endure this torture, which culminates usually in what little breakfast I have consumed being left on the playground floor, behind a bush, or in a sand bucket, if they have been fast enough. They never learn, they are determined to convert me to a happy swinger. They are determined to force me to conform to their particular image of child. *Then the afternoon activity, more a respite for supposedly hardworking teachers than something of value for already bored children, a compulsive mass nap on folding army cots with scratchy wool blankets, sleepy or not, the lights dimmed and the window shades lowered so that only the tips of the trees are visible in the yard, and finally Mommy arrives, worn and cranky after her long day of teaching and dealing with routine technical nonsense, to take me home. When she sees me, her face softens, and a wide smile appears.*

We walk slowly, hand in hand, to the bus stop. Her hand is soft and cool and pliant, as always; the feel of it is engraved on my memory, I can feel its touch whenever I am sad or ill. Her hand is love, security, and I cherish its brief tenure attached to mine. Warmth infuses my body just to be near her. Already the day has faded to a faint gray receding blur. I wish to cling to her, to never have to let go, but I know that is not going to happen. Did you have a nice day, she asks sweetly, her voice filled with love, and I nod yes, because I don't know what else to say that will not create more havoc than I am ready to deal with. My eyes give me away, huge and dark and sad. She tries not to notice, cannot face discord, dismay, in her barely tolerable, tightly controlled existence. The lines from the corners of my mouth to my chin are getting deeper; I look like a marionette, I think, when I look at myself in the bus window, the world darkening behind it as we pass under the elevated train structure. I open and close my mouth a few times experimentally, noticing that yes, strangely enough, I am turning, the opposite of Pinocchio, into a puppet. No, I think gravely. I will never let that happen. I know Pinocchio very well, since my mother takes me to see each and every child's movie and show that graces the theater. I am on first name basis with Dumbo, Babaar, Snow White, and Cinderella, and an assortment of adult musicals; The Secret Garden, The Little Princess, *and* Pollyanna, Anchors Aweigh. *Meet me in St Louis, Louis, I sing inside my head, meet me at the fair, I sing silently, remembering. I will never forget how Dumbo lost his mother, and Babaar, and there is Madeleine, the French orphan who lives with nuns in an orphanage, twelve little girls in two straight lines, which all fill me with terror. Mom was forced to leave me in the care of the nuns at the church on our corner a couple of times when the baby sitter didn't show and she had to leave for work. I am quite certain that I don't want to be sent to an orphanage and be cared for by nuns.*

On the last Friday of the month, I know the routine. I guard my secret knowledge tightly, allowing only the slightest suggestion of a gleeful grin to sneak across my face, which is otherwise engraved with that eternal image of sadness. I am constantly asked with grave concern, even by strangers, what is the matter, dear? We exit the rocking bus, and begin our voyage now on foot down the cracked cement hilly sidewalk. After a brief stop at Manufacturer's Trust Bank on the corner, we continue our walk, past Safeway and the dry cleaners, the Chinese laundry, Cristedes and Rexall, Mommy waving gaily at those proprietors who are nearly family, who have managed to steal a moment in a tedious and hectic existence for a breath of fresh air, this late winter afternoon, which sports a hint of Spring merged with the smell of melting snow mixed with traffic fumes. The somber stentorious disembodied voice of a newscaster relating the news can be heard continually spewing out the serious word of the day. The United States government has interned a million Japanese evacuated from miles and miles on the coast, I hear, what does that all mean? Everyone has a radio on; radios are never turned off. Everyone listens, continually, to the solemn deep serious voices that give the blow by blow recount of the affairs of the world in these difficult and dangerous times, one ear cocked at all times. Life is precarious, these days, and the future unknowable. A bit of information filtered through the screams of distance and secrecy is a treasure.

Whistle while you work, I sing loudly, off key as I skip down the sidewalk, Hitler is a jerk. Mussolini is a meanie and the Japs are worse. This is the verse that is going around my school, a variation on the ditty sung by the seven dwarfs of Snow White. I wish to drown out the deep serious voices and their mournful rant of doom and gloom. My mother winces and I have no idea why. It is obviously a secret, another secret. Mom has a lot of these secrets.

The immense filthy flatulent bus expels a huge noisy black puff of noxious exhaust, and glances exchanged, a titter ripples across the pedestrians and shopkeepers who are united in wartime angst, a welcome respite from tension, stress, and tightly contained days. The bus continues on its way, rumbling and snorting. I continue skipping down the hill. I am now singing my daddy's song, in a rasping deep throated imitation baritone. From the halls of Mont-e-zu-u-ma to the shores of Tri-po-li ... the words roll senselessly from my mouth like a fountain of multicolored jellybeans ... we will fight our country's ba-at-tles, on the land and on the sea ... My new mantra, louder and louder, becoming more and more distorted as the meaningless words are repeated

81

mindlessly, breathlessly, over and over again, jolting, bouncing with each breath as I go ahead skipping with abandon as we nearly reach the corner. Don't fall, be careful, sternly reprimands my mother, but she is smiling, thinking of other things. I believe that she is thinking that she is glad that he sent another record.

We follow the delightful fumes of pastry, which have at first blended with and then overwhelmed that of the bus exhaust as we have reached the corner, and enter the corner store, and Mommy is counting out her ration coupons, butter, eggs, milk, sugar, smiling happily. We are in Handscomb's Bakery, and the heady combined aromas of baking, bread and cake and pastry, overwhelm the senses. Always for me this smell is associated with the feeling of love. My mother hands over her bounty of coupons and a small amount of money, retrieved from what is left after she has deposited her precious paycheck in the bank, and I receive my token of love, a Lindser tart. Sometimes, only rarely, she buys two. That's how much she loves me. A Lindser tart, a concoction of raspberry jam between two giant circles of shortbread, a smaller circle cut out of the top one exposing the raspberry, the entire thing coated with powdered sugar, is a symbol that becomes engraved on my DNA, enmeshed in my atavistic memory for future generations, proof of love.

CHAPTER 14

July, 1958

Do I look different, I wonder, is there something unique, mature in my walk? I hold myself up straighter, Sadie, Sadie married lady, people might be looking at me, wondering. I know what you've been doing, they will taunt silently, as their accusing eyes slide across me, condemning me to perdition. I feel the hot red of blush creeping across my face. I also know what I have been doing. But now I am a married woman, a respectable matron, walking along streets that I have frequented since I was a child of ten. I am getting used to married life, making the best of everything. The medium is the message. I am married, therefore I am loved, and therefore I am happy. Maybe it is merely an absence of pre-marital, pre-wedding tension. Mom has ignored and deleted from memory or existence the desperate pleas I made upon returning from our honeymoon to have the marriage annulled, has pooh poohed my reasons for the plea. It's still that thing about the opinions of her friends and family, about the fate of gifts, the grand expense of the wedding. I am forced to put my head into the sand and be a good ostrich. So I adjust, live moment to moment, not thinking about the problems. I will be like Scarlet O'Hara from *Gone with the Wind*, I will think about it tomorrow. There are no choices. Things will get better, Pollyanna rules, I tell myself. I will have my name legally changed to Scarlet Pollyanna, I think sardonically.

Now, the July sun bakes me pleasantly, the fresh summer morning breeze wafts gently around me, caressing my bare arms and legs, tickling my nostrils in a most pleasant manner. I am en route to the Safeway supermarket to do my grocery shopping. Just like any other wife. If I act just like every other wife, will I become one? Do other new wives feel as disappointed as I do? Are their marriages so empty and strained? Is life around me just an insidious mythical illusion? What is marriage anyway? No one has told me. No one seems to know. Only songs continue their deceptively edifying promise. *Love and marriage, love and marriage, go together like a horse and carriage...I give to you and you give to me, true love, true love...my prayer is to linger with you...*

Life is continuing as ever. I am one with the program. Rote is the recipe, and attendance to it will prove the pudding. We have risen early, eager to begin our new protocol, like obedient robots, to create new habits. Steve as always has had his toasted English muffin and jelly, which he dunks in his morning Nescafe; I have once again watched the oily residue of butter and viscous melted fruit slide hideously into the waiting brown lake of coffee clamping my lips together to avoid gagging. He has taken his tightly packed new leather briefcase, and set off for work at Prudential Life Insurance, where he toils as an underwriter while he finishes his studies at Brooklyn Law School at night. Now, of course, it is summer vacation, so my new husband has summer school classes at night, and will not be coming home for dinner every night, and it will be worse when the fall semester begins. I will, of course, be going to Brooklyn every day also, in the fall, to my own art classes at Pratt Institute. But we are on vacation, now, and still honeymooning, and I am avoiding negativity, and looking forward into the future. I have purchased the entire package, swallowed the rhetoric whole; I am a Good Robot Wife, loving and beloved, playing the game, following the rules. You do what you have to do, and everything falls eventually into place. Things are never what they seem, skim milk masquerades as cream. A cold stone lies in my chest. It is in part due to thoughts that never leave me. And there is no telling if or when Steve may be called to the draft into the wartime army during this conflict in Korea. The food in this restaurant is so awful and the portions are so small.

In direct contrast to my discontent is this rising terror that I might lose him, my rock, my source of warmth, of life, at least the illusion of all this, that causes me to wish for a baby immediately, so that he might not need to leave, to be separated from me, so far away. Also, a baby will love me and let me love it without conditions or history. It will fill the chasm in my heart, in my life. Yet another reason for a baby, over and above the lifelong yearning that I can never remember being without. Steve suddenly and surprisingly says that he doesn't want children, at all, startling and shocking me. He has never voiced this feeling to me before, although I have talked about wanting babies forever, indeed, has always seemed to agree with my dreams and plans. I am intrigued by the genetic possibilities, and long to see the combinations of our genes. His best friend, Sandy, was married at seventeen to his fifteen year old bride, and they now have three babies. *Sandy* is not going to Korea because he has babies. Of course we will have babies, everyone has babies. What will my life be without babies? He is just saying that. He doesn't mean it. I close my eyes tightly, and see an ostrich. Squawk.

❧◦❧

I have folded the bedding and put it away in my sleek contemporary Herman Miller walnut dresser, and closed the teal faux silk sofa bed, replacing the loose cushions. These sparse furnishings have been acquired directly from the manufacturer's showrooms thanks to the connections of Aaron. Kitchen and bath accoutrements have been obtained under the direct and insistent husbandry of Steve's sister Elaine. I have washed the breakfast dishes, and run the vacuum over our sparse oak floor and small area carpet, in this tiny studio apartment in Forest Hills, across the street from the Stephen A. Halsey Junior High School which I attended way back in the early 1950s, actually left in 1953. An image flits across my mind, me and Frank Decker, coatless during winter lunch hour playing handball against the cement wall of the chain link fence wrapped handball court, returning to class panting with exertion and grinning with accomplishment. Now in the middle of 1958, I am light years away from that childishness. I am nineteen years old, but I swing my purse as I half walk, almost skipping down the street. My socks still crawl underneath my arches; adulthood, at least marriage has not cured me of that failing. I have a lot to be happy about, I think. I have my own apartment, I have my new dishes and gleaming copper bottom pots and color coordinated towels and sheets and blankets. I have a handsome husband, who will soon be a lawyer. Things will be fine. If there are any problems, I will think about them tomorrow. Just call me Scarlett-Pollyanna.

My first stop is the Kosher Butcher. Steve must have Kosher meat in his home, although he doesn't much care what he eats outside of home; in the beginning this is not so strange to me and it is not difficult for me to imagine or to follow. Kashris, the laws of keeping a Kosher home and all that goes with it are in the marrow of my bones, in every molecule of my blood, in every particle of my DNA; it is because it is all a part of me that I am able to understand and follow the rules.

1944

My mother takes my hand and we begin the long walk to Grandma's house. It is an especially long hike for me, at five years of age, anyway. Down the long winding back road behind our red brick apartment building, under the fire escapes and past the dark cold institutional laundry room. It's shorter this way, she says. This road is a kind of driveway, with parking spots on the building side, chain link fence covered by privet hedge and ivy hiding private homes on another street. What is a private home, I ask excited, not really caring. I am excited because we are going to Grandma's. That means noodle soup and pletsela and apple cake. It's not pie it's cake, I am repeatedly told. There is a difference, even if it looks like pie. Pletzela are cookies made from leftover cake dough.

Maybe, if I'm lucky, Grandma will save me one of those teenchy little yellow eggs that she sometimes finds in the chicken, and cooks in the soup. If I am good, I get to eat the little yellow egg. I am not exactly certain just what that little egg is doing in the chicken. And what has happened to the shell and the gooky stuff? Maybe, I can watch the magical incantation of the lighting of the Friday candles for the Sabbath, Grandma's head covered by a shawl as she rocks back and forth nearly inaudibly mouthing that familiar supplication. Maybe Grandpa will come home early from shule, and play with me. Not really play, like other days, because that would not be proper, but tell stories and hold me on his lap. You don't play on the Sabbath, I know that. We have reached the end of the austere red brick city of Parkchester, the macadam walkways and chained in lawns, and we are almost there.

Then that last turn around the corner, real houses, a normal street, and there is the Kosher butcher beneath the apartment in a taxpayer Mommy calls it, a two-story storefront with living space above, hence the name, she explains patiently, teacher for the moment; it pays for the taxes on the property, or something, she answers my insistent curiosity impatiently. I'm not certain just what a tax is, but fearing yet another lecture, keep this to myself, but I know this place. This is where Grandma gets her chickens. I go with her sometimes on Friday morning, when I am staying with Grandma and Grandpa, when there is no one else to watch me. Today, there is no school, and so I am with my mother. It is a special day for me. No nursery school, just my mother and me, just girl time, my mother calls it. Girl time is all there is for us with Daddy still away. So we are going to Grandma's house for dinner. The shop is closed now, because it is almost sundown on Friday, and soon the Sabbath will begin. My mother squeezes my hand, and we walk faster, swinging hands back and forth, bouncing a little as we walk. Every so often I find myself in the midst of an uncontrollable skip.

I glance in the darkened window, and think about my last visit there with Grandma. In the back of the butcher shop, is an old man with a long black beard, wearing a white coat that comes nearly to his ankles. Only his once highly polished black shoes show beneath the blood spattered coat, covered with the fine dust of many feathers. Feathers are all over the room, large medium and small fluffy wispy ones. The only job this man has, except for the ax *thing, is to remove the feathers from the freshly killed chickens. In my naiveté I do not realize that a living creature has been killed just for my dinner. Grandma chooses the one she likes in the magical hidden back room, and he whisks it away with a flourish, its head, complete with pointy yellow beak, and long lolling neck flopping behind, and begins his job. I look from face to face, in order to gauge the mood of my compatriots, and both Grandma and the chicken flicker are serious, their faces austere and expressionless. They seem to be somewhere else in time and place. I watch, fascinated, as feathers fly in all directions. Soon it appears to be snowing gray chicken feathers, like when you shake one of those glass snow scene balls that hold the piles of papers down on Mommy's desk. Grandma looks at my awed face, my huge eyes, and laughs, her entire body shaking with mirth. I join her, and soon, we are all laughing, including the stern-faced chicken flicker. The feathers stick to our wet faces, and cling to our clothes.*

The entire time, they speak in that strange guttural language, Yiddish, that I hear most times when the entire family is together at Grandma's house, or when Grandma and Grandpa are there together, and my mother. I recognize a lot of words, and understand some of it, but I cannot speak this language; the sounds get tangled between my tongue and my lips. I do believe that they laugh a lot, and they also argue, and scream at each other, a lot. Mommy says that this is because they love each other so much, but their loud voices frighten me, loud noises always frighten me. Sometimes I feel the need to hide under the dining table, already set for dinner, where I retire with a plate piled high with pletzela *or apple cake when things get too loud for me. The ancient white embroidered table cloth hangs down almost to the floor, hiding me completely. No matter what happens, I feel loved, as long as there is cake left on my plate.*

The bearded man in the long white coat carefully places the yellow egg with the small package of gizzard, neck, heart and liver, into the chicken. He throws in a few extra chicken livers, after a few murmured words from Grandma, shaking his head, yes. Grandma is going to make chopped liver. I feel a great smile taking over my body. My mouth is in a continual state of juiciness, as I think about the different delicacies that await me. He unrolls a length of reddish brown paper from a thick brown tube, and deftly spreads it on the huge wooden table, wrapping and folding and turning the chicken until it is a neat package, tied with a length of twine cut from a massive ball of the stuff that sits on a steel pipe attached to the table. He pulls two wiry-looking yellow three-toed chicken feet from somewhere under the paper, and wraps them separately. Grandma smacks her lips, and he smiles. Later, Grandma, Grandpa, my mother and all the uncles will fight over those feet. They will lick them and suck them and chew on them, with lots of noisy gusto. The thought makes me shudder. Don't they know where those feet have been walking, and in what? Have they never been to the zoo? He takes Grandma's large shopping bag from her, and carefully shoves the wrapped chicken down into the depths of it. After many polite exchanges of pleasantries and formalities, good wishes and blessings for all of their kin, alive and dead, they nod to each other, and we take our leave. My last sight is of him sweeping the shop, and once again he is enveloped in a cloud of soft feathers, like someone just shook the glass ball again.

Now, we go home to begin cooking. If I am lucky, Grandma will make an apple cake, and I will get to watch in awe as she peels the apples in one long fluid motion, leaving a single long curling strand of apple skin, which I am then permitted to eat. Then, I get to watch her make the dough for the crust. I stand close to the large wooden table, balancing, trying not to touch the surface. My nose barely reaches the top of it. She first makes a huge mound of flour, measures exactly one half of a jelly jar, the ones with the puffed out bottom, of sugar, onto the middle of the pile. Then she takes her fist and makes an indentation in the center of the pile, cracks an egg into that, and adds a dollop of oil. How much do you add, Grandma, I ask, making apple cake recipe notes in my head for the future, when I will make my own cakes, or maybe I will just tell Mommy about it so she can make some of those awesome cakes for us at home. A szhmenia, she says matter of factly. A szhmenia? I ask. What's that? That's how much you add. Isn't that what you asked me, she says with surprise? Well, Grandma, I ask, what exactly is it, how do you know how much it is? Grandma holds her hand out, and places her thumb against her other four fingers which are all together, and she says a little bit testily, THIS, is a szhmenia. It's just like a bissel, but different. A Szhmenia, she states emphatically! She takes my own small hand and attempts to place my uncooperative fingers in the correct position, finally giving up, kissing first my small hand on the inside and then closing it into a fist, on the knuckles, then the top of my head. Don't worry, momala, a szhmenia is just a szhmenia. Oh, I answer aspiring to exude knowledgeability and wisdom, as if this was something I should have always known, that was automatically a part of my inherited store of knowledge.

She rolls out immense sheets of dough the size of the kitchen table on which she is rolling them, spreads them on even more immense cookie sheets, fills them with her suddenly appearing mixture of apple filling from an immense glass bowl, and covers it all with another sheet of dough. Great quantities of these filled cookie sheets materialize, and are rotated in and out of the steaming oven until every counter and table space is covered with the now cooling tins. It is as though she is being helped by the Sorcerers Apprentices, who are juggling and carrying apple cake cookie sheets instead of pails of water. She sprinkles them with a mixture of cinnamon and sugar. Later, as the odor of apples, sugar, cinnamon and cake fill the apartment, intoxicating me with their joyous promise, I watch as she cuts square after square, and I am speechless with wonder because each one is the exact size as the last, and she piles them on platters in two three, four five layers, towering creations of architectural and gastronomic delight. Grandma is a sculptor.

Later, the pungent comforting odors of chicken soup and apple cake mingling in the air; grandma begins the task of making noodles for her soup. She repeats the mounding of the flour, and the punching of the center, and the breaking of the egg, this time, eggs, but there is no sugar. Once again, she punches and kneads and finally rolls it all out with her long worn wooden rolling pin, and then the best part. She takes a long heavy knife from a drawer, and begins slicing noodles, so thin and fine and even, that I wonder how she is able to do it, but suddenly there is a mound of ultra fine noodles, chopchopchopchopchop, which she throws into a pot of boiling water. I take reams and reams of mental notes for my future. It looks so easy, Grandma, I say, do you think I could do that? Grandma smiles, and moves on to the next task, the chopped liver. Sometimes, when I stay over, grandma has a giant pot boiling on the stove, all night, and the strangest smell comes out of it. What's that cooking all night, asks the nosy visitor, wrinkling that same freckled turned up nose? Gefilte fish, says grandma, smacking her lips. Do you remember that big fish, the carp, swimming in the bathtub yesterday? That is him, she says. I experience a moment of sadness for the executed fish. Sometimes, when grandpa is not there, she grates horse-radish and beets and mixes them together with vinegar, to put on the top of the cold fish cakes. Usually grandpa does this. I shudder, because I haven't yet developed a taste for this particular delicacy, along with pickled herring and sliced onions in cream sauce.

1958

I am thrilled to be able to cook for my new husband. I certainly have the instinct and second hand experience, the stash of mental notes, and I certainly love to eat. I already know that food means love. The ever present *they* say that the way to a man's heart is through his stomach, that old chestnut. Old clichés and anecdotes are what make up my pathetic store of knowledge, along with the ubiquitous popular ballads of the day, spewing from my ever resonating radio. And there are more than several protocols to the business of food. Steve insists that I keep Kosher. I of course do what he wishes, because I want him to be happy, even though it is rather a pain in the neck, and because I fear to disobey him. Maybe, if I please him if I make him happy, he will love me a little more. Any flaw in our marriage must be due to some failing of my own. My sense of security depends on pleasing him, no matter what. But the Kosher meat looks the same as any other meat; I fail to see the difference. Obviously, there is something important involved. All of this is engraved on my own DNA, and deeply tucked away in my memory. Oh, I know, it has to do with disease, and the rules about cleanliness going way back in history, animals with cloven hooves and all that stuff, but there appear to be other issues involving faith and custom and integrity that I am missing. Those rules were made a long, long time ago. Well, okay, I am game, if it will please my handsome new husband. It is necessary for him to be happy, so that he will make me happy. It's that simple. And it's not like I have a choice, since he is the lord and master. Butter and cheese, and other dairy products must live on the opposite side of the refrigerator from the meat. We must have two sets of dishes, cutlery, pots and pans, for never may the two be mixed, in any context.

Glass items are for some peculiar reason, exempt. I wonder, I think to myself, if he realizes just how ridiculous this is. And why must I play a part in his faith when I am not even permitted to attend religious services with him, when faith and tradition are never even discussed? I have so many questions about God and faith and the meanings of stuff. So, it is merely a matter of obeying orders, never my best thing, what I have so long sought respite from and now must accept anew.

I am now a new and different person existing in an old familiar world. I have my bags full of groceries, very proud of myself, and I walk briskly homeward, feeling very wifely. I have a Linzer Tart with its coating of powdered sugar in its folded wax paper in a tiny white paper bag tucked into my groceries, my reward for later for doing all of my appointed chores. I am a very efficient housewife, indeed. I do have a little experience shopping, for I have gone on such errands many times for Mom, pulling that old wire shopping cart behind me over these same rutted Queens streets when I was old enough. But this is different. Although I am still nineteen years old, in years, I am no longer a teenager, doing an errand for my mother. Now I am a woman with my own household to maintain, so I stand up straighter, puff my chest out for emphasis and smile at everyone I pass on the street. I have achieved the grand status of adulthood by attrition. I pass the old luncheonette where I stopped after school some days for a snack of a hamburger and a cherry coke that in 1953 cost fifteen cents, and glance at the kosher deli on the corner where I stopped on other afternoons for a frankfurter, mustard and sauerkraut, *two* for fifteen. The memories trigger thoughts of my uncle Irv who according to the family tale showed great business acumen when he sold Italian ices on the street during his youth in the depression, a nickel a piece, two for fifteen and one free, and makes me smile. When I notice the familiar Chinese restaurant across the street, looking exactly as it did three years ago when I was sixteen, a cold chill goes through me, and I turn the other way, and hurry to the safety of my new home. Thanks to my new marriage, I will no longer need to worry about Daddy's temper tantrums, his rejection. I will never be alone again. I have a husband, who loves me, and I love him, I chant inwardly. We will love each other and never hurt each other. We will always have a united front, in everything we do; the chorus from the theme song of the famous show. An old childhood mantra, but my childhood is over. I squeeze my eyes shut tightly, and ask the powers that be for help. What can I promise in return? Be careful, says a small voice deep inside, almost laughing, but not quite, remember what happened with *Rumplestiltskin*. He demanded a first born child in payment for a favor.

1955

A tinkling of wind chimes melds with a background of oriental music, chimes and flutes and cymbals. The red brocade walls are hung with scenes of China, delicate lines and washes, Chinese symbols, the details enhanced by gold leaf. The late afternoon light slides in from the street through large murky pane glass windows in the front throwing strange shadows and mingling with the dim atmospheric lighting. We sit awkwardly at the Naugahyde and Formica booth, a family akimbo, awaiting our exotic celebratory dinner. The celebration is for my sixteenth birthday.

It is late spring of my junior year in high school. Graduation is creeping up, and with it comes the imperative need to decide which of the favored and accepted colleges will be my choice. We have all taken CEEGs and SATs, etc., and we future graduates and college students are so numb that we begin to speak in multiple choice and thesaurean intricacy. This becomes our most favorite of many inside jokes. We, the future class of '56, await grades and percentages with bated breath, and secret fear that in this huge class of brilliant students, perhaps some of us won't even appear on the crucial list. The tension is as thick as the egg-drop soup I spoon automatically into my waiting mouth, and tempers run high.

I hide in a morose and desperate silence, for I am one of those, certain that in my wildest dreams that I will not qualify. I tell myself that this is a part of life, and that everyone cannot be recipient, especially in a school of such multitudinous talent, of a New York State scholarship. Let's face it; the odds are not in my favor, especially since I have filled my entire curriculum with art and writing classes, thus maximizing my grade quotient and avoiding the stress of more demanding classes. I am resigned to go to some lesser school than the hugely desirable Cornell University, desperately fearful even of the competition there, anyway, and happy to stay in the city, even though I look forward to the possible escape from life at home that out of town school will provide. In a sense, I cling to the stability of my old friendships and the known quantity of what I already have, because the thought of new challenges and possible failures of even greater magnitude are thoughts that are not even tenable.

I try to explain this to Mom and Dad as we wait for the waiter to bring our order, at my birthday celebration that is being held in this restaurant. I am trying to be mature, grown up and sensible and realistic. It is a tense time for me as well as for Mom, for one can never predict with any exactness Daddy's outbursts, and we sit under great strain, fervently wishing to get through the evening with no incident. We are accustomed to this; it has been an insistent dynamic of our life, since the end of the war.

We make small talk, stiffly, the conversation gradually slip sliding around to graduation and college. It begins reasonably enough, and I am lulled into the false belief that this is a normal discourse, that I can lower my defenses and express my true feelings and my very real doubts, and perhaps even get, for once, support in my goals. Are we not three adults having an ordinary conversation? Maybe this is youth, ignorance, naïveté, maybe it is just a terminal case of fervent wishful thinking.

I should have known better. I should have learned by now to keep my big mouth shut. I should have sensed that Mom's timing is as bad as ever, appears to be baiting, baiting, and her cringing and apologetic martyrdom are just begging for a shot. I make a big effort to ignore the growing tension, I pretend that it does not exist. Surely, he would not include me in their obsessive dynamic? Do I mimic, indulge in, the same old familiar programmed pattern as my mother? I definitely do not want to do that. Yet, I continue speaking, trying to be honest about my feelings, my truth, baring my soul, which is not that easy for me to do and gives me a uncommon sense of pride and accomplishment for once. I am merely being mature, realistic, I think. But isn't that what Mom thinks she is doing? Some message is attempting to get through to me from parts unknown, but I am not ready to understand it. So I muse that although I am in the first quartile of the graduating class, the chances are slight indeed that I will get one of those coveted scholarships, and as I begin to say that this is all right, that I have made peace with my inadequacies, Daddy seems to leap from his seat, and slapping me sharply on the face, in front of all the other diners, begins to berate me, his fury beyond imagination.

YOU TRAMP, he bellows, what the hell do you mean that my daughter can't manage to get a simple scholarship? The blood rises to his head and I tremble, watching the phenomenon of his fury in helpless and paralyzed fascination, mortification, terror. I have no identity, I am just His Daughter. In addition to the obvious injustice of his rant, I have difficulty understanding why my inadequacy makes me a tramp. In my adolescent world, tramp has a very different connotation. I jump from my own seat, tears pouring down my face. I run out blindly, senselessly through the streets, and finally turn towards the warm welcoming safety of my friend Emmy's house, a few blocks away, towards her normal, comforting family. I look around me, sense that there are families in this world that are loving and supportive and protective. This is what I crave. I must meet someone who will love me and want to marry me, as soon as possible, I tell Emmy. I have to get out on my own, away from them, my parents. If I stay there, I will die.

CHAPTER 15

1958

Today, it is just that old Chinese restaurant. I have reached my first and most pressing goal; I am out of that house. An entire encyclopedia of future achievements awaits. I avert my eyes and walk homeward, my arms aching pleasantly with the weight of my joyous bundles, my mind filled with plans for dinners. Like Mom had. But now, we will see what cooking expertise I have absorbed from my mother and my grandmother. I move dreamily, preoccupied, through the city landscape. I need to get one of those wire baskets with wheels for trips like this like Mom used to have, I think in the midst of my excursion and my wandering thoughts.

It is our first official day of marriage, here in the real world; I am officially a bride, a wife. I am resplendent in one of the outfits from my trousseau, feeling fresh and elegant and new. Having completed all my household chores, I am proudly cloaked in the vanity of my proficiency that has allowed me sufficient time to visit the local supermarket before Steve is arrives home. Glowing with the awareness of my domestic accomplishment, I am humming, singing popular tunes, daydreaming about home décor and exotic food, planning my mouth watering ingestion of my waiting tart. Absently I press the elevator button, balancing my two huge brown paper bags of groceries, smiling buoyantly at the kid that stands silently, maybe sixteen or seventeen years old, waiting with me; I am suddenly overflowing with joy. I am out of my parent's house of fury and turmoil, and independent, an adult, a wife in a grown up world. The memories recalled by the Chinese restaurant have reminded me of this. I strut into the elevator lugging my awkward bundles, lost in the reverie of my planned dinner. The doors shut with a bang, and we move unevenly upward.

The car stops between floors with a sharp jolt, a grinding of gears and I am shaken from my reverie; the boy whom I notice, now, for the first time, ludicrously for this neighborhood, for this time of day, dressed in addition to jeans and plaid shirt, cowboy boots and ten gallon hat, suddenly perilous, a strange expression on his face, rushes at me, knocking my pitiful groceries and me, to the floor, and begins to rip at my dress. My Linzer tart has been flung from the brown paper bag and has skittered across the black tile floor, leaving a wake of powdered sugar; he is sprawled on top of me, pressing his body against me, groping and grinding and grabbing and ripping at me, his hands and limbs all over me, the rough cold extensively laundered denim of his tight jeans brushes against my bare leg and I feel an incomprehensible sensation of anxiety directed at the remnants of my pastry. Then, for one short moment, the thought crosses my mind in an incongruous fugue that this is one of my favorite outfits, pale green floral embroidered ruffled cotton lawn, purchased with much care for my honeymoon, and in another moment I am scared to bloody death, retreat into the hidden recesses of my mind; all those years of walking in the middle of the road at night careful to stay under the beam of street lamps, watching the shadows creep and crawl from behind parked cars and bushes. All those fearful subway and bus rides listening for imaginary footsteps; all the frightful moments of walking into darkened vestibule and scurrying up three flights of stairs to fumble with an uncooperative key and lock in a murky hallway, trying to control the jumping of a queasy stomach and lurching elevator of internal chills. Now to come to this in broad daylight, my brand new husband due home in mere moments. Maybe he will get here in time I think for a second, a total non sequitur. Yes, Stevie will save me, I think feeling comforted, just a little, but my thoughts are jumping all around, anywhere but here in the elevator.

HAH HAH, I giggle to myself, my inner body tensing with terror, resigned to the inevitability of fate as fat tears overflow and stream down my face, you may rape me, you may even kill me, but you're too late to have my virginity, that which I protected it all those years, and at least I don't have that to worry about any more. Tears of some kind trickle down my cheeks. Triviality is commanding the situation, as I deal helplessly on a conscious level with my threatened mortality. The very idea of this ludicrous thought when my very life might be at stake somehow snaps me out of the helpless torpor that I have been allowing to take over my body, galvanizes me into action. Now, lying on my back on the filthy elevator floor, I am kicking, twisting, scrambling, scratching, and trying to find traction. My dress is ruined, my favorite dress, I muse, feeling the cold gritty steel pressing my back.

The elevator suddenly begins its ascent moving slowly upward, comes to a stop at the sixth and top floor which is ours. A thought flashes briefly across my consciousness, an impulse to thank the immutable unseen powers that be for whoever summoned it. I reach out for the door, with my leg, my foot, kicking at the door and finding air at first, trying to open it, and screaming at the same time, at the top of my lungs as we wrestle, a squirming mass of arms and legs and torsos; I can feel again the roughness of his jeans, the cold smoothness of his leather boots, the sharp prong of his belt buckle, still intact against my body through the thin fabric of my dress. Ultimately, fearing that by this time someone might have heard the commotion, my evil young cowboy leaps to his feet, slips through the swaying door, and disappears down the fire stairs before I have a chance to even get myself upright. Summoned by neighbors who have heard my screams, the police arrive to find me hysterical and incoherent, shaking uncontrollably. They question me for hours, filling out interminable papers and forms, staying with me until my impatiently awaited husband arrives. A kind neighbor helps me to gather up my groceries, just as Steve arrives home. Unfortunately, he is too late to save me, to be my knight in shining armor. But surely he will comfort me, offer me some tender consolation. Is that too much to ask?

I can see that dinner is not ready, he sneers as I shudder at his tone of voice, and I imagine that indeed compassion would be too much to ask. Always there is some trauma and drama, with you and your mother. I cringe a little, and shudder. My mother, I think? What does she have to do with anything? I don't understand.

Well, you must have done something to lure him on, says Steve a little bit later, after the police have written their report and gone, when he has heard the entire story, yet again. Men don't just attack a woman for no reason, with no provocation. What were you wearing? Was your hair all wild like that?

For a long time he doesn't let me forget what is supposed to be my fall from grace. He considers me tainted, even though nothing has even happened, and it is weeks before he so much as touches me again. I suffer in pained silence, longing not so much for his sexual touch as for the closeness of another warm human, of Steve, himself, the touch of his love. I can never get enough of that, it seems ... the feeling of being embraced by love. There is no price it seems that I am not willing to pay for even the appearance of love. I seem to suffer from interminable terminal *skin-hunger* as symptomized by this great need to be held.

ॐ

I lie on my chubby baby back feeling the somewhat pressing and musty warmth of the sun as it forces itself through the heavy coated canvas of the pram hood My eyes encompass everything that surrounds me in mere moments. I know every crack in the dreary gray canvas by heart; know every tarnished support rib also. The steaminess and the beating sun make me sleepy. The smell of the baking rubber offends my stomach. The good thing is that it feels so safe. I watch the clouds make lazy patterns across the sky, and sleep fitfully, on and off, lulled by the heat, the smell, the boredom. Awakening, I watch for the shadow of the figure, wish to see it back before my narrow field of vision. I do not cry out fretfully although I long to, for long ago I learned from constant ineffective repetition that this would be futile.

My hair lies damply in little corkscrews on my face and damp pillow; the sun scorched patchwork designs on my bare legs as it moves, unmindful of the delicately embroidered protective coverlet long since kicked impatiently off my small body. I am little more than one year old, not the infant one would expect to see in such a pram. I am really too old for it. Mommy insists firmly, however, that I need my nap. In the pram, I get to have it in the fresh air and sunshine. No one but me has experienced the inside of this pram. My mother believes firmly in the child rearing dictums of 1941. She would have been quite shocked had she been able to see past my small face, that spaniel-like expression of sadness, into my young mind.

Finally my patience is rewarded; the foot and a half square opening of the carriage hood becomes suddenly screened in shade as the longed for figure arrives. She bends over me, lovingly adjusting pillow, coverlet and curls, smiling sweetly. I look up with the biggest saddest expression I can make with my eyes, feeling restless and trapped, but not knowing what those feelings are or how to express them. I don't, can't, question Mommy's actions, of course, I am too young; I feel neither anger nor resentment ... because Mommy is perfect. I look through my private picture frame, through those liquid eyes that hungrily engulf the graceful figure. I have no idea as to the meaning of the words lovely, regal, or sweet, *but I do know that when Mommy is around, a soothing safe feeling envelopes me.*

I watch her long glowing hair, folded and curved into that early '40s upsweep glowing halo like as the late afternoon sun stands directly behind Mommy and the warm and musky odor of perfume wafts into the rubber and canvas mustiness around me, making me feel an incredible peace peppered with an ineffable sense of longing. I want very much to speak, but I cannot find the words; I feel a great need to express numerous overwhelming feelings, but when I open my mouth to speak I am overcome by an incredible sadness as nothing but coos and gurgles of baby talk come out. I close my eyes and pretend sleep, wishing that just this once Mommy would lift me out of the despised carriage early, and maybe even hold me tightly, making my day sweeter and safer. Soon I drift off to sleep.

You see, says my mother to her neighbor on the park bench, it's merely a matter of discipline and continuity. There's nothing that little girl would have loved more than to be taken from her carriage and coddled, but she's beginning to learn that this is the way it is. Children need to know what's expected of them and that they can't always have their own way and be cuddled just because they demand it. This is a very important preparatory lesson for life, she says sanctimoniously. Our family doctor taught me this. It's the newest discovery in child rearing. Later in life, I read it in a book, too.

Don't you think that's a bit harsh, asks her companion, wouldn't you think a child needs nothing nearly so much as love and a feeling of warmth and security? I know I do, she adds sadly.

That's your trouble, Etta, returns her sister severely, you're too soft. That's how you get yourself into trouble. If you had learned discipline years ago you wouldn't always need rescuing. You suffer from a surfeit of emotional weakness, she proclaims with a slightly supercilious authority.

Dear Sarah, her sister sighs. You know so little about me. What happened to me had nothing to do with discipline, and more to do with Poppa's rigid and puritanical beliefs, and his need to control me.

Without understanding or even being aware of any of this, somehow I begin to realize that Steve has quickly figured out that in my need for affection he has unwittingly acquired a useful tool to use in his battle to have power over me. Still, I love him. What I at least perceive to be love. I crave his presence, his touch. I am so needy. What is it that I need? Where do I find it? What does this need have to do with love? Is it Steve I love, or am I in love with love? I realize from our first day together that it is all wrong. I cry myself to sleep, then, and thereafter. No communication, no empathy, no consideration, as a matter of fact, no acknowledgment at all of my feelings, or that I have feelings at all. It is all an exercise in non-life. He is an automaton, moving by rote, preprogrammed, immovable and uncompromising; stingy, thick, rigid, demanding, ungiving, and unforgiving. It never changes; if anything, with the fading of the first glow, it gets worse. Where is the sweet affectionate boy I fell so in love with; where is love? Without hope of any solution, I begin to sublimate in kitchen gadgets, wallpaper remnants, crafty do-it-yourself projects and decor; almost as if, if I can create a proper home setting, the husband will emerge smiling and full of love, arms outstretched. Divorce is not only impossible, but unthinkable, in the 1950s. How would I accomplish it, anyway, my parents would undoubtedly refuse to help; what would their friends think? Steve doesn't appear to notice anything wrong. Everything is in its proper place. It is business as usual; he has never experienced anything different. Just who is this strange man to whom I am married?

The days go by slowly. I keep myself busy doing chores. Steve has delineated my responsibilities for me, annotated my chores. The days and weeks are choreographed in detail. I am expected to follow Steve's plan by rote, like an automaton, especially on Friday, the Sabbath. Oh, yeah, I know all about the Sabbath. And I know very well by now that Friday means chicken.

ॐ∾∾

It sits there propped up against the sides of the brand new, turquoise plastic, covered, wire basket dish drainer on the drain board of my kitchen sink. Its tiny headless body is solitary and pathetic, its poor dead skin cold and shriveling and beginning to turn from bilious yellow to gray. Tears are flooding senselessly down my face; I am choking on a lump of despair in my throat. Its little truncated arms and rounded footless haunches send a silent plea for pity.

I back away, and reach for the wall phone, trying not to look at the poor thing, and call Mom. Tears sluicing down my face again, I wail, it looks like a little baby, sitting there. What am I going to do? I mumble. What? Mom doesn't understand. The Chicken, I say, I'll never get it done before he gets home. It looks just like a baby, I repeat. I can't cook it; I can't even look at it. Today is Friday, chicken. What am I going to do? I hear the sounds of stifled laughter, as Mom attempts to get control of herself. The chicken, she gasps, the chicken, and collapses on the other end of the phone line in spasms of mirth. She is no help at all. Go out for dinner, she offers weakly.

Steve arrives home a short time later. I don't smell any dinner, he comments dryly. Could we go out for pizza, or something? I ask timidly. But it's Friday night, *Shabbos*, he says, the Sabbath. We always have chicken on Friday night. But we used to go out for pizza all the time on Friday night, I sigh softly, remembering, and we are practically still on our honeymoon; we are young and we are allowed to have fun, I say forlornly. We are married, now, we are adults, he comments. There is more to adult life than fun, he says. And then I tell him about the chicken. How it looked just like a tiny headless baby. You are as crazy as your mother and your Aunt Etta, he sighs. Okay, we'll go out, this time, but don't think I am going to allow you to make a habit of this. And if that is your way of bringing up the subject of babies, don't bother.

The shock of his words is incomprehensible. I look away, and don't answer. Rebellion and sarcasm stick in my throat, worse than my tears for the poor dead chicken. Dinner is solved, and the chicken has a temporary reprieve from the oven. And babies?

I think about our babies that will never see the light of day, about dying fantasies and lost dreams and broken promises; I think of the emptiness looming before me and all the years ahead, and think also about creative methods for solving problems. One lesson I have learned extremely well is that there is no end to creativity, and no finite method to solve problems. There is no prison, no trap from which one cannot escape. Look at Houdini. This man, my husband, believes he owns me, can control every part of my life, my dreams. He will find out who I am, some day. He will find out that no one will control me completely. There is something that I know. I have rights. They are delineated in the Constitution of our country by the Founding Fathers. This much, I learned at school. All I need is the courage of my convictions. So. There is also no method of birth control that is absolute. Now I am an adult who has the power to act. There are no other forms of adult higher up than me, to temper my decisions with loud resounding *noes*. At least when my babies are born I will have them to love as they will love me. I am an indulged only child, and I am in so many ways accustomed to getting what I want. And I have determined that I want babies. I have decided that this will be the way that I will finally find love, the only available way.

How could I have been so wrong about somebody? When I first met Steve, he reminded me so of Grandpa. Piety, dependability and conservatism appeared, in contrast to my father to be the most important of attributes. I believed at that time that his orthodoxy reflected a level of goodness and compassion not able to be breached, just like Grandpa, whom I know to be sweet and loving.

How have I ended up in this situation, I am beginning to allow myself to wonder. How did I end up with Steve, anyway? One moment I was a schoolgirl, my life looming ahead of me, needing only to escape from my parents' angry home, and then here I was, Steve's wife, a prisoner anew in a different Hell.

CHAPTER 16

1955

I am that most fortunate creature, a teenage girl in 1955!

Until recently, I have been content to cheer for the Giants, root against the Dodgers, at the Polo Grounds or Ebbet's Field. Chomp on awful hotdogs that taste somehow like something better than the revered by adults, filet mignon, passed along a row of fans from the white uniformed vendor in the aisle, fill out the score card, holler and scream. Letty and I can quote statistics with the best of them, argue good best better until we are hoarse, Letty is a Dodger fan, I am, a Giant. Letty and Shelly and I are the Three Musketeers, members of a prestigious club. The next moment, we are taking the subway to Manhattan to wait on line for *Gone with the Wind* at the Plaza, now long gone, *frankly, my dear, I don't give a damn,* we are fond of intoning in fake baritones and I'll think about it tomorrow, in exaggerated dulcet southern drawl; at the NBC studios to stand on line and hope for seats at the Pepsi Cola Hour to see Eddie Fisher in person, *any tiiimmme, you're feeling lonely... they're not making the sky so bluuuue, wish you were here... oh my papa to me you were so wonderful...* or waiting in the screaming throngs at the same Plaza to hear Frank Sinatra sing, *I saw you last night and got that oooldfeeling... my life is sad and lonely, I yearn for you and you dear only, you're all for me, body and soul...put your dreams away for another day...* and we grab each other to keep from falling over in a swoon. One time we got up front seats at the Pepsi Hour when I painted a portrait of Eddie Fisher, wrote a letter pleading to give it to him in person. We went back stage after the show, weak kneed and quivering with joy and expectation, and he gave us each one of his favorite striped ties, which we noticed and ignored what we saw, came from an immense carton of more of the same, as a memento, after accepting the portrait with grace and gratitude. He probably purchased the ties by the gross. I toss my pony tail and Mom tells me that I look just like Debbie Reynolds, and I think, yeah, but she has Eddie Fisher, maybe someday... My dreams and fantasies are filled with a romance with Eddie Fisher.

I abandon Eddie Fisher and Frank Sinatra, along with along with the Giants and Dodgers, the Gold twins, Gilbert and Edward, spin the bottle and the remainder of the remnants of youthful daydreams and fantasies. I move tentatively ahead onto the menacing and intangible stage of the grown up world with hesitant *pas de deux,* leaving behind to the high school corridors all of my gangly and acne marred, recently favored male buddies, and innocent enough would be and imagined paramours, real and celebrity. I hurry bag and baggage into the imposing and titillating terrain of Joe College. I am enchanted, tantalized by the promises of sophistication and an entire lifetime yet to come of privileged maturity. And I am not alone. I am traveling on this adventure, hip to hip, shoulder to shoulder, with my girlfriends. The JUGs are finally coming into their own.

That would be our club, *Just Us Girls*; the J.U.G.s for short. We are seriously impressed with our cleverness. We begin booking parties now with college fraternities, traveling *en masse* with giddy anticipation and fingers crossed. We pray with all that is holy in a *mélange* of mixed metaphors that this time, just this time, Mr. Right, Prince Charming on a silver charger will appear across a crowded room and fly us to the moon. There is no romantic fantasy that does not apply, no plan that is not valid in our journey toward reaching our goals.

Bitter bitter cold, colder than New York, really, much colder; it is frigid, by any standards. We have braved the long high-speed New York State Thruway and a host of additional obscure and insignificant to us roadways in our drive to Massachusetts, and stand here in the icy blackness of a winter night, in alien territory, mysterious and far reaching, unknowable, murky. The Tufts campus spreads around us, far and wide, disappears into the blackness, the curious strangeness. We walk along unaccustomed paths, approaching a forbidding silent alien house, the fraternity house, Alpha Epsilon Pi. Shelly's brother Sol has graciously invited us for the weekend; Shelly and I, two high school seniors, quaking in our boots, actually teetering on new Cuban heels, on the adventure of a lifetime. We are alight with anticipation, filled with our own sense of self-wonder, hoping to make the acquaintance of college men. My mouth is dry, my undulating stomach queasy, my anticipation tangible, an entire creature with its own body and soul.

The front door opens into chaos, a mob scene, loud and hot and moist and raucous, pervaded by an essence of testosterone. Everywhere, frenetic movement, everyone attempts to be heard over the blaring music by shouting above it. The result is a cacophonous bubbling popping pressure cooker stew of adolescent humanity, jiggling and swirling and jumping, perpetual motion. We slide into the churning mess, becoming instantly one with the movement, waiting for our minds to catch up with our bodies. Self-conscious as we are, no one notices us, no one at all. That was not the plan.

Solly comes over with a group of his brothers, shouting out some manner of introductions, this is my sister, Rochelle, and this is Lynne. Sol is an imposing figure, about six feet, close to three hundred pounds, broad and thick. No one in his right mind would dare to cross Sol. Treat them well, brother, he says fiercely, or you'll answer to me. Shel, meet Tom, Lynne, this is Bob. They look us up and down see Shelly, exotic, dark, buxom, sultry, and me, skinny, maybe just slim, but beginning to blossom, fresh faced, freckled, and ponytailed ... He disappears into the crowd, and we are left with two strapping handsome college boys in their Greek flocked lettered fraternity sweaters, a lifetime dream come true. We are helpless with a terror of the unknown, titillated by possibility, tongue tied by inexperience. Shelly wanders off with Tom to dance or find something to eat or drink, pretending to be right there in her element. I watch her walk away with trepidation and not a little apprehension, totally clueless, out of my league. Bob slips his arm comfortably proprietarily through mine, and as I cringe unseen, directs me to the middle of the room where there is a mob surrounding something on a table. Orange Blossoms, he says obliquely, shrugging, to my blank face. I look around, but see no flowers of any kind. He tugs me, and I follow meekly, obedient, having little choice, no other opportunity presenting itself. As we get closer, I make out the shape of a bathtub, set on top of this huge table. A glistening white claw foot steel tub sits at eye level, a spigot attached to the outer portion of the tub's drainpipe. The mob is because there is gin and orange juice in the tub, and they are looking for their fair share. Orange Blossoms says Bob again, smiling, here, let me get you some. Now I get it. A virtual light bulb lights up above my head, and I force a crooked grin. Sol appears as if from nowhere, and takes the glass out of my hand, hands me a Pepsi. Now Bob, he says, you know she's only sixteen. I told you about that. And Bob, worried, steps back a bit, smiles sheepishly and guides me awkwardly across the room where we can sit down.

We are going through the motions, trying to get to know each other, not really that interested and I am a little disappointed, there are none of those expected sparks, the automatic delicious thrills associated with liaisons with attractive older men have not appeared, but this is what you do at this kind of party. Mostly, with all the noise, we are reading lips and saying what, what, what, over and over again. We are both bored to tears, feeling the endlessness of looming time. Come on, says Bob, let's go for a drive, I know this great place, quiet and nice. This frat house is ridiculous, too loud, too crowded. I nod tentatively in agreement, smiling, warming up, knowing that Sol is near, and look around me for his comforting form. Still, I am too dumb to be concerned. He honors me with a sweet ingratiating smile, and I figure, what the heck, he has already been warned by Sol, and Sol is huge, powerful and not to be messed with.

I slide into the freezing car, missing already the warmth generated by so many bodies accumulated in an enclosed space, the looming unfamiliar darkness swirling around us, becoming aware of small inner admonitions, suddenly worried by the aura of unknown and alien place. What am I doing? This will not end well. Let's go back inside, I say, it's so cold out here. Don't worry, the heater will catch on quickly, it will warm up in no time at all, says Bob. Here, he says, taking off his camel's hair overcoat, climbing in from the other side, sliding closer to me. He covers both of us with the coat, and snuggles closer, laughing, pulling the coat over the two of us, and it's true, I am feeling warmer; just not more confident. Geez, he is smooth. In a moment he is reaching over under his coat, kissing me, his hands everywhere. No, I twist my head from side to side, no. But he is everywhere, his hands are everywhere. He is an octopus; I don't have enough hands to push him away. His octopus lips are planted over mine, pressing against me like a suction cup on a window pane, and I can't even speak, gasp. NO, I choke as I feel him reach under my skirt and begin to slide his hand up my thigh. I am beginning to feel that familiar intensifying aura of apprehension enveloping me and my thoughts begin to meander into areas of escape. The windshield is getting fogged over, the car is hot now, a sauna, and I am wrestling with an octopus; wrestling with an octopus in a sauna. I giggle, always in the visual. A car drives by bright lights flashing through the window, blinding us momentarily, he loosens his grip for a minute, and I am up, clambering over the console and the shift, and almost out of the car. Don't you dare, I spit at him as I put myself together, turn my head from side to side trying to figure out just where I am in the maze that is this immense campus, and where I am going now, Aw, come on, pleads Bob, probably thinking about big Sol, and the ramifications of his actions. I thought we were getting along fine. Don't worry, come on, get in, I'll take you back to the house. I am shivering, my lips are chattering in this incredible New England cold. Do I have a choice? Okay, I say, climbing back into the car.

We arrive back in moments, and Bob is the perfect escort, solicitous and gallant, a faint worry line tickling the corners of his eyes, marring his perfect face. His gaze is flicking back and forth and all around, looking for Sol, I think. But he is seeking someone else, anyone, it seems. Hey, Stan, he yells over the tumult, commanding, authoritatively, come over here and look after Sol's guest. A slim guy, youngish, rather ordinary, comes over, and Bob shakes his head, yes, and disappears. I'm a freshman, says Stan, shrugging, he's above me. He shrugs, and smiles, and guides me over to a doorway that leads to a sort of den, where there are banquets and tables, and few people, to a far corner in a little pocket of virtual quiet where you could sit and talk. And we do. And I am surprised at how decent and intelligent he is. He begins to look better, more attractive. It was my father's frat, he apologizes; it's not really my favorite thing. I can't really enjoy this fraternity thing. It's a family tradition. He shrugs. I smile. He asks me if I would give him my address, and would I mind if he writes to me, and I think, how sweet. Mostly, I like him. I don't expect to hear from him, but it was a nice thing to do. He is that rare commodity, a truly nice boy. Does this make him unattractive, unworthy? He walks me back to find my coat, kisses me softly and sweetly, briefly, and deposits me back with Shelly and Sol.

The postman, authoritative in his slick gray/blue uniform, his heavy brown leather mailbag hanging lightly on his shoulder, is slipping an assortment of junk and bills and correspondence that constitutes the daily mail belonging to each resident, into their respective compartments in the bank of mailboxes in this three story walk up garden apartment complex, where we live, as I am returning from school one afternoon the following week. He smiles at me, and hands me a letter. The return address, Waltham Massachusetts, and the unusual cartoon artwork all over the envelope tell me it is from Stan. A sweet newsy letter that makes me wish Waltham Mass. was closer to New York. I can barely remember what he looks like, but I am into the moment, into the spirit of the thing, and plan an answer. I feel obliged to respond in a manner that will uphold my reputation for being fey and artistic, the most original around. I am going to win him over, whatever that means, I will make him like me, want to see me again. He has put forth a challenge to me with his drawings, and I will heed the call to arms. We have an unheralded competition, we JUGs. Who is cuter, who is more clever; who will create the greatest shock waves. I send him a lengthy tome written on a roll of toilet paper. I re-roll it and slip it into a manila envelope and send it off. His phone call a couple of days later starts off with compressed laughter, tells me by the tone of his voice that my arrow has hit its mark. He tells me that he opened the letter in a lecture hall, and it unrolled down the auditorium stairs, disrupting the entire lecture. Let the fun begin. But geography and logistics contrive to throw their figurative monkey wrench into our promising romance, our budding hopes and plans; never mind Waltham, he lives with his family in Connecticut, too distant for normal interaction, too difficult to maneuver. Alas, we agree to end what has never begun, and vow with fervor and sincerity to meet again in the future. A truly nice boy and I must say goodbye. Will there ever be another nice boy in my life?

When Shelly and I reconnect at our hotel room, we decide that with all their obvious faults and shortcomings, college men are indeed far superior to our high school cohorts. It is simply a matter of finding the right ones. We are putting our heads together, and creating grand plans that include a whole rash of fraternity parties with our friends, just as soon as we return. Yet, I am wondering if this frat boy fantasy is all it is cracked up to be. But youth is nothing if not resilient, optimistic, and I am ever the personification of Pollyanna.

᚛ઓ᚜

The first official meeting of the JUGS comes to order that September afternoon in 1951. We all wear our purple satin jackets, the club name in white felt six inch letters on our backs, each with her name emblazoned in white script across the left breast. It is something to wonder at that our parents let us use the name, and that they have not addressed our innocent enough gaffe. It isn't clear whether they are more speechless or shy. They don't know what to do with us.

To the infamous members, twelve years old in post war Forest Hills, New York, of our number, Shelly is the only girl who quite qualifies yet physically, and though we all envy her full blown attributes, awesome compared to our own budding baby fat. We go through our days like society dowagers at the Ascots, parading in tandem, eyes turned towards anything that reflects, store windows, car windows, to check our profiles and the impact of our *look*, and to see if we are catching up to Shelley. Slowly but surely we are making progress, but overall we are sufficiently thrilled and self-impressed merely to have reached the plateau that is Junior High, and, we are occupied with questions of more staggering significance than mere physical endowment ... that would be BOYS.

Our world is populated by the usual flotsam and jetsam of pubescent candidates, including one or two popular jocks and a list of the others, declining gradually in rating. There are, of course, the twins, Gilbert and Edward Gold, who we have under surveillance at all times and could have recited any manner of information or scuttle-but about. Gilbert, of course, is the one that the other Shelly (Shelly 2), is stuck on. What is it about twins? This bunch would be there for a long time, so when tall slim provocative Annalee with her bouncing auburn curls and model's stance and gestures discovers someone new and different, a high school freshman, from Georgia, of all places, we all begin to sweat in an agony of discovery. Something very new and different and exciting is about to happen. Maybe it will happen to one of us. A great new distraction has arrived in our lives.

Annalee is very proud of her sophistication and experience, and if anyone has it, it is she who has the power to entice and attract an older boy. He is an enigma, tall and lantern jawed and taciturn, with a killer smile, and a disarming southern drawl. We watch her operate, in awe. As a matter of fact, we maneuver the meeting to her house in order to set eyes on this paragon, and watch and listen wide-eyed and intense, brimming over with envy, green and viscous, hoping to get a free lesson from the blatantly sexual insouciant and confident Annalee. We all finally agree that Marshall is indeed adorable, with his tall rangy body and his tumbling curls and turned up nose, his southern drawl, and register our various bilious shades of envy, all except the unswerving Shelly 2, who insists that there is no one in the world like her adorable Gil. Skinny, limpid eyed, striking Shelly, elegant patrician features, long thick black hair, who promises to become a stunning woman is unmoved by the astounding Marshall. But there is no contest and poor Gil fades into oblivion for the rest of us; even his name is remarkable, who has ever known a Marshall?

Annalee and Marshall and their friends hold court in one corner of the Grand Central Parkway Playground, and I attach myself to their clique, because they are exciting in their contrast, there is an element of danger because of their alien-ness, their ages, and their sophistication, nothing like the run-of-the-mill schoolboys of my association. They aren't wise guys, or budding criminals or anything, just different, from distant, different schools. Guy, for example, is French Canadian and goes to Catholic school. He and I have that chemistry, are drawn together as sometimes happens, and in the teen mating ritual of the time, we do a lot of standing around and smiling at each other, and sometimes holding hands lightly. Later on, standing close together in the gray winter chill, barely touching, feeling that strange tingling sensation, we exchange a few light experimental kisses, oh so sweet and gentle and innocent. But we are in a strange mood, exploring the unknown, reaching for the unusual and esoteric experience, inured somehow from fear or possible repercussion.

Frequently I ride my blue and white wide wheel Schwinn down to the playground there on the corner of Grand Central Parkway and Horace Harding Boulevard, what is now the famous LIE, in full view of the celebrated World's Fair Grounds built in 1939, the year of my birth, and the Old Aquacade, where sometimes in the summer, Janie and I used to gird our loins bravely, take deep breaths, and go swimming in an atmosphere fraught with danger. It is a time warp for us, a weird gap of time and space. The kids who frequent the place are from Astoria, a notorious inner city area. We are not accustomed to so many alien faces, of both ethnic and skin color diversity. The strangeness is tantalizing, titillating. Chills and thrills. I feel an odd connection to those alien cultures, Black, Latino, that rhythm, that music, the food. I can't place it; I don't question or examine it. I merely follow the path as it appears before me.

The playground, equipped for pre kindergarteners is rarely if ever filled with the little guys for whom it is intended. Hoards of pre-pubescent teens, however, claim their territory, hang out there in tightly ordered groups, practicing their swaggers and looks of disdainful boredom, bouncing their ideas of macho cool and adult sophistication off one another. Laughing and telling what pass for smutty jokes, showing off on monkey bar, slide and high chain link fence with daring feats of fearlessness. It is scene from *West Side Story*, without the war. No one can be the first to leave, and so we stay longer and longer, each facing reprimand for being late, no one able to leave first. We flaunt our opinion of authority and discipline.

Sometimes Guy is not there for long periods of time, and one boy or another will thoughtfully though offhandedly call out to me that Guy is again in the hospital for some treatment or other, or some illness or other that seems so natural that I wonder why he even requires a hospitalization, until one day

Marshall confides that Guy has leukemia and is not expected to live very long. This adds poignancy to our future meetings, as well as drawing us closer, for now we can talk of his pain and impending demise and often do, in barely audible, long, and frightfully depressing conversations, clinging to each other as if this will make the inevitable go away. But for all the talk, I cannot wrap my mind around the concept of mortality, struggling as I am still over the recent death of my beloved grandfather.

One afternoon, I ride whistling down the parkway service road, excited by the sensations of spring in the air, and Guy isn't there again, and Marshall tells me with tears in his eye, that Guy died the night before. I feel weak with helplessness. I am at a loss, don't know what to do or feel. All our intimate discussions have not prepared me for this inevitability, and I almost burst with the pain and fear and sense of loss that it imposes. A flash of memory, Grandpa's death, flits across my mind, and is quickly gone. I don't go to the funeral, engulfed in terror, partially because I don't know quite how to explain to my parents who this boy was and how I had met him, what was our connection, what has happened to him, or what I am feeling. I am fearful of some form of censure that I am unable to identify.

I ring his mother's doorbell one sunny afternoon a week later, the icy black tinged snow drifts and frozen ground already defrosting in glistening sloppy mud puddles. My stomach is lurching, there is a lump perched dangerously near my tonsils. The front door looms up before me, cold and bare and forbidding. I am about to turn tail and run for my life when the door opens. Guy's mother is standing there, pale, forlorn, limp. Her eyes are downcast and red-rimmed. I have forgotten the carefully prepared speech that I have been practicing all the way over. I swallow, take a deep breath, and mumble that I am so very sorry, and turn to leave before I can lose control and embarrass myself with my own undeserved tears. Things are changed forever. I can no longer go to the playground without remembering Guy and his gentle way, and his sweetness, and soon, I don't go there anymore at all. Summer comes along and there are other agendas.

But there are lessons to be learned in everything, I am coming to realize; I now know that you do not need to be old to die, like grandpa, and this reinforces my terror of everything, especially dying. Alone with no brothers or sisters, I have no one in whom to confide my growing terror, no one to explore my feelings, no one to talk to. It begins to appear to me that death is stalking me, following me around. And then there is that first of many summers in the Catskills the year I am thirteen...

❧❧

Bumper to bumper traffic on the old route 17 snaking north and west as we do battle with heat and gas fumes and the inevitable fatal nausea in Daddy's old metallic hunter green Kaiser, find a momentary respite in humor as we pass the famous Red Apple Stop which sports a sign reading: Eat Here, Get Gas. We are cursing the impetus that brought us to this time and place, wondering if there could be anything down the road that would validate the effort. Everyone has the same idea to escape to the country. For me this entire adventure signals a grand period of emergence. I transcend childhood, and moth-like emerge slowly from my metaphorical cocoon. We take the turnoff onto route 17B which brings us finally skidding onto a sharp barely noticeable turnoff to Zeigler's Hotel and Bungalow Colony. We have arrived in upstate Mongaup Valley in the Jewish so–called Mountains which is situated on this out–of–the–way dirt road strategically between Monticello, Swan and White Lakes and nestled in hills and valleys of undeniable charm. It boasts its own manmade lake. By this point in time, I am secure in my slowly but surely growing bosom, and the fact that I am now an indisputable teenager, almost by definition, an adult, having attained thirteen years of age. Daddy has other business at this time having given up the camping business. We are to spend the summer here, and he will join us for weekends. I embark on this, my first summer of relative freedom, meaning sans camp regimentation, with a joyfulness of anticipation that is rivaled only by my extreme ecstasy to be in the country once again. The relief to be separated from Daddy's temper tantrums and the incipient stress that always pervades our home is an added perk.

Slipping from my room next morning at the crack of dawn to explore our environment I inhale the fresh sweet damp morning mist as forms begin to emerge in the slowly brightening sun, the infinitely rising and disappearing rows of hills and ridges of trees, the occasional highlight of rustic barn or charmingly decrepit outbuilding. My great joy to be in the country is not only due to the smell of freshly cut grass drying sweetly in the pressing summer sunlight. There are the ridges of New England rocks delineating acreage, the miles and miles of gently curved and slowly disappearing fields covered with grasses and different varieties of weed and wildflower. It all enchants me and fills me with a soaring elation that almost never in my life has been equaled. This is the reason I will need to live in the country, always, I vow silently.

My old childhood friend, Ruthie, is there also with her parents, and all the fathers come up each Friday night to partake of Mrs. Zeigler's substantial and quality renowned Jewish cooking, and the charms and vagaries of the relaxing and city detoxifying countryside and all its recreational facilities. Kids our age begin to appear within hours of our respective arrivals, and soon there is a kernel of a haphazard peer group. Somehow though we move in unilateral motions and degrees, we manage to traverse the various scheduled day camp activities intact.

Of course, the usual camp activities are planned for us, to keep our energies well channeled. The translation of this is, to keep us out of trouble. Trouble is defined as potential experimentation with sex, a fear with which the adults of this small transient community are duly preoccupied. The adults go to great lengths to corral what they consider and fear to be our obsessive preoccupation and inclination, matters that concern us kids very little. *Our* heads are full of swimming and boating, volleyball, basketball, softball, hiking and exploring. The camp director, so–called, a mathematics teacher in winter, finally allows us to restructure the program for teens at least, on a less rigid basis, and soon we have all but taken over the place; we are having a ball.

The management arranges a *social night* on Fridays, and our group all rushes joyfully down to the old rec room to join in the festivities for the hour or so allotted to kids alone before the others, the adults begin arriving for the scheduled entertainment. The Catskills are renowned for what is called the *Borscht Belt* entertainment.

I spot him immediately, straight blond hair falling continually over expressionless features in bland ennui, a tough little Bronx budding hoodlum, street-wise and bright. His name is Joel, and he is the son of the camp director, one year younger than me; our eyes meet, there is an immediate connection and it is inevitable that we will become close as thieves; we are soon inseparable. What one of us lacks in imagination or direction, the other makes up for in daring and ambition. I still suffer from insecurity in general, and the remnants of my uber-self, the tomboy cling to me, are easily resurrected for this new venue. Symptoms are known to surface at strange moments generally precipitated by some minor or major loss of confidence or lapse of memory; that I am supposedly an emerging woman, perhaps. Or the arrival of my father. Or all three. Meanwhile, I alternate between practicing my newly acquired powers of seduction and showing off my considerable athletic prowess.

I challenge Joel, a fine athlete himself, compact and agile to horse, basket ball, one on one, and beat him a good deal of the time. Sometimes he brushes against me evoking a strange gaggle of feelings that short circuit my system for a moment or two. I vie with the best of them in the softball outfield, and swagger around with the most blatantly confident, some prescient though barely anachronistic propensity to be Daddy's favored son still nagging around the edges of impetus and prepubescent impulse alike. I struggle always with internal wars and external assault, real or imaginary.

When depressed or livid with helpless rage, or needing to be alone with my thoughts, and with some small at least desire to shock and dismay the enemy, e.g. adults, I blithely and agilely climb the highest tree that I can find, completely free from trepidation, enjoying the rough feel of the scraping bark against my sneaker soles and tightly clinging jeans, and reveling in the rustling branches and leaves and the feeling of the treetop breezes on my face.

Joel, however, becomes my dearest friend and staunchest ally. While the other girls are reading true confession magazines and experimenting with hair removal creams and tanning lotions, activities that only occupied me slightly, Joel and I use nearly every minute of every day in a perpetual motion of doing and discovering. We structure our day loosely, but manage tacitly with virtually no discussion, to cover the gamut of sports including long hours in the lake, diving off the raft and racing back and forth and early dawn fishing expeditions.

We hunt throughout the woods for Indian relics and cow skulls, remnants of the cold and brutal winters that we cannot even conceive of in this warm and balmy summer paradise. Ultimately one relaxed Friday night at one of Joel's father's ingenuously scheduled teen socials, we discover the covert pleasure involved in ballroom dancing face to face and with grave innocence realize that this is an activity not be ignored or neglected, with or without music. The adults have inadvertently organized us into the very activity they fear the most, one that we have not yet discovered on our own.

We now spend a lot of time lying hidden in the sweet summer grasses exchanging long and hungry embraces and wonderfully exciting kisses, reveling in this wondrous new previously inconceivable pleasure that we had only wondered at when observed in movies or the paper backed novels with their dog eared pages and saliva marks that made the rounds.

We never did identify with any of that stuff; we cumulatively believe that we ourselves have discovered this new gamut of sensations and that no one else in the world other than us is privy to them. The question of how far to go is academic, in those days. Just so far, and no farther...nice girls don't...no touching, no removal of clothing, no. There really is no question; we don't even know what comes next, despite the voluminous literature available. The most daring and exciting of our adventures concerns forbidden midnight swimming expeditions where discreetly covered with swim suits we manage to touch bodies without touching or doing anything tacitly forbidden in a scandalous frenzy of pleasure.

The strange thing is, that those summers exist in a hiatus that seems to have little or nothing to do with real life.... The one or two meetings that we manage to maneuver in the city fail for some reason that we are unable to identify. Perhaps it is the absence of soft and tender field and summer sun. Maybe it is the diversity in our city backgrounds and lives. In mere days it all fades into the background of regular life, becomes as faint as an old movie or a book read long ago...

Time passes, and the JUGs hone their skills, among which is the throwing of parties, which is basically the main reason for the existence of a club at all. One dark Friday night while playing post office, I discover the secret of the Gold twins in a delicate kiss when the bottle points to me, at least the imperturbable Gilbert, and become Shelly 2's rival. Why you can't just settle for his brother, she asks, and I shrug my shoulders. I don't know. They are different. They look exactly the same, but they are not. This raises an entire list of questions. Henceforth, my bike meandering takes me to other areas of Forest Hills, including Rego Park, where the boys practice their softball.

In earlier times, I had been welcome to play center-field or first base or pitch, but during the past summer, something bizarre has occurred that has changed the whole dynamic, I am no longer welcome. Maybe it's me, experiencing a budding awareness of the changes in myself as well as in the boys that suddenly excludes me from their male activities. Is this fair?

I spend a lot of time and energy riding all around and searching until I find them, and then watch from a discreet distance while they get to play ball and I get to yearn in an incomprehensible and ineffable way to be accepted. Or something.

CHAPTER 17

Sol, Shelly's brother? Not only a fraternity boy and college student, but our resident social *mavin*, drives us one night to someone's home, a fraternity member of a different fraternity from Queens College, in Flushing, in the borough of Queens, New York, where our newest party is scheduled to occur. We are mature competent self reliant high school juniors and at least we are in our own territory, surrounded by familiarity, fearless. Sol is a call away, and we know our buses and trains and taxi services. Our excitement is palpable. Shelly and I are remembering that weekend at Tufts. All we know is that we are about to meet ... *college men*, not mere boys, and therefore by any standards have obtained inadvertently in our world nearly godlike status. This will not be a free-for-all like the Tufts one; here, now, we are the ones in control.

Sol's car is filled to bursting with JUGs, in a party mood, high pitched voices, speaking all at once, loud and raucous and expectant. Any one of our lives can change on this momentous night. We drive through the neighborhood, through canyons created by the surrounding antique apartment buildings, brick and stone and concrete, both austere and gingerbread trimmed. But Ronnie's home is not one of these. Ronnie is a member of Tau Alpha Omega, at Queens College. He is one of the privileged, lives in a private house, with its own yard and garage and driveway. And finished basement, which is where we now stand in an awkward, befuddled hormonal cluster. I study the room, dark pine paneling, high windows looking out on nothing, casual old furniture of nondescript color or style, a ping-pong table pushed to the wall, an ancient television, a phonograph next to which stands a rack of records, 45s, 78s, 33 1/3s, the entire gamut. Records are already stacked on the top of the center rod of the phonograph, Jackie Gleason's *Music for Lovers Only – I Only Have Eyes For You, Body and Soul;* Frank Sinatra, Tony Bennett, *Strangers in the Night, Embraceable You, Come to Me My Melancholy Baby, Blue Velvet* and *Because of You....* The Platters *My Prayer (is to linger with you).And of course, Eddie Fisher who is still wishing I were there...*Somewhere in the far recesses of my mind Ezio Pinza is standing in the moonlight in the middle of a stage set of a South Pacific island during the war earnestly singing to me that some enchanted evening, I will meet a stranger, and a tingle of hope courses through my body followed by shivers of expectation. I look back at the tightly wound group of brothers, who are looking us up and down like cow carcasses hanging on meat hooks in an icy meat storage locker. We are staring back, with a not much different attitude. We are checking them all out, top to bottom, looking them over, who is worthy who is not. *Strangers in the night, exchanging glances...*

Svelte and a little sexy, neatly dressed in mid calf length sheaths or A-line skirts and sweaters, our hair curled and styled, our heels not too high, just high enough to enhance our our slim ankles and gently rounded calves, what can be seen of them, our stockings new and without ladders, seams straight, just the faintest hint of scent, pearls and drop earrings. We know how we look. We are exactly right; we have checked with the latest style magazine, and we are secure in our social correctness...*wondering in the night, what were the chances...*

The initial reconnaissance has been completed, amidst an awkward shuffling of feet, nervous jostling and squirming and stifling of giggles. There is the normal exchange of glimpse and unspoken consensus, and we experience that collective sinking of stomach, the moment we cast our first hopeful glances. It doesn't get any better with additional time. Now there is a problem...*we'd be sharing love, before the night was through...*

Omigod, a high pitched raspy whisper in my ear, I believe it is the other Shelly, skinny Shelly, or Annalee, or Joyce, *look at them, they are all drips.* We have somehow landed in the midst of the ultimate of dripdom. We react as one. Our lower extremities buckle in unison with dismay and foreboding. *This is it,* says Shelly, *this is one evening that is predestined to failure. Look at them,* says the voice behind me with silent chagrin, *they are all wearing ties!* Where are their letter sports shirts, their knit cardigans? There is no saving grace for this group.

There is no one who comes close to our dream standards, never mind simple acceptability. We retire to the walk-in closet, to confer, and decide that we have no choice but to be good sports, go along with the plan for the evening. We have our reputation to uphold; there will be other parties. So, we proceed with a quickly conceived ice-breaking routine that we have invented that promises to be a most viable schtick. We turn on the charm as if we are surrounded by Rock Hudson, James Dean, Sal Mineo, and the rest of our '50s teen idols at the height of their popularity, paragons of adolescent dream and aspiration. It is good practice, says one JUG, it won't be a total loss, repeats another, and it is necessary to at least do something to pass the time until Sol comes to collect us. Omelets out of broken eggs, I think sagely. *Something in your eyes, was so inviting...*

Look at this tie, I exclaim to Shelly in animated surprise, walking up to the least non-presentable of the guys, a boy actually not that bad looking, if you look beneath that drippy unpolished exterior, but ...

I can tell you this, Shelly, this one is pre-law!

How do you know that? he asks, a little startled. He crosses his arms in front of his chest as if to hide the telltale tie. His hair is parted nearly in the middle. His trousers are baggy enough for another person to share the space. *Something in your eyes was so exciting...*

By the direction of the stripes, and the color combination, of course, silly, I answer. *And from your* brother, *Ronnie, who has been convinced to conspire with us for the sake of the evening's success.*

Gee, that's great, but I'll bet you can't do it again, breaks in another of them, joining the gathering group. They are wondering how we are doing this, a bit wary, getting interested. A strange atmosphere of confusion, tinged by a little bit of wonder is beginning to permeate this crowded pine paneled rec room. They are crowding around us. Although there is a certain amount of glee involved in that uplifting sense of superiority, I am bored with it all, with their gullibility, especially. They are mostly pre-law, a couple of pre-meds, budding accountants, totally uncool and uninteresting. You'd think they would be a little more intelligent. But we are a little invigorated by their growing interest, attraction. It is a good feeling, no matter who they are. Feeling wanted. *Something in your smile, says I must have you...*

Well, of course we can, our method is foolproof.

Well, then, prove it! Totally inspired, biting our collective lips and chewing on the insides of our mouths, we continue to astound the entire membership until, Ronnie, our co-conspirator, unable to contain himself any longer, spills the beans, and a brief period of laughter, raucous on our side, polite on theirs ensues. By this time the ice is broken, and we break off into animated groups and dancing couples. They're not that bad, actually, bearable, if not inspiring.

It will not be a total loss. Although no true love connection has been produced, the best is made of an originally doomed evening. But far earlier than would be usual to end an evening, we decide that the time has come to leave. *Hey Solly*, Shelly yells into the telephone, *can you come and get us? We are ready to leave.* But it is not Sol, it is Shelly's father, and he says that Sol is still at the movies. He is not expecting us to be ready to leave quite so early, we guess. *Strangers in the night, two lonely people...*

A few well placed queries get us the information we need, which of the brothers has the car. I, who never win anything, defy the law of averages and win the short straw determining who will try and entice the guy of the first tie, who has his father's car, the pre-law, into chauffeuring us home. I am not thrilled by this assignment. I have no desire to flirt with some jerk wearing baggy trousers that parts his hair almost in the center, which can only make stilted conversation about nothing, and only knows one dance, a stiff boxy bouncy fox trot...*we were strangers in the night, up to the moment when we said our first hello, little did we know, love was just a glance away a warm embracing dance away...*

Stoically, since sportsmanship is imperative, and I pride myself in being a good sport, I take on the job at hand, and, we are on our way. The car is a late model, clean and comfortable and roomy. According to the protocol, I am taken home last. He makes what passes for polite conversation, asking me if I know what kind of car he is driving. It seems to be a matter of great pride. I look around for a moment, and baffled and disinterested, ask if it is a Chevy. For some reason he finds this to be extremely humorous, and corrects me sagely, and proudly, saying that it is, of course, a Cadillac. His father's Cadillac. If I was expected to be impressed, I fail that test. Cars mean nothing to me, nor does status, in general. In our family, status is an entirely different thing, has to do with intellect and creative achievement. Did anyone ever tell you that you look just like Debbie Reynolds, he asks innocently? (Celebrity, that's another one.) It must be the ponytail, I think, and just what does he think that's going to get him?

Oh, I know what to expect, I am here according to design with yet another Joe College, and they are perpetually on the make. Well, this one isn't getting anywhere. This will not be another Bob incident. To my surprise, he never even tries to kiss me, but walks me sedately and properly to the door, and asks nervously if he can see me again. I am a little impressed, and a little apprehensive, what is his game, what should I expect next, when will he make his move? We stand in the dull yellow glow of the vestibule light, narrow metal stairs rising, zigzagging austere and ugly above us; I toss my ponytail, uncomfortable, as he jots down my phone number. I am unable to hurt his feelings by turning him down outright, figuring that it will be easier to accomplish that with the courage created by distance and impersonality of the telephone. But I am chicken, unable to inflict the final punishing blow, aware myself of the sensations arising from rejection, and I continue reassuring him in many phone conversations in ensuing weeks, that yes, I really do want to see him, punishing myself in my thoughts for not being more honest. Finally, in weeks to come when I have refused him a total of five times with the most absurd excuses I can manage to invent, he asks me nervously and tentatively if he should call again. He has received the message, but, oh, boy, am I assailed by Guilt. The guilt melts me just a little, just enough to get into trouble. I am sensing how rejected he must be feeling. Rejection is a sensation that is as familiar to me as breathing, has come into being from my father's long abandonment during the big war, my mother's long days away at work, the camp kids who found me unacceptable, the residue of all my faults and guilts and failures. I never want to be responsible for someone feeling like I do. In a moment of madness, I say yes, and how about Saturday night? I imagine I am a little flattered by his persistence, and I thereby, cast the die for the rest of my life and probably into perpetuity. *Ever since that night, we've been together, lovers at first sight, in love together, it turned out all right, for strangers in the night…*

Guys and Dolls, Picnic, pizza, first tentative embraces, kisses, necking in the front seat of the Cadillac, or his sister's Chevy; dances. How good it feels, how comfortable it is, talking with him. We visit Sandy and Alice in the Bronx, pass sunny summer days at Rockaway beach; attend my senior prom. We eat cherry cheese knishes on the Rockaway boardwalk, he makes me ride the cyclone against my better instincts after which I gamely manage to resist. Sun and sand and love and companionship, a close tie with a peer, male appreciation, tantalizing for an only child whose father was absent for so long. There is nothing to compare with that feeling of content when we are embracing, our bodies touching, exchanging warmth, I cannot get enough of it; warmth, and that very personal very private sense of intimacy with another human being, belonging to someone, having someone that belongs to me. This is what I have waited for, it seems, all of my life.

If Steve is not as sophisticated or smooth as he could be, that isn't of primary concern; his wife will never have to want, he will never desert or neglect a family. It is *beshert*, written. By whom, I don't know, but that's the expression that is so familiar to me. But he is a strange boy, he acts silly, has a rather bizarre sense of humor that I don't exactly understand, wears those incredibly distasteful ill fitting baggy pants and seems to be unaware of the existence even of what I consider to be typical teenage activities. He doesn't ride a bike to play ball after school, he doesn't seem to have friends, to hang out anywhere. The rules and regulations of orthodoxy seem to dictate his actions excessively. But he is a welcome change from the aggressive and pugilistic, insipid and inane (albeit sophisticated and smooth) *Joe College* sort of fellow who appears to be the only breed around. Who knows I may never get another chance. This is the guiding force in my world, a dynamic that I recognize as being more important than any other.

But I am sensing something under the radar, there is something solid, something sweet, something real about him in spite of his nerd factor. I would like to question my feelings, explore that tiny thread that suggests something of value to be discovered, but peer pressure, the fear of being found to not be cool, shakes me from any diversion; on with the program.

Strangely, I begin to see so many wonderful qualities in Steve as I get to know him better. He is sincere and honest, sweet and not conceited. He is responsible and reliable, focused on his education, his career, and his future. He is nothing like Daddy; and he decidedly is not one of those *Joe College on the make* types. As a matter of fact, he is more insecure even than I am, as if that were possible. His mother rules him with an iron hand, something that turns my stomach to jelly, and he cannot make even the simplest decision without her carping advice; when to wash his hands, when to eat, what to eat, what to wear. It takes me quite some time during the course of our relationship to teach him how to dress and comb his hair, stand on his own, make his own decisions, convince him that he is indeed someone special, to infuse him with confidence. I barely notice that he has taken his new power and has begun to belittle me, to treat me in the exact same way that his mother has treated him. I think it is a phase, something that will pass; nothing to worry about. But for a very long time, he is just nice, so nice, so comfortable, so different from the rest of the threatening world of males; so easy to be with, to relax with, to enjoy; the ever illusive nice boy.

Familiarity and habit spawn a strange kind of intimacy. Before I know what has happened, we are a couple, closer and closer every day. Close joins hands with like, and morphs into love. I begin to love him with all the desperation that has been saved up in the empty years of my father's forced absence, neglect, and abuse. At least, it feels like love. What does love feel like? I do not know. But I do know that I feel safe and protected when I am with him, and I begin to see a comfortable future with him. I never think about my father any more, just feel the new promise of male affection, protection. A proliferation of raging hormones takes up the slack.

Yet, I go to that first dance at Queens College with Steve still unsure of whether or not I wish to pursue this infant relationship with him. He is too strange, too drippy, too shy … and yet he possesses all of the qualities that are prerequisite to a successful future that have been drilled into me for as long as I can remember. Obviously, he meets the vital parental criteria of being Jewish, wealthy, and pre-law. In addition, he is responsible, respectful, ambitious, and handsome, conservative, and not the least bit risky. I am going to be oh so careful not to repeat my mother's mistakes, and to insure a safe and insulated life, for myself and for my future children. I am excited by the idea of children, still haunted by my old dreams. He seems to be as excited by the idea of children as I am. I can barely wait. He will be a wonderful father, I think. Security is the focus of the moment.

There seems to be some sort of pressure hovering in the atmosphere, inciting me to make a decision as soon as possible. Time appears to be galloping onward. My future needs to be cemented, because Fate can step in and ruin things in a moment, wars and strangers and illness. It is the better part of valor to have one's future planned and locked up. I have learned well the lesson that I am in some way damaged goods, unworthy of the routine rewards that are heaped on normal girls. What if no one else ever wants me? Here is my future handed to me on a silver platter, and it is up to me to make a rapid and prompt decision. Look at my mother, at all her plans and dreams that never happened, because she was unable to make timely and courageous decisions. Haven't I vowed forever to let my sins be of commission, rather than omission?

Steve is the consummate good Jewish boy, Yeshiva schooled and conservative. He is a practicing member of the Jewish community; he is planning to be an attorney, which is second in line to a doctor for desirability, according to the Jewish book of rules for choosing a husband, and he is responsible and reliable, two qualities that endear him to me immediately for their importance as well as their contrast to my own volatile and charming father. He is like my Grandpa.

CHAPTER 18

Steve and I arrive at the dance with the entire TAΩ brotherhood, the same motley bunch of goofy, socially inept misfits, either too shy or unable to get dates, and I bask in the glory of being surrounded by default by so many adoring *men*, whatever their flaws, at one time. They converge lovingly on me, protective and related by brotherhood, my ersatz boyfriends, by privilege and chance providence, by merit of my relationship with Steve. I now have seven boyfriends, by default, and it feels great. In the confusion of dancing with them merely to spare their tender feelings, I am located when the music stops, across the floor from where Steve is involved in a loud and spirited, boisterous college boy conversation. He has delegated my care to his brothers, seems to have forgotten for the moment that I am here with him, that he has a date.

I look around, studying the faces in the crowd, and suddenly I see a familiar one right in front of me. I can't believe my eyes, here is Dave Warrenbrand, my first unrequited adolescent fantasy love. The hall is vibrating with shock waves; it is the kind of providence to which I am unaccustomed. I stare, speechless, in a momentary limbo of indecision and for moments I have forgotten all about Steve. Dave comes over to me drawn no doubt by my intense scrutiny, apparently genuinely puzzled yet flattered and intrigued, and with a small ingenuous smile asks has he met me somewhere before. Smooth, I think, smiling inwardly. As a matter of fact, yes, I smile, this time at him.

Even though this is the glibbest most quintessential of lines, he really does know me, that's what's so funny. He just can't equate me to the freckled skinny twelve-year-old who followed him around mooning with great puppy dog loyalty and tenacity that summer four long years ago. Four years! I reintroduce myself to him with solemn giddy confidence, adopting the ultimate of sophistication that I can summon, given the circumstances, figuring quickly in my head that if he was eighteen then, he would be twenty-*two* now, oh my God, that is so *old*. A little strange, that he would fancy me, a little scary. I am not afraid, I am sixteen, and I am immortal. I pull my stomach in as flat as I am able, hoping to enhance my ever hopeful bosom, and hold my breath with as much blasé as I can muster, making light conversation, struggling to talk while holding my breath, enjoying the way his glance flicks admiringly over my newly blossoming and grownup person. What does he see? It is imperative that he appreciates my physical maturity; I know no other basis for relationships.

I tell him that I am here with a date; I have snapped back from the midst of my old daydream, horseback riding at Highpoint in the Adirondacks, Dave. Lithe and tall and svelte, riding beside me, his dark hair flying in the breeze, his wide and brilliant smile warming me, into the present. I apologize silently in my head to Steve for my deliberate perfidy, my disrespect to our budding, barely begun relationship, when Dave invites me out for lunch one afternoon, and I find myself accepting. Too bad, Stevie dear, this is business that needs finishing, says that oh so smart voice in my head, and I feel quite grown up and wise beyond my years to think that the paragon that is Dave is interested in me. He has seen my potential, obviously bought my charade of experience, and has accepted my maturity and sophistication. I have arrived.

Dave is the riding counselor at Camp Highpoint this year, 1951. Tall and confident and handsome with matinee idol features and characteristics and a smile that impacts directly on my knees, making them weak, and causing strange sensations in areas of my twelve-year-old body that I can't even identify, never mind acknowledge or understand.

My one goal becomes to impress this paragon. I sweep stalls and shovel, and polish stubborn leather; I ride with ultra confidence and gay bravado, hoping to impress him with my newly acquired horsemanship and thereby with my ultimate desirability, whatever that is. I reprogram my fantasies of families of multiple children with matching names including those mellifluous with Dave's surname, and with tentative scenarios of romantic interlude, the protagonists being myself and Dave. My fantasies are based upon romance novels I have read, and popular movies and songs.

The daydreams become so real to me as they are repeated again and again for the sheer pleasure and ultra viable escape valve that they afford me that I begin to believe them. I almost can accept that Dave at eighteen years of age can fall in love with my twelve-year-old unformed and inexperienced self that I mistake his tenderness, kindness, and solicitude for romantic attentiveness.

I saunter coolly into the bunk reeking of the stable that I have just shoveled out. I am cruelly taunted by my bunkmates for my supposed slavish immature blindness. Wishing to impress the giggling taunting group with my status and import, I weakly allow myself to boast with great aplomb and casual boredom that I will be Dave's date for the upcoming social. *The wave of adulation that is supposed to occur according to my internal script is suddenly and embarrassingly supplanted by the unexpected shock of a great uproarious onslaught of knee slapping and laughter. The ringleader of the group, obviously unaware of the scenario of my daydreams informs me between guffaws that everyone knows that Dave is an item with Helene. Helene is the sultry bombshell of sixteen years who is counselor in training of seniors bunk eight. Upon hearing these words and as their meaning registers on me, I run from the bunk, hot tears scalding my cheeks. A cloud of inescapable embarrassment follows closely behind me. I run into the woods behind our bunk, needing to get away from the source of my agony. Finally, I find refuge behind some thick shrubbery near the stable.*

When I exhaust my supply of furious self-conscious tears, I turn my mind to the necessity of fabricating a story that will cover both my sudden and lengthy disappearance and my swollen eyes. The other ignominy could simply be ignored; I will say simply that I have been joking. But what would be a shocking enough story to elicit not only belief but the sympathy that was by now to my thinking my actual due?

I begin to think about what will be the ultimate loss for which I could demand compensation? Who can I depend on to help me out of any trouble? Grandpa; he would help me if he were here. Isn't he the one person in the world who cares the most about me and whom I worship? I return to the bunk slowly, red eyed and nose blowing, clutching a gaggle of Kleenex, unaware that Dave has heard of my indiscretion and in his infinite kindness, informs the gaping bunkmates that he has indeed asked me to the social, but that there is a camp rule about such things and so he is being forced against his will to take Helene, when he would rather take me. Helene herself, declawed and defanged by Dave's stern insistence, is coerced over to his side, in the noble effort to do me a kindness, and disarm the monsters.

117

The girls are noticeably subdued when I enter the bunk, but I am so engrossed in my new scenario that I am oblivious to the change in the air, and proceed to present my dramatic tale to them with all the drama I can summon up, made easier by the realization of what the impact would be if my fabrication were indeed true.

I just received a long distance call, I weep, projecting a genuine grief, my grandfather died today. And I dissolve in heartfelt tears as if the horrible thing has indeed occurred. My sojourn at Highpoint goes much better from that day onward. My mother and father pick me up from the bus stop after camp ended and take me to Jahn's famous ice cream parlor in Jamaica. After a period of time notable for its awkwardness and stiff conversation, my mother tells me in a somewhat choked and restrained manner that my beloved grandfather had indeed died of a massive cerebral hemorrhage on that very day.

The paralyzing horror of that moment; the feelings of guilt, the certain knowledge that I have caused his death is a screaming siren in my head for years and years and years until I manage to tuck it away out of sight and hearing so that I can survive, and leave it to torment my subconscious instead. *Many years later, I wonder briefly if my outburst has been some form of precognition, rather than random burst of desperate invention.*

But finally here is Dave, in the flesh, the Dave of my earliest fantasies. My memory of that cavalier pompadour that was his trademark in an earlier time is somewhat mitigated by a slightly receding hairline, even at twenty-two, that he now sports. I don't notice until later, that he isn't as tall as I remember him, and has grown a trifle pudgy, the merest hint of a threatening muffin top. Cuddly, I think. Overall, he actually looks a bit shabby, even seedy. I wipe that unworthy thought from my mind. Is it possible that this slick *older man* is interested in me?

I make a deal with myself that this will be a sort of test, to see if I should continue with this Steve thing, or take the big chance on maybe never finding anyone else and ending up an old maid and childless. Dave meets me in front of my house, picks me up in his convertible. *A **convertible**; an excess of sophistication, over the top!* I have no idea what kind, and hope fervently that he won't ask. I am nervous, apprehensive; this is a new and uncharted embarkation for me, and I'm not sure if my parents would approve, even though my father knows Dave's family, a fact that I use to rationalize the situation in my own mind.

We talk over sandwiches at an uncomfortably distant and obscure diner, the obligatory red plastic upholstered seats, round aluminum barstools, Formica topped tables, the quintessential mini juke boxes on every table, sporting the most popular and updated songs, but I cover my uneasiness with a veneer of what I consider to be sophistication. *I'm a fool, to want you...* moans Frank Sinatra as I feel my cheeks burning and will them to stop. I think that he must find me totally transparent, but he smiles at me. I am enjoying my moment of triumph too much to be aware of any innuendo that might have caught a more practiced eye, too impressed with my own sophistication and desirability. When we finish lunch he tells me enthusiastically that his mother is dying to see me, and without missing a beat, whisks me away into his car, his convertible, once again, and confidentially brings me to his mother's apartment on 67th Street, as familiar to me as my own street, where, I gather, he still lives. It doesn't occur to me that I don't know his mother. Why would she want to meet *me*?

The ride up in the elevator unnerves me, as elevator rides always do, but we arrive at the apartment without incident, to my relief, although I don't know what I expected to happen right there in public, protected though I am by this hefty young bull. But there is that underlying current of nerves, fear of the unknown. I will not let it show. So preoccupied am I with the mechanics of covering up my fear, appearing sophisticated and confident beyond my years, that am startled by his somewhat clumsily feigned surprise that his mother isn't home.

He quickly reassures me with aplomb that she will undoubtedly return within moments, she must have run down for some milk, or something, he smiles glibly. He puts his warm hefty arm around my shoulders, as I tense, rigid with discomfort; allow him to ensconce me at the kitchen table. His manner is so protective that it soothes my sudden mistrust. He smoothly goes about the business of putting up tea, an action so respectable, so commonplace that it allays my fears, as it is indeed intended to do, and I begin to relax. With sudden gaiety that masks a calculating eye, he turns off the singing tea kettle, deciding casually, gaily, that wine will be nicer than tea. He is insistent, firm. He will not permit me to decline. For me to show my discomfort would puncture the delicate balloon that is my uneasily worn essence of sophistication.

When his mother does not arrive by the time the third glass has been consumed and the heat of the alcohol is spreading through my limbs, turning them to mush, creating a smooth hot feeling between my legs, my doubts begin to grow once again, but he ushers me and my wobbly knees gently to the sofa and disarmingly begins to serenade me with his guitar with an array of charming ditties, both serious and silly, and a captivating smile. He soon has me at my ease, wondering how I ever have been able to mistrust this lovely handsome paragon of a man.

I am mellow with the wine and relaxed, and after all, it is Manischevitz, leftover from Passover, what could be bad. I don't expect him to slowly, gently put down the guitar, after just a little while, and oh so smoothly, reach for me, his huge arms enfolding and capturing me, and his well schooled and experienced lips, soft and supple and gentle, seeking mine with a dexterity that thrills me, and scares the living daylights out of me. I must have responded to him, as what young woman would not have, especially one with a head full of unused fantasies. But not so deftly or enthusiastically that he couldn't know that he is with innocent Miss Sweet Sixteen herself, and not some older more experienced woman of the world, or just some trashy pickup.

Frightened, I pull myself away, and tell him shakily that I think that it is time for me to leave, because he knows, because we have discussed it all in our lengthy conversations of life and philosophy and plans and dreams of the preceding afternoon, about my values, my limits, that there is no area for compromise. To my chagrin and terror, his gentle and kindly exterior falls suddenly and sharply away. Quickly he pushes me back on the sofa, covering my slight body with his own, and begins writhing and grinding and groping all at the same time. His brow drips with sweat, his heavy arms and hands are everywhere at once, and his mouth is clamped tightly on my own as if to preclude the emission of a possible scream. I feel that hot, hard part of him pressing against me. I am frightened, I am dismayed, and I am disgusted. I am unable to move.

I feel my body go limp with the inertia of defeat, terrorized by both the suddenness of his transformation and his strength, horrified by this metamorphosis that has occurred before my very eyes, idol to monster, revolted by the tawdriness, the sweaty vulgarity of the scene. It is only for an instant. When I sense his grip loosen for a moment as he assumes that his dexterity has weakened my resolve, I wrench myself away from his heaving, rooting bulk and gagging with revulsion, lunge for the door, taking only the time to grab my shoes and bag and jacket. Once again, I seem to have avoided the executioner. Sobbing, I head for the elevator and the street. I rearrange my disheveled clothes, put on my shoes, in the elevator, under the questioning glances of the other occupants, staid, responsible, judgmental, their eyebrows raised.

Luckily there is a great mob of people in the street by this late afternoon hour, walking here and there, in every direction, busily, as they return from their various jobs and errands. I mix right in with them, and when I see Dave's figure approaching frantically from the distance, I continue to move along with the cluster of strangers that I have come down with, one of their group, glancing over my shoulder as though burdened with a kind of uncontrollable tic. I am too embarrassed to say a word to anyone, and soon I notice that he is no longer following me. What is it about these guys? What am I missing?

No, this is not how I had imagined my initiation into the world of adult love.

The next day, a dozen red roses arrive, complete with effusive apology, but I want no part of Dave, now or ever. I think of quiet, conservative, obedient, law abiding, unthreatening Steve, and resolve at that moment to continue my plan to win him. What could be bad? I think, shuddering. I might never get another opportunity to be loved, by the right boy, a good boy. That is the most convincing and overriding argument for perseverance.

The adaptation of Jules Pfeiffer's novel, *Little Murders* is being seen off Broadway, and I am thinking that my life seems to be a succession of small rapes. Small, because they have never materialized, never become a reality, but have threatened and frightened just the same, infected my views of life and my ability to cope.

∾∾

I am only seventeen in 1956 when we are *pinned*. Steve has given me his TAΩ fraternity pin. We are engaged to be engaged in the vernacular of the time. Now I am virtually a member presumptive of the family and frequently find myself babysitting for his small niece, Amy. Amy, the daughter of Steve's sister, Elaine. Amy of the huge turquoise eyes, straw colored tresses, and precious heart shaped china doll face. She calls Steve Zshu-Zshu, because she was unable as a baby to say Stevie. Now, I call him that also, finding it cute. Look Uncle Zshu-Zshu, a flying red horse, warbles Amy in her sweet treble as we pass a Mobilgas station, and he crumples with emotion, with joy. Isn't she adorable, he squeaks with joy? This is good, he loves children. I feel warmth coursing through my body as I think of him and our future children.

Amy and I walk to the park where the swings are, hand in hand. Amy is never still. She wants to know everything there is to know, about everything.

Are you a teacher? Amy asks with great innocence and ingenuousness. No, I answer softly thinking how much my mother wishes for me to follow in her own footsteps, to have permanent security, to fulfill her own aborted dreams.

Well, then, Amy insists, are you a mother? It is more statement than question. Her experiences in her short life has to do most certainly with mothers and teachers.

No, I'm not a mother, either, I answer again quite gently, musing on what the future has indeed to bring or promise.

Well, then, says Amy with a great exasperation and boredom, WHAT ARE YOU?

What am I? Nothing, I muse to myself, and then look into the past, then forward into the future ...

I am nothing. I am hiding from the battling of my parents in my room, frantically painting. Am I an artist? I will be a famous artist. But to do this I will need to compete in a forbidding world. No, then I guess I will not, for I am nothing. Okay, then I will have children and never be lonely. I decide all this at twelve years of age. I will be a wife and a mother, and hide from the fear of competition, the fear of failure. But I don't know who I am, who I will become. I don't want to become, I fear to become. I know that I want to be somebody very special, but I don't know how to do this. No, I change my mind, again.

I don't want to compete any more, I want to hide. Maybe I should just hope to die and to be free ... yet, I wish to live forever. But I am so afraid of dying. Oh, God, I am so afraid of both these things, living and dying.

Stevie will hold me and love me, I will be his wife. I will have lots of babies, and never be lonely again. I will be a mother. I will be someone. He will take good care of me; envelop me with love, like Grandpa.

CHAPTER 19

1944

There is a photograph in an ornate slightly tarnished silver frame that sits omnipresently throughout my childhood, so it seems, on as assortment of mahogany or blond oak end tables adjacent to various overstuffed or patently contemporary sofas in my life; it is of me as a small child of three, seated on a small *Super Flyer* sled wearing a carefully and lovingly tailored mouton fur coat that my grandfather had fashioned for me, the latest in my short life to date in a long collection of elegant fur wear; it is enhanced by leather leggings that Mom has anxiously sewn, zippers up each side. A wide hood surrounds those ever present fat bouncing golden sausage curls, framing that soulful worried face adorned with huge shining hazel eyes, squashed button nose, permanently frowning rosebud mouth. And another photo opposite it, of me at one wearing a carefully, lovingly crafted pure white rabbit cape with tassels made of tiny rabbit feet, the hood covering my head. My grandfather, a tailor in the old country which was Bessarabia (now Russia) or Karamov, now a furrier by trade, creator of masterpieces of needle and pelt, a tall man with regal bearing, himself topped with black fur Russian Cossack cap, pulls the sled along the snow coated sidewalks of 1942 Bronx, New York, in that first photo, spinning tales of the old country as we progress through canyons of sun-and-years-bleached red brick apartment houses. Friendly windows frame extended families of neighbors from similar backgrounds. Upon second glance at this silent patriarch, one might see the original face, the prototype for the serious look that seemed so incongruous on a child of three. The excursion has a serious intent, being one more in a series of family rituals, made sacred in my memory as a small child being reared in awesome times, under extraordinary conditions. We return apple cheeked and tingling to partake of another of Grandma's feasts.

World War II continues. My father has been gone for most of my short life, in fact since that earlier photo that was taken in the white rabbit cap when I was one. I barely remember him. My mother toils in the public school system of New York City struggling with the rest of the country to adjust to a world gone berserk, a life turned topsy-turvy. While I can barely remember the legend that continues to spin that is my father this silent looming nurturing enigma cloaked in more than his long black topcoat and steeped in the customs and mores of middle Europe and Judaism becomes my father figure and almost my God. When anyone mentions God I think of Grandpa. A *shonda*, he would say, a shame, irreverent, but not to me. Reverence is an imperative in this way of life.

❧◆❧

I stand on tippy toes my little face barely above the busy tabletop watching her ministrations to the familiar ritual Friday afternoon preparations. Grandma, why don't you turn off the stove tonight and tomorrow, I ask in some kind of wonderment, perturbed, vividly recalling images of bears in broad hat and uniform standing in the midst of charred forests, of accidental death and destruction by carelessness and errant flame. It's the Sabbath, Momala, and the Lord our God commanded us to rest on the Sabbath. She continues to dish out the hot broth, fine noodles and clumps of parsley swimming in their golden steaming glistening pond that Grandpa calls *fishies* for my amusement, and much later I ask wonderingly again, and what about smoking cigars, remembering Grandpa's fury and wrath when Daddy after returning from the war and exhibiting his characteristic irreverence defies this particular edict. And driving and writing and even playing the huge old upright piano in the dining room on the Sabbath, also forbidden.

And why do you do that, I ask, curiosity bursting from me once again, a torrent of impending questions waiting impatiently in line for answers on a small platform on the back of my tongue. Hush, murmurs Grandma, rocking back and forth her scarf floating gently over her lowered head, her arms raised in the ancient traditional gesture of prayer. *Boruch atah adonoy...Blessed art though oh Lord our God, King of the universe, who has commanded us to kindle the Sabbath lights.* The flickering flames of the long white candles cast glistening shadows over the chalky faded pastel painted walls in the deepening shadows of creeping dusk, growing and shrinking and implying otherworldliness. Grandma utters her magical incantations, her indiscernible pleas, her ancient promises and declarations and I stand awed and fascinated, watching. I am *benching lecht*, Momala, lighting the Sabbath candles, she says matter of factly her ritual ministrations completed; effused, glowing with an aura of peace and some other ineffable essence that fills me with nameless unfathomable envy... maybe contentment.

Grandpa returns earlier than usual this Friday afternoon from the place where he works making coats and hats and capes and muffs from the fur of exotic animals. He first blesses the golden braided bread, the challah, and then the wine. *Boruch attah adoney, elohanu melach ho-olum, ha moces lechem min horetz* or *boreh pre ha go-fen. Blessed art thou oh Lord our God, King of the universe, who bringeth forth bread from the earth; who bringeth forth grapes from the vine...* I listen to his familiar incantations with the same awe that overcomes me when I observe Grandma lighting the candles. I see my grandfather as a holy being, a man of paradox, gentleness combined with authority, power, quiet strength that I find myself drawn into his presence by a force more powerful that any I have ever imagined, could imagine. He finishes his simple repast of soup with noodles, boiled chicken or meat and a glass of wine, ripping off chunks of the egg bread, the challah. Much later after a proscribed period of time after partaking of meat, he will drink a glass of tea which is half milk, sipping it through the cube of sugar which he holds between his teeth.

On the Sabbath on Friday nights and Saturday mornings, or the Holy Days, he walks to Shule for driving on the Sabbath is against Jewish Law; he hoists me up onto his great shoulders and carries me silently so that I may accompany him (a duty and privilege that I wear as a heavier cloak than my customized animal skin garment) the distance to the Synagogue my huge hazel eyes shining and my golden sausage curls bouncing with the motion of his powerful stride. He lifts me down when we arrives to offer Shabbos greetings to the other elders and a host of acquaintances. Good Shabbos, Abram, and a good Shabbos to you Harron. And we would enter the tabernacle and wait silently amidst the faint rustle of preparations for services to begin. Almost immediately Grandpa would begin his pre-ritual ritual. Everything in Grandpa's life revolves around ritual.

I sit near him next to the huge garden window by the Eastern Wall, oh prized location. Women are only permitted upstairs but I don't count as a woman yet as I am merely a little girl. I worry what I will do when that day comes, but it seems to be so far off in the future that the worry just slips away. I alternate studying the marvelous stained glass windows and highly polished woodworking, listening enthralled to the fascinating mystical inexorable chanting of that strange ancient language of the draped and rocking black draped men in the congregation, and studying the vines and blooms and later the grapes of the arbor just outside my window. The droning of the entire congregation begins to make me drowsy aided and abetted by the great quantities of food we have just consumed at Grandma's table. The rising and falling cadences of the ancient words accompanied by the rote and uniformity of the chants and the gyrating shadows doing their own macabre dance across the walls seemed to take on a life of their own. I sit mesmerized, captured, enraptured by the emotion it all invokes, lifted to some other dimension by a powerful spiritual force in this intricately carved and gilded cavernous place of worship.

One year, there is a nest of robins in the grape leaves, and I watch mesmerized for months and follow their growth with bated breath ... overcome by tenderness at the tininess of their feathered vulnerability. I am devastated when the babies are suddenly gone one week, convulsed with tears. They've learned to fly, *momala*, says Grandpa, and gone on to make their lives. But I am inconsolable. Why did they have to leave, I cry silently. They have touched a deeply planted maternal nerve in me. I go home and sobbing; hug my dolls to my chest.

Grandpa's existence is simple. He works long hours, and on the Sabbath he attends Shule. At home, he does his praying, dovening every morning and evening, as a matter of course, with no exceptions, ever. His tightly curled gray hair is always covered indoors by a stiff round black yarmulka. He dons his tefillin, a black prayer box attached to braided black silk string of indeterminate purpose, to me, and his tallis, a black and white striped prayer shawl with its long silk fringe, and reads his prayers, barely under his breath, as he rocks back and forth, lost in a trance of divinity. He holds his worn prayer book in front of him, but the words have long long ago been committed to memory. I watch his face as he chants, oblivious to my presence, memorizing his beloved chiseled Middle Eastern features, his calm controlled expression. His adherence to his orthodox religious practice is just one side of his total orthodoxy, his tight control and rigidity is the other.

Each evening when he returns home from his work as a furrier downtown, he first removes his salt and pepper tweed suit jacket, and loosens the matching vest. He sits down at his seat at the table in front of the kitchen window, settles his large frame on the ancient wooden chair. He sits stiffly, even when relaxing. He never slouches, except on Pesach, Passover, when this is required. He wears his freedom, acquired with such difficulty, as the uniform of some obscure army of survivors. I know his next move by heart. He glances at his pocket watch, and reaches back to open the carved cast iron door to the cabinet built into the flaking plaster wall under the window where he keeps the schnapps. This is also where he keeps his seltzer, in plain quart bottles. The seltzer is delivered to the house in crates, and is the primary drink in the household, except for the schnapps, and the ritual wine. He keeps the special pressurized tops in a small wooden box. I watch in fascination, my small hands pressed to the tablecloth, mesmerized, as he screws on the magic apparatus that spews tiny pressurized bubbles through the bottle, and turns water into soda. My drink of choice is seltzer squirted onto a teaspoon of grape jam in one of those globby bottomed jelly jars that accumulate in droves and are limited by choice as opposed to availability to a classy glassware service for twenty-four. It is the best drink I have ever had. Nothing has ever or will ever compare with that taste. Maybe, Dr. Brown's Cherry soda, found along with Celery Tonic, only in kosher delis.

Everything he does is controlled, organized, encapsulated within a rigid format and schedule dictated by orthodox Jewish law. On Friday afternoon, before preparing himself for shule, if there is none, he makes horseradish. He carefully shreds, slices, minces the fresh root, and grinds it into almost a grainy paste. He mashes freshly cooked red beets, and adds these with a dollop of vinegar to the pulverized horse radish, and carefully, methodically mixes them together until they are emulsified. He moves then onto his next carefully scheduled chore.

*Shma Yisroel adoney Elohenu, Adoney echod...*Hear O Israel, the Lord our God, the Lord is one. What does that mean, Grandpa, I ask? It means just what it says, Momala (making that automatic assumption that I understand the language). There is only one God, and he belongs to *us*, we are different from all others. We are Jews. God made us and has anointed us; we are the Chosen People. Stay away from the others, the Goyim, they will only hurt us, contaminate us with their own otherness; we cleave only onto our own. When I begin to ask another question, what have they ever done to us, he tells me sternly that this is not open for discussion. It is written, he intones. So I have learned something new in the lesson of life. I am Jewish, and I am different. I begin to feel this in the way my outer shell reflects back what I see around me. I begin to see it in the way that other people respond to me. I don't know if I like feeling different, I would much rather that I were like everyone else and not need to worry about being chosen or stuff like that. Shma Yisroel Adoney Elohenu Adoney Echod...I am chosen, I am different, I am alone.

My life is filled with the accouterments of Jewish Orthodoxy, and I grow and prosper safely and gently in its warm embrace, quite certain of my identity, at least in that respect. *I am totally unaware of this monstrous thing called the* Holocaust *until many years later.* There is never any question of my continuing Jewish education and even after my father's return in 1945 at the termination of the war, I move onward into my future as a good Jewish girl.

I love my grandfather with all my baby heart. He is the most important of persons in my young life. My father overseas for the duration of the great but distant war has receded into a shadow world less real than the storybooks that I voraciously consume or even my private world of fantasy. My grandfather is tall and stately, solid, in his salt and pepper tweed three piece suit. He radiates a sense of safety and security, warmth that pulls me into its aura like a magnet. Grandpa holds me on his lap for hours playing a tickling game. He walks his fingers as if they are little men, across my arm, tickling me, repeating the chant, kesila mesila something, something, until he suddenly reaches across, pretending to pounce with great ferocity, and tickles my stomach, and while I am giggling, looking down at my stomach, he catches my nose with his finger, whoops. I am convulsing with uncontrollable laughter. I never see it coming. No matter how many times he does it. Kesila mesila, kesila mesila, it is the anticipation of the unknown that creates the excitement Then he continues telling and retelling ancient middle European fables, Bible stories, deftly Americanized in his best and cleverest manner so that I may relate to them, but sprinkled with Yiddish. He is Tevya from *Fiddler on the Roof*, Americanized, a little; he is only one half a generations removed from the *shtetls* of Russia, Rumania, a blink away from pogroms and aching poverty, a hair's breadth away from the cultural mores of ancient people who own their wives, and beat them, and work them to death, who assign them no rights at all.

The two of us spend many happy hours seated on Grandma's old upholstered dressing table bench that we pull conspiratorially over to the window of the ancient brick apartment dwelling. We spend the hours gazing down from the third floor to people watch and generally observe the outside world. People walking back and forth, doing their assorted chores and business, great cement sidewalks going from building to street with no respite of vegetation or adornment. Sometimes we draw horses. Grandpa's horse's race through the wind, their manes waving, their muscles rippling, their nostrils flared. They are racing through the fields of Russia free from care. Grandpa has disappeared into a world of memories. He teaches me to draw the horses, but I wonder that these are only things that he draws. This is a fact that puzzles and fascinates me.

Grandpa, how come you draw such good horses and you don't draw anything else, like people? I ask. I don't know, *momala*, I just never learned anything else. But I bet you could, if you tried, I state firmly. I have been taught that a person can do anything he or she wants if they want to badly enough. You could draw people, I bet, I tell him. Please, could you show me how to draw people? I can only draw horses, replies Grandpa with finality. When Grandpa makes up his mind, it is all over. Grandpa's word is law. And that is that. But Auntie Etta, I begin, and stop short with chagrin, realizing that I have crossed a delicate line, fearing some strange and unknown repercussion, but Grandpa has not heard my tiny voice. Or he has just ignored me.

Sometimes he watches me play with a small cigar box filled with a collection of Grandma's discarded costume jewelry. It is a treasure chest full of jewels and riches, creating many hours of delightful fantasy, so much so that I don't even seem to care when Grandpa drifts away to steal his precious nap.

Then, looking up from my game, I notice that he is gone, snoring gently in the big high bed, and I slip in beside him and snuggle up against his broad, strong back and sigh contentedly, luxuriating in the alien, exotic male warmth and strength and smell of him. He is nearly the only man in my life, and this slight contact is precious. This is his personal bed; Grandma has hers in another room. I don't wonder why, because my own father is far away, and I have no frame of reference for marriage beds. What is this, this feeling of safety, of pure bliss I have when snuggled up against his strong male back? Somewhere in my subconscious, this memory is stored as a gold standard for ultimate joy, in the game of life.

Occasionally, he allows me to comb his thick graying curls, a privilege that fills me with an ineffable and inexplicable sense of tenderness and delight. I can do anything I want to him, he just smiles. The family members are all enchanted by the tender and serious look that comes over my face when I am brushing Grandpa's thick tight graying curls. She doesn't know, says Aunt Harriet, Uncle Irv's wife, she has no idea, she adds sadly, glancing at the long dark hallway. Irv says, sha, loudly, emphatically. Oblivious, I reach for another piece of apple cake.

My grandfather was born Aaron Appleman, or what translates as Appleman, Yablonsky, in what was then called Rumania, a small pocket of Europe sandwiched between Russia and Germany. His father was named Elia Jakob, scarce and vague family memories recall that his two older brothers were Duggy and David and his sisters were Minka and Fega. His family and the extended family of the *shtetl*, tiny village, shared the same sad though culturally rich existence scratching a bare survival in their dirt floored mud huts, or if you were *well to do*, wood shack, from pitiful vegetable patches on tiny parcels of land. The families banded together for strength and support, in these times of pogrom and extermination, fighting vaingloriously to survive. Aaron was fortunate in that he was able to apprentice himself to a furrier, and gradually to parlay his talent for design and construction, aided no doubt by his grand good looks and incredible charm, into a fair business creating warm yet stylish garments for the local upper class, such as it was. No one in his community lacked for winter coverage, either, able or not to pay for his service and the pelts needed. He continued to ply his trade and build his fortunes, but fearing the continuing pogroms and hearing rumors of a great war coming, he managed to save the necessary amount of money, perhaps borrowed the rest and sought passage to the promising land of America. This was accomplished with the help of the rest of the large family. There was a promise made that they would send for the rest of the family, cousins, aunts, uncles, his father when they were established, when they were able, a promise that was kept.

When he arrived in New York in the early nineteenth century, the harried clerk who took his information and unfortunately had very little understanding of the strange guttural and exotic tongue of these immigrants, mistook his pronunciation of *Aaron*, and he was then and forever onward known as Harron. His future wife, found later through the traditional services of a matchmaker, Hannah, became Anna. Go figure.

Harron and Anna were married and found lodgings in the burgeoning Russian community on the lower east side of New York, but in no time, with his looks, charm, and astonishing ability with needle and fur, worked their way uptown. Their first child, a daughter, Sarah, as brilliant as she was beautiful, was destined for greatness. She would at least have the best education available to any child of the early twentieth century. Sarah would be educated and successful and famous, and she would take care of the family in their seemingly futile efforts to survive. Sarah was the quintessential good Jewish girl! She would be successful in her chosen profession as a teacher and would marry well. The boys would be all right, after all, they were men, but what about Sarah's younger sister, Etta?

When the teeming city and the pressures of city life became overbearing, Harron purchased a farm upstate in Nyack, which became the basis for caring for incoming émigrés. Anna worked nonstop to feed and care for these multitudes of relocating family members and friends. God had provided for her, and she would repay this seemingly endless debt. In 1920 when finally her multitudinous responsibilities became too much for her to bear any longer and she was in danger of falling completely apart, they sold the farm and moved back to the city. Ultimately they ended up here in the Bronx. Sarah was married by that time, and Etta …?

1944

I stand at the end of a long dark hallway, Grandpa's familiar bedroom on my right, the tall dark austere dining room with its dark mahogany furniture, immense upright piano, crystal chandelier, never used, to my left. Grandma's familiar silhouette blocks the light streaming from the large kitchen window, hiding her clothesline hung with drying Lipton tea bags and paper toweling as well as laundry, as she prepares some delicacy or other; she has not forgotten the overwhelming hardship and poverty of her former life in the shtetls. Grandpa is out for a while at some nameless faceless unidentifiable place on some urgent business of the moment; it does not concern her. My grandparents are in charge of me while Mom is at work, but they are busy, and I am left to my own devices. While there exists nothing at all pertaining to the entertainment of children in the apartment, there is a lot for a small child to explore in the rabbit warren of this strange complex abode.

A tiny dim light bulb hangs from the solitary fixture in the center of the high ceilinged hallway, throwing the barest glimmer of a light on the large white door at the end. The door is slightly ajar. It is the entrance to Aunt Etta's bedroom, and I am forbidden to *bother* Aunt Etta, Auntie. But I feel an undeniable magnetic force, pulling me against my will toward the doorway. I am struggling with conflicting emotions. Part of me is trembling with fear from the stories I have overheard of Etta's madness, the admonitions I have been given, and I hesitate, torn.

The door opens, and Etta is standing there, pale and thin, her tall frame slumping slightly, almost caved in on itself. Her black hair is piled on her head in a fashion similar to my mother, and although you can see a resemblance between the sisters, her face is gaunt and has a ravaged look. But her expression is soft and sweet.

Her face is framed by a halo of errant strands of hair that fly around her head surrounded by sparkling dust motes, highlighted by that same afternoon light that silhouettes Grandma. I am frozen by a sense of magic, and of something more, not only forbidden, but slightly bizarre. She crooks her index finger, and beckons me to her, and mesmerized, I move slowly towards her. The other part of me craves the warmth and love that I find with her.

Come here, precious, and let me see you, says Auntie, her voice bursting with tenderness and joy. I move in for a hug, all fear and hesitation gone, and rejoice in the grand feeling of being held. Haven't seen you in a while, she croons, stroking my hair, you've grown. I smile, and sigh just a little. Come, she says, pulling me into the room, pointing to a small ottoman beside a low table. Sit. She drags over a large suitcase, and opens it up, and rifles through it. Look, she says with growing excitement, Look at this, and this, and this. She has brought out photos of landscapes and flowers, dancers and children, paintings by well known artists, Van Gogh, Degas, Cezanne, Matisse, Monet, Renoir, Bonnard, Rembrandt and Reynolds; mothers and their babies. These are my favorites.

This room with its dingy faded cream colored walls covered with networks of fine lines and cracks is Etta's safe haven, her escape from the world and all it has done to her. It is sacrosanct, filled with her treasures and collections carefully arranged in their austere otherwise nondescript *insignificant* setting. This is all that remains of her life. A bed, a dresser, and a chair, and her collections of postcards and books and magazines, reproductions attached to the walls with yellowing tape, the bed covered with odds and ends of ancient spread and scarf, intricately patterned pillows.

Auntie pulls me onto her lap and picks up a worn book from a small table. Do you want me to read to you, she asks? Yes, I reply, read about Mowgli. Yes, she says infusing me with affection, *Just So Stories,* and she opens the book and begins with my favorite part. Dearly Beloved, she murmurs sweetly, and I snuggle up against her thin chest smiling into the scent of her to hear all about the small boy, and how the leopard got his spots, the elephant his trunk, the zebra his stripes, and all the rest.

Now, she rummages deep down, and pulls out sets of water colors, pastels, a pile of thick white paper. Come, she puts out her arms to me, come and draw with Auntie. I move into the circle of her arms, and allow her to show me, to guide me, to teach me how to draw, to paint. At first, she puts her hand over mine and guides me. Later, she lets me experiment. I am enthralled, enchanted, I cannot get enough. More, Auntie, more, I cry with glee. I am in the right world, finally, I think. I am home.

In the background, we each hear the voice calling, Lynne, Lynne where are you, and our eyes meet. Hurry, Auntie says urgency in her voice. You have to go now. I will see you another time, again. Go now. I slip through the cracked door, and pretend that I have just left the bathroom, which is right next door to Auntie's room. A small deception that frightens me, but I tuck the guilt away and gauge quickly the sense of my best interests. I'm right here, Grandma, I say, and continue ingenuously. Are we going to make apple cake now? A change of subject that constitutes a white lie; I am young and I am small, but instinct takes over so that I may protect my beloved aunt, my precious secret time with her. Grandma takes my hand in her firm grasp, and leads me to the kitchen. Does she know where I have been? Will Auntie get into trouble? I do not know. I only know that I cannot wait to go back into that room of delight and creativity and love. Sometimes I don't see Auntie for a long, long time. She has been forbidden to entertain me, say the voices of adults when they do not know I can hear. I don't understand.

❧❧

Grandpa adheres completely and strictly to the accepted orthodoxy regarding the rules about art: Art is verboten, unacceptable in any circumstance, period. It is frivolous, wasteful, of no value whatsoever. My Aunt Etta's brief and brilliantly promising art career is quickly nipped in the bud, yet another family *shonda*. Then the family, with Grandpa in the lead, spearheads the annulment of her brief marriage to a lovely man whose name is Henry, because he is crippled by muscular dystrophy and she is going to have to take extensive care of him in the near future. He is deemed unsuitable, and Etta's feelings and desires on the matter are not even considered. Grandpa's wishes are sacrosanct, and his word is law. Etta owes to her parents, her father in particular, her descent into madness and depression because she is unable to do battle with the tight control he has over her. But Etta is more resilient than she is given credit for, and she has her own library of survival mechanisms. And she is crazy like a fox. And she adores me, sees me as the child she will never have. I am not certain where I would be without her subtle loving influence on me, and my art.

The reason that art is wrong in the confines of Jewish orthodoxy I am told is because of the Bible's prohibition of worshipping any so-called graven image. Images are forbidden in the home, are not even acknowledged in any situation, except for two austere sepia photos of both maternal and paternal forefathers, in oval frames. In addition, since Grandpa considers such occupation to be the height of foolishness and time wasting, Etta is a heretic, a fool, a silly time wasting girl, who is unable to choose a proper life partner, and is to be tightly controlled, guided, led, and punished when necessary, for her failings and failures, past, present, and future.

Sarah, my mother, is perfect. In the eyes of her doting parents, anyway. And to tell the complete truth, she is revered in professional circles for all her life. She is the oldest, the prodigal child, who goes to school, college and graduate school, and does the family proud. She is a teacher, even if it is in a *goyishe* school, God forgive her. There is no way that Etta will or even could ever live up to the paragon of perfection that is Sarah.

My uncle Sammy, Mom's baby brother, youngest of five, is the greatest source of pain for my grandparents. Still, I adore him, even to causing myself damage when racing to hear his voice on the phone when he calls to surprise me on my birthday when I am four, and I trip on a rug and hit my head on the side of the sofa. I wear the resultant bandage on my forehead like a badge of honor, bask in my temporary importance as the wounded soldier; complete the image of injury with my usual poignant and tragic facial expression. There is a lot of chest beating and hair pulling out over Sammy. Although he is a brilliant mechanic, actually an engineer, and has an awesome baritone and love of opera, which he does proud, he is considered a disgrace to the family. While serving honorably in Japan during WWII, he falls in love with a Japanese artist, and marries her. His father refuses to acknowledge him or the marriage. He is dead to Harron, after whom Sam and Midori name their first son. When they want to move back to New York, after many years in Japan, after all, the oldest son is now five; Sam's father turns his back and will not discuss the matter. Sam desperately misses his home and his family, and wants to provide a proper future for his sons, preferably in the United States of America, but Harron has long since closed his mind, and there is no crack in his rigidity.

After Grandpa dies when I am twelve the conflict alters. Now, the rest of the family is beseeching Grandma to allow her son to return to the family, but she wishes not to dishonor her late husband's wishes. They pressure her mercilessly and fight a good fight, outnumbering her four to one. Etta even comes out of her solitary confinement to add her two cents, now that her father is no longer there to scare the bejeebers out of her. The combat continues for years, and the sound of voices rising and falling with pleading and anger and even fury becomes the background accompaniment to my personal evolution.

Finally, years later, when I am married with still only one child, they persevere, and Sam returns with his family, his wife and four sons, Harron, David, Abraham, and Michael. They stay with my husband and me, at our house, for a while, while Sam restructures his life. He is a exceptional engineer, an inventor. It is from Sam that I get that feel and desire to save used stuff, to accumulate good things that are no longer wanted by somebody. I get the instincts from Sam. Sam's four boys grow up to be musical virtuosos and successful businessmen. Midori, bright, soft spoken, loving, and gentle, restores violins and builds violin bows for the remainder of her life. She is a amazing artist, and she prepares awesome sushi. Ultimately, Grandma embraces her, and her beautiful brilliant children, and welcomes her precious baby son, now over three hundred pounds back into her life.

~•~

When I sit quietly watching Grandma engage in her never ending chores, I study her worn, flowered house dress and apron, her poor swollen legs wrapped with cloth bandages that she unrolls and applies deftly, round and round until both legs are tightly covered, and her plump feet shoved into worn slippers. Her long gray hair is twisted and turned and wound around her head, and pinned into place with a huge gray bone comb. She is the caretaker of a continuing parade of immigrants from the old country, relatives from both sides, and friends, whom she and Grandpa sponsor and bankroll in their escapes from tyranny and poverty. She is exhausted and worn, her body unable to sustain much more abuse.

She can create almost anything out of nothing. In a moment, a crying child is silenced by a rabbit that moments before was just a handkerchief, and now wriggles in her arms, complete with jiggling ears and nose. String beans and hard boiled eggs and onions are suddenly vegetarian chopped liver for an unexpected visitor, the day before the weekly butcher visit, when fresh meat has run out. She leaves the kitchen light on, and one burner on her ancient gas stove turned to low, from sundown Friday evening, to sundown Saturday night, in case something needs to be heated. It is forbidden to do any form of labor on the Sabbath, and the turning on of a switch is considered to be labor.

Although weary and faded, remnants of her early beauty prevail, shining through her sagging skin. Now plump, worn and preoccupied, she dispenses foodstuffs and hugs, and is generally as wrapped up in her multitudinous responsibilities of cooking and preparing for meals as her legs are in that cloth bandage. Her entire existence is concerned with the administration of the various prescribed and sacred rites of living including ritual family gathering of monumental and staggering impact.

৵৽৽

The family arrives piecemeal, section by section. Each arrival sends out electrical currents of expectation and excitement. Here are Himey [Herman] and Beatrice, Healy [Irv] and Harriet; Sarah and Lynne, that's me, have arrived first, as usual and hold court. I will get to see my cousins, Dale and Dicky, Susan and Glen, the closest thing I have to siblings. Although they are at least six years younger than me, an inescapable logistical phenomenon, I adore them. Even though they have now usurped my position of only child, sole grandchild, I still retain seniority. I am the favorite, child of the favorite. I accept my position with grace, secure in my absolute status. Finally, there are Sam and Midori; Etta stays in her room, most times, she is not fond of turmoil, knows that her presence is merely tolerated, somewhat dreaded; the persona she has promulgated over the years for protection has achieved such status that she is disparaged, disdained. Poor old crazy Etta; Etta and her fate are frequently the subject of family discussions.

More likely than not, one such gathering will dissolve into a screaming match of monstrous proportions made mystical by the fact that the screaming is done in that strange sounding foreign language that is by turns funny and menacing. I have come to understand many of the words, but the secret of the Yiddish language eludes me, and ultimately the rising and falling cadences become merely a sort of background accompaniment for my world of fantasy. The familiar words are comforting in their cadency, redundancy and omnipresence. I have tried to wrap my tongue around those sounds, but find this impossible. As a small child, I hover in the perimeter of activity, and nibble constantly on the cookies, pletzela, that seem to regenerate faster than I can consume them, and I move deeper into my private world.

I spend a lot of time at my grandparents' home, which is just a few blocks from our own apartment, for with my mother working and having important places to go, someone has to watch me. I look forward to these sojourns with the old people, because they constitute the mainstay of peace and security for me; one can never tell what kind of mood my mother will be in and I dread the times when I become wincing repository for her fears, agonies, and frustrations. Her loneliness.

134

Sometimes I climb right out of myself to gauge a situation, and look out from sad eyes in a thoughtful serious face, again making special vows to my inner being, complete with stern instructions that they not be forgotten in the vast and looming future when I will be … they tell me … grown up. Quite seriously, I watch these supposedly infallible adults go through the motions of their lives as if they are in some play that exists in one single stage set that is a room with no exits. Each actor has the wrong lines, the wrong actions, and the director waves his arms and shouts at them but they are oblivious to his words and motions. *Tower of Babel,* I think, remembering the stories that Grandpa told me, and vow to stay aware of reality when I grow up. And above all, to avoid anything that remotely mirrors these family battles.

CHAPTER 20

When I am eight years old, I fall into Hebrew school lessons after school with the enthusiasm born of a great need to cleave to something representing security, and my ties to Jewishness through Grandpa are the most powerful feelings that I possess. It feels so good to belong to so great and cohesive a whole. To know that there is a force of spiritual intensity that belongs through the ages; and here I am, part of the Chosen People.

How can anyone ask for more, be more fortunate. I sublimate all of my feelings at that time, all of that yearning for family, into the great mysterious province of Judaic heritage and history, and begin to fantasize about when I will move to the Promised Land and become one with a brave new world that symbolizes everything that is fine and valid about living. Zion becomes my guiding light. I excel in reading and writing Hebrew, entranced by the magical imagery of the strange characters and the words, the spirituality of the mysterious incantations. Green fields of waving grain thrust from an unwilling desert, and everyone is equal.

The rest of the children are singing Christmas carols at the top of their lungs and I am closing my eyes and ears and mouth tightly and thinking about planting olive tree seedlings in Israel. Shma Yisroel Adonoy Elohenu Adonoy echod, I am chanting in my head, warding off the evil of the Goyim and their world, they are the strangers. This entire thing permeates my thoughts and my life and it frightens me, repels me, draws me to it… round yon virgin, mother and child… a great sense of warmth encompasses me, and envy claws at me for not being able to share in this great universal tenderness. I am enveloped by a joyous heat when Mommy sings and plays carols at the piano, and confused. She speaks sanctimoniously of seasonal cheer, as if it all had nothing to do with this Christ-child or this entire faith system. Splendidly decorated pine trees and the rest of the glitter and special traditions are locked out of the closed abode of the chosen people. I do not feel so chosen at Christmas time.

I am under extreme sanction, escorted with horror and distaste to the office of the principal of our school during assembly because I refuse to put my hand over my heart and pledge allegiance to the United States of America, in school, because I am a child of Zion, a citizen of *V'Eretz Yisroel*. My real ritual Hebrew name is Leah Shulamith after ancient royalty ... I am a Hebrew princess, royalty, I am special. I dream of a world of waving olive branches where no one ever hurts the ones they love, and voices are not raised. Someday I will travel to the Promised Land and live and work on a Kibbutz and be an honor and richness to the chosen people. And I will not partake of this heathen ritual filled with meaningless pomp and circumstance forced upon us by the Goyim who have taken over the world and who torture and destroy Jews in every corner of it.

I pass by Woolworths and stop at the giant Christmas window display and press my nose against the glass devouring the essence of a baby doll and coveting the possibility of ownership, likening it to the infant Jesus himself, and resume my journey home with the certain knowledge that this dream will never be realized. Once home I am lighting the last of the familiar orange Chanukah candles set in the tarnished brass Menorah which sits on the top of the television console and I sigh, for I have received the last of my Chanukah gelt, holiday money, and the baby doll still sits in Woolworth's window and I know it will never find a home in my arms.

I walk home from the religious school on the extreme opposite side of our neighborhood in the pre-dinner dark of winter, smelling the various different meals wafting out the Bronx apartment house windows like some 1947 late day scent specific to that moment in time. City bouquet stamps its identity over even the airways, as I play my games of imagined fancy and assorted maneuvers to kill both elements of time and space that challenge me with their tedium during my walk home.

I steel myself against the long walk, and think about the meal ahead and about the paints that wait in that warm and private space, in the sanctity of my bedroom *cum* studio. We all sit at the table, either watching *Kukla, Fran, and Ollie*, or listening to classical music on WQXR, the perfect picture of a cozy family meal. The only thing is, I can already feel the squeezing jumping insides of me threatening to destroy my entire body from the inside out; as usual ... the tension is as thick as the steak that my mother puts on the table. How do you expect me to eat this steak? My father inquires sternly, loudly, tightly, amusedly, quizzical ... steel, a grenade waiting to go off. What is it? What is it? Sarah inquires tensely, watch spring sprung hysteria tight. What's wrong, Albert? I look at my mother; she studiously avoids my glance, overcome with terror. It is the same old-same old. I CAN'T EAT THIS STEAK! His voice booms, the room filling with the poison of his fury. But what ...? The tension and fear is palpable, all invading. His stern features relax; soften into a comical and amused grin. You forgot to give me a fork, he murmurs innocently, greatly amused at our chagrin; his eyebrows, mustache dance with amusement, doing charming things to his face.

My stomach gets off the roller coaster that my insides have become, and weird sensations of spasmed horror shoot through the different parts of me. We relax, but only for a moment, and only on the surface, for God only knows what will be forthcoming next. Every part of my gut is still clenched in tension, it is impossible to let go. This time it is only a joke. Some joke!

Then there are the real episodes. One day, there is the argument over the amount of fat that should be on a piece of meat, or where anyone purchases so tough and/or tasteless a piece of food, or how could it have been so badly over/undercooked. Then it is ginger ale that has not properly chilled. It can be anything. Anything can set off one of those temper tantrums that are so astonishing and paralyzing in nature as to decimate entire bunches of observers who blend and fade into the walls or furniture as tightly as they can will their molecules of being to push. Mom and I are those observers.

Some days I am sternly admonished to eat every single carrot and pea on my plate, emphasis on *pea*, and my confusion would result in great thigh slapping laughter. Mostly I sit in uneasy trepidation awaiting those explosions that can come erupting right out of the top of Daddy's looming Vesuvius presence, unable to take my eyes off of the red flushed to bursting face atop the huge flailing form, at any moment.

Each time I am paralyzed into nonbeing, unable to tolerate not even one more thrusting pain inflicting word or sound. Great hot tears spill over the tops of my eyes and roll hotly down my face onto my shirtfront, and I am still more fearful to look up, hoping against all that was holy that he will not spot my tears, for then the invective is redirected against my babyness, my over sensitivity, my spoiled rottenness, and I am ordered in that sharp captain's bark to stop crying that minute. I grip the edges of my chair and pray to die right on the spot. I am a peculiar mixture of fearlessness and trepidation. Such is the family that I am a part of.

Although I fear my father to distraction, I inexplicably adore and crave his presence and attention intensely. I am all alone, no one, no brother or sister to confide in, to compare angst with, real or imagined. I feel this aloneness, loneliness so intensely that it becomes a major focal point of my entire being.

I have finally realized that there is no chance that Mom and Dad will ever have another child, thereby dashing all my hopes and dreams with a healthy splash of icy water. I come to this conclusion by subtracting the ages of the youngest of my friends' siblings from the ages of their mothers, then comparing the result with my mother's age. It is obvious that relative to the information at hand, she is just out of time. I would thus somehow need to survive without a household baby until such time in the far distant future that I will be able to produce one myself.

My parents try to console their inconsolable child, covering the guilt associated with their obvious inadequacy along with their mirth at my intensity in the matter. They refuse my counter offer that maybe a puppy will help to fill the void, because it is so obvious that puppies and tall elevator attended apartment buildings are not compatible, and that it would be therefore inappropriate to have a dog. They try with great intensity and sincerity to compromise with gold fish and guppies, but alas I find it impossible to bond with something so tiny in a bowl of water and besides it seems to be very difficult to keep these creatures alive.

The next brainstorm arrives at after much whispering, heads close together feigning intimacy, a grand show, is a canary. I name him Dicky-bird, and I say to him (with proper allegiance to the grand deities of my parents, the impresarios Gilbert and Sullivan) *Dickybird why do you sit, singing willow, tit willow, tit willow*, talk to him, confide in him, feed him, clean his cage religiously, love him dearly until he perishes one morning following a frigid March night from a chill breeze that has attacked his delicate constitution. With proper decorum and appropriate seriousness Daddy and I climb the steep steel stairway, walk over the pedestrian crosswalk to the great park, actually merely a long deep field of weeds bordering Flushing Meadow Lake in the shadow of the World's Fair grounds and the Aquacade swimming pool and Daddy reminds me once again feigning a closeness that remains stiff and elusive that it was all created in 1939 the year I was born. I carry a White Owl cigar box, lined with wads of Kleenex and scraps of velvet left from Mom's latest sewing project, in which Dickybird lies in state. Tears well up from my tight and aching chest, seep from my scratchy reddened eyes and roll down my face. This is one time when Daddy doesn't attack my babyness although I am beyond caring, instead places a firm warm hand on my shoulder and squeezes lightly. We bury Dickybird at the edge of the field, counting off the cyclone fence posts from the crosswalk gateway, and I sedately place a rock that I had painted with his name, Dickybird, and the dates of his acquisition and death, September 1949-March 1950 on the top of the small mound. Dickybird is replaced by Petey after a reasonable period of mourning, like three days. Petey survived for a year and some, until he was attacked by a rodent in his cage while we summered at one of Daddy's multiple camps. Probably Winneshawauka, in New Hampshire. By this time, I was all cried out, all used up, no longer willing to put myself out there in plain view of fate and disaster and disappointment.

҈

Time passes, and things change. I am now ten years old, and we have left the Bronx for the country, we are living in Forest Hills, in Queens, where living is supposedly, according to rumor, better in quality and where more opportunities for success prevail. We have discovered this apartment while I am visiting with my new friend Jane one weekend. Mom is impressed with the schools here, and the surge of post-war new construction tantalizes her with the possibilities of more commodious living space. And the Bronx is changing, the notorious *they* say.

I love our new apartment. It's in something brand new that had appeared with many of the new post-war innovations, a *garden apartment complex*. Three-story brick walk ups containing three bright sunny apartments on each level, the buildings arranged in serpentine complexity around grassy, landscaped courtyards. The schools in the area are supposed to be the top in the country. Despite all of these attributes, which include the fact that I have my own personal room, the sudden and glaring separation from my grandparents is wearing heavily.

I continue to attend Synagogue on High Holy Days, and my mother keeps up the practice of all tradition and custom attending all the holidays. On *Rosh Hashanah* and *Yom Kippur*, we have our special dinners, dress up and join in services, also on *Simcus Torah*, the celebration of the receiving of the Torah; we eat *Humantoshan*, three-cornered prune pastries on Purim Which is especially symbolic because my mother's middle name is Esther after the queen, visit the charming Succah built at the temple to celebrate autumn harvest on Succoth, hold Seders and eat *mazzah* and other special foods on *Pesach*, Passover. My father is peripherally involved in those customs that he likes, ignores with determined insouciance those that he eschews.

My fears of my father do not manifest themselves upon the other facets of my existence, indeed, by the time I reach ten years of age I am willing and able to take long trips of mysterious destination with a total lack of trepidation and with spontaneous fearlessness and joy of exploration.

One sunny Friday afternoon, when the housekeeper whom Mom employs is to take me to the Bronx to Grandma's house after school as usual on her way home, I arrive home to find that for some reason the woman hasn't even shown up. It is too late to reach Mom at her job, so that leaves only one thing for me to do.

139

The smell of chicken soup and apple pie and *pletselah* and the thought of sitting pleasantly with Grandma and Grandpa in that place of warmth and security draws me like a magnet, blinds me to any thoughts of danger. Maybe I will get to see Etta. Am I not the child of brave immigrants, fighters for a new life in a new world? Surely I can deal with such a minor setback in plans.

I concentrate on the memory of many such trips taken with my chaperone, focus on the details, shake all of the change from my gaily painted piggy bank and stuff it into my pocket and plan out all of the steps in advance, strike out on my way. I take the Kew Gardens bus on 67th Street, across Jewel Avenue to Main Street in Kew Garden Hills, where I pick up the Q44, which takes me to the Bronx. Once there, I disembark at the familiar stop, and walk the rest of the way. My heart is in my throat, but I feel that surely I am able to face this so simple of tasks compared to facing my father, the lion, in his den, the dragon in his lair. I walk through familiar streets and courtyards, open the familiar front door, step into the same old aged decrepit rattling elevator, heart in throat, and go to the third floor, walk through the drab dark hallway to the familiar apartment, knock on the door. Hello, Grandma, I say, when she answers the door. I am received with astonishment and shock. My adventure is met with much horror and admonition, and just a little pride at my awesome courage. Isn't this at least in some part, genetic? Did my ancestors not escape the pogroms of early century eastern Europe? I am looked at with new eyes, if not a little trepidation. Mom arrives as planned at our mutual destination and does not stop staring at me with combined terror and pride throughout the rest of the visit and through the hour long bus trip home later that evening, and when it is all over and I am safely home I am of course reamed out and punished, sent sternly to my room. When I am in bed I can hear the rhythmic melody formed by the rise and fall of my mother's and father's muted chagrined voices for a long while. What will I do next, they wonder, the little rascal? She's our daughter, all right, look what we have accomplished, created.

The following week, high on my success and the thrill of striking out on my own, the accepting of challenges and the capture of them, I charge this time into the cavernous and moldy depths of the Eighth Avenue subway. I am on my way, this time, to visit my uncle's office where I have my dental appointment. Uncle Hal has continued the family tradition of dentistry, and has a thriving elite practice on Madison Avenue and Forty-Sixth Street. Again, I have no choice but to miss the appointment if I falter. My parents, somewhat mellowed by time, have agreed, their hearts obviously in their throats.

A shame that the Big Apple is no longer safe for a ten-year-old to chance such intrepidity, I tell myself in the seventies. I would have liked Lynnie to have had the opportunity for such exalted challenge. And then there is Wendi, the fearless, the inappropriate; her forages into Central Park at sixteen, her openness and invitation to the Latino population, as personified by this new flavored generation of young mobsters hanging in the park. Wendi is completely without fear is missing that important bone of self-preservation, or is it merely common sense.

CHAPTER 21

1951

Have you visited your other grandmother who lives in Manhattan, asks Grandma-in-the-Bronx, the merest suggestion of self-righteous jealousy tingeing her soft voice? My father grew up in the city; his mother has always been a city person. We visited her often, and when she was younger she would travel to see us in the Bronx at our apartment, sometimes care for me when I was sick and Mom had to go to work. When she was younger, she took me out to lunch, on occasion, and to the theater or the movies. I can still hear the songs being belted out across the rows of seats from the giant colorful screen, of *Annie Get Your Gun.* Our visits have become sporadic, since Mom's job has taken on new and time consuming responsibilities. I miss her.

I have now traveled solo from our new home, the garden apartment in Forest Hills, just one street away from my good new friend Jane, whom I have met at summer camp, to Grandma Anna's house in the Bronx, and Uncle Hal's dental office on Forty-Sixth Street and Madison Avenue, Downtown. It seems the next most logical thing for me to do is to attempt a visit to Grandma Julia. Daddy has helped to relocate his mother recently from her immense elegant traditional family apartment on East Sixty-Third, to a studio apartment on Amsterdam and Ninety-Something. He can occasionally be relied upon, in a crisis. I have made this trip with Mom, but never really paid attention to the route. Yeah, Daddy, I remember, I lie, don't worry. I'll be fine. More little white lies, survival. I choose not to risk the potential of his fierce refusal of permission for my trip if he has the slightest suspicion that I am flying blindly with no evident flight plan.

I once again swallow fear; let my sins be of commission … and brave the New York subway system, following Daddy's instructions, scrawled, nearly illegible, carefully. If his handwriting is any indication, maybe he should have reconsidered his decision not to be a doctor. I emerge from the dark, dank gut of the city, back out into fresh air in a new and alien environment. I walk along the wide cement pedestrian walks, in this grand manmade canyon, trying not to step on the cracks between sections, not wanting to compromise my mother's back. Uptown Amsterdam Avenue is wide and busy, great ancient edifices rising with stature and pedigree, boasting grand and elegant details of cornice and carved stone gingerbread, wrought iron grilled windows on lower levels, and doormen.

The gentleman standing guard over the entrance to Grandma's new home greets me with taciturn stone face, staring straight ahead as if there is no one else there. His uniform attempts to disguise a frail and bony ancient body. His bland and expressionless face stares inward, concentrating on his main goal, which is to appear to guard this building while disdaining identity. I step under a maroon canvas canopy and approach the impressive glass front door going through extensive facial contortions trying to match expressions with the doorman, who stands ramrod straight, fighting the corners of my mouth which refuse to remain properly pointed seriously downward, trying hard not to make eye contact. I make an elaborate issue out of checking and rechecking the address on my folded slip of paper more than a few times and as I reach for the door handle I find another hand already there and giggle nervously.

Can I help you, madam, asks the doorman in his stiff most professional tone of voice, bending his head to look downward and meet my eyes, struggling with errant facial muscles. I'm here to see my grandmother, Julia Addelston, on the sixth floor, I respond with my most haughty voice, making my face stiff and supercilious all at once. I am trying to match his tone and mood so that there is no question of the appropriateness of my presence. Ah, he answers, the Duchess. Let me help you find her. I try to restrain a titter, looking around me at the faded elegance, remnant of an earlier time; paintings a la Fragonard, thick rococo gold leaf frames, dusky heavily trimmed wood walls and soffits, the latter hiding soft lighting, carved wooden balusters on rising worn carpeted stairs. He slips around the open door, to a podium, and reaches for a huge black telephone, presses a number, and waits a moment. Ah (he says again) Madam, he speaks into the phone, there is a young lady to see you, shall I send her up? There is a sharp squawking chattering sort of sound, and he says, very well Madam. He hangs up the receiver, and guides me over to the elevator with his hand on my back. I am chewing on the inside of my mouth to keep from laughing out loud, and looking up at him, see that he is struggling, himself, to maintain the charade. Is that a slight twinkle in his watery blue eyes?

I find myself once again in the belly of the beast a frightening bouncing clanking elevator, whose huge accordion gate is closing me into its maw with its brass teeth. I've been here, and survived, back in the Carnegie Hall days, when I was younger and more vulnerable. I am the fearless explorer, now, conquering new worlds, and there is no time or energy for fear. The doors close, the grinding sound of ancient machinery begins, and I am swooped, stomach first, upward, and set down feet first, released from the vacuum of spacial movement onto the sixth floor. My stomach follows, slowly and tenderly. Grandma Julia is waiting for me at her open door. She gives me a cool, stiff, perfunctory hug, and I follow her inside. She points at a brocade velvet chair with carved walnut arms, and I slip onto it, pushing myself back into the depth of it, my feet dangling, barely touching the floor. I am seriously uncomfortable. Beauty is not always commensurate with comfort.

I have arrived early, and I have interrupted her in the ministrations of her toilette, and try as I may to act with due respect, I cannot resist watching. I am mesmerized by the length of her gleaming silver white hair that cascades down her back nearly to her ankles. She reaches back under her neck with one arm, and runs a bone handled hairbrush through it with the other hand, over and over again, finally placing the brush carefully on an ornate silver tray. I continue to watch, as she lifts the mass of hair with her arms and hands, faster than I can figure out just what she is doing, She twirls and winds and tosses and corrals this cloud of hair that although it seems to have a mind of its own, has come up against someone with more power. The Duchess controls the moment. In a flash she has wound the mass around her head, tucked the end somewhere under itself, and secured it with a curved ivory comb.

Her regal figure ensconced in a gauzy black silk dress, pulled together at the waist with a tie, her pendulous breasts resting over the waistband, her chest flat on top as her breasts begin lower down than one would think possible. The skirt over its stiff iron-like under slip goes nearly straight down to her ankles, appearing as though solid, primly denying the possibility of a human body beneath it, where it barely covers thick black cotton stockings over elastic support hose, tucked into neat black polished oxford shoes with slight two-inch heels. Her body is tightly corseted, in an ancient garment that permits no pursuit of imagination. Around her neck is an elaborate concoction of crocheted white lace, covering an area nearly from one shoulder to the other, and at least eight inches from her neck downward; a collection of chins rest comfortably in this nest. Her face is covered with a bare coating of face powder, which accentuates the elaborate network of creases, a crosshatch of fine lines when she speaks. She sports an elaborate silver lorgnette, which she uses from time to time, to examine something closely, or to read.

Grandma Julia is obviously royalty. Her statuesque carriage, the details of self and surrounding suggest this. Her apartment is filled with antiques and pedigreed furniture, salvaged from the huge family space that she has inhabited previously, for so many years. There is so much to look at, so much of interest and beauty. This is the only place that I have seen outside of a museum that is so opulent, so weighty with implied history. A heavily carved mahogany glass-front credenza holds a variety of figurines and patterned dishes, table tops are covered with samples of her crocheted cloths and doilies. Here and there are figurines, obviously painted with nail polish, of famous personalities. She removes a piece of well chewed Wrigley Spearmint from her mouth, and delicately places it on an evolving figure, carefully pressing into the previous mass, molding it deftly, quite obviously in progress that sits on her personal table, beside the chair in which she holds court. She pokes and prods it into the desired position and shape, and pops another piece into her mouth. I cannot quite tell yet who this will be. I turn and look at a rendition of H.L. Mencken, the philosopher-author, who is Grandma's cousin, it is said. It is also said, whispered amongst family members that Julia is in reality the long lost Princess or Grand Duchess Anastasia, the czarina, who was allegedly killed in the revolution in Russia so many years ago. Julia herself has perpetuated this story, and we wonder. Mostly we wonder how a Jewish woman could have been the czarina. Julia just smiles enigmatically. There are many claimants to that title, many of what are called pretenders to the throne. When asked about it, Julia allows that secret smile to crack her usually still features, and I see a bit of Daddy in her; the naughty reprobate. It is probably no secret that he is her favorite of the three boys, her firstborn, and that she secretly indulges him despite his failings.

I summon up the courage to ask her a question that has been tormenting me, wasting space in my conscious mind. Can you tell me about that spittoon that Daddy talks about, that my Grandpa used to have, I ask her. Spittoon she asks, puzzled? Yes, I say earnestly, the big ceramic pot by the front door, the musical spittoon that plays a song when Grandpa spits into it just right. Grandma struggles to keep another smile from escaping her stern countenance. Albert. What are you going to do with that Albert? Oh, yes, she says, that one. I had almost forgotten. And she repeats the story to me, stifling her mirth, her demeanor stern and controlled and as she repeats it exactly I realize that it must be true.

And is it true, I continue, emboldened by her cooperation, is your name, Addelston from the *Duke of Athelstain*, in England, where your parents come from? Now she is genuinely puzzled. No, she says, we are from Russia. We are descendant from Russian royalty. She leans forward conspiratorially and whispers. I, she says firmly, am really the czar's daughter, Anastasia. It is not wise to discuss this, she says piously, straightening her back, and draping herself with an air of cool sophistication. But my husband's family came from England, I believe, she adds with a slight twinkle flickering in her staunch bland countenance, or passed through, at least.

The czarina takes out a deck of cards, and hands it to me. I obediently remove them from the box and spread out the cards in the form appropriate for a game of solitaire, which she taught me years ago, to fill the boring time when adults talk about things that children have no interest in. This is what I am to do while she prepares a pot of tea. I know the ritual. I am happy, because I am busy. Nothing annoys my spoiled and arrogant young self more that one of those vacuums that occurs when there is nothing to do. I lift my eyes for a moment, intrigued by one of Grandma's chairs that has just caught my eye once again, a strange apparatus which I can never figure out. It is a triangle, or a square, I can't decide, but the back is rounded. Actually, four of them would create a perfect circle. Why would anyone want to design a chair like this one? I ask myself, fearful to pose the question to Grandma. They are impossible to sit on, you never know which side to hang your legs, and of course, you cannot, under any circumstances put one on each side. I never do find out. I return to my game, frustrated because I am stuck. Outside, the sun has managed to filter through the rising canyons and the gray shadows of the city, illuminating an eerie slanted column of light, dust motes floating in this strange shape in the middle of the shadowed room. I stare at the dancing specks of light, puzzling over whether or not anyone will ever know if I cheat at solitaire, but decide on the route of caution, the path of least resistance. How can you know the answer to a question such as that? I always have a lot of questions.

Soon, she returns with a tea service of delicate china, painted with sprays of tiny roses and leaves, intertwined with one another. There is the obligatory teapot, and plate of refreshments. Today, there are tiny cakes, coated with shiny chocolate or vanilla *ganache* and decorated with carefully placed flowers of colored almond-flavored frosting. Sometimes there are thin delicate cookies, and other times there are tiny elegant strudel filled with apples, strange yellow raisins, crushed walnuts. These cakes have no resemblance at all to those made by my other grandma. I have never seen yellow raisins anywhere else in my life. She fills my cup with milk from the elegant pitcher.

Have you practiced your crocheting, she asks solicitously, between sips of tea, and I nod yes, my mouth full of cake. Did you bring something to show me? No, I shake my head, embarrassed, feeling the red begin to creep up my neck to my face. I have not been very successful with my few attempts. Very well, then; she finishes her tea and puts away the tray, and a ball of heavy white thread and a crochet hook from somewhere under her skirt or behind the chair, and I move closer, for my lesson will now begin.

She proceeds to show me how it is done. She takes her thread, and makes a loop, slips the silver hook through it winds the thread around it and pulls it through. That much, I've got. She continues to poke and wind and pull, and soon there is a string of chains. Then she begins to reach into the chain with her hook, and continues the winding and pulling through, until she has an entire mass of interwoven chains. Now, she is getting more elaborate, and I watch fascinated as loops and chains evolve, and become curved borders and ruffles and flower forms. Now, she hands the hook to me, and a ball of thread, and guides me through the same maneuver, and thrilled, I see the same forms emerge. Do it again now by yourself, she tells me, and I do. Now I cannot stop, I want to continue spinning flowers of thread forever.

But she is tired, now, and it is time for me to leave. She hugs me, runs her hand over my short hair with a tsk, tsk, and phones down to the doorman that I am on my way down. Thank you, Grandma, for a lovely time, I say formally, the way one would address royalty, and she smiles, and bends down for a kiss. Her cheek is soft and dry, like a fine parchment or old silk, exuding a faint breath of lavender scent.

The doorman is waiting for me when I step out of the elevator, breathless, and the door clanks shut behind me. How is the Duchess, today, have you enjoyed your visit, he asks, and I say, fine, and yes thank you, and he almost smiles, and I reverse my steps back to the subway. I walk down the steps to the giant underground system and pray that I can remember where to get on, when to get off, and when to make those three changes. My mind is turmoil of confused dancing letters, a veritable alphabet soup, A, E, F, R, GG, the different subway lines. If I cannot pull this off, God only knows where I will end up. In the hidden caverns of sleep in the deep dark night, this is the very theme of one of my most terrifying nightmares. I take in an enormous deep breath; stand up at least as straight as the doorman, maybe as straight as Grandma, sucking my stomach in. I can do this. I am descendant from the Czar of Russia. I am royalty.

᠗᠙

My father is the prodigal son, in more ways than one. In the years when he is gone, during the war, life consists of my symbiotic connection between my mother and me; when he returns, everything about our existence changes.

He brings himself home from the war that memorable day and something else, with him. He brings a gift for my mother, a raging case of gonorrhea, which hospitalizes her for several weeks of serious antibiotic treatment. He also brings his war baggage, a French girlfriend, and a vacuum created by the end to his law career. Actually, his law career ended some years earlier. Story has it, that he had graduated from law school right into the Great Depression, received a scholarship and then a doctorate in International Law from the University of Switzerland, in Geneva, and unable to find employment, turned to selling insurance. With his charm, personality, brilliance, and silver tongue, Daddy was a natural. The problem was, after selling policies to friends and family, the most accessible and easy targets, who was left? And considering Daddy's avocation and passion, gin rummy and poker, it was easy to see what would follow. So he owed some money, borrowed a small amount, temporarily, from a premium he had just received from a client, someone's uncle, really meaning to replace it as soon as his luck changed, which of course, it didn't. Of course, the uncle had occasion to file a claim and found that indeed he did not have a policy.

So Daddy lost his job. And he was disbarred before he ever began practicing law, which was a great loss, not only to Daddy, but to the hoards of potential clients whose legal problems he could have addressed with his vast knowledge, brilliant and clever

146

mind, and silver tongue. He had enlisted in the armed forces, and disingenuously applied to JAG, without their ever knowing about his disgrace, and served the country with distinction, reenlisting several times. Here, he was in his glory. When the war was over, he had very little choice; perhaps they had finally discovered his perfidy, and expelled him, I don't know, I'll probably never know. All those who are privy to these facts are long gone, as is Daddy. Since 1975.

But now, his future life as he has foreseen it is over. Still, he continues onward, selling encyclopedias, vacuum cleaners, the first televisions, and real estate. We have multi editions of World Book and Britannica, with their associate yearbooks and atlases as time unfolds, and a new Electrolux each year. It is all amortized by Mom, who is moving inexorably upward in the New York City School system, respected and revered for her abilities and accomplishments, ever supportive of her husband. Daddy becomes more and more morose and angry, directly proportionate to the level of success attained by Mom, and the quantity of product he is forced to sell her in order to meet quotas. It is as if she has slapped him in the face each and every time she receives an award or promotion, each and every time she writes a check to one of his employers, and each slap is a tacit permission for him to slack off, add another gin rummy night to his already overloaded schedule, and ruin the potential of yet another job. (He could have retaken the bar exam at any time in those forty years, but his stubborn pride forbade it.)

He would gather slights and insults, real and imaginary, allow his self-loathing to escalate into a tremendous volatile mass inside of him. He was like a pressure cooker, a time bomb. When would Albert explode again? His temper tantrums became legend. The strange thing, at least to me, was how Mom appeared to bait him, to do or say exactly the wrong thing, even I knew what not to do or say, so that an explosion was inevitable. What was it that caused her to appear to enjoy these attacks? Did she feel guilt for her own success in the face of his failures? Was it that Middle European phenomenon, a post Holocaust Jewish survivor's guilt, causing a need to suffer, to be martyred? Perhaps a need to seek sympathy as a substitute for what passed for love and affection? All in all, her timing was awful, her seemingly innocent comments made me cringe for what I knew would inevitably follow. Even as a child, I had more sense of how to avoid the wrath of Albert.

So, the saga continues. Instead of attempting to remedy his early error of judgment and move forward with his life and career to fulfill his promised destiny, he chooses to fill his empty existence, hide from his self-loathing and self-recrimination, with sports, gambling, and a stream of women that Mom never knows about until he is gone. So he pays his money, and he makes his choice. So he is a salesman, and he could have been a contender, but he is determined to fail. So instead of demeaning himself more and more by cold canvassing, or following carefully sales leads handed down by his main office, Daddy chooses to sit at home, watching baseball, football, basketball, or whatever sport is on. He would be watching one game on the television, and have two portable radios tuned to two other different games. It is an ordinary sight for me, arriving home from school, to see Daddy, ensconced on the sofa in his shorts and T-shirt, feet up on the coffee table, smoking his cigar, eating a sandwich and drinking a beer, cheering three games at one time. A nearby ashtray would be filled with apple cores and grape rinds and cigar butts. I knew that the fathers of my friends were all at work. I was unable to have friends over after school, not only for the abhorrent visual scene, but for the embarrassment caused by having a father who did not appear to work.

I would stand in the front hallway of our tiny four-room garden apartment in Forest Hills, Queens, in terror of him, of his award-winning, awe-inspiring tantrums. The blood would rush to his face, he would rise from his seat and loom over me in all his six-foot glory. I would look up at his contorted face, rigid with terror. Awful words would burst from his mouth, in a voice so harsh and deep and loud that it had the power to paralyze me. It was impossible to know just what would set him off, because the reasons were not the issue, it was just about his need to blow off steam, a bloodletting of self-loathing. But I did need to cross in front of the table that held the television to get to my room, or to the bathroom, a more immediate need. Crossing in front of him was certain to initiate an *event*. I would stand with my eyes tightly closed, hopping up and down, waiting for a commercial, or for his attention to temporarily shift, and race like the devil for my room. Sometimes I made it, all too frequently, I did not, and I would stand there, subject of his wrath, clenching everything on my body there was to clench, until the moment passed, and I could continue, shaking with combination of fear and relief, about my own activities. Temporarily relieved of his burden, Daddy would return to his occupation, maybe throw me a grin, or make a joke or an attempt at conversation, oblivious to my state of mind, or to the result of his performance. I had no clue what was happening, and took the full brunt of the blame (this was my fault, wasn't it?) adding more and more to the burgeoning downward spiraling self-image that was an ever weightier anchor around my hopes and aspirations.

CHAPTER 22

This is the year, when I am high school sophomore, when I study the adorable and vivacious, bright well adapted and brilliant Emmy Perl and Joy Holtzman, wondering with awe if their knee socks will stay up there forever without rubber bands, or slide downward as mine always do to come finally to rest under callused and unrepentant heels, and at the inequity of their having those bright and perfectly shaped eyes and luminous unblemished skin, and imperturbable confidence, and most of all, perfectly functioning loving supportive families. The fragility of my morale must have been obvious...

Incongruously and finally to my shock one day after all this time that I had continued to pester Mom and Dad for a dog especially now that we lived in a garden apartment here in Forest Hills which is practically country compared to the Bronx, they hesitantly agree that I may indeed be able to assume the implicit and inherent responsibilities of pet ownership and husbandry including running up and down stairs at all hours to attend to the personal needs of a small mammal. They succumb to my pleas and blatant manipulations. So at fifteen I finally get my puppy.

With casual endurance Daddy takes me to the ASPCA in Jamaica, Queens where I ignore all the raucous tumbling members of this litter fighting for supremacy and choose the tiny quivering black fur ball that sits cowering, pressed against the wire walls in the rear of the pen. I stroke her silky fur and bury my nose in her pungent puppy body, name her Cindy, my little black cinder, and she becomes my closest companion, sleeps tight against me all night. I continue my existence in a room covered with newspapers, have a new itinerary rising earlier than usual to take her out for her walk, returning directly after school.

It is our junior year in high school, and we are deeply involved in Play Production, spend all our free time and some that belongs to other interests back stage doing more hanging out than production; we are the Wiffenpoofers, lost and rudderless, most of us from varying degrees of dysfunctional home, we cling together seeking solidarity, *we are poor little lambs who have lost our way, baa, baa, baa...*

Being a member of Play Pro bestows on us the epitome of elite labels, which comes along with special advantage and license, work passes from class, unlimited privileged hall passes, the self-importance that comes with the exhilaration of a successful fabrication. William Kerr is faculty advisor, engenders hero worship in all of us, is responsible for bringing me out of my shell, conquering my shyness, giving me self confidence, enabling me to speak in front of the class. With Mom's guidance, I prepare to emote the indelible words of Robert Browning's *My Last Duchess* for his much coveted Drama class; *that's my last duchess hanging on the wall, looking as if she were alive...*easier said than done. Mom is exactly the right person to be helping me, since she is a drama coach par excellence in her own venue. She teaches her class on the skills and secrets of emoting, with a special exercise which involves the repetition of a sentence with the emphasis on a different syllable each time; **what** are you doing, what **are** you doing, what are **you** doing, what are you **doing?** Then there is the direction for the proper presentation of the smirk as delineated in her favorite how to drama textbook; raise upper left lip over upper jaw...and when the class attempts it, chaos and laughter reign. My own attempts at reciting Browning are not all that successful, but I have conquered some of the shyness.

Michael Hamburg portrays his wacky version of Harvey the invisible rabbit, and stars again in the biography of Harriet Beecher Stowe; Frank Decker guides us in building and executing the most exquisite of scenery, along with stage crew Mike Lecterman and Billy Accles, Buddy Short and John Huntington. Emmy Perl and Joy Holtzman excel in leading parts, as we all float on joyful adolescent currents of notoriety and renown...*those were the days, my friend, we thought they'd never end...*

My senior year of high school is iconic, immersed as I am in Play Pro laboring over scenery, as editor of the senior yearbook, and other senior activities. I wield my celebrity power with aplomb, adopt that arrogant swinging senior who the hell I am walk, and flaunt my status for the entire school to see. Seniors rule.

It is the year that John Huntington, rangy and dark and handsome and shy, possessing those thick and bushy eyebrows covering huge and timid eyes who ingenuously eats Daffodil Day blooms in April, chose me for his sweetheart. We spend large blocks of time hiding in the costume room back stage, holding hands, staring into each other's eyes, and sharing sweaty embraces and awkward kisses. This romance lasts for at least one joyful and unexpected month, before John finally moves on to diminutive, soft, round, doe-eyed Emmy, with her impish perfection.

My best friend, the object of my deepest secret envy. I fall back painfully but protected into the embracing cushion of Richie Spivak and Michael Hamburg, and the rest of the group, and there safely nurse my various wounds in relative safety. Long hours are spent in walking and talking and some comfortable and comforting platonic smooching with them, but this is merely an expression of friendship and support, and never approaches anything more serious. I carry memories of those days, and especially those close times of soul baring and mutual support with me for years, wanting to contact them to reminisce and perhaps bring back that easy camaraderie and safety that are remembered in times those two qualities are sorely lacking in my life. *It is twenty-five years, until the organization of the twenty-fifth high school graduation anniversary reunion, before I see any of them again.*

This is the year of realization that I am in serious trouble, and there is nowhere to turn ... it is the year that I realize that to escape from my parents home will be the first step in an odyssey toward mental health and sanity. It is the year I meet Steve.

It is some sort of miracle in my own eyes, that I have been accepted into the hallowed halls of the immortal Pratt Institute, especially in view of my well known inadequacies and shortcomings. This is after the Chinese restaurant debacle, and after my feelings of humiliation are reinforced by the resultant CEEB and SAT, New York State Scholarship test results; and after the coming out of the newly revealed list of 984 graduates flaunting such superlative achievement that at what I perceive to be my very most brilliant; I have only achieved the top quartile. This is not sufficient for acceptance to Cornell University or Sarah Lawrence or Skidmore ... and has left me the ignominious choice between Syracuse or Pratt or Queens, where Steve goes, and assorted non-desirable obscure and distant out-of-towners.

Syracuse has become an almost certainty, even to my going through the tedious processes of registration. This includes traveling the long, chillingly boring and apprehensive roads alongside Daddy with his rank cigar-and-business-paper-junk-littered, heavy-footed Oldsmobile for the obligatory interview. When I finally I graduate from high school I am awarded a *St. Gauden's Award* for art at the ceremony, all of which brings no more than a lukewarm reception.   My fear of losing Steve to the outnumbering girls at Queens College and my desperate need for weekly administration of the reinforcing warmth of his arms propels me to register at Queens College where I manage to finish that first year of academic classes with Steve. We eat our lunch sprawled on the quad lawn, a feast of egg salad on whole wheat bread, coffee milk and immense scarlet Delicious apples from vending machines; lounge between classes on the grass telling stories, sharing dreams, talking and laughing. And dreaming. The campus is comprised of a series of elderly old world Frisco-like stucco buildings ringing the center quad, faded peachy gold with red tile roofs... I am studying Calculus, the French philosophers in French, History of Art...and I continue to acquire my academic credits with summer classes at CCNY, the College of the City of New York, and with his graduation to the world of work and law school and our engagement, I continue with my own goal, art and discover that to transfer to Pratt in my sophomore year is easy. Both Queens and Pratt are, though lacking snob appeal, actually highly accredited and well reputed schools. With all my academics under my belt, I am now free to concentrate on my art. During this time it appears to be perfectly all right for me to be engrossed with my art.

ॐॐ

Fear holds me paralyzed in its taunting grasp, fear of competing with the *crème de la crème* of the art student population of New York City and the world at large. This fear owes its efficacy and potency to the insistent and voluble hype that emanates from the dingy but hallowed place itself.   I brave the first of uncountable trips by bus and train and to what was once a most elegant and desirable section of Brooklyn that still cries out sadly through its faded tortured brownstone, carpenter gingerbread, magnificent sculpted detail of cornice and wrought iron, for recognition.

I enter my first class in a chilled and trembling sweat, glancing around at the threatening competition who suffer, unknown to me, from the same fears and qualms as I do myself. I try to appear more cool and confident than I feel. I watch my adversaries out of the corner of my eye, throwing discreetly casual and sweeping glances at their sketch pads to see what genius lurks right at my elbow ready to strike a death blow to my frail ego and spurious class standing. Soon the teacher strides briskly into the room, and contemptuously introduces himself, and the entire group, in great awe, chokes and gulps a little, waits for its first directive, wondering if it will be equal to it, certain that even collectively they will not.

I want you to take one of these sheets, he orders crisply authoritative, holding up a large intimidating newsprint pad, and then pausing dramatically, says, and I want you to draw a living cube! There is a cessation of breath, and after a moment of shock, heads begin tentatively and ever so subtly, delicately turning, each pupil fearing to make a wrong move, no one knowing what the hell he means. The collective beating of thirty hearts must be audible down in the cafeteria, even through the well-built and thick and ancient walls of the venerable institute. The professor must have bitten a hole right through his inner mouth trying not to laugh out loud at our gullibility, ignorance, tenderness of spirit.

Well, he makes his point, although it is a while before we are relaxed enough to become aware of it. Finally some several hours later, the desks and tables and floors are littered with pages of newsprint covered with cubes of varying degrees of sensitivity and cleverness. Many of them are also covered with a dashing and cavalier F or D, superciliously left there with grave flourish by the aloof and contemptuous instructor. We heave simultaneous sighs of relief and, smiling sheepishly and conspiratorially, unite in the endurance of success over adversity, move on en masse to the next challenge.

Alan Ginsberg and Jack Kerouac; Charlie Parker, Dizzie Gillespie, Miles Davis are the voices that are being heard in the literary and music worlds that accompany our travail. Literature, poetry, music are transported into another strata of sound and meaning; stream of conscious and jazz, wild and beyond sensation, comprehension and experience. Abstract Expressionism is the two dimensional translation of all of that; it is the passion of the art world now, something that I have no understanding of, curiosity about, or interest in doing. Jackson Pollack, Mark Rothko, Robert Motherwell, Lee Krasner, Willem de Kooning ... these are the giants in the field; they are worshipped by the art elite for their bold exciting dangerously innovative works, and I am smirking with contempt and disinterest, interested in my own need to master the limitations of paint and canvas and my dreams of future success and fame.

We are doing our learning in the height of the *avante garde* movement of the arts, yet few of us ever realize what an opportunity this is in terms of art history and growth ... all I can see are Titans everywhere, and established successful talented and well taught brilliance, with which and whom I am fully aware I can never compete. My failure is a foregone conclusion. If I didn't know this by merely looking around me, I have learned it by osmosis all my life. I struggle gamely, surrounded everywhere by huge impenetrable walls of fear and inadequacy. Not that anyone else in the class is distinguishing him or herself in any way, save for the few whose graphic design sense is acute or who have well used their high school years at Music and Art or Art and Design. Even their minor successes are sufficient to intimidate me, although I am excelling in other areas in which they flounder sadly. I do not, however, notice this.

The second class is actually *Two-Dimensional Design*, a frighteningly exacting technical drawing course where I ultimately learn about *happy accidents* and the unacceptability of using *up-ness for in-ness*. In *3D design*, we build a thing called an *architectonic*, which is a mad conglomeration of carefully glued-together cardboard or plastic squares or toothpicks or whatever inspired genius has been given birth to, forming some sprawling or burgeoning structure of mind boggling complexity and painstaking effort. Frequently, these are known to disassemble piece by aggravating sullen piece on the way to school, most probably in the crowded swaying tunnels of the downtown Eighth Avenue subway.

Free painting class is, of course, my favorite, I say, of course, because that is what I have been doing for as long as I can remember, and that is what has brought me to this school in the first place; the desire to paint, the need to learn how to do it right. I need not have worried, this is not the protocol, and instruction is not to be. Although we spend entire days in intense uninterrupted painting, I fume that there is no guidance to speak of, save an occasional critique. I feel the struggle to paint looming ahead for eons and know in my soul that I will not outlive the discovery of technique that resists, eludes my concentrated efforts. This *laisse faire* theory of teaching that inspires such gut tearing frustration in us all is part and parcel of the gestalt philosophy of art that permeates the art world at this time. Discovery must be a part of the entire experience. I spend much of my painting time staring out of the window of the vast musty high ceilinged studio which is filled with laboring novitiates staring at local boys playing baseball on the school field below, wondering about the future, breathing deeply of the intoxicating odor of turpentine, linseed oil and varnish.

I continually struggle with my painting technique, and I know that I have a long long way to go, but I feel myself making progress. I finally bring home a huge painting that claims for its pedigree eight weeks of daily work of tedious concentration and painfully struggling execution. We labor over the trademark *setups* that appear like fungus after a long summer rain, on the huge platform in the front of the studio. The subject this time is a diabolically elaborate still life that includes a giant harp draped with a deep blue velvet and a red and white checked cloth in front of which sits a chipped and ancient stone sculpture of a small cherubic boy drawing several fish from a bubbling stream, surrounded by samples of Romanesque, Greek, and Corinthian cornice and balustrade, casually sprinkled with carefully placed groups of several dozen persimmons and apples.

I am radiating pride, as I maneuver the monster canvas through the subway rush hour, impatient to even let the paint dry, for I am going to shock the socks off my parents, and show them that I am not the failure they think me to be, even though I study art, instead of some more worthy subject like education or law. Like a girl could major in law in the 1950s! The carved stone fishing cherub in my painting seems so real, that you want to reach out and rub the stone surface to check ... the harp strings flow and glisten as if gently moving with the air currents of the room ... the checks on the scarf move in and out of the shadows and folds of fabric changing tone and value and losing themselves in the deep pockets of the shadows ... the other small chunks of antiquity move out of the picture plane and also defy touch ... the persimmons and apples are left blocked in and merely suggested as they have been from the first day of work, for somehow their importance has palled in the demanding challenge of the other subjects. I have finally run out of time, and the apples and persimmons have suffered from incompletion ... I rationalize that one can always paint apples.

When I reach home and with a tight smile and a flourish set the thing up against the lifted piano bench for my mother to see, I have keyed myself to a fever pitch of anxiety, desperate for the words of approval that I know I deserve, needing my parents to be proud of me. My mother backs away thoughtfully, and studies the painting for a long long time, during which I die several deaths, and finally she voices her opinion. It's nice, I guess, but how come you didn't finish the apples? The *kinnehurrah* is implicit, not verbalized, so I do not hear it. I turn my head, after the moment when the words finally sink in, so my mother will not see the stricken expression on my face, and blinking back a tear or two, carry the huge painting silently into my room, where I throw myself on my bed after locking the door, and I am unable to come out of the room for a long time. Is this the best she can do? Is this just another *kinnehurrah* moment? Either way, I am devastated. So this is what it means to have been damned with faint praise.

Now, I always think more than once before I show my mother any of my work, but sometimes I forget in my excitement or enthusiasm of the moment, and before I know it, I have pulled out some wretched piece and am again knocked to the floor by some ascorbic and inconsequential comment. What is it, jealousy of a new love for me? Failure to comprehend? Fear of making me too self-satisfied, or even over confident? It never occurs to me to question why in this and other ways my mother continually puts me down, and it isn't until years later that I begin to understand some of the dynamics involved, or to rise above them, even to be guilty of the same indiscretions, all of my vows notwithstanding. And none of this contradicts the truth, that I am my mother's pride and joy, that I am dearly and deeply loved and adored. And confused.

Part II

Steve

CHAPTER 23

The Present Day, 2009

Along with our literary contributions to the cause célèbre, our enthusiastic writing workshop, we obediently each bring something for the table, homage to our new guru, Herstory. I have left my personal muse and mentor Hope at the door, a rejected look on her face. Don't worry, I tell her, fearing her wrath, it's just for now, you can come back later. She runs her slight fingers through those wings of black hair that fall around her serene Basque face in that familiar gesture, and smiles her enigmatic smile, restacking and then carefully stashing her tarot cards in a pocket deep in the recesses of her long gown; she then dissolves into the dark.

I listen to the readers, spinning their tales, rich with detail and anecdote. When it is my turn I am filled with a burgeoning sense of inadequacy. I wish to leave, making some excuse, fearing humiliation, that old hairy bête noir failure, growling at my heels. But they support me with their sisterhood, their love, and I begin. As I proceed, my words seem empty, puerile, meaningless, my story simplistic, my voice whiny and self centered. I hold my breath. Back in the day fearing my mother's consistent censure I found Hope who became a surrogate mom. Hope encouraged me, praised me. What now, now that she is gone, they are both gone, and there are only strangers who know nothing of me to guide me?

First, I am encouraged, like a small child learning my ABCs. I struggle with new approaches. I feel a sense of progress. Failure fades away, conquered. My words are my newest children. Once again I am birthing one infant after another. Then, I am told, I need to choose one child to live; the others must die. This is an impossibility. But, they insist, choose one child, one child of my heart, my mind; one element of a lengthy, complicated story. Choose one part of a fractious fragmented personality, favor one element of a complex existence where all parts are intricately intertwined. Tell about my children, the agonies and the ecstasies, my art, or my preoccupation with the law? About building houses, living different places, one love or another, not all. How can I do that? Wait!

What was the manifesto and thrust of art in the '50s when I was getting my education, what was the prevailing mantra at the revered Pratt Institute where I put forward my very first tentative steps into art, *real* art; it was all about the *gestault,* the entirety.

My *gestault* is a composite of years of feelings, surreal and evocative that together flesh out my whole person. Efforts at recollection bring back ancient emotions almost from other much earlier lives. Recently maturity of art as well as person affords my work strength and sophistication that has been hard earned. I emerge from the thresher a pure kernel; discarded shards of painfully acquired experience lie beneath my feet on the threshing room floor. Khalil Gibran merges with Robert Graves as I wander incessantly insensate in new worlds of spirituality and esoterica and experience. My White Goddess paintings and etchings based upon the writings of Gibran and Graves done in the Art Deco and Art Nouveau traditions of Mucha and Erte illustrate all of this. Painting my feelings has always been my best means of expression. So all I can really do is paint a picture, a series of pictures, that's what I do. It is what I am accustomed to doing. Now, I must learn how to delve into the past, to seek whatever support is available, to paint a picture with words.

Among the earliest recollection that can be dredged from the annals of my memory I recall an intense and driven twelve year old staring deeply back at me from my own reflection emerging from night darkness behind my bedroom window above my easel-desk; big sad almond hazel eyes straining to see beyond pain and disappointment and perhaps fear. Those same eyes that stared out from an earlier photo of me wearing that lovingly, painstakingly constructed fur coat and hood as I perched on my small Super Flyer sled, my beloved grandfather behind me. A later photo shows a radiant smiling bride tiers of eyelet spreading around her, gauzy white lace flowing gently from a veil covered with white rosebuds framed around her face, standing next to a very serious striking dark young man.

CHAPTER 24

1958

I am a voyeur enveloped in pillows and quilts lurking in cool dawn shadows invisible in our bed watching my bridegroom, Steve, prepare for work. Awful, lonely, and tense as the time is when he is home the thought of his being gone fills me with a sense of dread that I am unable to overcome. At least when he is here I can pretend I am a part of a real functioning entity. When he is gone I am alone with myself in the vacuum created by the general failure as a human being that I know myself to be. Only when there is someone to cleave to do I have identity. Steve is all I have to cleave to. No one, parents, friends, or even Steve knows how I feel about myself, has any interest in finding out, in helping me. I am unable to express my angst.

Debonair, and alien and untouchable, he is already not here, but in his other place, his inviolate distant ineffable world of law and business; an image flits across my mind of my mother preparing for her school day signaling another impending desertion when I barely reached the level of her thigh. He looks so handsome in his well tailored suit, his hair combed and wet and gleaming; his crisp white collar held in place by the perfectly adjusted tie. A brief sense of incomprehensible envy washes over me. Still, at these moments, a wave of love for him encompasses me or is it desperation, chagrin to be left so quickly and easily behind, forgotten, and I leap from the bed and run over to him slipping my arms around his waist. I hold onto him tightly pressing my face against his wool jacket feeling the roughness of the fabric against my cheek, inhaling the crisp pungent soapy essence of his carefully starched shirt wishing with all my might that I could just somehow melt into his body, disappear under his skin, into his bones, his body, and travel with him throughout his busy day absorbed, infused, attached; involved and safe, not responsible for any other action or activity than to remain just beneath his skin. Not deserted, left alone to freefall. Finally, impatiently he pushes me away, tells me not to be silly, and off he strides. Just like Daddy; strangely enough that controlled bouncing gait as unlike my father as he could be in most ways, his build, his manner of walking, is a perfect replica of Daddy. When Steve deserts me, again and again, it is Daddy all over again away in a distant war deserting me, severing comfort and sustenance leaving me to flounder alone in an alien and lonely world in which I do not belong. And I recall…

My dearest Lynnie… I love you, my Lynnie, can't wait till you're home again with me… I'm getting kind of envious hearing those wedding bells ringing for everyone else. But my day will come soon, (I hope). I've got my bride all picked out, the only girl for me. I never thought I could love someone as much as I love you…

What happened to all that love and exultation and expectation? It's confusing; this is not what I thought marriage would be. The reality is that my husband is a symbol of someone to love. I love him because he is mine, because he is the perfect player in my fantasy. It is a fantasy of love, marriage, home and hearth, and children. It is as though I recall some faint murky film of jumping rope to that popular ditty: *Lynne and Stevie sitting in a tree, K-I-S-S-I-N-G. First comes love, then comes marriage, then comes Lynne with a baby carriage.* The day is empty, except for school, homework, chores and home decoration projects, sewing and painting and cooking. That keeps me busy, this complex activity called nesting. Then it is evening, and my husband is home, mostly, except when he is at one of those countless meetings. Meetings are where you make those important contacts that are so vital to future careers, to power and control, to winning.

I wash the suds down the drain, scour the sink with cleanser, roll my sleeves down over damp reddened arms; not my idea of pleasurable entertainment. The dishes are done, along with all the rest of my allotted chores, folding laundry. Now, with luck I may expect my husband to join me in bed where we can be anticipated to make love. How strange is this expression; we are going to make love, create it as if from nothing as though it doesn't already exist. So for ten minutes of my day I *make* love; I am loved or have the illusion that I am. In a moment it is again morning and the entire itinerary begins again. *Second verse same as the first, a little bit slower and a little bit worse...*But what is marriage anyway except for being together, sharing life? What more is there to know?

> *Today I counted the days until we can see each other again ...It's hard to find words to express how lonely I am or how much I miss you, my dearest babe. I'm sure you understand how much I love you and need you...*

Immersion in business and career is Steve's *modus operandi* and for my part I am expected to immerse myself in all that is housekeeping and nothing more. He has invested his $60,000 inheritance from his mother in the purchase of an estates practice from a retiring attorney which I don't find out until years later and has merely to wait for people to die to cash in by filing some standardized papers and collecting his fee and percentage. He does an occasional real estate closing and rarely takes any other case. He does not venture into court or deal in civil litigation of any kind. When he attempts it he falls quickly on his handsome face. He is what is called in certain circles a pencil pusher, has no aptitude for trial law. Still he works on creating and enhancing his law career flitting from one civic or political organizational luncheon or meeting to another, creating and cementing his power base, making and *shmoozing* contacts. You never know when you might need one of these in the ongoing drama of life and business. He invests most of his profits in stocks, and watches his portfolio grow. The less he allows to be spent on his wife, children, and family in general the more he has to invest. I am oblivious; I am more or less, barefoot and pregnant although the pregnant part is by my own choice.

Before I loved you, my life had no real meaning or significance. Now I have something that makes my life worthwhile…you, my dearest Lynnie.

Whatever happened to *my prayer is to linger with you*? What about all that stuff that came just before *PS I love you*? *Dear, I thought I'd drop a line, the weather's cool, the folks are fine* … that entire image of family … If I am good, and do all my chores I am allowed to kiss him goodbye in the morning. If I fail to fulfill my responsibilities according to his solemn creed, his dictates, I don't even ask for I know my required punishment; more rejection; more banishment. I hear Mom somewhere in my periphery reciting in gleeful singsong, *and when she was good she was very very good and when she was bad she was horrid…*

… I am writing this letter right after talking to you on the phone. I don't know why, but I always feel terrible after talking to you on the phone. Maybe it's because you're so near and yet so very far away. Hearing your voice makes me want to hold you so badly I could scream. I'll be able to love you full time again, and have you near me all the time. Then, all the loneliness I feel when I'm not with you will be gone. I get such a glow inside of me when you tell me how much you love me. It is such a wonderful feeling to have the one you love tell you how much she loves you. It made me feel secure and wanted. You're the most wonderful thing that ever happened to me, my Lynnie, and I love you so much. Before I loved you, my life had no real meaning or significance. Now I have something that makes my life worthwhile…you, my dearest Lynnie. So don't tell me ever that telling me how much you love me is 'silly'. All the way home I kept thinking how lucky I am to have such a wonderful person like you loving me. I love you, I love you, I love you…

It was magical. That word, *magical,* describes those early courting days, those days at Camp Paradise. Maybe the reality is that life changes to a remote tightly encompassed zone away from true life. This in some way could be because so much of my childhood involved summer camp; camp was a big part of my life as a child, as Daddy's avocation was utilizing his war experience in running summer camps for children, a creative solution if just for the summer to his eternal post war employment dilemma.

Beads threaded on a string, those childhood summers are a never ending succession of camps as daddy now home from the ravages of the war years tries to put his life and fortunes back into some frame of normalcy. He wheels and deals and puts his marvelous skills of organization to work, basing the structure of these vacation delights on his army experience. I can't even remember one summer spent in the city, which is all right with me because in those days I remember the city as being an intolerable oven fit for neither man nor beast. In those days there is also still the specter of Polio that lingers in the air along with the ghost of F.D.R. The main problem for me once they have accomplished the getting of the child out of the city into the healthy country, *is that being an only child, a loner, never having had either the privilege or the experience of sharing space or anything else, confidence and closeness included, is in adapting to the concept of a multi-dwelling...the bunk house. The trauma of this experience is a downhill roller coaster ride that never ends. My bunkmates are a strange conglomerate of disparate beings, imbued with the usual amount of viciousness of children enhanced by the diversity of their number and the unique ability that children possess to single out the weakest of their number and submit him to the most voracious of ceremonial rites.*

�❧

Save for the chirping of the ever insistent crickets and the maniacally screaming cicadas the night is damp and still. The moonlight glimmers on the black and shining lake; the raft enameled green and white in the camp colors, sways ever so gently with the slight breeze that causes the occasional ripple on the smooth and glassy surface. Taps has sounded, and not even one yellow glow issues forth from one bunkhouse; silence reigns, and an essence of peace. Gone are the raucous yelling and cheering and hailing, the high spirits of one hundred and eighty rambunctious and high spirited campers.

Beneath their hospital cornered blankets, they have sunk gratefully into their camp cots, and sleep exhaustedly dreaming about small victories and tooled leather key cases, swimming laps and nature walks. That is most of them. In one small and cramped white bunk, a caucus is being held quite surreptitiously in the john. A flashlight is held half beneath a bathrobe as one by one the inhabitants slip into the damp wooden cubicle. All except one; I cling paralyzed to my own tightly tucked cot, fear gripping my throat like muscled parental talons. Oh no, Oh no, I will not even consider the ramifications or possible retribution of the action being proposed. I close my eyes tightly, and pretend to be asleep.

Excited whispers and plans are peppered with hoots of derision directed towards my rigid figure now alone in the deserted room; they aren't fooled. I am torn with the desire to be one with the group, but fear roots me to the spot. Finally, they slip out of the rear window one by one, and dart and slither from one bush to another like a rear flank army maneuver, until they reach the silent rowboats, pulled up safely on the beach for the night.

Quickly, they push one into the silent black and waiting water, and manning the oars, row hard and silently towards the waiting raft. Once there, they plant a flag of sorts, shout the camp cheer with hysterical manic glee, and are rapidly on their way back to shore and their bunk before even the staff realizes what has occurred, chortling with success, high on excitement and danger, and are tucked back in their beds before anything is discovered amiss.

Only the flush of their small faces bears witness to their valiant and shocking wickedness. When someone discovers (by whatever means) and confronted by the massive and angry flashlights of the staff, they are marched out in front of the bunk, all of them including the innocent one, and lambasted by the head-counselor ... Daddy. He does not choose to punish the group as a whole; this issue for some obscure reason is clouded, and something else is happening. Someone is to be a scapegoat; a matter of pride and protocol succeed even the great issue of disobedience.

Daddy makes me step forward, before the others, and before I can open my mouth in defense of my innocence, he brings his arm back and delivers a stinging slap across my face. What the hell do you think you're doing he demands? Haven't you any more sense than to do a fool thing like this? Don't you realize how dangerous and stupid a thing that was to do? He is shrieking now, his face infused with blood, his eyes piercing, his body rigid with fury and terror grips me silencing my tongue, short circuiting my limbs; any defense that may or should have been forthcoming is aborted before even gaining impetus. I have firsthand knowledge of the capacity and volatility of Daddy's epic temper. The others, happy to have achieved non-visibility, gleeful to see the spoilsport take the major rap, remain silent. I am unwilling to be a fink, a character flaw I refuse to have added to my other failings as a campmate and good sport. Suffering from terminal paralysis, I keep silent.

The spot where the slap landed stings hotly and prickly red in the moonlight, and I cannot concentrate on anything else save the awful ignominy of that slap. When it is all over, I will the whole incident to the far recesses of my mind, unwilling to remember. Of course, I cannot complain to Daddy, the head counselor, about the tormenting of the other children, because that is one reason that I am being singled out. Since my Mom is also there, being his wife, I am taunted, and called Mommy's Baby.

Silent tears soaking into my pillow become my new nightly reality, while I endure a barrage of short sheeting and tooth paste–corn flake tortures and other various razzings, and the humiliation of being of late the bunks' chief resident bed-wetter. I awaken each morning to the acrid stench of stale urine as I lay in the warm comforting wetness. I endure these ignoble days as punishment due for past crimes,

৵৽৻

Intense yearning masquerades as love; I am a small child, barely able to see over the counters at Woolworth, and I have become enamored of a tiny plastic doll no longer than an inch long, complete with tiny layette and infant related paraphernalia, wrapped in a carefully formed clear plastic package. After much agonizing and conscious wrestling, the desire to possess overcomes any knowledge of morality or propriety and fear of retribution and blushing crimson beneath my hand knitted cap and hood, slip the precious goods, trembling, into my waiting pocket, and covet its contents for a lengthy and painful time. I surreptitiously remove the tiny figure and its accessories; cradle, comb and brush and miniscule milk bottle, rattle and one inch square of cloth, presumable a diaper, and tenderly administer to the creature as though it were a living baby.

Later, having accomplished this first loathsome act with such ease no detection, and no punishment, I move ahead in my criminal career to the delicate purloining of a selection coveted library books and one or two bright and shiny irresistible Book Fair treasures that my inner soul finds overwhelmingly enticing. It has become so easy, this acquisition of that which I cannot live without and the reward is undeniably worth the anguish of knowing that I have done something egregiously wrong. For a long time I suffer the torments of a Hell of my own making for these transgressions. My irredeemable guilt manifests itself in a great jumpiness and irritability and a spate of vicious and vindictive nightmares of dreadful intensity. In the end, unable to bear the pressure and onus of the awful deeds any longer, I carefully wrap the guilty items, baby doll and books in an old towel. I then stuff them in a large paper bag, and one sunny morning on the way to school, in a fever of apprehension, I heave the guilty package surreptitiously over the fence of an empty lot. Then, I stand up straight, my small body straightening out like Atlas shedding his earthly burden to some other axis after that painful time of shouldering it alone.

I feel the absence of missing siblings with added intensity at this time needing desperately to confide my horrid and weighty guilt in someone whom I can trust. I am ever fearful that my parents, in finding out, will further relegate me to the Hades of Failure and Disapproval that is my anathema. I wear my loneliness and misery on my face, feel as if there is a label engraved across my forehead; people stop constantly in those days and stare at me with such concern, are always asking me what is wrong. I come across a photo taken around that time, and see a sad and wistful large eyed waif, button down shirt and pleated skirt, knee socks slipped down in wrinkles under feet encased in scuffed brown oxfords, Band Aids on both knobby knees. A bright red barrette restraining straight hair tightly pulled back serves merely to accentuate the downward curve of the corners of a tightly pursed mouth. I hear people talk about my eyes, they are said to be deep pools that just pull you into them, twin giant pools of quicksand, brimming over with unspeakable pain. Oh, my dear child, what is the matter? Please tell me, this minute. The burst of sympathy only causes me to cast my eyes downward, and allowing a trickle of fat tears to slide over my vulnerable cheeks. I respond, however, with no delicious confidence; I merely draw further inward.

∂∽⟨

Anything that happens in the country is a highlight in my life once I have survived that first camp season; the country stands alone as my most favorite place to be, and bad or good, summer camp provides one memorable experience after another. I meet Janie Sterinbach at Camp Rondax who much later becomes my maid of honor at my wedding to Steve. Janie is probably my first real friend, my dearest friend for years to come, and actually is pivotal in our move to Forest Hills. To be sure, that move is of paramount importance in terms of choices and pathways, for it is beginning with that time, when my life begins to take form. When I meet Janie that summer of my tenth year, hesitant to trust in another child, especially at a summer camp after the Narragansett experiences, I approach the offer of friendship with a tentative restraint, which is fine with Jane, for she is a painfully shy middle sister of three, unaccustomed to a limelight which is generally taken over by one of her two more flamboyant siblings. Her mother Natalie is an artist of brilliance and success, although at the time my appreciation as well as knowledge of the avante garde is limited; I can sense, though, that her work is fine, and enjoy her vibrant impasto pastel colors which interact perfectly through her elaborate sense of pattern, form, and texture. I keep my distance, a little in awe of its power and mystical hidden meanings.

I fall into the rhythms and patterns of our friendship with an ease that confers upon me a sense of security that covers over my growing fear of approaching pubescence and its inherent responsibilities; Jane is a tomboy, an athlete, probably why we fit so well together. I begin to work earnestly on my athletic prowess, for I have recently come to the conclusion that Daddy's coolness and contempt at are apparently directed at me are unequivocally responsible to the fact that he had not wanted a girl, but a boy to share with him his lifelong obsession with sports. Already s I am an expert in caddying his golf clubs, and tag along to many baseball and football games with him, so anxious am I to please him and so fearful of failing. I adopt a boyish swagger, cut my hair into that short bob that becomes my trademark for years, with some exceptions, involve myself in playing and perfecting my performance in as many sports as possible, even attempt at one early time to pee standing up which doesn't work to my great chagrin. I will be his boy, his precious favorite boy; maybe then he will love me.

After the first shy tentative overtures on both sides, Jane and I become fast friends, sharing almost everything, and rarely are apart from that day on, except that though we share the same birthday, we are a year and a grade apart. She is as fair and blond as I am brunette and freckled.

A giant pickle jar requisitioned from the kitchen lives beneath the floor—boards of our bunk in Camp Rondax and now holds a collection of spring peepers; we nurse an abandoned infant rat in a tiny cotton lined locket box until it dies...more probably due to our over-conscientious ministrations than to natural causes. When we return to the city and my mother arranges for the momentous move to Forest Hills certain that the influences that I encounter in a neighborhood so posh and well heeled and intellectual, will only bear me in good stead for my life to come, Janie and I immediately build a packing crate go cart that we laboriously push up the steepest hills and wildly fly down with no care or fear, plant a vegetable garden, and finally when winter arrives in all its suburban splendor, build a monumental snow sculpture, a massive icy St. Bernard. I spend most of my waking hours save for school at her house, become a fixture.

Bike riding from dawn to literally dusk, stickball in the street with vengeance, building, and running and tennis, and hikes, picnics, project; we are an energetic driven nonstop duo. I adopt Jane's family, or maybe they adopt me; I nearly live at her house, I am there so frequently, probably to the chagrin in her family; I am not aware of any tension, only of the feeling that I get when surrounded by a normal a family. At least in my mind, by comparison to mine, and to families I have seen on the movies. I need, crave a real storybook family, and so I play at adopting one, something that continues in the future, until I have my own, and when I am alone again, and again, and again.

Marriage is supposed to have cured that need, to have filled my life with all that missing love. Isn't that the implied promise? Instead, old memories surface in the vacuum of my days and I exist in a morass of anguish and disappointment.

I love you, my dearest Lynnie. I'm getting kind of envious hearing those wedding bells ringing for everyone else. But my day will come soon, (I hope). I've got my bride all picked out, too. She's the most wonderful girl in the whole world and the only girl for me. Her name is Lynnie, and I love her so much... I get such a glow inside of me when you tell me how much you love me... It made me feel secure and wanted... Before I loved you, my life had no real meaning or significance. Now I have something that makes my life worthwhile... From now on, I'll be telling you how much I love you in person (for about sixty years).

I love you, I love you, I love you...

An almost nonexistent membrane separates me from reality as I inhabit my own private little bubble believing in Steve's love for me, believing that Steve and I will be my fantasy family. The main problem is, it is all a fantasy indeed, having very little foundation in reality. I go through all the proper motions, confide in him, talk to Steve about my dreams out loud, again and again; he won't listen, nor will he tell me anything he is thinking about is planning or desires. He doesn't hear me, refuses to listen, turns off his personal incoming audio utility with the flick of an invisible switch that no one knows about but him, no one experiences but me, just as he turns off my phonograph or radio first thing when he arrives home in the evening as Frank Sinatra and Dean Martin moan about imminent love...

Barbara Streisand sings *People, people who love people, are the luckiest people, in the world...he touched me, he put his hand on mine and then he touched me... Second Hand*

Rose, they call me second hand Rose... and pop stuff, when he is not around; this is the time I get to hear my favored music, and periodically the news is presented. I am peripherally aware of what is happening in the world. Alaska becomes the forty-ninth state, Buddy Holly, The Big Bopper, and Richie Valens are killed in a small plane crash; it is the day the music died, everyone says. Indira Gandhi is named to lead the Indian party, and Charles de Gaulle has become president of France; *Raisin in the Sun* and *Sweet Bird of Youth* can be seen on Broadway and while Steve conquers the business world and the legal community I continue onward, sublimate all my frustration and insecurity and loneliness in my art, in the art world, still a student at Pratt Institute, moving through the days zombielike yet absorbing particular and varied precepts of art.

⤙⤚

I am developing a new understanding of formerly enigmatic though tantalizing works such as *Hide and Seek* and *White on White* at the MOMA which we visit after my painting classes. *White on White* originally painted eons ago by Kazimir Malevich in 1918 speaks for itself, a huge canvas painted...white; *Hide and Seek* also quite large is a fantastical tree, a kind of tree of life whose negative areas contain frightening figurative images in rich startling glowing colors. With some chagrin and not a little embarrassment I leave Norman Rockwell my first muse crying out to me feebly as he recedes gasping for breath into the distance. Illustrations from *Cosmopolitan* magazine, revered in my teen years follow quickly. Also retreating into the past is that omnipresent familiar correspondence art school test blatantly available for all to see on the backs of matchbooks, a contest offering free art instruction at a touted art school entered with much hope and excitement when I was twelve. I of course win and am offered a reduced tuition if I sign up for a vast amount of expensive instruction. I am now being dutifully exposed to a treatment that is intended to plant the seeds of *avant garde* art in the hopeful artist, me. Still, Mom is fond of repeating her favorite story that she has heard at a recent Hadassah meeting about the white on white issue that sums up all that she knows or wants to know about contemporary art; a Jewish matron who has been grudgingly schooled in art by her sophisticated son declares smugly and virtuously that she does not like a painting at a new show to which he has taken her in order to test her new knowledge, all white with one small dot in the lower left hand corner because it is *tsee fere ungepotchkt*, too busy. The punch line loses something in its translation from the Yiddish, as these generally do. The lesson my mother presents with her anecdote serves little more than to confuse me further; she is there in the background, directing my education in the arts, as ever.

Bracketed by giant cement lions, we climb the immense steps of the imposing 42nd Street Library as Mom assures that my school assignments are worthy of her own status as English teacher and do her own brilliance justice. Young as I am I am taught to do proper research, define chapters, create a proper bibliography; my reports are replete with artwork and presented with seriously artistic covers. My research on the United States Constitution has for its cover the American Flag, waving, the entire project is cut to the shape of the waving flag. When my assignment is to write about the controversy over Shakespeare and Bacon and just who wrote Shakespeare's works it appears to be pro forma *a college paper while I am still in high school. When I am still in the eighth grade I am recruited to do the scenery for Mom's omnipresent school productions of her beloved Gilbert and Sullivan operas,* HMS Pinafore, The Mikado, *which I work on evenings at her school to which we have returned after school hours.*

I can remember as a very young child scribbling by the hour, pasting together masses of booklets, manufacturing great piles of stories and play-lets and dioramas and wallowing sensuously in great gooey globs of brilliant pigment. Covering piles of paper and most of my smock and me...but I can't say honestly that I heard the Muse call until much later. When did you know that you were going to be an artist the ubiquitous they *always ask with grave interest, and I answer after delving backwards into the annals of my memory that it seems to have always been so. I remember clearly as far back as I can recall throughout my childhood, my mother dragging and prodding me through every kind of cultural activity imaginable from piano and theory through ballet, interpretive, and on and on...*

There is that resolute young girl peering back at me from the reflection in my bedroom window and I am painting what I see, dabbing passionately, painstakingly at a small canvas board. There is no question, it is what I do. From the time I was a small child I needed to create. Is it Mom's insistence on classes, art in school projects, or some innate force driving me? I think that's what it is. I draw self-portraits, using the darkened bedroom window for my mirror. I paint peculiar still lifes in an attempt to express to myself the meaning of my life, the terrors and the unexplained. I put my old baby dolls who still sit on a chair in my bedroom into the compositions to show my helplessness and sense of imprisonment, an unconscious bookmark to my dreams of the future and my wistful still embryonic need for babies. When we visit the country in spring and summer, by train in those early days, I paint landscapes.

From early on, I am enchanted, captivated by landscape. That summer at Camp Rondax when I meet Jane, I am thrust into a painting class and suddenly find to my own surprise that a little watercolor landscape done under the auspices of the counselor, a middle eastern European refugee Jan (pronounced Yan*) de Ruth (Ruth is his beloved sister) an artist of some repute shows a hint of artistic promise and the teacher insists with intense sincerity to my exultant and enthusiastic parents that I need to continue lessons in oil painting when I return to the city. We travel by train to his studio in Washington*

Heights way up there in the northwest Bronx and I am instructed how to do this painting thing right. I am joined by Michael Fried, the son of my mother and father's best friend. His mother is regal and overbearing, another balabusta. *His father is a renowned and successful attorney. Although my father both loves and hates the elder Fried, hates him because he is a constant reminder of Daddy's own failings and defeats their friendship has endured for many years. So did mine with Michael. We even had a fleeting romance one year at summer camp, short lived and without the passion that it had promised. This was a major disappointment to both of us, but even more to our parents who had betrothed us at one year old, when we played together and hugged each other in charming baby cuteness.*

Michael and I are brought to the studio of our former camp counselor, now our art teacher. We are surrounded by walls hung with immense canvases, lush classically done portraits and figures with glowing skin draped in rich velvets and tapestries; there is a pervasive odor of oils and varnish and turpentine that is both exotic and intoxicating. He sets us up in front of easels, our paints and palettes sitting on sturdy stools, our small canvas boards on the easels; before us is the proverbial Chianti bottle, one apple, one pear, one banana and one orange sitting on a crumpled piece of red velvet. We begin to transfer our model onto canvas with Jan's gentle direction. It isn't the same as painting giant pine trees in front of an immense lake in the Adirondacks but there is a certain sense of power that wells up from somewhere deep inside me to recreate real life with my own hand, an oblique promise of unplumbed horizons awaiting my attention. The sensation is as addictive as the essence of the fumes from our oils.

Michael went on to make his very successful career as an art historian and critic which belied the fact that his artistic talent was tremendous. I always considered this a poor choice because he could have gone so far as an artist. Maybe I am feeling rejected, deserted, again. For Michael it is a brilliant move. He excels in his career, conquers all manner of esoteric disciplines. In fact he has only recently in 1967 written his emblematic essay, Art and Objecthood *criticizing among others popular new art titan Robert Rauschenberg about whom I am in a few short years to write a critique for an art appreciation course when I return to a local university.*

Sausage is what my mother is making, zealously forcing into me every manner of cultural and artistic exposure conceivably available in our world like so much ground meat and garlic and whatever else, pushing, pushing, waiting for the finished product that is her child to be extruded as a true cultural frontrunner and leader in her new skin. She gives me every advantage possible to insure my intellectual growth and preparation for what she perceives to be a full life for me. I will be successful, very successful, earn loads of money, beyond her wildest dreams; her dreams. To my great dismay and chagrin I am offered every manner of artistic temptation and instruction known to man; woman. To become an artist of any genre is the ultimate of successes, as a matter of fact, the only acceptable direction that a worthwhile person will attempt to follow assuming that this person has any intelligence at all. Something tickles my memory, something about

Aunt Etta. That's it. She was not permitted to be an artist. What has changed in one generation? That is something I would like to know.

૭૦જ

That small modicum of success that summer at camp plants a tiny seed. After our return to the city that fall, my education in art begins in earnest. My mother has latched voraciously onto my sudden show of real enthusiasm. Her goal is born of her indirect ambition, so intense that it almost always has the reverse effect on me and turns me off. So enticing are the ineffable rewards inherent in creation of the visual that I ignore my usual perverse desire to thwart the ever insistent prodding and allow myself to be sucked into the vortex of the ever demanding, ever pulling, progressively escalating creative syndrome, heralded and controlled by the Call of the Muse.

Once enticed into the Muse's ever tightening grasp I become increasingly subservient to her demanding whim. My ever present ever demanding need to escape the pressures around me causes me to find succor in the delightful comforting soft cushioning flow of the creative process. I lock myself into my room for long hours at a time, and become so involved in form, pigment, pattern, that I become oblivious to the rest of the world. What balm, what escape, what safety. What an opiate and what a demanding master. The more I do, the more I want to do; the more I learn, the more I need and want to learn. There is never lack of inspiration but instead an ever escalating progression of new ideas and their uncountable corollaries.

A few years after beginning to paint, I am studying with those titans at the Art Students League in New York; I am attempting my new favorite subject, still life now, in a new and difficult medium, water color, wet on wet, colors flowing into one another, rich and sensual. My efforts are immediately framed and hung by my doting parents despite my knowledge that they are really not very good. What does this say about the value of my parent's continual praise? What does it say about me? I ask myself these questions and miss the part about being appreciated and encouraged.

૭૦જ

OBSSSERVE! This is the barking Teutonic order of Richard Lindner, one of my most recent art professors who is teaching representational drawing; *Realism.* I am studying now in 1957 at Pratt Institute. I suffer gamely the outrageous slings and arrows of his brutal criticism which he inflicts with delightful sadistic intent in his eternal quest for meticulous detail and the perfect performance of his students. We take field trips to the Museum of Art as well as the Museum of Natural History to spend long tedious days copying masters and drawing detailed costumed period figures onto paper with well sharpened pencils and pastels. I am realizing somehow that I am in the presence of genius though I am not at all familiar with his work which would have frightened and repelled me had I been; startlingly graphic and grotesquely detailed woman-hating humanoid fetish paintings with pornographic overtones. I never think to check him out; he is the esteemed teacher and teach he does. The other class that he instructs is *Expressionism* which is a joy and a delight for it opens up new areas of thought and concept that I have never realized existed. I paint a city scene that is completely consumed by flocks of swarming white pigeons created by overlapping slashes of heavily textured white paint, they are the entire painting, the city barely shows; it is a monumentally *avante garde* experiment for me. I find out about using too much up-ness for in-ness, the colorful explanation by another professor concerning misapplied perspective. I also discover the meaning of the *happy accident*, the use of happenstance in a positive manner. But I have no one with whom to share my successes and my failures; I am so alone.

On many nights I sit on the edge of the tub in the close privacy of my preferred refuge, the bathroom, arms hugging my knees to my chest and sobbing long lonely tirades into the night and the clothes hamper, stuck in my prison, unable to speak with my husband for fear of reprimand. Is this, then, the way it is supposed to be? Will this be the end as well as the beginning of my life? Perhaps when I have my baby I will have someone I can love and have that love reciprocated. Just like I love my mother and she loves me; it will be just like those years when Daddy was away; we will be so close and loved and loving, my baby and me. Anyway, it is true that I have wanted a baby for a very long time, since I was a tiny child. This was where those early dreams were conceived.

I sit comfortably on the seat of the bowl day dreaming. I am passing time and soon I will go back to the more pressing matters at hand...like the new Gothic mystery novel I have secreted together with the obligatory flashlight beneath the bunched and rumpled quilt of my bed awaiting another all-night reading spree. Tomorrow my reddened eyes will tell the tale of delicious escape and the strain of reading in the dark. I run my hands impatiently over my flat twelve-year-old body searching for the most minuscule of promising swellings and find none. Once again, my mind wanders toward exotic fantasies of shapeliness and beauty. My collection of magazines tells me all about what will be expected of me in the future.

Disenchanted and bored I change the game. I am standing on a slight angle in front of the mirror that hangs on the back of the door. Now I arch my back, puffing out my flat belly into a straining curve before me, and acknowledge my breastlessness with a shrug. Arching and puffing again I think this is what it would look like to be pregnant; to have a whole entire cuddly infant growing under that straining curve of skin, what a wondrous phenomenon. I can almost feel him (her) kick if I really concentrate, gas from overeating Mom's dinner helps the illusion.

171

Then concentrating even more fiercely I slowly allow the belly to recede so that I can continue my carefully formatted script. Seated once more on the toilet I think that if I can get just the right balance and angle of abdomen overlap and squint a little I can see the tender head of my emerging newborn in the new downy covering of the pubescent mound between my legs. I stare very hard and very long, squinting, willing this fantasy into reality and smile blocking out everything around me but this deliciously tingling preview of the future.

Finally with a sigh I acknowledge to myself that the experiment has indeed failed. Dreams need more time to be willed into reality and with a shrug I exhale the pregnant puff of air. I wonder anyway if the pains of childbirth are as horrible as myth has it. I wonder what they really feel like. Lynne? A shout emerges from the nether places of the apartment. What are you doing in there all this time? Startled, I jump up, flush the toilet noisily to make it look good for the time spent hogging the bathroom, the only one in our apartment, and run the bath water. If I let it run for just the proper amount of time and dampen the towel Mommy will believe that I have bathed. Are you taking a bath in there? I hear somewhere in the distance. I have never liked being told when to bathe and the truth is that fantasy and daydreams of the future seem always to demand my attention.

The water runs at full blast. Standing before the bathroom mirror once again as if in the few moments that have just passed some monumental change may have occurred. I turn semi-sideways to check my profile, yet again, turning slowly so as not to miss any promising new bump. As deeply as I can inhale, as provocatively as I arch my back, there is precious little new to observe. Sighing resignedly but impatiently I fold three triple hems lengthwise on the bath towel and with a bothered jerk, another, carefully wrapping the padding around my chest. Turning and preening I decided that this is a distinct improvement. It won't be much longer now I hope; I imagine that I will be quite a knockout. This I know will be power. But deep in my heart of hearts I know also that soft downy baby's head will be the ultimate joy.

CHAPTER 25

The introduction of the happy accident to real life; I am pregnant, the first realization of my most essential earliest daydream and I am beside myself with joy and anticipation. The truth is that this miracle was not indeed planned but has resulted from a matter of inadvertent slippage, happily enough. I cannot tell if Steve is chagrined; he is so full of pompous pride for his plus-obvious super potency and prowess and overwhelming masculinity. If he is angry with me for this then he can add it to the by now long, ever growing list of my misdemeanors. But now I am someone! Not just any girl, not just someone's indistinguishable worthless insignificant wife, not just anyone; someone's MOTHER. I know from personal experience that mothers are remarkable, special, deserving of pedestals. Now I am going to find fulfillment. Now, I am going to be loved. Now I have someone who needs me, who will not judge me, to whom I can give my whole self, who in return will love me unreservedly. I dig back into the past for inspiration and again practice sticking my stomach out and waddling, joyously feel for gas bubbles and call the sensation *Life*. I sew quantities of maternity clothes as though nine months is eternity and begin squirreling away layette items in two colors, pink and blue (yellow and mint green are verboten in my mind as unworthy and nondescript) months too soon, the tags still attached for convenient return of the inappropriate color.

Nausea violently incapacitates me twenty-four hours of every day for nine full months and I accept it as due punishment for my guilt for having a child so soon, husband still in law school, tight budget, before my college graduation. College degrees suddenly seem meaningless from my lofty perch of high status as a MOTHER. I am going to be a mother!

Waiting for my baby is my only reality, the only thing that makes any sense to me. The rest, whether it is the entire institution of marriage, the current mode of art philosophy, or dealing with my parents' seeming lack of comprehension or empathy in regard to either my art or my marriage hovers nonsensically in the atmosphere in a fugue of irrelevance. When it comes to my art in these days my mind is centuries away from the *gestalt* of it which had I been more aware and focused might have unified the diverse elements of my Pratt experience for me and perhaps created thereby an artist of note…but in addition to the distraction of my pregnancy there were those massive walls of fear that invade my heart and soul and the thought of facing all that superb competition out there in the real world freezes me. I ignore the blaring sirens that warn me of danger ahead and choose to lose myself in the safe fantasy world of vine-covered cottages and those other pervading instincts that are part and parcel of impending motherhood, the great cure-all. My pregnancy begins before the first term of the second year is finished, and now with luck no one will be able to argue with me about 3D design or perfection of balance and in addition I will never be lonely or unloved again. That is what I am thinking.

The most important ramification of this truly happy accident is that this pregnancy will keep Steve (who has responded to the news with inchoate blasé) out of the Army and the fighting in Korea and that causes me reverberating waves of untold relief because in my mind he is all I have and I don't believe that I can survive alone without him even with all his flaws, with all my misery. Hah! I recall one of my mother's favorite one liner Yiddish anecdotes, *the food in this restaurant is sooo bad…and such small portions!* Now he will be available to continue nurturing me in his fashion, to wrap a cocoon of security around me that will keep me from worry about competition or failure. It will be fine. We will discover the secrets of marriage. We just need time. It will get better, won't it?

While I await the birth I make the daily trek to Brooklyn to my classes at Pratt and revel in Calvin Albert's figure drawing and sculpture classes, for the figure with all its inherent complexities and spatial movements and mysteries is said to be truly the basis of all art and the quintessence of sculpture although I do not quite understand the evocative sensuous abstract clay constructs that he is famous for; gargantuan, geometric and amorphic, ripped and gauged and globbed.

⋙⋘

A lithesome young man has taken his place on the large upturned wooden box painted battle ship gray enamel that is the model stand and dropped his robe. There he stands in all his glory and I don't know where to look first. Now that I am married and no longer ignorant as to physiological realities that had until recently been a deep dark frightening mystery, I should have been totally blasé and even smug to be a part of the initiate, wise and experienced. But no, I am so embarrassed that I am rendered incapable of movement, unable to begin my work. Because they are aware that I am now married, *they* know that *I* know that…not that this makes any difference considering the level of promiscuity that exists in our so Bohemian artistic environment. But here I am, a foot at least away from the work stand where my armature awaits the application of mounds of clay, the child I am carrying in my belly that should have been a reminder that I am no stranger to the entire syndrome of male plumbing and its preferred use and application, a massive wedge between me and the job at hand. Not that there haven't been models in my experience before but they have mostly been women and the few males have always taken discreet poses; bent legs, knees carefully leaning inward, no penis has been evident at least not in a obvious manner. *(Once at the Art Students League there was a gentleman who deftly slid from beneath his robe and lifted a large handkerchief into the air cavalierly allowing it to fall onto the waiting protuberance where it lay for the duration of the class only fluttering discreetly with the breezes caused by the ancient heating system and causing caught breaths and collective hearts to beat faster with delicious panic at thoughts that the pale square of cloth might become dislodged, yet I was unable to witness the most titillating part of the performance because his back was to me.)* Now here this model is, standing in that open arrogant pose in all his glory and sculpture is done in the round so I cannot as I usually do in sketch classes, change my seat and do a back view. When finally I manage to look around the studio I notice that no one

174

appears to be suffering the same embarrassment that I am; everyone male and female is concentrating on his work and I make a massive effort to rise above my mortification, work at that casual blasé artist at work facade and soon I am right there with the rest of the class immersed in applying clay to wire lost in structure and form. Still I am loath to work on the delicate details in front of my peers, blush at the thought of touching and poking, articulating the details of some stranger's penis, even just in clay, in public.

Once I have conquered my original discomfort over a naked male who is not my husband the sculpture class is my greatest joy; working in three dimensions and pulling and pushing and gouging and adding is being involved in the creation of art to the ultimate degree. Just as the living sculpture that I am creating and nurturing in my belly my own personal happy accident elates me and raises my self-esteem and especially as I proudly draw the grade of A+ in all four clay figurative attempts in class. My Uncle Irv has them cast in plaster for me, keeps a copy of each one for his own to my great pride. My mother's brother Irving is an artist of some accomplishment, owns his own advertising agency. His early renditions of Cezanne have hung in my parents' home for as long as I can remember. At the same time, my breakthroughs in painting, while the rest of the class (in general) struggles with incipiently muddy colors and escaping forms, ever cognizant of the need to be unique and excellent begin to thrill me also.

With the advent of our child Steve and I move to our own home on the cusp of Forest Hills Gardens, English Tudor, attached in a row; ours is the last in the line so I can access the backyard by merely walking around the side of the property without going through the entire house; tiny front porch, the garage going down a slanted driveway under the porch and then the house. Steve's father and mother purchased it for his older sister Elaine years before. She has moved to her mother's larger more commodious home in Rego Park inherited on her mother's death upon which the small house reverted to Steve according to plan, and thus to me. It is charming, tiny, adorable. On the sole issue of having my own home my cup runneth over. It is the fulfillment of a dream acquired through my mother whether pre or post natal which is intrinsic to the very essence of my existence. I nest with added fervor. I garden, a lifetime first and find peace in the warm and crumbling earth and the new green shoots pushing through it, and awaiting the birth of my first baby. I get lost in the busywork of gardening, revel in the results; living, growing things. I can feel their life essence, see their joy at living in their flamboyant colors and I am part of making this happen. I do have power. There is strength in the ability to create life. In the meanwhile when the new school term begins the next fall I continue my art studies at Pratt. In general except for gardening and art school and awaiting and preparing for the baby life is otherwise bleak. I am as alone as if I were single. Not what I had hoped or expected of marriage, or desired. But as an adult who is married I am free to do what I want, I think. Am I?

॰৵৵৽

Small and dark, Cher-like and shy with masses of black curly hair, Jackie Ferrara also alumni of Forest Hills High School and fellow student with me at Pratt and still single, listens patiently, blankly and impotently to my whining rants as the Metropolitan Avenue elevated train rocks and rolls from side to side on our daily voyage to Brooklyn to attend our art classes, brings to the conversation only her brief and pathetic experiences listening to her parents' petty battles at home. Our major point of communion is the fact that we are both only children, lacking that vital ability, experience, comfort of commiseration with siblings; our home experience is exactly the same, except for the minor differences of Italian and Jewish heritage, and the pointed educational contrast between our parents. But we are connected in truth by our mutual passion for art and hunger to learn all there is to know of the why and how, particularly the how of it. Finally, I have someone who comprehends, shares my dedication.

With Steve still occupied with law school most nights and me lacking a driver's license, accompanied by my growing stomach I hop blithely onto my bicycle as any teenager would and ignoring the lump that threatens to impede my effort at pedaling traverse the several miles up good old Continental Avenue, past the old Midway theatre through Forest Hills Gardens to Jackie's house, one of many identical tiny three story shingled cottages in this area located at the further end past Metropolitan Avenue, to do homework and discuss our art and lives; finally a friend from a similar family, although her parents are nothing like mine. She is almost a sister. I am hoping this baby will be a girl, and the one after that another, so that my daughters will always have a sister to confide in, to share with.

We snack on bologna (which I have never tasted before in my life) sandwiches and *caponatina*, her mother's brilliant and esoteric, to me, combination of tuna and canned eggplant appetizer, and I try to explain with an affectation of authority to Jackie that which I do not understand myself about love and marriage and the expectance of a baby. I am home long before I hear Steve's key in the lock, taking a position that suggests I have never left. There is no particular rule regarding consent for me to socialize or to leave the house in the evening but instinctively I am aware that if permission were to be requested the response would be *no*. One thing I am certain about; he will be too tired and preoccupied to pay any attention to me anyway. If he knew where I had been I would probably be forbidden to go again; I can't take that chance. I rejoice in a modicum of independence in a life encompassed by rote and captivity. It is my first attempt at civil disobedience or defensive combat in my battle for my inalienable civil rights in what later comes to be known as the Feminist Movement.

Conquering new worlds at Pratt Institute in the late '50s, preparing to vanquish the world in coming days Jackie and I are joined at the hip, and with Barbara Domroe now along we are the Three Musketeers. We are spending glorious times hanging out at Jakes Art Supplies before Patti Smith and Robert Mapplethorpe were ever around; we are passing the time of day touching, fondling, deep in lust with the varied and intoxicating art supplies, paints, pastels, rice papers, brushes themselves. We mercilessly tease Barbara who is always telling us with vociferous gusto about the newest particular work she is *gonna* create which she describes in mouth-watering detail. Olive green, yellow ochre, burnt sienna, her preferred colors, touches of teal and crimson, strong cascading shapes connected with strong slashes of black a la Roualt; she has it all planned. Just do it we say with exasperation, stop talking about it. I tuck this barely cogent lesson learned away for future reference. I am totally absorbed for weeks in an assignment for the class called 2D Design, rendering detailed copies of a magazine advertisement containing many faceted crystal wine glasses, bunches of grapes, strawberries, every seed and reflection and highlight delineated; a mechanical rendition of the cross section of an old hand-operated pencil sharpener rendered in fluorescent pastels on taupish gray oatmeal paper. These are days of glory, full and exhausting. At the end of each school day I exit my schoolgirl world and return to the other part of my schizoid existence, my marriage, home to my ersatz loving husband. There is not that much to do; a quick stop at the super market, a bit of laundry, vacuum the small wood floor area, straighten the bed. Neither of us is home all day, Steve does not return until eleven at night.

ै❀ॐ

I open the windows wide and get into bed, at night as we retire to sleep and Steve gets up and closes them. I can't sleep without fresh air, I tell him at which point he informs me that night air causes pneumonia.

Germs cause pneumonia, I say...

...I want that window shut, he answers firmly.

The battle continues, I am Laurel or Abbot, Steve is Hardy or Costello until one of us waiting for the slow and even breathing of the other drops off to sleep and the other wins by default. The window is then either wide open or tightly closed. We have been considering ourselves since our marriage to be adults but right now we are two little kids in the midst of a schoolyard squabble: *Oh yeah? Yeah!* One of us is smirking with self-congratulation; I am frequently victorious but distraught even in victory.

177

We blindly follow custom and rote sharing the morning breakfast ritual; each morning is exactly the same. I make the coffee and the pitiful comic drama plays out as usual. I pour two cups of coffee. He tells me not to stir my coffee, the cup is too full. I look him in the eye brimming over with repressed frustration and hostility and after adding the milk stir the cup until it overflows. Then I drink some staring directly at him as I perform my ritual act and pour the leftover coffee from the saucer back into my cup and drink it watching him wince as I do. The next morning he rushes to be the first for the coffee pot and pours me only half a cup.

I want a whole cup Steve, I say to him, controlling my facial muscles, craving some manner of power.

You can't have a full cup because you'll only spill it when you stir it. Besides, you only drink half a cup anyway.

But I want the TOP half Steve. And I get up and pour the second half filling the cup, pour in the milk watching him every moment and finally stir the coffee with deliberation so that the liquid spills over into the saucer. He recoils. It is a small measure of rebellion but keeps somehow some bizarre and delicate measure of sanity for me. And is too innocuous and unimportant an issue for him to make much more of a fuss.

You're crazy, he mumbles. I'm done with this. He gets up to leave, mumbling under his breath about my mother and my aunt Etta, that old familiar refrain.

Something strange happens, a shot of adrenalin, maybe, maybe just that elusive sense of self realized, of the return however slight of power lost or found maybe for the first time. I always feel stronger and more confident after one of these—what I fondly refer to as—*coffee episodes* as though they are a part of a favorite sitcom, *I Love Lucy,* or *The Honeymooners*, a Milton Berle sketch; the famous coffee episode. *To the moon, Alice,* would be his obvious retort if he was aware of my fantasy.

But it is not just the humiliation and criticism. Day to day reality is an intolerable weight to bear. The end pieces of packaged bread may not be eaten because they are there for the sole purpose of protecting the rest of the loaf, my husband informs me. I live in a rigid world of constraint horrific to me. I have dubbed myself a free spirit. I have waited all my life to be out of my parents' house, out from under their control, waiting to have my own life, but I have gone from the frying pan into the fire. Now I am captive in another jail. What good has it all done me? I am prisoner in a dungeon surrounded by walls of tight unyielding rules. What about finally being an adult? What about that long sought freedom that meant so much to me? What about my creative nature, my craving for diversity, my artistic soul? Everything in my new world goes against my nature. How can I even to please the most insistent insipient chauvinist restrict my laundry, shopping, cleaning, ironing, meal planning to rigid calendar blueprints, have no initiative or inspiration of my own?

How can you make chicken on Wednesday, he demands astonished. Chicken is on Friday, Wednesday is lamb chops; *my mother always*...he stops in the middle of the sentence recalling his own edict that his mother is not to be mentioned. This doesn't change the agenda. Washing is done on Monday, ironing belongs to Tuesday. Underwear, towels, and even socks must be ironed. These are not guidelines but rules and the rules are absolute. My innate sense of rebellion will not allow me to comply. So, I am punished for failures and misdemeanors and aberrations. I am refused a goodnight kiss. For a girl who has never learned that sex and love are not one and the same I feel unloved when sexual communication is denied to me, live for those moments of warmth ensconced in my beloved's arms. The knowledge of this phenomenon gives Steve his most useful tool in the battle to control me which he considers his right and duty. It reinforces my knowledge that physical contact is equal to love. If the chore program for the day hasn't been fulfilled I am in trouble. This criteria carries over into even my most intimate and personal ablutions; I am not permitted into bed if I have not showered in the evening. Neither the morning nor the afternoon is sufficient. I am right back there in the home of my parents the recalcitrant child taking orders from an adult.

But still I love. And love. Why? Is it Steve or Love that is my passion? Do I even know what Love is or should be? Such a lovely boy, a good boy, responsible and ambitious, everyone says. How lucky you are. But Steve will not speak to me about it, about anything; there is only sparse conversation on the most mundane level between us, during the rare times when he is home. I am helpless to know what to do to change things. There is no source of information to seek or to obtain in 1959. Days continue, filled with routine and sameness. Weekends roll around and there is protocol to be followed, no matter what.

৵৵

Friendly jubilant dinners are prepared and hosted with expectation weekend after weekend, become an undertaking done ultimately by rote and habit; our guests are couples we have met on our honeymoon, Steve's old college and law school buddies. None of my old friends or new ones are ever included; they are deemed unworthy, lacking in one way or the other, superfluous. These social evenings are born of my incipient need accomplished at my insistence; for some inexplicable reason he does not object. This becomes my only human contact, companionship, apart from school where I am that other person; Saturday night dinners for our married friends followed by Monopoly or Scrabble. Steve refuses to be my partner in these games. I horse around too much, constantly make jokes; I do not play well enough; I am not serious enough about winning. Winning is everything, along with the pursuit of his superiority and control over me; he is somehow compelled to continually embarrass and belittle me. Soon, it becomes obvious to everyone but Steve that he is humiliating no one but himself. I am taken to one side again and again and told I need to do something, that they are on my side. *They* are all Steve's friends. But I am an ostrich, a large ugly ungainly bird in love. I only want Steve to love me. I love *security*; I need his love to insure it. I am unaware of all of this. All I know or want to know is love. That is all I want. I smile and thank them for their concern and walk away. I dare not do anything that might cause me to lose him, to lose the security that he represents; this grand illusion.

The little house in Forest Hills begins to symbolize the approaching fulfillment of all my surface dreams or maybe my mother's; finally my own home, a garden and a shade tree, a patio and an entire yard. With this new reason for boundless joy I can hide my personal misery and fear away deep inside, while I wallow in homemaking and gardening with a passion that replaces all of that frustrated unrequited love that I have always thought was part and parcel of marriage, the birthright of loving. I pick up my mother's magazine clipping obsession, thirsting for ideas, paint room and doors and trim in assortments of different colors, purple, teal, olive green, make drapes from mill end remnants and create my stage set for happiness. I take long walks through the famous Forest Hills Gardens as well, and rediscover Joyce Keller now Mrs. Reese Galyon of the original JUGs in the supermarket one day also awaiting the birth of her own first child. We soon find that we are kindred spirits, refinish furniture, sew maternity dresses first and then tiny baby outfits, knit piles of tiny sweaters, caps, mittens, coverlets. We become devotees of all the home magazines and their amalgam of recipes and craft projects and fill the hours with tasks and keep-busy jobs vying for the ultimate in creativity, seeking identity. We have no clue what that is, or where to find it. She is enhancing her existence, I am hiding from mine mimicking my mother's pet avocation.

Steve has finally arrived home after my long day alone and he is enveloped by the arms of his huge deep easy chair feet up on the ottoman covered by his New York Times *which is opened before him like the sails of a small sloop, content in his private world. I crawl under the billowing carefully balanced paper and slither up onto his chest beguilingly. What are you doing behind all this paper, Stevie, I whine in my most alluring voice; tell me about your day. I am hungry for information about the real world, needing stories and anecdotes to fill the void in me, in my sterile existence. What are you doing, he gripes back at me? Can't I read my paper I peace? Leave me alone now, go on, go. I try to seduce him with soft kisses, gentle sensuous strokes, to no avail. He brushes me off as if I am a gnat crawling on him with tiny hair like feet, tickling him, something to be swept away. Go on now, he says, go make dinner or something. Sometimes he can be cajoled into some brief snuggling, a few kisses, not for long. Sometimes he relaxes, softens into my old Stevie smiles and does his crackly off key imitation of Frank Sinatra... when it rains it always rains, pennies from heaven...*

There is barely time for me to dwell upon my sad and empty marriage. Between our two schedules Steve and I are proverbial ships passing in the night. We come together for that customary nightly session of automatic scheduled lovemaking, daily dose of connection, feeling proud of our obedience to rote, to the institution of marriage, our failure to miss one opportunity to indulge in adult marital activity as though this bestows upon us the mantle of maturity, finding momentary comfort in connecting. The sex part is the only part of this union that works. Since love and sex are still confused issues in my mind, I continue to believe that I have love and I am willing to fight to keep it. We are still making love but we are not manufacturing a credible product.

But we are manufacturing something after all. To my hands spread across my swollen abdomen it feels like a barrel or maybe a knapsack full of monkeys. I keep my hands most times on my belly feeling the activity inside. I giggle at the incongruous thought that I am a massive industrial capsule a fact that is mirthfully corroborated when I read that two monkeys have survived an American space trip in May while Joyce and I are walking all over the neighborhood waiting impatiently in a kind of sisterly tandem for our first babies to be born, completely ignorant of babies, inclined to relate more to thoughts of gamboling monkeys, probably see little difference between the two. We watch the changing forms of spring and summer gardens along our path, and finally the repetition on every block in every garden of the colorful August pastel blooms of the popular Rose of Sharon tree exploring, killing time; waiting. This baby is trying my patience, gestates for nearly ten incomprehensible months and appears to be doing calisthenics inside of me in jarring and un-cadenced tempo to the hands of the clock.

Steve and I do battle over his name when Bruce finally arrives on August 12, 1959. I am cheering for David, it was the name of my beloved grandfather's brother, after all, but Steve says David is too ordinary, everyone is named David. It is not, I complain it's a beautiful name right there in the bible, David the Giant killer; he finally agrees with grave condescension. You may use it for his middle name. I give you permission. I am aghast, I have just learned an important life lesson; I need to have permission from my husband to even name my child. Something is very wrong here. It is impossible for me to ignore the other new mothers and the way they are treated with respect, consideration, adoration, and reverence, wondering why I am not.

I have noticed the headlines on page one of Steve's times which he has left folded on his armchair the next day when I bring the new baby home and hovering in the periphery of my existence is the news that work is beginning on the three hundred and twenty million dollar Verrazano Bridge connecting Brooklyn to Staten Island; in my own world this is a million miles away. In September Little Rock restrains mobs as schools open now integrated by law and the Guggenheim Museum opens in New York in October but not being a great fan of modern art *per se* and being totally involved in the wonder that is my new baby son I am underwhelmed by the opening, have no desire whatsoever to visit this phenomenon, remain disinterested in the rest. The Verrazano Bridge is of negative interest to me, I can barely visualize that part of the city, Bay Ridge or something, don't recall ever being there. I am also ambivalent about the fact that rock and roll is being accepted as a new transformative music form, I still listen to classical pop, ballad and swing, show tunes; these are both my oracle and my instruction manual. It is all floating about on the fringes of my world now that I am finally a mother and this new motherhood is my entire existence.

࿐

I lean into the cradling security of crisp antiseptic and institutional efficiency and concentrate my every sense onto the minute being that I hold so neatly and securely in the crook of my arm. I am encased immobile in the crisp white tightly tucked sheets in this hard hospital bed. I think sadly and despairingly as I poke at the jelly soft flesh of my belly that tight and hard again will never describe my own body again. The clean antiseptic smell is strong, efficient, yet comforting at the same time. I rub my face against his tiny creature warmth. I delicately draw my nostrils through the warm silky down of his head, still somewhat pointed from the intensity of his expulsion. I look deeply into his dark gray liquid eyes as his tiny hand curves around my finger and as incredible concoctions of emotions surge through my body, become thoughts that bounce and tumble through my mind; I vow my unspoken and undying fealty to this tender and innocent creature. The overpowering feelings well up from somewhere in my toes and ankles and don't even begin to wane until like a surging tide they have risen to the top of my head nearly choking me en route and leaving in their wake a powerful sensation almost totally ineffable. I know at that moment that I will be his willing slave for life and I don't care. It is a kind of *rush* that for me has no choice but to become addictive. Another addiction; I must have an addictive personality.

As if it were second nature to me, I reach with one hand for the pastels and sketch pad that I have carefully placed on the bedside table, knowing in advance that my innate nature will surface and I will want to capture his likeness on paper, and while balancing the soft and fragrant package that is this infant, begin a drawing of that precious face. My obsessive need to express myself through my art is so instinctive, so implicit to my being, that I give the process, the impulse, no conscious thought. Within a few years more, I have piles of them, sketches of the different children at different phases, starting with each one, mere moments after birth. They are my most treasured possessions.

Steve regards my avocation as something that diminishes my capacity as a mother, a wife, as a human being as if there is only so much to draw on from within, doesn't wish me to waste my resources and he admonishes me accordingly. He has confiscated or maybe just adopted my precious and extensive childhood stamp collection filled with the most artistic and colorful stamps with little regard to value purchased with meticulously accumulated allowance and babysitting monies from assorted catalogues and abundant solicitations, added it to his own painstakingly filled with contributions from relatives, nothing bought. Any activity that is not directed precisely at the chores and responsibilities of existence not on the joys is wasteful and verboten.

Years later, his new wife discovers the stash of drawings stored at the house, my old home, her new home and destroys them as though the doing so will banish all remnants of memory of his former life with me from existence, will somehow destroy my own memory as though she had stuck pins into dolls in some insane voodoo rite and delights in telling me so.

Celebrity is mine for three days and then it is home to reality. The first hurdle when the baby is eight days old is Bruce's *briss*, ritual circumcision, performed at home by a rabbi specialist, called a *Moyel*. Steve and Aaron politely joined by the obligatory audience are laughing uproariously over the quintessential *Cross Eyed Moyel* Joke that Aaron regurgitates on cue whenever a boy is born. *At a public urinal, the cockeyed Moyel lacking aim accidentally pisses into his neighbor's shoe*, har, har. Not only am I underwhelmed but the entire thought of what is to happen makes my blood run cold. I am ordered to hold the tiny penis of my baby son while this greasy looking bearded monster who reeks of alcohol, a form of schnapps, cuts off a part of him after slightly sedating him with dark red syrupy wine that portends a bloodletting yet to come. Crying, I refuse creating astonishment disappointment and fury in my husband. This is what I am supposed to *do* as a Jewish mother. Bruce's father finally steps in shaking his head from side to side, what is this world coming to, to do the honor but I am made to watch. I close my eyes in revolt as well as revulsion. Then there is the nurse that Aaron gets that I don't want to make certain that his grandson is properly taken care of because I am obviously considered inept for some reason, who completely takes over all aspects of my baby's care to the point where I must ask her permission to hold him, or even visit him in his nursery. But after a couple of days of this I take a deep breath, utilize my innate right as mother; I fire her, and take over the job. Once again both Steve and Aaron are aghast that I have made such a move of my own volition contrary to their wishes and direction. I find that caring for an infant is all instinct for me, which is a real relief; I have a new revelation, it is all about logic. I give my babies Pablum and strained bananas from the very beginning; they are never hungry, never suffer from colic, I never need to walk them all night long to control constant screaming. My theory is that everything in life is based on the simple logical fact that is they are clean and dry and their stomachs are full and they are loved they will be fine. They all sleep through the night at five days old. It is so easy, makes it so simple to have so many.

❧❧

During these times of gestating and birthing babies, except for those portraits of the babies, my artwork suffers from some neglect since all my creativity is being absorbed into my babies' growth and in the enhancement of my nest. Now and then, I manage to do something but can't really sustain the interest or concentration. Being a homemaker is such mindless contentment. Waiting for the births of babies is so smugly satisfying. It is almost enough to hide the obvious deficiencies of my subsistence.

This doesn't last forever. Soon, I am fighting off ideas for paintings, and find myself being pulled back into my world of art albeit a narrow one. One of the attributes of having our own home tiny as it is is that now I have space to work on my paintings and when the first bloom of excitement owing to motherhood wears off and life settles into routine I feel that odd tickle, that urge to begin again a tentative search for the ultimate painting expression. Suddenly all Steve's pretense of pride, approval, or interest in my art has disappeared. A new dynamic has arrived. I am at first chastened for allowing the dirty smelly paints into the pure and sanctified home to contaminate the environment of his child and then finally forbidden actually to paint at all. But I have always been willful and stubborn, and denying me art is like denying me breath. I find ways to work when he is not around, and hide my supplies and paintings carefully when he is expected home seeking further hiding places with each of Steve's furiously jubilant discoveries of the last. Discovery results in expulsion to the trash bin. It is a balancing act, marriage, motherhood and art; I teeter on the high wire juggling all the elements of my fragile existence.

I used to treasure those moments early in the morning when Steve was getting ready for work. Now I watch tense, impatient, for him to leave, that is when my private time with my son Bruce David begins. He casts that wide gleeful smile at me, rapidly kicking his arms and legs in excitement. I pick him up, change him, feed him, and bring him to the bedroom. I am lying on the bed, propped up on pillows, my legs bent like a mountain, baby against my

184

thighs. He has his fingers curled around mine, pulling my hands up and down. He is strong. He should be, he was nearly nine pounds at birth, 32 inches long, after a nearly ten-month gestation. For a while I make faces at him enjoying as he giggles until he is helpless with mirth, and sighs. I make sounds at him, mamama, dadada, bababa. He moves his lips, concentrating. I begin to exercise his arms, back and forth like scissors and then his beefy little legs. Back and forth, up and down. I pull forward on his chunky arms when he strains against me and he favors me with a huge grin as he nearly sits then stands. Wobbling, he stands there holding on of course, grinning from ear to ear, swaying. And I gradually ease him down to sit, to rest. He begins to kick his legs and wave his arms, reaching out to me, making a strange grunting sort of cry; he wants more.

Hickory dickory … DOCK…the mouse ran up the CLOCK. He is filling in the words of nursery rhymes by six months, walking all over the house like a sand crab in this strange low, four-wheeled apparatus, a walker, scurrying flying bumping when he is five months. Don't rush him, they say, you will ruin his legs and spine, but he is a small ox, a tank, strong and healthy. At eight months he is walking by himself. Letting go of tables and chairs and running across the room to the other side. Steve and I have all we can do to keep up with him, to catch him. He runs all over giggling like mad, and we are all laughing and tears are rolling down our cheeks. My baby son is like a bumble bee, he is physiologically unable to walk but doesn't know it so he keeps on walking just as the aeronautically challenged bumble bee keeps right on flying. He has brought us closer together in spite of ourselves sharing in the enjoyment of this constant stage show that is the baby.

᷾·᷾

He is very busy at sixteen months, seriously carries his pail and tools around the house pretending to fix things. We watch him and *qvell* at our small son's brilliance. He has a screw driver and pliers that he has taken from my tool box, his treasures. He has no patience for plastic imitations in bright colors. But he is not fixing things. He is surreptitiously removing as many screws and nuts from as many pieces of furniture or toys that he can find, he is collecting hardware in his pail. Soon, we are experiencing the ultimate inevitable collapse of our belongings in rapid sequence like a long secession of falling dominoes.

Well into 1960, there are other dominos falling. I am reclaiming Steve's Times from the day before and reading them with my second cup of morning coffee after he has left. I read about black sit-ins at lunch counters in North Carolina, an U2 spy plane is captured, and Nazi death-camp chief Adolph Eichmann has been captured in Buenos Aires. What does it mean to me right now when the Supreme Court rules that using illegally acquired evidence is unconstitutional? I live in the United States of America, I am blessed; we have Justice in a world where that is something unique. Although I am excited when John Fitzgerald Kennedy is elected president this November especially since I have voted for him this colossally exhilarating first time I have ever been able to vote I am preoccupied with my growing family.

The art world is reveling in the new Minimalism…what you see is what you get. It is said that this could be an answer to President John Fitzgerald Kennedy's fervent plea that we *ask not what your country can do for you, ask what you can do for your country*. I take this under advisement and begin a series of three landscapes with simplistic nearly geometric designs painted in flat modulated colors devolving into a years' long frustrating struggle. This new young progressive president has devised the new deal, proposed a new frontier, is opening doors for a Civil Rights movement and for the leadership in these matters of Martin Luther King Junior. It is all very exciting, but what does this have to do with me? Will it help me with my painting; will it make my husband pay attention to me?

࿐

Night law school continues for Steve, and its natural evolution is multiple meetings of Bar Association, Kiwanis, Knights of Pythias, and on and on for Steve has learned well his father's lesson that it is not what you know but whom you know. In earlier years I hear that catechism many times and never cease to shudder. I never realize what far-reaching ramifications it will have in my future, and in the lives of our children.

But my general discontent with everything that marriage has turned out to be, as well as with my sporadic and tentative attempts and the resultant failures in my artistic aspirations, has another aspect. All of a sudden I am a master creator. My painting which is so cruelly forbidden and needs to be attended to with great cunning and duplicity and accomplished in the gravest secrecy is frustratingly out of reach as well in terms of achieving my creative visions is nearly too much trouble to even attempt. As much as I try, as intensely as I experiment and redo entire paintings over and over again I am unable to make those colors do what I want them to do, sing and interact with each other; forms do not take their required shape and volume, lines fail to obey my direction. However, this absence and failure becomes sublimated in the totally satisfying and infallible act of creating the perfect living breathing sculpture that not only is faultless in its design and execution but surpasses all other sculpture or other art forms in that it is able to grow and change and emerge into something else. It is a veritable chrysalis, as well as an exquisitely perfect work of art. Each excursion into this new media brings forth a combination

186

of genes from two sides, an infinite Chinese menu of choices that is a surprise right up until the last moment, one from column A, one from column B, and then continues to emerge and change before our very eyes. Then relatives, friends, and passersby can indulge in that common game of comparing eyes, noses, ears, mouths, hair, etc., to various relatives, and the guessing game begins. No one, however, ever criticizes this work of art, no one would dare presume to. It is automatically considered to be perfect. Suddenly, in at least one facet of my life I cannot be criticized; at least for the creature itself. What I do now, now that the production part is done is fair game. Everything depends on my actions which is in some ways a daunting responsibility given my well publicized inadequacies.

CHAPTER 26

It is all a jumble of technical mystical Black Magic words that are only peripherally available to me at this time, permitted to be used and understood by a select brotherhood that has no relation to any part of my conscious life; they never occur to me in part because I have no familiarity at all with them and even less comprehension. I don't even *begin* to understand, the one course I have not taken in my desire to inundate my world with art is Psych 101; I don't even know that it exists. I dare not even venture into thoughts of analyzing his behavior in fact this never crosses my mind. I have come to believe that Steve is and always will be, I muse, a total emotional cripple and I suspect something worse than that. I have somehow become aware that there is no marriage and never will be. I have finally realized this, and spend long hours trying to make my peace with the knowledge.

There are certain accepted verities. Marriage is forever and divorce anathema and unspeakable. That's it in a nutshell, period; the end. I know this one thing at this grand age, 20 years. But I have solved the problem. I will be surrounded by my adored and adoring children and we will all live happily after. Steve will continue as he likes best as a peripheral apparition hovering in the background and will have no bearing on our existence. This fiction allows me to survive in a world of my own making that grows more and more schizoid and intolerable day by day in spite of its promise as somewhere in the real world Bob Dylan scores in Greenwich Village, Chubby Checker introduces the twist, and gentle artist-writer James Thurber, who is one of Mom's favorites, dies. Fiction will never be the same, she mourns. Mr. Blandings has built his dream house, I have mine, and she has finally abandoned that dream.

I have given up trying to elude Steve's sharp eye and nose and eschewed my art at least for now too dispirited and exhausted by the battle to continue. Soon fiction becomes my method of sublimation and piles of completed novels lie on every surface, the latest lies face down awaiting completion. I read, escape into fantasy every living daylight and nighttime moment that can be stolen from Steve's precious *chores* and deep into the sleepless nights. I have found the ultimate of weapon in passivity. Many times the chores are left undone because fantasy has become more acceptable than reality. I have long since ceased to care if Steve is or is not approving of my housekeeping. There are many forms of escape.

We hang out at this playground behind the local school, this group of young mothers and our toddlers and infants in their carriages mostly from our own block. Soon these women become an integral part of my life on Selfridge Street. There is Barbara who has her babies in the house naturally, and lets them eat dirt in the yard in the same spot that their drooping diapers leak into; there is cousin Susan's friend another Barbara whose son Kevin is so over cared for and over cleaned and overprotected that in turns I feel inadequate or horrified. I swear that I will never be guilty of strangling my children this way and I never have been. I don't believe in extremes of either kind. It doesn't seem reasonable. I am becoming obsessed with the idea of reason. Reason which is the greatest thing missing from my life in general. Then there is Mira whose child is the tiny precious doe-eyed Heidi. It is into Mira's sympathetic and patient ear that I pour tales of Steve's neglect and abuse. There is one other girl whose name escapes me at this late time who never becomes a friend because she is DIVORCED.

I hold her in contempt for any marriage can work according to pompously self-righteous inadequate unsuccessful me if the two people involved will only work at it. This does not it appears apply to me possibly because I am willing, although Steve is not, to work at it. She is a tarnished and scarlet person in my own intolerant eyes. And yet, with great sanctimony and carefully adjusted blinders on I ignore my own precipitously precarious situation. It will work, soon, it will work, everything will change, whispers my alter ego Pollyanna into my waiting ear.

ॐ✑

Any visit at all is always welcome, breaks the monotony, places a small vibrant crack in the fragile though rigid wall of survival that contains my existence. Aaron visits frequently which has become almost tolerable and Steve's grandmother Nany makes the trip from Cedarhurst by train and bus and taxi from time to time. Nany is his family, all that there is on his mother's side since she is gone except for his Aunt Rose with whom Nany lives. Steve and I drive some Sunday mornings in rare moments of marital interaction and intimacy between pregnancies to play tennis at the high school in Laurence near where Nany and Rose and her family live while Mom joyfully babysits but former tomboy and promising athlete that I have always been I am an unworthy adversary not sufficiently adept or competitive for the Olympic star that Steve sees himself to be. But we still visit the family anyway.

CHAPTER 27

Quaint age darkened shingled cottages with green shutters and white trim, fragrant rolling rich green lawns surrounded by masses of fluffy azure and violet hydrangeas and brilliant orange day lilies provide the background for Bruce's first summer; we spend a week at a bungalow colony in the Catskills with Alice and Sandy and their kids chasing baby Bruce barely one year old, full of energy and invention, all over the place totally exhausted with this activity. I am feeling a certain numbness, wondering why I am so depressed. His platinum blond curls bouncing with his every move, Bruce toddles all over the place charming everyone with his beaming smile, walking and talking at ten months old. There was an old woman who lived in a shoe, Jack be nimble Jack be quick, Mary had a little lamb, Hickory dickory dock... He has a complete repertoire which I have taught him, worked on since he was born playing with him all day long. Now that Bruce is growing, turning into an actual child, I need a baby; crave that tiny creature growing beneath my skin, that tiny helpless creature swaddled in my arms, visualize the high and glory of the birth and its attending days and rewards. I manage this feat of daring by the judicious and carefully directed use of a straight pin to the contents of Steve's bedside table top drawer. As a reward for my ingenuity I am cursed with morning sickness again.

The green countryside and distant mountains highlighted by a glorious summer sky are witness to our erstwhile enjoyment of our vacation, planting ideas for future art in my subconscious. In the company of his old friends Steve is clowning around with his usual goofy aplomb, dives into the glistening blue pool and hits bottom with a jolting thud nearly kills himself, indeed, knocks himself out. Left alone as he plays and cavorts like a child himself I have been going through empty motions of enjoying our vacation, really somewhere else. I have mixed feelings as they drag him from the frigid water, icy chills running through my arms and legs and stomach; with luck, maybe he's dead. Omigod, what will I do if he's dead! Panic at thoughts that I could lose Steve, lose my loved one, my husband, be alone begin to overwhelm me. I watch in combined terror and wonder as they administer to the victim who instantly becomes the hero of the day and life continues as usual.

Thick heavy steaming summer air diffused with petroleum fumes, auto horns vies for honors for loudest and most obnoxious aural assault as trapped in Sunday morning traffic some time later that year we attempt the awful drive to Aunt Rose's house in Cedarhurst; Steve refuses to pull over for a moment as I am overcome with nausea never a good traveler, even worse now that I am pregnant once again. I grit my teeth and clamp my hand over my mouth, threaten to vomit in his car or right out of the window and he has a second thought and finally stops. Hurry, get out of the car and get it over with, he says impatiently. And watch the car...

Life on Selfridge Street is an exercise in performance art; I perform the role of suburban matron all the elements in play; baby carriages, pregnancy, maternity clothing. I am performing the part, cooking and crafting and nesting; talking baby care and clothes and recipes, taking gourmet cooking classes with friends. Watching the children in the sandbox and the swings, teaching my child about life, and being important; ambiguous about wanting the pregnancy to be finished desperately wanting to know if it is another boy or the girl I crave. I am waiting for labor to begin, hopefully and fearfully. Desiring and dreading; wanting the baby, not wanting for this respected condition to be over. Secret stash of pink little girl outfits, sweaters with hoods and button on mittens, my own design, knitting in front of the television while Steve is out late at his meetings, watching cheesy old movies like *An Affair to Remember* and *Peter Ibbetsen*; dreaming my favorite fantasies.

Bruce though is a challenge escapes in the middle of the night as we sleep the deep exhausted sleep of long busy days despite a deadlock at the top of the front door. The police bring him back at two a.m. I place a huge sheet of plywood over his crib and confine him with harnesses; I am a monster. I am a mother alone without support or help from father who only undermines my efforts. But there are very real terrors associated with the guardianship of children.

Chocolate covered cherries; this intense craving that I have developed for them has become the feature of this pregnancy. I am known to leave the house in desperation at any hour of night or day assuming Steve has arrived home consumed by my obsession for them. I have secret hidden emergency rations, stashes all over the house to make certain that I am never faced with a scarcity of them. Aside from the cherries the next best thing happening for the second time is that once again I am no longer lonely; the only time I am not alone it seems is when I am pregnant. I will presently have my new baby, and this is the ultimate bond; this is my realer than life addiction.

We become a family for rare moments raucous and hysterical with laughter chasing Bruce around the house Bruce giggling madly. It never lasts beyond the moment. Now I am moving ahead, Joyce is driving, Bruce is in the car bed attached to the back seat of Steve's Chevy and I am on my way to take the test for my longed for and coveted driver's license. Although she is driving now with Steve's tentative permission, has acquired her own license, she does not have access to a car; her husband takes theirs to work each day. How much longer can Joyce and I go shopping with both babies by bus and subway folding and unfolding strollers babies sleeping on the floor nestled into our spread coats while we try on clothing, the best cost-free activity that we can imagine.

☙◊❧

The future looms like a Technicolor movie preview in slow motion; the days appear longer, the nights interminable as time passes and the date for the birth comes closer and closer. To the horror of my elders and contemporaries, I make the trip to New York City with Mira for a grand Italian luncheon in a murky basement *trattoria* aptly named *The Grotto*, Chianti bottles hanging in raffia twists from the ceiling, and the popular Broadway show, *Camelot* starring Bob Goulet. The food which I have gorged upon sits like a pile of hot rocks on top of my baby who is pressing sharply and heavily on my pelvis as the story unfolds in music and song, and wishfully seeking the advent of labor pains in indigestion I wonder if I will make it back home or go into labor in the theater. Strangely, somewhat disappointed I do. Make it home.

Politically correct and realistically expedient as it seems in these times to schedule births by appointment the date selected for the birth finally arrives. Fortuitously or not there is a major snowstorm the day before and I tempt fate yet again by spending the entire day building a giant St. Bernard sculpture in front of the house the proverbial keg hanging from his neck, reminiscent of the one Janie and I built not so many years ago. Are you crazy? My friends express their horror and dismay yet again at my aberrant behavior. What self-respecting pregnant woman does this sort of thing? *They* are all sitting around being pampered and fussed over and waited on... *Beulah, peel me a grape, get me a boy to fan me.* They are channeling *May West* and I am someone else maybe George Gershwin's *Porgy's Bess*. I am bad for the gender. A surge of adrenalin makes me redo the tile floor of the entire dining room, blue and green checkerboard; Bruce gets into the mastic when I am not paying full attention looking forward at my job in progress fat and awkward, unable to twist and look behind me, he sneaks away with the can and he *shmears* up the ivory ceramic tile that covers the entire bathroom with his beefy little hands. Then I need to clean it up; it, and all of him, hands and clothes and face and hair. My appointment is at nine am. I am tired and I have tile mastic on my hands, under my fingernails, but I am on time, with bells on.

Remembering that sweet connection with my mother, musing pleasurably about mothers and daughters I am ecstatic when Wendi is finally born; a daughter is what I have been craving. I am filled with great joy and plans for our future, remembering my own childhood. They inundate me with flowers and gifts and then they fight over her name, Mom and Aaron. Aaron says, Vindi, what kind of name is that after he and Mom are reduced to tears of mirth but it is better than Kim. Their hilarity knows no bounds when they dramatize the possible future act of calling my little daughter to dinner, what will you call out, Kim, come, squeals my mother dramatically barely able to speak, or, come, Kim, or maybe Kim, Kim. Kim is the Yiddish word for come of course. There follows a great slapping of thighs and wiping of wet red faces. You want to laugh I ask them silently as usual in my head? Go see a movie. My pitiful life is not here for your amusement, a naughty voice whines in my head. There is enough entertainment out there. Truman Capote's *Breakfast at Tiffany's* is being filmed in New York, Paul Newman is starring in *The Hustler*, and *West Side Story* is debuting on Broadway. You find my life so amusing? Don't bother to see a show, better still, write one.

The very next day after Wendi's birth which is March 20, I hear on the radio that President Kennedy is increasing aid to South-East Asia. How nice for them, I think. Then, on April 12 when Wendi is barely three weeks old the USSR puts the first man in space. I am neither supposed to know about these things or to care; there is no one to discuss it all with. This changes for a while when my Uncle Sam and his wife Midori come to stay with us with their boys, it is the only place they have to go like Uncle Irv and Aunt Harriet lived with Mom and Daddy and me after the end of World War II, all of us in Parkchester in that tiny apartment in the Bronx. The greater my responsibilities become the more intensely I feel those vibrations of insecurity enveloping me. I am earning without any effort on my part Steve's caustic moniker, *Mother of the Year* directed at me more and more frequently by him with great sarcasm.

Wendi is a tiny kewpie doll, button nose and ice blue eyes, and one lock of tawny hair that loops naturally into a curl right on top of her head screaming out for a pink bow. Finally I have a baby girl. I am mad with acquiring baby girl outfits, buy them, sew them, knit them; I dress her and redress her, parade her around, show her off. Cuddle her. Talk to her, exercise her, just like her brother. But she is never mine; she is *Daddy's Little Girl* from the moment of her birth.

Steve's Precious Baby Girl...she begins manipulating him, and me, very early, with his help and blessing. I look into her ice blue eyes, and she stares back at me with what appears to be a challenge of some sort. I feel a chill. Something strange is happening; there is some sort of competition in play. Two women fighting for rank. Who will be the victor?

Bruce graduates to the seat on the top of the pram; in a very short time, life is back to normal and I assume my new position of second-class citizen, assistant to the princess. I am having trouble understanding the politics of my family, my marriage. I still don't know what to do. Joyce has a perfect marriage, a perfect husband, and two perfect children. What am I doing wrong?

I cry myself to sleep silently night after night. When will the changes begin, when will I be happy? Knowing how tight Steve is about money I get my small revenge by opening charge accounts at a few local department stores to compensate for the stuff I am unable to buy for the kids with the tiny stipend he gives me weekly. The more money I spend to compensate Steve's neglect and my low self-esteem and depression the more uptight and rigid Steve becomes and the more I spend to compensate for the resultant rejection with a blind and helpless anger. Somehow peripherally I am aware that this is a visceral target, his Achilles heel. In real time I have no knowledge of what is causing the problem because he never talks to me. He never confides anything of our financial status, his plans, his hopes, his dreams, goals and plans for our family. He refuses to converse with me at all on any level. I do not in his judgment have the mental capacity or intellect to comprehend these deeply esoteric matters. I am relegated to house help, chattel status; privately owned and operated, solely the property of my husband. Credit becomes my new metaphorical coffee cup, or open window.

∂∽⧸

It is a time however in the real world out there of monumental actions. Krukschev bangs his shoe on his desk during a United Nations session, war criminal Adolph Eichmann goes on trial in Jerusalem, there is a Soviet-American Summit meeting, Berlin is cut in two by the Berlin Wall, and birth control pills go on sale in the United States. I yearn to talk with someone about it all. What does it all mean? Steve gravely contemplates the first of these although he will not discuss any of it with me and exhales a massive sigh of relief over the last but my mind is racing forward. Steve's mind is elsewhere as we settle into mindless daily ritual.

I'm going into town for an ice cream cone, calls Steve searching his pockets for his keys, What kind do you want?

Strawberry, I shout from the bathroom where I towel the babies dry after their bath.

I think chocolate is better, he answers, appearing in the doorway.

No, come on, Steve, you know I like strawberry, I want strawberry, I say absently, concentrating on pajama buttons.

Well, I'll bring you chocolate, you'll see, you will like it better.

Bring me strawberry or don't bring me anything, I fling back at his receding figure without hope as he heads for the stairs. Damn, I mutter to myself, stuffing the damp and soggy towel over the rack, wondering if this time at least my desire will be regarded.

Steve arrives back in his customary five minutes carrying two covered cones. He begins to remove the foil paper and hand me one and my mouth waters thinking of the cold, creamy smoothness and the icy red fruit chunks. He hands me a chocolate cone. Here, don't you like that better?

I resist a strong impulse to grind the business of the cone into his face, giggle inwardly at the thought; cower at my general terror of defying him.

∂∞∽

Night blackness itself hovers silently inside and out as I lay sleepless and wide eyed listening the only sounds the loudspeaker and the thump thump thump of tennis balls from racket to clay, to racket to clay during matches blocks away. Joyce and I pass the mornings walking through Forest Hills Gardens in the shadow of the tennis stadium. She and her husband rent a tiny apartment adjacent to one of the classic homes just a couple of blocks away from us. We are inseparable back and forth from one home to another taking part with relish in our young matron activities. One morning we pass through the Gardens beneath the rows of leafy bowers of ancient trees along the rows of old classic homes, Tudor and Georgian finding Queen Anne chairs along the street on big garbage day and pile them on the top of the respective carriages, bring them home to reupholster, a new challenge, a new craft. We have been enjoying an ongoing friendly competition of knitting and sewing for our children, and now something different, upholstery. There is a lot to do, adapting new styles, playing at home décor.

Our respective basements house the peripatetic chairs for years as we never have the proper time or inspiration to attack this major job. When Joyce's husband voices a considerable complaint about hers she brings it over to my house and now joyfully I have two to dream and obsess about. Finally one by one we drag and heave the treasured chairs upstairs and out to the curb, garbage day again. Later we are sipping tea, nibbling on newly baked pastries, watching the babies play. Bruce and Robby are out front on their bikes, pink cheeks and red noses in the early winter weather, up and down, up and down in front of the house; the little ones sitting in their carriages outside the window watching also.

A station wagon drives quickly by passing our house, comes to as screeching halt, backs up. The driver gets out, looks around left and right, glances at the window behind which we sit and quickly opens his rear hatch, drags the chairs over, and places them inside rapidly disappearing down the street as if he has stolen something of great value. The next year, another bright sunny morning children piled into carriages older ones following down the rutted sidewalks on their tricycles we see a familiar configuration of color, texture, shape and bulk piled at the curb. There they are, our chairs, there is no disputing this fact. Once again, they are up for adoption. Another car pulls up and stops quickly, the driver looks around and loads them into the trunk, half closes it and ties it down, takes off with a great squealing of tires. I often wonder where they are today; are they still making the rounds, house to house, waiting for that perfect renovation?

෴

Like Lemmings rushing towards the edge of a cliff my friends are leaving the city one by one. Joyce moves first to Flushing and then upstate to Nyack in the shadow of the farm that Grandpa once owned which is now a suburban community of rows and rows of tract houses. Another example of that old six degrees of separation syndrome pushes itself into the picture. Lonely, my sole connection to adult companionship gone, as soon as my license arrives in the mail I bravely set out in the old Chevy to visit my friend my heart in my throat the babies in the back of the car. Here I go onto parkways and expressways lickety split, heart in throat, lump in chest; damn the torpedoes. Life is for living; there must be something out in the world that will fill this hollow in me. There is nothing to fear but fear itself. It is a long trip, not one to be made too frequently but one to be savored. There is a certain excitement in the vision of brand new homes sprouting like mushrooms in checkerboard patterns and ever widening circles across the countryside. I feel a hot oily trickle of envy seeping through me as I am treated to the entire Cooke's Tour of the new house and the neighborhood, stroke gleaming cabinets still smelling of varnish, pastel painted walls exuding plaster and paint; sit on new furniture still bouncy and crisp, and sigh. Joyce puts out a simple lunch of cold cuts and salads and fresh rolls, pours two mugs of tea, and for moments I have my friend back.

Joyce and I watch the little ones playing in the soft damp sweetly smelling grass, still carefully dressed against the early spring weather; the sun presses warmly on their chubby bodies, heating their skin and their soft hair. I watch the older children play on the brightly painted aluminum swing set recalling with nostalgia that swings have never been my personal favorite. I breathe deeply again of the fresh spring air, and feel a great joy. What more can anyone want in life, I remark to my friend, contented...

෨ೕ

Huge chickens sculpted of chopped liver sitting on their lettuce beds on platters with their celery stalk tails, roasted pepper combs, carrot beaks; slices of olive with pimento centers for eyes; standing rib roasts with all the proper accouterments. My new friend Judy and I have conquered the world of gastronomy and are pleased to find ourselves armed with several new and esoteric recipes and the certain knowledge that we are able to prepare them to the proverbial T. This has all occurred during our induction into an adult education gourmet cooking class which is held in the same Forest Hills High School auditorium, the same stage where I painted scenery in sublime innocence short years ago. We are quite pleased with ourselves. Steve's friend Dave has married and now I have the occasional company of Judy who has no children yet, lives in a tiny garden apartment in Kew Gardens Hills and I am now prepared to entertain Steve's business acquaintances to help him get ahead. Soon I am in business, ready to prove myself, show my value as an attorney's wife. I cook and set up all the food and dishes for forty guests proud of the job I have done, waiting for any praise or gratitude and for thanks I am sent to my room. This meeting is business and none of mine. As I slink off, humiliated, I hear through ringing ears the names of the guests as each is greeted, Kohn, Thom, Albert, Dikman; I slip into bed with my clothes on, pulling the quilts up to my chin knowing I will need to arise and clean up the mess, not tomorrow, now, as per the rules. I do not want to get *the look,* or that reviled moniker, *Mother of the Year.* I am an obedient wife. But I sigh knowing that at six in the morning I will need to arise again and take care of the children, *Mother of the Year* is what he will call me no matter what with groggy knowing contempt as I awaken slowly.

That this is a harbinger of things to come it is too soon for me to know. This concept of payoffs and influence; it is too soon for me to fear it all when Mark Van Doren is found guilty in a quiz show fix. What is happening in our world, I ask myself; where is integrity? Thank God that is one thing about Steve, his integrity. Then we are stunned when the Flying Wallendas and popular comic Ernie Kovacs die, tsk tsk we mutter, neither talent nor celebrity are able to defeat death it appears, but the mortality of strangers really doesn't collate; life continues in the Heffner household, Ernie and the Wallendas fly off pin-wheeling into space like the wicked witch from Oz, disappear in a puff of wind.

෨ೕ

The house is filling with a thick gray haze as I cough and gasp for breath. I watch Steve's grandmother, Nany, with awe when she visits as she continues chain smoking, hour after hour. Bruce toddles over to the cellar about to turn around as I have taught him in order to inch crab like feet first backwards downstairs to the playroom to find a favorite toy but Nany notices him in mid-turn and shrieks, the baby, and startled he falls down the cellar stairs, is rescued with a bleeding lip and bruised cheeks. It is my fault, of course even though Nany is the one who frightened him and screamed. He has been going up and down now for weeks with no problem. I gird myself for the barrage of funny looks and tsk, tsks and caustic references to my status as mother of the year.

෯๏๙

Here comes that artist again, cries the entire nursing staff; they know me very well. I am there nearly every year, every eighteen months, at least although there is a mere eleven months between the two girls which thrills me since they will have each other always. It is a pattern that will seemingly go on forever with each successive child. As soon as one innocent cuddly totally dependent being begins to be mobile and verbalize and be aware of his identity the craving overcomes me to replace him with another worshipful and again totally dependent. The old baby moves up to the next notch is another chapter in the series becoming a new and different creature altogether to be cherished on this different level. The entire house full of babies is like a big basket of warm cuddly, frolicking puppies. A cradle full of baby dolls.

They race across the lawn, wander through shrubs and trees, gambol on monkey bars and swings, spend inordinate incomprehensible time digging in their sandbox. As I observe I breathe deeply again of the pristine and promising early spring air which still holds a hint of winter frost, and feel a great joy...

෯๏๙

One baby becomes two and three as I seek that illusive quantity of love needed to fill my empty existence and compensate for having no sense of self. I fight to have an image that will stand above others. First child in the group, youngest mother around, first with two, three, four...the winner and still champion... how does she do it...she looks so young...my glory. Alas, my only glory, my glory and my nightmare; my salvation and my death. With little help from the sorcerer's apprentices I shovel up mounds of toys and toy parts all day long robotically wash and dry basket after basket of clothing and bedding

197

and towels; do battle with the rancid buckets of omnipresent diapers that are everywhere. We choose our daily clothing from the mound that threatens to spread from the daybed in the den and overtake the entire house as I struggle to catch up with sorting and folding that never ends. It is getting worse every day. Now, I am surviving in the *no exit* of all time, trapped by the very creatures who I love the most that are my entire life that has become by attrition with apology to Sartre, the no exit of all time.

But there is something else happening. Nothing can fill that empty void of my spirit like that throbbing growing entity, flesh of my flesh, beneath my heart. Each child is a combination of the genes of both of us that proves that we are a vital viable couple, a true marriage. We have this connection that proves that we are together, two halves of a whole. Our baby connects and completes us. It is the quintessence of illusion. I always feel complete when I am pregnant and then I always feel a great vacuum post–partum. It is also at this moment, the moment of becoming a new mother, probably the only time my life that I hold myself in any esteem. The only time that anyone truly reveres me. I am young, I will always be just as I am today, nothing will ever change; I have created the stage set of my life and so it will remain. The show will continue each day and night with the same script into perpetuity. Aging and the rapid passing of time are attributes of the unimaginable distant future; my life as it is right now is what I have designed to be will never change, will never go away. Divine Providence has designed life so that to youth time passes practically at a standstill.

Ah, that little hand that curves trustingly around my finger, those deep all knowing eyes that search my face adoringly. I can't get enough of being needed, of being worshipped, of being infallible to another being. I am accustomed to being viewed as the incarnate screw-up. Everyone knows it. I know it. The belief is reinforced daily, by my beloved husband, in case my faith is waning.

My parents, as ever, fill the remaining void. Mom checks furniture tops for dust and appraises the strewn toys as though they are piles of dung. Here, baby, let Grandma wipe your little nose; are you going to give him *that* for dinner; is that a *dirt* rash on his face or is he allergic to something he is eating; tsk, tsk, when did your mamma last change your diaper? Maybe Grandma should give you a nice little bath. Daddy just raises a quizzical eyebrow, sits simmering like the time bomb I know him to be.

It is what it is. I make of it what I want it to be.

⥸⥷

His platinum hair a beacon bobbing up and down behind the privet that lines the homes on this street Bruce, two, rides his small tricycle up and down the cracked rutted sidewalk; as he pedals, back and forth, up and down, his brow furrowed with concentration, his lips pursed; I watch from the kitchen window. He stops at each house, leaves his tricycle, walks up the front walk and stands at the front door; each neighbor comes to the door, smiling, brings something, hands it to him; a piece of fruit, a piece of cheese, a cookie, a bagel, a roll, a sandwich. He continues on his way, riding and eating and stopping for more. When nature calls he does what comes naturally and then pulls off his clothes and leaves them on the street. But I am watching and I run right out and grab hold of him, swoop him off the street his platinum mop bouncing and flopping in time with his giggles and the motion of my rapid progress. A little later if I have been changing the baby or turning on the washing machine or answering the phone. His timing is exquisite; he always seems to know when I have turned my head for a split second. I collect my cleanup apparatus and a large towel and race out to trouble shoot. Bath time again, hose down the street; wash the tricycle seat.

The rest of the time, Bruce plays silently, almost not there while I do chores, obey orders, he listens to Steve criticize me, berate me, put me down, in silence. I look at his serious little face, so inscrutable, and wonder what he is thinking, what is happening to his precious little mind.

෫෬෯

We need to call the fire department, this time the fire has gotten out of hand. Somehow he has obtained matches, although I don't smoke and he has found a quiet spot behind a bush to experiment and now there is a fine blaze and he is looking at us with that completely innocent face and denying that he is the culprit even with the evidence all over his shorts and T-shirt. I didn't do it, Mom, I would never do that. I don't even have any matches. But his hands are behind his back, and sure enough there is a book of matches clutched in his guilty little hands. He still denies involvement. So the chief steps forward and clears his throat and Brucie looks up at his six-foot-five frame with no trepidation at all innocence beaming from him and the chief glances over at us and we nod and he looks back and clears his throat again and begins his riot act. Do you know how much damage you could do, he thunders, if we didn't get here in time or if no one called us? Do you realize, huh, do you? And Bruce begins to wonder if he is really in trouble this time. He looks down at his scruffy sneakers. The chief falters for a moment but I accidentally brush against him and he clears his throat again and bends down his beefy chest now nearly even with Brucie's face. I am warning you for the very last time, mister, he says, better watch your step. You could do heavy jail time. He gets up and shrugs stifling a grin. I don't really know how to deal with toddlers, he says. Brucie is four. I live in an armed camp in order to survive my child's energy and innovation.

CHAPTER 28

At least there is an occasional Saturday night out. The babies are asleep and the baby sitter will arrive momentarily.

Aren't you ready yet, hollers Steve from the living room, she'll be here in a minute. He paces in his usual circle round and round throughout the kitchen into the front hall around the living room then the dining room and finally back to start again only to continue with never a change in tempo or rhythm.

One more second, I shout back from the tiny bath where I try desperately to make my hair curve counter to its natural bent intent on replicating the newest style of the day. Finally it flows softly around my face bouncing and swaying jauntily as I walk. I smile to myself beginning to feel a sense of confidence, feeling my enthusiasm for this evening begin to grow. Why don't you reverse your walk, start in the living room and go to the kitchen, instead, to make it a little more interesting, I call out impulsively unable to control this small comeback feeble attempt at revolt, his compulsive pacing makes me nervous and a little hysterical. And I am tense with expectation. Not in a good way.

What, he shouts, Oh. He lowers his voice as I mince tentatively into the room in my high heels glancing at anything reflective as I move, ready now, and pleased with the effect but knowing from experience that the ritual deflowering is yet to come. His eyes dissect me, travel all over my body. Isn't that dress a little long, he asks innocently, a slight edge to his voice. It looks like a shroud. Last time it had been, Isn't that dress too short, your entire legs are showing. I can practically see your tonsils. It's obscene.

I thought this one would please you, I sigh, looking down at my feet, deflating rapidly.

Well, why is your hair loose? You know I like it pinned up. You look like a slut with it swirling around your face like that.

Slut? I blush. Well, last time it had been pinned up and was too severe. I can't win. I run quickly into the bedroom that familiar sinking sensation in the pit of my stomach. All right, I change into a slightly shorter dress, rifle carelessly through my dresser drawers, redo all of my accessories and pin up my hair in a French twist, my hands shaking uncontrollably. The mirror tells the tale. He may have done me a favor, I muse to myself, turning this way and that, observing my reflection in the mirror. This does look rather great. How bad could it look? I am young and full of life and ready for anything. I leave my room feeling confident again about the way I look, but by the time I have negotiated the short hallway and anticipated all of his potential responses based on old experience my self-assurance has left, but then I am never quite prepared for his inevitable admonishments.

THAT'S what you change into as an improvement? He sneers. Who are you trying to impress with that cleavage down to your belly button. I guess you are who you are. I guess you just can't help looking cheap.

What is with this *slut*, and *cheap* stuff? Where is this coming from? What does he mean? What's wrong with it, I almost whine like a chastened child, my voice whole octaves lower than normal. I am growing smaller like Alice, shrinking away to nothing. An instant recall of Daddy, my sixteenth birthday at the Chinese restaurant slips into my mind. This is a perfectly run of the mill normal neckline…it looks…nice…

Well if you want to show your entire chest to the whole world, *mother of the year*, then go ahead. But don't expect me to introduce you to my business associates even acknowledge that you are my wife or even with me. I won't be seen dead with you looking like that.

I am choking with the tears that struggle to bubble up into my throat from somewhere in my aching heart. I'll change again, I say. No, no, he says, we're late enough now because of you. Why can't you ever be on time?

I was on time, you made me change. I am whining. If you had any taste, we wouldn't have these problems. He is carping. Why did you marry me if I am so inept? I don't know, I should have had my head examined first. I run into the bedroom of the kids and kiss them, hug them, tears threatening to overflow and ruin my makeup, can't have that, we're late already but just the feel of their warm soft bodies, their smell, their sleepy faces soothes me and I am regenerated, able to move on.

Here we are at yet another Kiwanis dinner dance after a long cold auto ride through Queens traffic, like so many others, recollections of them haunt my dreams and fill my memory, long lines of dreary intolerable business cum social occasions. They read like a list from the oh so familiar Gilbert and Sullivan recitative; *I've got a little list, and they'll none of them be missed.* I walk stiffly and slowly, feeling that sensation of anticipation mixed with terror that such occasions demand. I get no support from Steve. The ride has been a long and chilled silence of interminable duration, icy and tense with no conversation. I spend the time playing with the beading on my evening purse, running my fingers over the ridges and bumps, over and over.

The phony welcome and ebullient effusive gestures; I brave the pretense of amenities with a bored and heavy feeling inside but reinforce my armored shell with contrived warmth and my best simulation of charm. I am out in public at a fancy affair, I am not home alone folding laundry and changing diapers and washing floors. I am going to enjoy every moment, by God. Hello! I greet one of Steve's friends with an effusive smile, lighting up, glad to see a familiar face.

Don't *BUBBLE,* says Steve into my ear with testy impatience. Put a cork in it. You always have to *BUBBLE.* What do you think you are a newly opened bottle of champagne? He is speaking through the slit of a mouth that pretends to smile jovially as though he is not speaking at all his eyes pointed somewhere other than me.

He has hit pay-dirt; his blade has found its mark. Now, I feel thoroughly insecure as if I didn't already. All of Steve's earlier observations rush forward to the present and paralyze me. Now there is no longer any doubt that I am truly an embarrassment, it is a certainty that my outfit, my image is ungainly, gauche, offensive, and all wrong. I am totally apprehensive about my neckline, which hasn't concerned me in the least until this moment, keep pulling at it looking down to check that nothing is out of place. The misery that grips me sinks into my chest, grabs me around my middle like a giant's steel monkey wrench, to remain there throughout the entire dinner; I have all I can do to go through all of those motions of required conviviality, to even continue breathing. The delicious food sticks in my throat, I am unable to swallow. My eyes are flicking from one person to another sitting at our table, combinations of words are beginning to filter through my flushed head, my stuffed ears. I am becoming interested in the conversation, forgetting about my anxiety and status. Isn't it amazing about John Kennedy, isn't he doing a great job? I begin to relax a little, forget for the moment that I am stupid and inept sufficiently to allow myself to become a part of the continuing discussion forgetting that I am forbidden to speak. My vote for him in the presidential election was my very first time. Kennedy is now at a popularity peak, also, Eichmann has been hanged, and public TV has received thirty three million dollars. It is all the talk of the table. It is good to be involved in conversation with adults. I am almost beginning to forget my discomfort and actually enjoy the banter, interaction, conviviality, when I glance up to see Steve standing across from me, behind the businessman with whom I am conversing. He has left his seat and maneuvered around to send me a message.

He is shaking his head *no* motioning to his mouth and then points at me pinches his lips shut all the while that same shaking his head no then pretends to turn a key and throw it away; Steve dramatically performs an elaborate mime, stages an entire message for me. I feel as though a blood red stain is creeping obviously up my neck to my face and the words that I have prepared in my mind for my next contribution to the conversation disappear suddenly leaving a void where once there has been sense. My words dissolve into a meaningless garble of mumbles. I try not to draw further attention to myself, fighting the initial fury that rises quickly from the pit of my stomach into my chest and head, the desire to retaliate, to fight back but am brought back to the present by the certain knowledge that disobedience will only bring as its reprisal further unwarranted punishment. I remain silent for the remainder of the evening feeling the seed of a horrible rage beginning to burst and grow inside of me, a tiny embryonic organism of rebellion too immature yet for viability but there is a tiny promise lurking that says that its inevitable birthday will come as do they all eventually.

I experience a sudden thirst and want to order a drink at this moment from the suddenly appearing waiter with his generous smile, his small round tray of assorted cocktails; I picture myself motioning to the waiter imperiously my voice firm and clear. May I have one of those, please? I don't even want one, have never even tasted one of these, have no craving except for that engendered by having been forbidden to have one. I have never been a drinker, never had a drink, to speak of just a little Manichewitz on Passover but I remember that warm numbing feeling running through my stomach and veins calming, anesthetizing feelings. I know that it will soothe the agitation that is threatening to blow me apart at the seams, will numb the jumpiness and knifing pain that runs right through the middle of my body. But that is just a fantasy and quickly fades away leaving me in the midst of nowhere. I have been enticed once again to attempt the forbidden. No cocktail. I already know that. It is engraved on my DNA; it is an intricate part of the catechism of my upbringing. Nice girls don't drink. I have already earlier been prohibited wordlessly by a simple glance, raised eyebrows, and nod from helping myself to one of the scotch sours that sit enticingly unclaimed at the open bar. I have no experience with alcohol but there is a mystique; a promise of nirvana, a carelessly disguised assurance that eludes me becomes more attractive because of its being forbidden. And there is another vitally important matter concerning Steve. There is an unwritten rule hanging in the ether, please do not do anything that might ruin the promising career of this budding attorney, destroy his parents' dreams, a career that depends almost entirely on the social skills and prospective sterling reputation of his wife, her ability to mimic a robot. Yes. And a man needs to establish control, to exhibit to those in the world of industry that he is master of his domain. His domain is my prison. Steve has asserted his superiority, his control of his home camp, his mastery of the moment. A trap, an endless trap, a little voice inside me screams, over and over, a dungeon with that old familiar no exit. No Exit. No Exit. My most familiar mantra; another apology is due to Sartre. The elements of my life are fragmented and separate; exist in tightly attended compartments having no conscious relationship to one another.

Maybe not for someone else but for me it is the norm to begin thinking about another baby. A new baby will fill this void, will give me some sense of importance, will provide me with another creature to love and nurture; fill that vacuum that is my life with being adored and needed. Steve has no clue that this is what I am thinking about, how would he, he never listens to me when I speak, never talks to me at all, never confides in me nor the corollary, I in him, has no idea what I want or need. So according to Steve's master plan it appears to be necessary to find a more reliable birth control method if we are to continue even our empty and pitiful love life. The new solution seems to be that new invention, a diaphragm, awkward and difficult to use renowned for its proclivity to flying across the room during attempts at insertion; but the doctor says it is foolproof, I tell Steve, if you use it, I say under my breath. And wonder of wonders, I am soon pregnant again.

Still in the shadow of the tennis stadium, we live yet on Selfridge Street in Forest Hills and Janet Something Or Other is our fifteen-year-old baby sitter, carrot top hair, slim and schoolgirl. Steve thinks she is the cat's pajamas, she can do no wrong. He nicknames her in his typical quirky manner, *Jant.* It is Jant this and Jant that, singing her praises, all day and night. He compares my manner of caring for my children with her fifteen-year-old after-school style which he finds to be perfect. He is obsessed with her, infatuated, can't wait to drive her home after our evening out; can't wait to get into the car alone with her. What is really going on here? Why do her parents refuse to my great relief, puzzlement, and consternation, to allow her to sit for us any more suddenly one day? Steve blames me for Janet's disappearance, mourns her loss incessantly. And I smile to myself and wait for my new child to appear, hiding from the everyday angst, sublimating in the mechanics of baby waiting.

We fool ourselves for a time, heads in the sand, cooperative little ostriches but we are merely continuing to go through the motions. To all outsiders we appear to be a perfect family doing the things that families do; even take yearly family photo portraits which we hand out to all comers as if to prove the point. Mom covets her photos, places them all around in expensive frames and joyfully offers to babysit when a friend tells us about the neat and cheap cabins available in the mountains of New Hampshire on the border of Vermont, a quaint and charming escape. So we vacation in a rustic cabin in with an old fashioned Icebox, no electricity, our first time, alone together in eons enamored of the place, Caryn is just a bump. Lake Sunapee is a quick jaunt away complete with gorgeous waterfalls and beaches. We are barbequing on the porch in the deep pine woods, storing our groceries on blocks of ice in the ancient box. Except for the work it is idyllic. We have no choice but to pass the time together. When I am totally ignored I pick up a paperback and cuddle up somewhere to read.

enchanted with the spot and filled with overflowing optimism we take a second trip a few weeks later with Bruce and Wendi along, all together, hoping to share the experience with the entire family. We dine and sleep in our quaint cabin high above the forest floor, keep the Icebox full of ice and stocked with kiddies favorites and barbecue nearly everything except corn flakes. We contend with the dirt and ever present insect life and mice. We pack up early in the morning and spend the day lounging and playing at the beach; the kids do their digging thing. Steve does his own thing; I have all the childcare as usual, including the delightful insufficiencies of laundry at a Laundromat in town in a time of the most rudimentary disposable diapers, he just relaxes. I arrive home exhausted. Isn't vacation grand? Still the excursion has given me some measure of hope for the future. Escape has proven to be a positive measure; a spark of romance has been lit then flickers, sputters and goes out.

CHAPTER 29

But my oldest escape and safe haven, harkening way back to my childhood still exists. Working secretly in Steve's absence on new paintings I manage to reach a plateau after much sweat and tears of something near what I envision in my mind's eye. I fear or rather evade the issue of showing these pieces to anyone for I am that sure that they are worthless and too immature to stand up in the world of art of today. As I am emerging into art discovery in '61, Claes Oldenberg is doing more than painting successful as he is, his new medium is plaster; he is creating sculpture whose main subject is food, clothing, furniture, other items blown up into massive reproductions of themselves. Strangely enough during this time he is coexistent with my first inspiration, Norman Rockwell, a confusing dichotomy! My disdain is endless and complete; I still struggle with flowers and landscape. I have been working tirelessly still in all my spare time on those three-color field minimalist landscape paintings, large and flat with softly modulated colors, greens and blues and golds, applying paint in layers, over and over again, unable to know when to stop. Then another technique, more of that flat modulated color somewhat monochrome in feeling, using a delicately brushed black outline as a crutch to delineate flowers, a cop out, to get past the inadequacies that frustratingly still existed in my technical vocabulary of form and modeling. I apply it once again to my other stealthy crutch, the mosaic or stained glass window approach using palette knife, and heavy outline, a harbinger of some sort. In the back of my mind is the memory of my mother's criticism of the apples in that first successful painting. It has been purchased by Steve's friend Harry Freedman and his wife Linda, who like the apples and persimmons just as they are. Still, my mother's words sting, in retrospect. They have a power to paralyze me, to destroy all my confidence in myself, in my art.

❧

Strange and eerie late afternoon winter shadows are being cast by sunlight all around the room as I sit at the kitchen table; the mood that is evolving only serves to enhance the weird sensation that I have been feeling of late, sort of a cross between boredom and restlessness that keeps me twirling like a dervish in a tornado of constantly painting and redecorating rooms. I sew piles of probably never to be worn high fashion clothing and outfits for the babies, and fretfully repaint already finished canvasses which I then store away angrily, cranky when I am unable to identify their worth or function. Wait with tingling anticipation the delivery of my most recently designed and ordered sculpture now in the process of fabrication, the latest baby. Long morning walks through Forest Hills Gardens and long afternoon naps engendered by all that fresh air give me time to work until the children awaken.

It feels like my hundredth at least cup of instant coffee that I have just finished. Feeling the baby moving restlessly in its crowded and over extended home, I place one hand over the pointy protruding lump and smile, idly wondering at the same time whether it is a heel or elbow or knee or what. I wonder too how much longer this particular pregnancy will continue. Part of me wants to keep that precious cargo to me, finding comfort in our oneness and mutual company. The other part of me insists with an impatience that belies reality that even one day longer is more than I can bear until I hold that marvelous tiny presence in my arms. I close my eyes and imagine that baby hair smell, those liquid eyes, that clinging hand around my finger. I pray silently that this baby will be a girl, so that Wendi will have a sister close to her own age; these last two babies will be thirteen months apart. Diaphragms are indeed useful apparatuses. What I wouldn't have done for a sister especially one close in age.

CHAPTER 30

This is my third baby and already I am smug self-important mistress of the patterns that attend the entire syndrome and regimen...as I perceive it, according to my experience and programming. I know that something about my own experience is distorted, seen through Sylvia Plath's already well documented bell jar, but I still revel in whatever bounty magnanimously comes my way. In the greater scheme of things from what I am able to see it is precious little. I know that I am lucky to be getting even that much. I am coveting the feeling of the growing baby filling that empty void that is my spirit feeling closer to Steve as my partner in this act of creation, feeling complete, dreading that inevitable post-partum vacuum. I am again awaiting with combined anticipation and dread those few precious moments of importance and status that will be mine when I hold my newborn in my arms. A gut tightening sensation of expected joy races through me each time I picture that little hand curling around my finger, those intense gray eyes studying my face.

Trying to fill the hours until Steve is due to arrive home I idly reopen the afternoon newspaper and re-scan the news articles eager to find one that I may have missed,. The other two babies are still peacefully and innocently asleep in their cribs and I relish the silence and inactivity that are so infrequently mine but today nearly at the end of this pregnancy time and space need filling. I glance absently at the coming events listings and find myself stopping instantly at the notice of a newly opening gallery in Bayside founded by two women artists...former housewives...who are seeking an outlet for their own work as well as others...and I think, *why not*. I feel a sudden soaring sense of joy and hope. I sense a new goal on the horizon, something to aim for, a reason to go on living. I phone the number listed in the article feeling that rising excitement in my gut, to inquire about the competition they are sponsoring. Fearful again of the same old rejection I almost don't complete that first call but it appears that added dollop of adrenaline floating throughout my system maybe aided and abetted by the caffeine pushes me right over the edge and a feeling of devil-may-care audacity spurs me onward. Before I am aware what I have done, I have made an appointment to deliver my work. My excitement is more than palpable; it is rampant, and spurs me ahead into action.

I am *stripping* the edges of the pile of canvasses that have been gathering dust in the closet the very next afternoon, working at a frantic pace; I dress the babies, Bruce and Wendi, in their layers of knits and quilts and blankets and strap them into their car seats. Piling the paintings gingerly in the trunk of the old Chevy I head for the Gallery Downstairs. The gallery turns out to be somebody's basement in a residential area. Well, it was called the Gallery Downstairs. What did I expect? So what? I think. I am already seething with envy because they thought of it first and were able to follow through on the idea.

Among the groping amateur and striving almost professional works that cover the walls, are a collection of *still lifes* and *florals* and *nudes* that take my breath away; new world opens for me that afternoon They have all been studying with the same artist and I am compelled to discover his name; I am anxiously salivating at the thought of joining the class. I know that I am wasting my time to even ask for Steve will never permit me to take any lessons but my flapping tongue defies my better judgment once again. Before I know what has happened I have spoken and I am busy tucking a piece of paper with the instructor's name and address into my purse. I argue with myself all the way home, stating first my own question and then Steve's answer, back and forth. The babies, two silent and outerwear stuffed zombies in their tiny seats are as usual happy to be riding in Daddy's Car. I sound out various sentences, trying to find a way to convince Steve that I need desperately to take this class for not only all the obvious reasons but because if I cannot answer the insistent keening call of that demanding muse my soul will probably shrivel up and dry as dust just disappear into the atmosphere, leaving me with no self at all. I imagine complete conversations with him, taking both sides, beginning with a simple request moving on to cajoling and knowing his natural response sense the mounting fury begin to rise in my chest. The result always ends with me begging and defending myself. The only good thing about that, is that suddenly put on the defensive by my own imagined narrative that grows more and more petulant and combative with each word a niggling flame of anger begins to flicker fanned by my own growing outrage at all the restrictions and directives I am forced to follow as his chattel. The flame spawns an undeniable stubbornness that has already decided resolutely and without compromise that I am taking that class.

Steve fights and screams and inflicts his favorite punishment of ignoring me and forbidding me sex and affection but I clench my teeth and I hold firm. It is my first venture into the world of actual revolt. I unabashedly use the pregnancy as leverage. In my ninth month of pregnancy, his favorite weapon, denial of sexual contact, is moot, so what do I have to lose?

Waddling along, my huge belly leading the way proudly, I begin the class, heady with the joy of the coming taste of knowledge and technique and membership in a secret society of artisanship that tantalizes me with its rosy promise. I do my best imitation of a sidle in between the wooden church basement chairs, easels, palette- and paint-covered bar stools, and intent fellow students. The heady smell of linseed oil, dammar varnish, and turpentine combined with the promise, the anticipation, and joy of the next three hours, is intoxicating beyond anything else I know. Old feelings are encompassing me in a lovely way. I have been compelled to hire a baby sitter for the evening for Steve is at yet another meeting, to be paid out of my carefully squirreled away pennies, but it will be worth it for I feel alive again. I ignore the many voices that inform me that it is both folly and dangerous to be out running around in the ninth month of a pregnancy. I just shrug my shoulders and coast on an adrenaline high, which is enhanced by the inadvertent additional high engendered by distilled petroleum fumes.

❧❧

Friday the thirteenth, once again as per the trend of the day my child will be delivered by appointment, the date itself presenting only the most minor of apprehensions. The traditional fight over her name, Cara is stupid, it means dear in Italian, what's wrong with English, call her Karen, that's close enough, but I look through the venerated baby name book and discover Caryn, and ask Steve ingenuously over the phone if it is all right and he answers tersely that he has already said so, hasn't he, just fill out the birth certificate and get it over with, stop bothering him, he is trying to work. So thinking about overflowing cups of coffee and Steve's other attempts to control me, I do, and I have not really disobeyed him, have I? So, my second daughter's name is Caryn. This year there is yet another snowstorm, even in the middle of April but this time I get no visits; who cares, not Steve. Do I care at all at this very moment in time that President Kennedy has ordered the United States to invade Cuba via the Bay of Pigs or later that the invaders have been sentenced, to be flown back to U.S.? I never even heard of any bay of pigs; don't even know what that means. All I can think about is missing my older two children, about my baby, about going home. Finally, Mom brings the two little ones to the hospital, and I get to wave to them from the window since they are not permitted to come up to my room and Steve shows up joylessly but on time of course with all my carefully prepared newborn paraphernalia to bring us home.

A crisp and frigid Sunday morning, gray and inauspicious is the day after we bring Caryn home from the hospital when she has attained all of three days of life. I awaken early to attend to this new treasure as well as the other two babies, and find to my distress that I have begun bleeding quite heavily again, and soon I am all out of Kotex. The doctor has directed me to stay off my feet, his favorite bromide for every ailment; fat chance of that with two toddlers and a newborn.

Steve, I shake his shoulder as he sleeps, you've got to go down to the drugstore for me, hurry. I stuff an old bath towel between my legs and will him to rush; the children call from the other room.

Don't be stupid, he snipes; you know I don't buy THAT. Anyway, it's Sunday! And you weren't so delicate when you ran out to your painting classes, were you?

But Stevie, this is an EMERGENCY, and that was different. I just had a baby, I'm bleeding. Last week, I was just pregnant.

Look, I'm NOT going, so just forget it. If you need something and you are stupid and incompetent enough not to plan for it, then the result is your responsibility. It's about time you develop some sense of organization and responsibility, he says sanctimoniously. If you can go to classes up until the last minute, you can do your own errands. Really, you could learn to be a little more efficient. And you're not leaving those kids with me. Take them along with you.

I am twenty-three years old. I have three babies; the oldest is two and a half years old. But I wanted them and I love them and their father did not, did not want them, although I am certain he does love them, in his way, and this was my choice. Maybe that respect and compassion that I crave is just not due me. I grit my teeth together and dress the babies. It is mid April but still there is that chill in the air, and it is one of those dreary early spring mornings that has not yet remembered that it is supposed to be warm and sunny. I wrap tiny Caryn in her blanket sleeper and slide her into a hooded snowsuit bag with a zipper; Wendi, bundled and tucked into blankets, rides on a seat affixed to the carriage, and Brucie sits astride his small red tricycle that is tied to the carriage with a piece of clothesline rope. I pin the unwieldy wadded towel to my old corduroy maternity dress and slip into a full cut winter coat that I designed and sewed several years ago especially to account for the idiosyncrasies of pregnancy. Wendi as usual commences her furious howl at being brought out into the cold for any reason, stiff in her seat her icy blue eyes rimmed with vermillion, and continues until we return home, as usual. Bruce stoically pedals, concentrating on maneuvering the uneven sidewalk. Caryn three days old is insensate and unaware. We walk past the Old Age Home where my grandma Julia spent her last days, Caryn's namesake, Caryn Jill; Jill for Julia, Grandma Julia. Wendi is Wendi Arlene; the A for Anna, Grandma Anna, the Hebrew translation of her first name is for Steve's mother, Ida, of whom I am still forbidden to speak.

We walk the three blocks over cracked and rutted concrete sidewalk to the local drug store briskly. I am on yet another adventure in the still Sunday emptiness. Filthy formerly white remnants of the last snow storm fringe the yards and walkways. Touches of brave green spikes push up through the brown grayness of the bare frigid winter ground. I make my purchase rapidly, and push the heavy English pram that has been willing servant since the birth of Bruce. I maneuver the bumpy rutted uneven sidewalks and the ancient curbs as well with a forced bravado and determination that belie the weakness of belly and limb that I still experience, post-partum three days. It is time for me to change, to grow up, to deal with it, to rise above all this, to be strong, to grow a thicker hide; if I am to survive.

The least you could have done if you were going out anyway was to pick up the *Times* and some bagels, barks Steve at me. My fury has ebbed right along with my fragile energy, taking with it any resolve, any sense of revolt. I weakly unload the children, unpeel their wraps, placer them in cribs and high chairs with bottles or snacks, willing myself the energy to continue until I am able to fall onto the soft comforter adorning my mattress and recover from the ordeal. I am too exhausted to give vent to the invective that resides in the private recesses of my mind begging to be released and too aware of the potential consequences to even think about it. I am afraid to anger my Lord and Master. But something subtle is happening to me that I am not even aware of.

Caryn's birth interrupts the pattern of my classes but only for a week; I attend classes right up until the night before her birth. Now, after my Sunday morning enforced adventure, the obvious lack of compassion or respect that has been doled out to me I feel no guilt or compunction, and determine that turnabout is fair play especially in the name of survival, survival of self. I have gotten over feeling guilty for her conception and birth. She is here and she is Steve's child also. My Sunday forage has given me food for thought, caused a minor stiffening to occur in my backbone. Leaving the infant with her perfectly capable father for three hours I go back to class the very Tuesday night following my return from the hospital. Forget about babysitters, baby Caryn has her own father to care for her. I return to find a naked baby lying in a wet bed. I don't do diapers, Steve tells me. That's your department. Look what you have made me do, now, look what you have done to your baby. There was no one here to care for your baby. You are an unnatural mother, one who neglects and deserts her children. Note, that at this moment, it is my baby, not his, and notice the continuation of a familiar theme.

My motherhood is already suspect, my entire value appears to be nonexistent. As a mother, I am already considered to be unnatural. I am the only one it seems that is aware of what I feel, what I do; my instincts to jump up instinctively in the middle of the night to tend to unheard needs of my babies are unnoticed. Nobody notices that I do not frequent beauty shops or spend hours shopping. It is something suspect that I would rather read to the kids, sit on the floor and build blocks, play cars, play house, or play outside with them in our yard than join the other young mothers on the block for lunch or coffee rather paint than go shopping. It is odd when I am excited that Picasso has received a peace prize, that I am less than impressed when John Glenn orbits the earth, it is expected. No one speculates about why I don't play mahjong or bridge, attend or hold Tupperware parties. Babysitters are a requirement for all of these activities and I am looking for a replacement for the irreplaceable Jant who will pass Steve's impossible rigid criteria, Mom cannot be counted on all the time, and Steve cannot be counted on at all. The only time out that I treasure is for my painting class; any available sitter is saved for then. Days out are few and far between. I have no decorator, despise beauty parlors and makeup, and am bored by afternoon coffee klatches. I am not like all the other women, never notice the difference, I only know who I am. In addition to my babies, I am only interested in the unholy worthless thing that is art; I love my art so I am unnatural. It is the only satisfaction besides my babies in my life. Why are these two things mutually exclusive?

CHAPTER 31

The promise of the class is well fulfilled and I pass the week attending to my usual responsibilities while waiting expectantly for Tuesday nights. Working steadily in the class I learn more from the amazing Paul Puzinis than I have managed to learn about technique in all the years that I have been painting including those at Pratt. Suddenly even the landscapes that have frustrated me, eluded my capture come alive with the secret glazes I have been taught. These glazes are the thing that brings to life the nude figures, renditions of the models posing for the class. They work as well I find for other subjects. As a matter of fact they are the missing link, the element that has been lacking in my attempts. Uncle Irv purchases a heavily encrusted realistic nautical scene with much flurry and fanfare. I am so proud of my new work that I have the canvasses leaning against the walls in every possible space despite Steve's disapproval and disdain. Aaron, Steve's father in his rare moments at the house although he lives with us now passes the glowing bodies on their flat canvas beds and giggles self-consciously and disapproving shaking his head from side to side and wondering at the reason for such immoral and unacceptable work. Naked ladies, he mumbles, shaking his head from side to side. Maybe it's because he has a girlfriend now which is where he is spending all his free time, why he is never home; he is making up for lost time, getting familiar with love. He has his own oblique naked lady waiting for him. So he giggles.

Aaron has become acquainted with the widow Miriam and a grand romance ensues. Dinners out, assignations at her home, weekends in the Catskills; his life has become a rich one. Steve is consumed with jealousy on behalf of his sainted mother, Ida. His wicked inappropriate humor is no more evident than at that Thanksgiving dinner at Miriam's house when after a thorough investigation of all her drawers and closets, he arrives triumphantly in the dining room with her very private telltale red rubber apparatus of personal hygiene waving it around for all to see with a mischievous grin; Steve has reverted to adolescence, maybe he has never left.

And Steve ignores my work altogether as if it doesn't exist. Did he even then believe me to be an unfit mother because of my involvement in my artwork?

Deserting your baby already *mother of the year*, he sneers as I leave and withholds *his* pretext for *love* for as long as he finds humanly possible weakening only with a usual softening of manner and momentary tenderness as usual when his own need overwhelms his agenda. This is our obedience to the concept of love within the convention of marriage. His need, the chronology of his need, creates the pattern of our physical attendance to love, or sex, which is all that this is, and dictates the rhythm of our relationship and our home and the world of our children. I try to hold onto that moment, the one just before capitulation whatever it is for tenderness and affection are rarely dispensed and greatly needed, to be guarded and treasured. I try to hold back, to ensure a slightly longer period of gentility but usually, my own need takes over and hungry for closeness I am easily won, left with a sense of unworthiness. Isn't this a major role reversal? In all of the books I have read, all of the movies, stories, I have seen, heard, it is the woman who tantalizes the man, teases, denies, controls. I am a failure at being a woman, obviously. It doesn't matter, I still have the classes, and the babies are as dear and loving as I always hoped for them to be; they take up most of my time. They are my life.

One baby has become two and now three as I still seek that illusive quantity of love needed to fill my empty existence and compensate for having no sense of self, my bottomless pit, seeking to fill the space with babies, the love of and for babies. The issue of responsibility, necessary down time, babysitters is given very little thought, is lost in the intensity of my main focus. Originally I fight to have an image that will stand above others. First child in the group, youngest mother around, first with two, three, four...the winner and still champion... how does she do it...she looks so young...my glory. Alas, my only glory. It is my glory and my nightmare, my salvation and my death. Now I am addicted to the process, the only part of my life that contains any satisfaction. It is getting worse every day. Now, I am surviving in the *no exit* of all time trapped by the very creatures that I love the most in a trap of my own ignorant making.

I fill the emptiness with gardening, crafts, my art, sewing, reading, decoration. I wander haphazardly into an occasional adult education class; caring for the children uses up most of the time. I play with them, read to them, teach them, entertain and feed them and keep them clean. Is there supposed to be something more? This is all there is, there is nothing in my life to compare it with. I am to keep my mouth closed, not speak to or in front of Steve's, our friends or his business associates. I am to do my chores. I am not to paint or to bring paint into the house. Seen and not heard. Not ask any questions about our finances or other fiscal information. Not bother him when he is watching television or reading his paper. Not question where he is going or where he has been. I am put down regularly, kept in my place. My self-esteem falls lower and lower until it results in unavoidable depression which grows and grows until it completely takes over my sense of self. I am so engulfed in malaise after several years that there is very little left of me at all. I can barely move and manage to complete my chores with only the very minimum of motion surviving in almost a state of paralysis. No one notices, no one cares, or seems to care.

I have decided that Steve needs to pay more attention to them, be more involved in caring for his babies and under duress he has taken over the bath time business in his way, fills the tub with warm water piled high with bubbles, dumps them quickly full of protest into the soapy soup and when he leaves them alone to watch the ballgame, Wendi, furious that Daddy has walked away from her in her usual manner when not getting her way cries at the top of her lungs, takes a deep breath, holds it, turns the same shade of blue as her icy eyes, and falls over into the water. Mommy, Mommy, cries Bruce, Wendi is under the water, and I hear him faintly but that incomprehensible innate maternal instinct brings me to attention and I race into the bathroom, swoop her up out of the water and I hold her upside down and smack her on her soft pink wet behind and water pours out of her mouth and she is wailing once again. Steve rushes into the room chagrined and terrified totally innocent of any responsibility, what have you done to my precious baby now, *mother of the year*, and she holds her wet arms out to him glaring daggers at me, Daddy, Daddy, Daddy, she cries. What has the mean Mommy done to my precious baby girl, he croons into her wet ringlets. Tsk or something similar, says Mom when I relate this story to her, I can sense her shaking her head in disapproval of Steve's behavior on the other side of the line. *All you need is love, da da da da da...*

❧◈❧

Mom is devastated when Eleanor Roosevelt dies, in 1963; it is the end of an era, she moans, and then gorgeous, sexy Marilyn Monroe commits suicide under spurious circumstances that stun me, ghosts of conspiracy theories haunt, raise all kinds of questions. Was there something ominous about her relationships with both Kennedy brothers, and was The Mob involved somehow? Was there something sinister about the tastes and proclivities of our sainted president and his brilliant brother? Are other sinister political forces at work? But these things do not touch us and our routine continues. Their daddy arrives home at 11:30 p.m., wakes the finally quiet babies to kiss them picking them up one by one, dumping them back down crying in their cribs, walks out and leaves them crying. Exhausted, finally done with my chores now I have to get up and soothe them, get them back to sleep. He asks me the exact same routine questions twenty times each in a private third degree, inquisition, turns his back to me and snores. I am left with my angst, my exhaustion, and my swirling thoughts unable to fall back to sleep. I am rarely kissed goodnight anymore for my infractions are many. When I can force myself to ignore fatigue I stay up sewing, painting, reading; I am back to my childhood addiction and escape but now it's paperback mysteries and thrillers and old time movies on the Late Show. I never miss my old favorites, *An Affair to Remember* and *Peter Ibbetsen*! In my favorite fantasy world escape I am Deborah Kerr locking eyes with gorgeous unattainable Cary Grant on the deck of an ocean liner returning from a European vacation, or staring into the deep sensitive eyes of Gary Cooper on an idyllic flower strewn hillside, warm summer breezes tickling my barely exposed Victorian limbs.

∾∾

Restless and seeking I am painting now with a vengeance, fierce and focused, Steve's displeasure ignored. Now my frustration added to those of my empty marriage is the inability to express my feelings with brush and paint to the degree that I desire, thirst for. I have built a wall around myself to protect myself from my husband and his barbs and coldness. We still sit close together in rare moments sometimes absorb some warmth but when I try to talk about anything he will not answer. He still uses his newspaper as cover, is distraught when New York newspapers strike for 114 days and his routine is threatened and won't discuss with me the intriguing ruling of the Supreme Court that the poor must be entitled to lawyers. Am I foolish to be excited by this? What does it mean to me, as a woman?

A very young, very handsome Gary Cooper waits for me by a garden bower and I meet him on the top of the hill and we walk smiling happily off into the sunset. Although I am already married I begin to daydream myself to sleep with the same fantasy, different leading character, I cannot help it, it is all beyond my control: I will meet, fall in love with, and marry, someone who loves me forever although I never even begin to believe that there is the most remote possibility that this could or would happen. Some day he'll come along, the man I love and he'll be big and strong, the man I love…Without these daydreams and fantasies I do not possess the reserves of strength to survive. I always fall asleep before the inevitable consummation scene. With all of this, I am still rigid and puritanical, the thought of Divorce remaining unspeakable. All those with whom I've come in contact who have gone this route are leprous and contemptible for their weakness, their quitting, their immorality. Marriage is forever. And so defiant I continue painting, take more classes, make a few sales actually and secure part time work for a few dollars here and there adding oil color to communion photo portraits; it is not much but sufficient to feed and clothe the kids, pay for my classes and art supplies. As I work on the complex and mind-numbing minutiae recording the joyful realities of others tightly focused and methodical deep into the night my thoughts roil and swirl in my brain, *someday he'll come along*...seeking understanding and solutions, finding none...*the man I love, and he'll be big and strong, the man I love*...One eye is always pealed for something ineffable and without identity. *He'll look at me and then I'll know*...

I don't know quite what or who I'm looking for or why, what I would do if I found him but somehow it becomes the most imperative of meaningless drills, a survival-mechanism maneuver related to the filling of the great inner vacuum that grows deeper and more cavernously echoing with every passing day and each cutting rejection.

Among friends Steve delights in chastising me, shutting me up, putting me down; I am always either up or down. The wall I am building is very high. Occasionally a chink falls loose and I find myself begging to be loved; always I am rejected...but I am learning, slowly.

Caryn is growing, and I sense that keening siren call from somewhere in the depths of me, from my womb. I have been using birth control pills for a while, and they have done their job; now they have another job to do with their absence.

It gives me food for thought when Nelson Rockefeller divorces his long time wife and remarries his mistress making headlines; there is the faint sound of a tiny bell ringing. I am having even more numerous envious fantasies of escape when the USSR sends the first woman into space. Food for thought but I still suffer from insipient motion sickness. There is a massive wondrous excitement all around as a new pope, John XXIII, after the death of Paul VI, Martin Luther King makes his famous *I have a dream* speech, I feel the agony of the president and his wife when they have a baby who dies soon after birth.

Steve is hysterical with mirth when he reads that Alexander Calder has completed and is showing a sculpture entitled *The Pregnant Whale* and tells me between gasps how I don't need to be an artist, I can just be a sculpture. My pregnancy when I am carrying Andrew is a breeze. Bruce and Wendi are perpetual motion and Caryn lingers behind sits down and smiles that beatific grin at me lifts up her arms and murmurs sweetly, Cawwy Cawwyn, and I have no choice but to heave her up onto the shelf that is Andrew. And then the day of the appointment for his birth is here. Surprisingly this number four is a quick birth; shockingly the doctor catches him like a football moments after administering the obligatory Pitocin and warning me that we have a long, long siege ahead of us. Then there is the usual fight of course over his name. We have resurrected Bruce and Wendi's and Caryn's old bassinet with its triple tiered eyelet cover and matching pillow cover that I have designed and sewed; my mother's daughter. My favorite photo of the day is baby Andrew lying there surrounded by eyelet and pale blue quilts and pillow shams and stuffed rabbits and puppies watching wide eyed as the mobile floats and waves above him surrounded by his three older siblings; Bruce, four, serious and proud, finally a brother; Wendi, cute and fluffy, sparkling ice blue eyes; Caryn, pixie hair and huge dark eyes, her thumb firmly and thoroughly inserted into her mouth.

Andrew is one month old on November 22, 1963. I am holding him in my arms watching a movie on the television while I feed him as John Kennedy is assassinated in Dallas; I am stunned with horror, paralyzed by sorrow. The moment of the shooting is captured on a home movie and we are treated to the awful gut-wrenching sight on an endless loop on our television screens. Then his murderer Lee Harvey Oswald is murdered by Jack Ruby. More conspiracy theories abound as former vice president Linden Baines Johnson is inaugurated; is this the embodiment of the fictional story of the terrifying Manchurian Candidate, engineered, by whom? Thoughts of conspiracy become common as the world becomes more and more bizarre. On November 25 we watch the burial at Arlington National Cemetery after the procession of horse led caisson and there is that famous poignant photo of tiny brave JFK Jr. saluting his father. I hold my infant son tightly and hug the other three to my body. Strange formless fantasies drift through my mind and are blocked out of consciousness as even stranger sensations of terror and guilt engulf them. I cannot encompass even these unworthy horrifying thoughts. It is even more difficult to focus on the evil and ugliness in the world. Later, young Frank Sinatra Jr. is snatched for ransom, released after it is paid. Once again I clutch my three children to my lonely (newly empty) whale's stomach thinking about beginnings and endings and what lies between, and of MORTALITY, a concept important enough to be thought of in capital letters. I am the antithesis of ee cummings, I muse, who thought that *capitals* are superfluous and wrote of childhood and mortality: *life's not a paragraph, and death I think is not parenthesis.* I know I read it *somewhere.* I am stilled troubled by thoughts of mortality, find solace in literature; Steve scoffs, only reads non-fiction.

Salmon are spawning and swimming upstream acting certainly in response to some remote biological urge, maybe an arcane atavistic memory and I am experiencing the first of many such sensations in the pit of my stomach that portend a need for geographical escape or at least movement and somehow convince Steve to move out East to Long Island for the good of the children oh hallowed phrase. Technically it is the second of my geographical escapes the first being marrying Steve. More and more I find myself inadvertently searching faces in a crowd; it becomes one of my favorite fixations, romantic fantasies, I am barely conscious of what I am doing. Have I made a horrendous mistake? Is there still someone out there who is destined to be my true love? What are the odds? And what will I do then? I am already in a trap that offers no chance of escape. It is all a waste of time and effort. There is no one, there is no way that anything will ever change; it is all an exercise in futility. So I am a still, mute and chastened spectator when the Beatles invade America, making their long anticipated melodic way into our hearts and souls, when Lee Oswald's murderer Jack Ruby is sentenced to death and then himself murdered. And when there is a furor over the USSR using spy satellites. What does all this have to do with me? It affects neither my happiness nor my existence. Only the music reverberates. I am married to Nowhere Man and like Eleanor Rigby I keep my face in a jar by the door. I can only think of the lost dreams of Yesterday.

We brave the weekend traffic on the Northern State Parkway as we spend weekends looking all around now that we have formulated our plan to move, and finally find the East Northport house *way out on the island*, that's what it is considered in that time. Actually we purchase the property, the house to be built just like the model home we have visited. We are exhilarated by our forage into the deep raw woods, envisioning a new life on this virgin land. I am enthralled with the juxtaposition of rough hewn cedar shingles and antique brick, travertine floors and trimmed wooden cabinets that look like furniture, two levels, four bedrooms, three bathrooms, a sunken den and a rear deck and a half acre of woods. It is the answer to every one of Mom's stagnant dreams. The long wait for the completion of the house is as tedious as a pregnancy, lacking the gestating infant beneath my heart existing so distant as to be nearly imaginary. We endure the despairing terrified comments of Aaron and Elaine about the fact that most of the names depicted on the mailboxes at the curbs of homes in this neighborhood are Italian and Irish. How will we survive in this desert of non-Judaism? *And it is common knowledge that it is located at the end of the world.*

Somewhere over the rainbow skies are blue, and the dreams that you wish for really do come true...

Carrying an assortment of babies and imminently necessary paraphernalia we struggle to maneuver around a disarray of cartons and furniture piled high throughout the house as the sound of the straining and chugging of a struggling engine and air breaks invades our usual routine and an immense van backs up to the house early that morning on our moving day in 1964 which falls on the July Fourth weekend. Andrew is eight months old; the girls are two and three. Bruce is five. The main problem is that the house is not quite ready although we have been forced to close on the sale of the old house by a certain date; the varnish on the wood floors is still wet, our belongings have been left by the movers in the den, we are all sleeping on mattresses on the kitchen floor. We play go fish and

Chinese checkers, tell ghost stories and sing songs at the top of our lungs; there are no neighbors to hear us. It is very late, but finally the kids are all asleep. Here we are stranded in this brand new house, one of sixty, the only one occupied, in the middle of a storm, mud and ruts where roads are supposed to be, far from stores, in particular, drug stores, birth control pills and diaphragms still packed away who knows where. The spirit of adventure, the newness and promise of a clean slate, a new beginning, engender a sense of excitement; the sparkling masses of fireworks are visible over the tops of our woods. Camping out in an unfinished house creates a romantic devil-may-care mood, Steve throws caution to the wind and Kevin is conceived in the midst of the ensuing excitement, feelings of future expectation and joy sudden surge of mutual affection and divine inspiration. Have no fear; in mere days we are back to normal.

But we are out here living in the country surrounded by trees and fields and I am in my glory; the kids are exploring the neighborhood, playing outside in the cul de sac without fear of traffic, getting filthy in mud and building debris, hunting for treasures. We are all savoring the emptiness all around out here in the woods; the house is spacious and roomy, all set up for the care and entertainment of five children. There is this special room called a den just for their toys and projects. Everything is located on the main level, laundry, coat room, well planned kitchen, room for me to paint and to sew; organization is a cinch. Every new home today has an automatic dishwasher. We are inundated with all kinds of new inventions, the split level house, cellophane wrapped crackers and the H bomb. I and many of my sisters although I am unaware that they exist am undervalued by patriarchal conceit, ignored, just like I have been for my entire life, while I was fighting Steve; I am just as oblivious to the new and burgeoning world of feminist art programs that are being formed, rooted in the larger women's liberation movement. NOW, the National Organization for Women is not to be formed until 1966; my Puzinis nudes in 1962 were way early and never seen. Bruce is building all sorts of things from scrap lumber, has made friends with the Polish farmer next door, Mr. Orange, a direct translation whom he refers to as the farmer who becomes a surrogate father to my son in the absence of his own father's time or interest. The others soon follow. The couple is referred to by the kids as Boshie and Bopshie, in their own permutation of the Polish words for Grandma and Grandpa. Wendi and Caryn have set up their dolls and play housekeeping in a corner of the rear deck, and are enjoying walking their doll strollers up and down the driveway. Andy is toddling all over looking for trouble, finding it with ease, more inventive even that his older brother, Bruce.

I endure by my wits; logic and common sense have evolved a series of survival techniques now that there are four babies under five. Drinks are poured only an inch at a time so when inevitably spilled there is less waste and less mess. Glasses are placed away from spastic baby elbows and careless movements. Mostly, there is order, efficiency works. But Wendi, vying constantly for control, supremacy, a gleam in her icy blue eyes challenges me on every point, demands more juice which Steve gives to her, insists, moves her glass to the edge of the table, I move it back, she moves it to the edge again, a battle of wills ensues. She gets the last move occupied as I am with cutting everyone's meat and her glass topples over juice flying all over, covering the table, dripping on the floor. Wendi throws me a look of glee, of radiating triumph. I clean up, reset the table, re-pour one inch of juice, place the glass behind her plate, and she repeats the entire show with another look of accomplishment augmented by a giggle. The other kids join in giggling. Fury is a hot hard knot sitting in the bottom of my stomach. I warn her that if she does it again, she will not have dinner; that she will be put into her crib for the duration of the meal, and then some and still she repeats the entire thing again staring directly into my eyes all the time. Into the crib she goes; I curl my arm around her waist, carry her like a limb flailing animated football up the stairs and toss her into her crib, return to the kitchen. Steve disappears stiffly disapproving up the stairs; I can hear the heavy clump of his angry steps. He returns in moments Wendi enveloped in his arms her limbs curled around his body and neck her tiny hands grasping his face and neck radiating victory, what did the mean Mommy do to you, croons Steve his voice dripping with honey into her face, that familiar mantra. I feel myself go rigid with resentment and frustration. It is not easy being a proper mother when you are the enemy, when you are not supported. You cannot undermine my control, I tell him.

He now has a new schtick, something to instill discipline in the kids, he says. Steve insists they complete any request to us with *please Mommy dear, please Daddy dear*. Mom is horrified, I am helpless as usual and Steve won't listen anyway; this is how he wants it. He thinks it's clever and swell. And I am wondering why Lenny Bruce has been put on trial for obscenity when what Steve is doing is so much worse. What *is* in a name?

I was completely traumatized when Daddy nicknamed me, addressed me as Schtunk and Freckles, or called me Bacciagaloupe actually just a typical Italian surname that he found amusing. I remember fearing him, hating him, at the same time that I was loving him...I still hear him singing *how are things in Glockamora*, in his deep rich baritone...*is that willow tree still weeping there, is that laddie with the laughing eyes still laughing there*...And I have other memories, good ones, bad ones, mixed blessings...Daddy taking me with him to play tennis or golf on Sunday mornings or accompanying him to baseball and football games. When I cut my hair short that first time when I was twelve and he first saw the haircut he lost it, yelled at me, you slut, his favorite epithet, a kind of involuntary response. But I only wanted to please him. What did I do wrong? How will Steve's children feel about him after being forced to call him Daddy dear? Just who will they blame for being forced to call me Mommy dear?

I am given minimum cash for groceries and nothing for any possible extras for example, children's clothing, my own nylon stockings. I rarely go to the beauty parlor as my friends and family do and even more rarely have the special treat of a housekeeper. This is a rare gift received for special occasions. I am so immersed in my own private little world and away from the mainstream of art that I am completely oblivious to the fact that my old friend Michael Fried is defending the outrageous artist Frank Stella in *Artforum*. Our new president, Johnson, is very busy instigating the enacting of legislation for social welfare, pushing the Civil Rights Act, the NEA, is selling his new concept the Great Society. The nightmare that life has become continues, of diapers, pails and pails of them, a suburban variation of the *Sorcerer's Apprentice* fermenting in every bathroom of the house. Toddlers, toys, bottles, milk stains, baby food, and turmoil.

And, I am forbidden to keep even plastic ivy in the house because plants eat oxygen. Plants are a new symbol, my new coffee.

I thought marriage was give and take, I scream at Steve, unable to control the feeling anger rising out of the top of my head once again. I pick up the pieces of my flowerpots and broken bits of philodendron from the sparse lawn of the front yard my usual unwieldy belly handicapping my every move.

I don't want plants in the house and that's final. He barks the words at me, turns and goes back into the house picking up the paper and automatically turning off the invisible little knobs that regulate the volume of his hearing. Imaginary knobs to be certain and I am the only person who knows about or experiences them but I know that they are there. Then, back to the plants.

But they don't bother anyone and they look so nice, I plead following him into the living room, missing the touches of green cascading from the shelves already.

Obviously they bother me. Otherwise I wouldn't insist, he mumbles reasonably, returning to his paper. But I won't have PLANTS eating all my oxygen while I sleep and growing bugs to invade the house.

Oh Stevie, I answer, trying to control my anger, frustration, and disappointment, don't you remember your biology class? Plants don't consume oxygen. At night, they produce it.

I don't care, they still grow in DIRT.

Finally I give up, for each day there is the same scene and the poor plants are by now decimated from the trauma of continual flinging and transplanting.

I replace them with plastic ivy in plastic pots. I'm not happy but at least they *resemble* green living things.

He throws these into the yard also one day saying that they are still plants, plants imply dirt, insects do not know the difference and hadn't he told me already that there were to be no plants in the house? The same scene is repeated again and again for one time longer than the human spirit can bear, my human spirit, anyway. Then he is off to the real world, where he lives, away from all of us and I am left speechless and hobbled and helpless in my self-designed prison as he roars off to mingle with the living.

⇜⇝

A gigantic mound of plastic ivy is piled in the tub filling it completely. Soaking in ammonia and suds it floats buoyantly on the murky soapy water. I at least can be reasonable. Fighting to maintain some semblance of dignity in the face of unreason I decide to show Steve that plastic plants at least can be clean. Is it at all unnatural that I forget in the midst of my usual ongoing projects and responsibilities that I have done this? Dusk and Steve both return the former exhausted after a long day wishing nothing more than a good soak in the bathtub. He mumbles under his breath and slouches his way to the tiny bathroom and not until I hear his unearthly shriek do I recall the bathtub jungle that I have left. I roar with laughter nearly doubling over with overflowing mirth along with strange incomprehensible tears. When he comes tearing into the kitchen looking ridiculous wrapped in bath towels in an unfathomable fury I am still too helpless with laughter to respond to his anger and I wave him weakly away. I take my victories where I find them in this life. The trouble is I always pay for each and every one eventually. It no longer matters, it has become worth the cost. Tears of laughter become all too quickly tears of misery.

⇜⇝

Steve still turns off my stereo the moment that he enters the house each evening, without ever breaking his stride. I am forbidden to have it on when he is home; he doesn't like my music. I remember when he used to sing along with Frank Sinatra, when it rains it only rains, pennies from heaven… This is the price I pay for having him back at the end of a long day. You pays your money and you makes your choice and in the end you pays anyways, isn't that what someone wise said once? But it's after dinner and the children are all tucked in and the television is playing although I would prefer music. There is a background hum about boat attacks on U.S. ships, about the Verrazano Bridge opening and I try to be interested but I don't really care. All I want is some attention from my husband. He is all I have

222

all I will ever have. I am willing to make this sacrifice, swallow my pride no matter how his action jolts me, affects me deep inside. I am now sitting at his side on the sofa and I am leaning my head on his shoulder. I am still Pollyanna, ever hopeful. Do I have any choice?

How was your day? I ask conversationally the perpetual optimist trying to guess what would engage his attention. Did anything interesting happen out there in your world? Did you know that Bobby Kennedy resigned as United States Attorney General to run for the Senate in New York? What is he thinking, is this a safe thing to do? That poor mother, she has lost so many of her children. Do you think they're right to call him a carpetbagger? What is a carpetbagger, anyway?

He doesn't hear me, isn't interested in anything I have to say. Leave me alone, he answers, anything that might have happened is beyond your scope and intelligence anyway, so why bother to talk about it. This is an old story. I already know that as a woman I am of a lesser species lacking value or brainpower good for nothing but household chores.

I want to tell him that I am not so dumb, that I read books and articles, read the newspapers but my tongue is tied. But I go on anyway. This is important isn't it? President Lyndon Baines Johnson has signed the Civil Rights Act, I offer in a conversational tone trying to hide my excitement. We could talk about something else, I continue, lamely already knowing the outcome of this old and redundant scenario, like something you've read, or whatever. Chagall is painting a mural on the ceiling of the Paris Opera House, I mumble, did you know that?

Don't you have any chores to do he answers impatiently? He hasn't heard a word I have said. Why do you always bother me? I work hard all day, spend the day talking to intelligent adults, I don't need to come home to have to talk to *you*. I'm tired. Before the words leave his mouth, his attention is already absorbed by the moving patterns and bleating noises issuing from the glowing brown box. And yet, I am supposed to be the one with nothing to talk about.

I may burn the house down or maybe I'll go uptown and rob a bank, I suggest in a very normal conversational tone.

SHHHHHHHH. He hisses at me, pushing at me with his hand but removing it rather quickly as if I am a sizzling stovetop or possess some virulent skin lesions.

I stand up rather balefully and wander out into the yard and pull weeds from between my flowers and shrubs for a while. Then I turn on the hose and water and water and water my garden plants for hours mindlessly holding and turning the hose almost subconsciously, drifting with the mindlessness of the task into some other level of awareness far from the emptiness which surrounds me.

I cannot tell you what goes through my mind at these times only that it is nothing on a conscious level. Much later when the entire neighborhood is silent and the accusing moon and I are the only inhabitants of the moonlit tree-filled world I turn off the water and silently, numbly, go inside to bed. Steve only grunts as I slip in beside him and I know better than to wake him looking for some warmth for I have been bad. I am forbidden to digress from Steve's agenda of chores; gardening may not be done until laundry and dishes, mopping and vacuuming of floors are complete. I have chosen to disobey, to do something that I want to do myself defying my lord and master. I don't care except that I do. I am also a little afraid.

CHAPTER 32

I continue with a taut sightless desperation to sublimate my angst in the usual gardening and nesting, crafts and redecoration, and my painting. I am sustained by the embraces and adulation of my children. What else do I have? Just so much satisfaction can be derived from laundry and reading of children's books. Maybe I could do something that might please Steve, something that might bring back my Stevie, my loving husband or my continuing fantasy of him. The early Stevie of our courtship before his mother's death whom I miss desperately am grossly unable to retrieve through some grave shortcoming and inadequacy of femaleness of my own. Despite the promises of everyone I have confided in he has never gotten over his grief or it appears blaming me for it. I never stop trying to make up for it, trying to do things that will please him. The fourth bedroom would make a great combination office/den for him; I will surprise him for his birthday.

The carpenter is working now on the closet in Steve's so-called study. He is a strange and inarticulate breed of man, a new type in my experience given to hanging out in something called a *gin mill* drinking beer, exchanging toilet humor, and guffawing with the other guys until his shrewish wife comes in and drags him out by the ear filling the same poor ear at the same time with a string of vituperative invective that would make a truck driver blush and usually does. He has told me about all this in brusque macho vernacular colored by his own point of view of course while he measures and cuts and fits shelves exuding testosterone mixed with a grubby kind of camaraderie. He is singularly unattractive to me bearing no attribute that would under any circumstances cause me to take an interest in him, a skinny rangy fellow with lank greasy hair constantly sweeping down before his eyes while he is working, and he certainly doesn't move very fast. But he has a kind of genius with wood and has been highly recommended by the local lumberyard. He does not even come close to anyone in my frequent fantasies. But I am so lonely so needy of conversation that I find myself hanging around the area where he is working drawn to any adult male interaction at all. He entertains me while he does his crafty magic with an ongoing narrative of his experiences so strange to me that I listen fascinated by this new area of my continuing education. I am powerless to leave this scene drawn to his expertise at his craft, mesmerized by his adept hands, so hungry for adult companionship of any kind. Nothing romantic or prurient is on my mind at all.

I stand in awe of him partially because men who work with their hands, who have those large, competent, magic hands, are alien to me and partly because he is of a breed that is so unknown to my experience that I have trouble compartmentalizing him, as is my wont. Steve's first and only attempt at handiwork, the installation of a curtain rod in our old house resulted in his drilling through the drill motor wire so that it split and curled burning out all the fuses of that area of the house. So the carpenter installs distressed beams in the den, decks on the patio, shelves in the laundry room and assorted and sundry goodies all over the rest of the house. This is all paid for by my mother as a gift in her desperate efforts to cure me of my misery. She has long ago lost whatever respect for Steve she had ever had and her sole interest now is in her impotence to make her only child happy. I also continue to earn some cash from the tinting of confirmation pictures. I have found a local photographer with whom to work.

This is my first real house and I bubble over like champagne as Steve is so fond of complaining with clever little efficient ideas gleaned from the piles of home magazines that I devour voraciously, my mother's daughter. Devour and sublimate in like *House and Garden*. I am so very pleased with this carpenter's work that I recommend him again to my sister-in-law Elaine, when she surprises me with her first call of the year, certain that he will please even her. I am anxious to establish credentials with her so that I might be accepted by her into her life, she is the new matriarch of Steve's world. On the last day that he is to work for us before starting Elaine's job I follow him up into the study like an obedient puppy to see what he has accomplished on the closet. I listen to all of the little technical details that he feels proudly impelled to relate to me, listen with what I think is the proper amount of sincere interest although I strain inwardly to have him leave me to the private space of my home once more. I am distracted by the amount of concentration that seems to be involved in mere politeness. I certainly don't expect him to be suddenly face to face, mere inches away from me, nor to be wrapping his arms around my body, pulling me closer to him, kissing me with an intensity that bruises my teeth with his, forcing his tongue between my lips and backing me, backing me backing me across the room to send us both sprawling across the daybed nestled against the window wall with its gaily patterned covering. I fight with him as gamely as I am able, but his great strength (those able hands) and the element of surprise with which he has moved in to attack leaves me veritably helpless. I twist my head from side to side trying to free my bruised mouth, to speak, to beg him to stop.

Aren't you the cutie pie, he snarls at me with a sarcastic grin as he continues assaulting my mouth, wrestling with me, pushing his body obscenely against mine…You know you want this just as much as I do. You know you've been lookin' for it. Give, now.

No! I shout, wrenching my head away from him finally, you must be crazy! I've never given you the slightest inclination that I could be interested in you. How can you think or say such a thing. I am sobbing now, repelled and at the same time looking back in time wondering which of my actions have been misconstrued, have spoken to him of lust and seeing none still doubt myself for that is what I have been always taught to do. Get out of here, I say to him tightly in a very low voice filled with all the menace and disgust that I can bring to bear. And never, never come anywhere near me again. Your check will be in the mail. A cliché delivered with an almost ludicrous flourish of righteous melodrama.

He becomes suddenly frightened by my fury it seems; maybe he just has second thoughts, or suddenly begins to question his own reading of me for a sheepish expression comes over his features and rearranging his clothes he all but scurries out of the house and leaves as quickly as he can get his old truck to start. I have other things to think about, the little ones are waking up from their naps and Bruce is expected home from school. Yes, here comes the school bus.

ঙ৵৶

Whatever did you have in mind, asks my mother some time later on one of her myriad phone calls to check, direct, question? How could you have done that to poor Steve? Oh. Now, he is *Poor Steve*. And I am always suspect, always presumed guilty; don't bother to *ask*, I think.

I am truly puzzled and ask her what she is talking about. That carpenter, she says, why of course, the carpenter. I met Steve's Aunt Rose at a Hadassah luncheon this afternoon, and SHE said that ELAINE said the carpenter told her that he was having an affair with you and felt sorry (she said he said) for poor Steve to be married to a tramp like you. He is a *goy,* a carpenter, after all. I'm not certain which is worse. How could you have shown such poor taste or done something so WRONG? I am so mortified.

How could you think so little of me, I mumble under my breath. I don't even try to defend myself to her, not until much later. I am paralyzed by shock. How could she believe that I would even have an affair, especially with a man like him, a construction worker, so lacking in class and intellect and worst of all, not even Jewish? Who does she think I am?

I have not wanted to have anything to do with the carpenter, I know that. But I have to admit that I am a little bit flattered by his attention. Maybe I'm not the totally unattractive woman that Steve makes me feel I am. After reconsidering what I had been wearing all that week I could still not figure out just what had made him see me as provocative. But if that innocent appearance is able to cause such a reaction what would happen if I really tried? Maybe I could get Steve to notice me. It never occurred to me that the fault is in the observer in his own particular warp; both the carpenter and Steve, one positive, one negative. *The fault, dear Brutus, is not in the stars but in ourselves that we are underlings.* Who, here, is the underling? Not me. Am I?

I think long and hard about Elaine's story, the source of her information, the reasons for her enthusiasm for inserting a wedge between us, between Steve and me. In truth by this time there is a void so wide and deep that a wedge would simply fall through a bottomless vacuum. But there was a distance, an iciness, a lack of connection between Elaine and me, such a shame because I had had high hopes that she would be sort of like a sister to me, the sister I had never had.

And a thought occurs to me that just maybe there *is* someone out there waiting for me, someone who will want me, is that too absurd a thing to believe? *Somewhere, beyond the sea; somewhere, waiting for me...*

CHAPTER 33

How does anyone continue to survive in a vacuum of love, support, of acceptance? Mindlessly and full of hope it would seem. The days are filled with a blur of tedium. And the years pass by. Every now and then the faithless, devious hand of Tantalus reaches out and offers a sprig of olive branch, an orange blossom. Who can refuse this offering?

There is evidently still hope for me, for us. Pollyanna is still alive and well and living in East Northport.

I run down to the bookstore as quickly as I can. Excitement permeates every atom of my being. This book is going to be the solution to all my problems; at least the one that causes me the most pain, the one that is at the root of every other. Thank God SOMEONE has discovered and written about this subject, its solution, in time! Thank God it has been reviewed in *Newsday* the night before and I have found and read and reread the review.

I have hardly been able to get through the night, waiting for Steve to leave so that I could run right down to get my copy. With shaking hand I open the cover, having wasted enough precious time procrastinating over the back and inside jacket and heaving a huge sigh attack the meat of it with a voracity born of desperation. Which is what it is.

The Complete Woman: How Every Woman Can Fulfill Her Destiny, How to Please Your Man. A giant chill shivers across my back. Maybe now I will be able to get Steve to respond to me. It does seem a little bizarre at this point in time to dress up in pink lace baby dolls and white boots and greet him at the door with a martini. I don't know about this martini thing especially since he doesn't drink but maybe I ought to defer to greater minds than mine even though it goes against all my better instincts. LOVE is what I really want and if this is the only way to get it, then this is what I will do.

I already know that I am a failure as a woman, a mother, and every other important thing in my life. My mother and Steve keep up an unending stream of criticism and derision on that score so I am not all that optimistic but I don't have too many alternatives, do I? I am stuck in this trap with no exit, a trap of my own making but nonetheless an impossible situation and if this opportunity is to be offered to me then I will take it. I'm still not exactly sure how that is going to be accomplished but I'm not going to leave many stones unturned in my quest for the Holy Grail.

By the time I have finished the entire book I am not sure whether to laugh or to cry but I am certainly going to give it my best shot according to my own very non-literal translation of what I have just read.

It is evening. I sit down next to Steve in the den; the children are mercifully off to sleep, finally and I have both dreaded and awaited this moment for the entire afternoon. My palms are damp, as well as my underarms and my hands are shaking. I have slipped into what I considered to be a provocative position my newly curled hairdo fluffed out around my made-up face; I eschew the book's proscribed plastic wrap over naked body and choose the transparent lace nightgown that is now carefully arranged around my body. The lights are dimmed, and my perfume that I never wear except for special occasions wafts across the sofa and environs. I slip a little closer to him leaning my head seductively on his shoulder willing him to notice the changes I have scrupulously effected obviously for him. After all it is obviously my fault; there are some failings in ME that have rendered him disinterested, cold, distant. A momentary recollection of my wedding night, my honeymoon flits across my mind but I push it fretfully away. This is no time for negative thoughts. Is there some sort of lesson I should have learned? Is there something I am missing?

After a few moments of deliberately snuggling closer and closer so as to draw his somewhat unwilling attention, he shrugs me away from him as you would shake off an annoying insect and says, what's with you anyway, are you a nymphomaniac or something?

I leap up, tears of embarrassment as well as disappointment stinging my lids and make a vow never to humiliate myself before my husband again. I will keep so busy that I will not have time to think about it all. The worst thing is that I have no one to confide in, upon whom to dump my misery and fear; not even Mom, certainly not Mom.

⊰⊱

Shelly Moskowitz's kitchen table is gleaming with its layers of furniture polish and this is where I now sit sipping a cup of freshly brewed coffee afraid to drip a drop on that pristine and gleaming surface as I await the return of Bruce on the kindergarten bus. The girls are expected a while later from Nursery school in their own minibus. Outside is a panorama of construction in a background of woods and piles of dirt and construction material a rudimentary rutted dirt road winding in two directions as far as the eye can see. What shall I do with my dripping spoon? I glance out of the window from time to time where Andrew lies bundled and sleeping in his carriage running my hand soothingly over the tightly stretched skin of my again distended abdomen willing labor pains to begin. I know it is still much too soon to even hope but my impatience is legendary now and the tedium of both the wait and the burden is too much to bear. My entire being is now tied up in this awaited baby, the awaited moment of his birth is the guiding light that keeps me focused on staying alive. Now I will have five babies to love. My babies are the mainstay and purpose of my life. I will live for them and teach myself not to think about Steve and our marriage.

I am looking forward to this new baby for my usual reasons. Andrew is getting too unwieldy to schlep around anymore as well as too large and active and impatient to rock any longer on the Foamland version imitation Eames chair in the den. The two girls, Wendi and Caryn, at three and four have each other and are very involved in playing together and in nursery school and I need that new little creature to fondle and care for. Also I can well use the upcoming vacation that my confinement promises. I have a huge bag of mending ready though to polish off in the boredom of the hospital stay and an entire suitcase loaded with art supplies and mystery novels. You would not think that the entire confinement consists of three days.

I watch Shelly with awe and a little bit of annoyance tempered by jealousy as she pushes that heavy waxer around the kitchen removing yesterday's coat zealously so that she may apply a newer and fresher one and wonder at her. She wears the same distended though smaller proportioned stomach even though her baby is due only a short time after mine. My baby is due to what I recall as nothing more than an accident of laziness in the midst of a July Fourth rainstorm in the middle of the night on the weekend we moved into the new house. Though this is only her third, and my fifth, I can tell you that there is no motivation that will get me to strip and wax floors or anything else, ever. I feel exhausted just watching her. I am a little annoyed too, for I have endured the long lumpy walk over to visit for a while and as usual she can't stop cleaning long enough to talk or anything though she never has anything to say anyway. In Steve's world she is perfect.

The only thing that we have in common besides our mutual pregnancies and Jewish heritage is the fact that out of some sixty odd homes in this new development we are the only two families that have moved in to date. The roads aren't even paved yet and I can tell you it's no easy job pushing a baby carriage over those ruts. It's even worse than the uneven cement sidewalks of Queens. This time though it is my choice, which is different because....

Shelly has moved here from Brooklyn, and her heavy accent both tickles and repels me but even that doesn't irk me as much as the trivia that issues forth from between her lips. When she is moved to speak, she has me glassy eyed with boredom in mere moments. Her entire preoccupation is with the objects of TV commercials: wax, laundry soap, diapers, breakfast cereal. These are subjects on whose relative qualities she can expound for hours; she parrots the various commercials nearly verbatim in an annoying sing song, which I hear as the squawk of chalk on a blackboard. Then there is the discussion of the *pieces* ordered by her cousin's friend the decorator who is a little, *you know*, but very, very talented, and the great cost and quality of craftsmanship inherent in each and how it is worthwhile to live in an empty house while waiting for only the finest and costliest of accessories. I really wouldn't know.

Ultimately I wander back to my eclectic mish–mash of Salvation Army discard do–it–yourselfer décor in my certainly never empty house. Repressing a tinge of jealousy I remind myself that there is no way that I will ever possess the type of stuff that Shelly finds essential for a full life. Steve has a fit when I order blinds for the windows so that no one can see in from the street and then cannot understand why there need to be drapes in front of the blinds, to him it is redundant. Why pay for two things that do the same thing? He does not comprehend, or does not wish to, that the drapes I have sewn myself have cost nearly nothing, make the room look homey. Shelly's elegant version has cost a king's ransom. There is also no way that Steve will ever treat me with the deference and awe that Shelly both expects and demands and receives without question. She is that most awesome of creatures an original *Jewish American Princess*. The famous acronym is JAP. I am the first to admit that in the University of Life I have failed JAP and must go on now to master that tenuous and ungraspable essence Survival. Although it is a well known acronym I still find the word distasteful; Uncle Sam was after all married to Midori and my four cousins are half Japanese. How cold and insensitive we all were during that old war World War II when we were children. An old tune flits distantly across my mind, *Whistle while you work, Hitler is a jerk, Mussolini is a meanie, and the Japs are worse...* I feel a slight blush creeping up my neck.

Anyway my way is more creative and individualistic and imaginative and it keeps me from crawling up the walls with frustration and dismay for I am always busy with some project or other. At least, I have something material to show for my efforts. I wander over to her house on many evenings for a long period of time desperate to escape Steve's rejection or harping criticism and the all encompassing aura of tedious responsibility at the house. And Steve glued to the TV set never misses me unless one of the babies awakens and then I receive a cold insistent demeaning and sarcastic phone call and scurry immediately homeward an obedient wife, a conscientious mother. I am permitted the luxury of this activity solely because there is no coherent argument under the circumstances that could deny it. Shelly is everything that Steve wishes I were although he is unwilling to give me in return what Shelly expects without question from her husband as well as the world at large, excesses of respect and the material remuneration it demands.

Still, Steve deeply resents this insignificant liaison because it detracts my attention from my first allegiance which has no choice but to be him and the kids; housework. Even if I am being ignored, I must remain in house to endure it. It is unthinkable that I could have any other interest even one friend. Even my work at the Jewish Center which has become another innocently sanctimonious escape that he is hard pressed to exact fault with is looked upon with censure. As far as any social life this is limited to an occasional gathering with the other upwardly mobile attorneys of his acquaintance most probably of law school days. Stu Namm, Dave Judlowitz, Lenny Brownstein, most of them old fraternity brothers. Anything new is patently unacceptable to him...in fact he resists all attempts to get together socially with the Moskowitzes as a couple because not only are they new but they are not of his own personal affiliation. Even their Jewishness in a despised and ignored suburban Gentile world is not sufficient to break through his barrier of disinterest. And my career as a *Sisterhoodnick* (member of the sisterhood) at the Temple is short, since I cannot abide the abundant hypocrisy. The entire reason for its existence is to raise money to expand the Jewish Center so that our children will not need to mix with the *goyem*, the Gentiles in the neighborhood; the chosen people must be kept pure so that they may grow up to raise money to expand the center so that...I am soon done with that something that makes my normalcy even more suspect.

So I bribe these people to visit with good food, warm welcome and the promise of camaraderie. It's something of a busman's holiday there is a tendency to talk shop. Hey Stevo, hear you finally won a case this week. What are the odds that a drug using hooker will keep her kids, he snickers. Steve is renowned for never winning in court, usually avoids trials like the plague. His expertise is in more clerical areas; he is known in non legal terms as a pencil pusher. Well I guess I just lucked out this time, Steve answers somewhat smugly, you know they never take children away from the mother.

But even when his own friends visit with their spouses, spend Saturday evening, share dinner, converse and play the old standard board games, Scrabble and Monopoly at a certain moment Steve is suddenly missing, makes an odd implausible detour then across the living room with a huge garbage can ostensibly bringing it out to the curb as his last chore of the evening then disappears, and is discovered after a long perplexing absence already in bed in his pajamas without even saying good night. Our guests have a somewhat stiffly performed laugh at the bizarre behavior of their friend Steve and murmur words of commiseration to me, take their uncomfortable leave shaking their collective heads in sympathy and chagrin. You really need to do something, says Stu Namm, the future judge.

CHAPTER 34

Dreaming up ways to survive is what I do. It always seemed to be a one-gag joke when I let people know that I have so many kids. First there would be the astonished gasp then the comment about how I look young enough to be their sister but certainly not old enough to be mother to so many…then the evil leer and the suggestion about our tremendous sexuality, Steve's great masculine potency. What happened did your TV break down? Har, Har. And the inevitable reference to our name Heffner any relation to Hugh? And the overly obvious jokes about the habits of bunnies. Bunnies, get it? I laugh politely most of the time but the moment comes when I am driven to actually consider the possible satisfaction associated with the commission of murder. Steve of course basks in the implication of his sexual expertise and the quantity of his testosterone, the quality and quantity of his sperm, and lowers his eyes with mock humility all the while preening with importance, extremely flattered. I try to stifle my laughter and look down at the floor counting specks in the travertine.

The rationale that I have for not being the best of housekeepers is that I am not only having too much fun playing with the children and teaching them to walk and talk and read but find the day dissolving away to nothing in just romping with them on the playroom floor or somewhere out in the yard investigating the wonders of nature. Whatever time is left I treasure for painting. Ever regenerating laundry remains piled on the day bed in the corner of the den awaiting the impossible task of folding; it becomes the norm to pick through for what you need. There will always be housework, tomorrow, anyway and reading fills whatever time is left not always after the obedience to chores. This is my most effective perhaps sole tool of rebellion and of course of survival and I am perversely titillated by Steve's dismay.

But survival in my world means organization whenever possible and that old standby logic. I have six large wicker laundry baskets sitting in the den and a wicker rake and a snow shovel...and I have a system that evolved during my last pregnancy when I had had trouble bending over to clean up their innumerable toys, which seem to come in multiplicities of separate pieces usually spread as far and wide as ten little hands can get them in the course of fourteen short hours...First I rake the pieces into the snow shovel, and then dump them into the laundry basket...as each basket fill up it is pushed up against the wall and when they are all lined up I throw a tarp over them. First thing in the morning as they watch the old Early Bird cartoons the kids go about the serious business of dumping them all out on the floor so they can find whichever single little goodie is required for the game at hand. By the time I come down for breakfast the downstairs is already in a shambles of toys and cornflakes and spilled milk and banana peels and upside down baby bottles leaking milk over all and frequently pajama bottoms rank and sour complete with diaper and pins, left where ever they had been walked out of.

It is all about organization. I always put the upstairs quickly in order before coming down, after which I begin the Herculean effort required to rearrange the den and kitchen. The constant maneuvering of stairs is not the most sought after activity and I plan to avoid this as much as humanly possible.

Usually the well developed sixth sense that I have acquired cumulatively with each consecutive pregnancy would tell me when something was not just right. I always know for instance when someone awakens in the night or isn't feeling well. I even seem to know when someone is about to open the back door with a scraped knee. There is no logical explanation; I just seem to know, that's all. But even the most sophisticated machinery breaks down, sometimes.

∽⚬∾

The difference between this day and any other is my preoccupation with the ugly words that Steve and I exchange before he leaves for work which leave me depressed and angry. I grumble through the kitchen and hit the den, and move temporarily to the laundry room to move each load up a slot...dry to the dry basket to be folded, wet to the drier, diaper pail to the washer...ten loads a day is the average it seems. And back to the den. Grumbling under my breath continuing my version of the dialogue in my head I attack the most basic mess avoiding the omnipresent and it is mere moments until I notice that the children are not here.

They are forbidden to play upstairs during the day, this is a failsafe for the obvious reasons so when I call them they come scurrying down instantly. They can't have been gone five minutes.

The long winter day drags slowly and my temper is sorely on edge a phenomenon that the children always seem to sense and play to the fullest. It is called *there's—nothing—on—TV—and—we're—bored—so let's—see—if—we—can—get—a—rise—out—of—mom!* Usually I can control the game and channel their interest into more productive areas, but today they seem strange.

I find out what the trouble is when I run quickly to the upstairs bath for an extra roll of paper and stop short to see an open aspirin bottle lying on the floor, its contents spilled. My hands shaking I gather the remaining orangey pills together and count them. Damn that bottle is brand new and there are only six out of fifty left.

Stuffing the bottle remaining pills and all into the pocket of my jeans I yell for the kids to come upstairs. They hang back a little, all four of them exuding guilt. There are only the four at this time; Kevin is still in the process of gestation, safe and cozy in my stomach. Bruce is only five and a half, Wendi four, Caryn three, and Andrew eighteen months. When I demand to know who has eaten the pills they all deny complicity or knowledge. It is just like a Bill Cosby routine. I don't know, I don't know. When I cajole, and reassure them that no one will be punished for this grave and verboten misdemeanor they still remain mute, their small faces blank. I beg and plead with the older ones that whoever has taken them will be very sick and I have to know but still no response. I run downstairs and call the pediatrician as quickly as possible and ask him what to do…there is a silence at the other end when I report that I don't know, that they won't tell me which one is the culprit.

Well, he says, the one that turns a grayish green and begins to act listless and cold first, that's probably the one.

Thanks a lot. I group them all together in the kitchen and read to them, the meanwhile watching, watching for any unusual signs. At about six p.m. just as Steve is arriving home I begin to notice that Andrew usually pudgy and pink and boisterous to a fault is wan and clammy and shaky looking and lifting him up in my arms realize that something is very, very, wrong…he is the one.

Steve, Steve, I run with Andrew in my arms to greet him at the door my heart pumping frantically fear rising and with growing momentum in my chest and head. *We have to go to the hospital, right now, Andrew swallowed a whole bottle of aspirin, hurry up, we have to hurry...omigod, if anything happens,* I choke back the words and feel the tears of fear spilling from my eyes, grabbing at Steve's coat as he continues into the kitchen.

What are you yammering about now, *mother of the year*. I'm not going anywhere right now. I just drove home from Jamaica, and I'm hungry and tired and I want my dinner.

But DIDN'T YOU HEAR ME I repeat tersely he ate an entire bottle of aspirins and he could die. We have to get him to the hospital right away. Will you please listen to me?

I told you...I am not going to go anyplace right now. He is not in any danger, everyone takes aspirin; *everyone* knows aspirin are harmless. If you're so worried, then *you* take him, I'm tired, I've had a busy day WORKING not just sitting around the house thinking up ways to kill my children. Can't you be trusted with anything? He opens the newspaper in front of his face and shuts his ears to me. I can almost hear the click as the switch falls into place.

The doctor warns me to hurry, I plead. I'm not exaggerating, Steve, we have to go right now. I feel hot tears sliding down my face now and a great feeling of helplessness takes over my body.

He puts a corner of the paper aside and looks at me carrying his child with disgust, irritation and warns me very carefully, I do–not–want–to–be–bothered–with–this–any–longer–do–you–hear–me–mother–of–the–year and replaces the paper in front of his face closing the issue. I dress Andrew in his outer garments quickly and admonish Bruce to look after the two girls and bundling Andrew in a blanket race as fast as I can, heart in mouth to the emergency room. The moment that I arrive they are already waiting and immediately swoop him upstairs and began working over him. I sit in that hospital all night twisting and twisting a corner of my shirt pressing my hand over my bulging belly protectively and fighting back alternating bursts of tears and rising strangling panic.

A couple of times I phone home to make sure that the others are safely asleep and Steve assures me that in his care they will be. He refuses to come down and sit with me and says that it won't change anything; and that if Andrew doesn't survive I can have it on my own conscience alone.

How can you talk to me like that, I cry, in an agony of fear and dismay, your wife whom you are supposed to love, about your own child? Before I finish speaking, he has hung up the phone.

Andrew is strapped into the large steel crib with its high steel bars hooked up to the tubes and bottles so pale and shrunken in the tight white sterile bed when they allow me up finally to see him. They explain to me about the massive doses of adrenalin that have to be administered whenever the white blood count, monitored every minute sinks below a certain number. They warn me that the chances are 50–50, but that the reality is that he will not survive. The only thing that he has going for him is that he is an unusually sturdy and solid boy and has slightly more of a chance due to this. They are not able to pump his stomach which is the usual procedure because so much time has elapsed since the ingestion of the pills. I didn't know which one took the aspirins, I cry to a nonexistent audience.

Oh God I think, Steve is right, I don't deserve to be a mother. What have I done, what have I done? I pray with all the intensity that I possess and promise, vow to all that is holy to never let anything happen again that could endanger any of my babies. Fresh sluices of tears start whenever the impact of the reality of what is happening begins to dawn again. Finally a nurse puts her hand gently on my hunched and shaking shoulder, and suggests softly that since we won't know 'til morning what the outcome will be I might be better off with a good night's sleep and might be of more use at home where the other children need me. I see that the nurse is right, and after being reassured once again that there is nothing that I can do at the hospital, I go weakly, trembling, tearfully and exhaustedly home where I spend the night in fitfully sweaty slumber interrupted by fearfully ominous nightmares only to fall once again into the same restless sleep and finally awaken early in the morning, dawn barely slipping over the tops of the naked trees and pace and count minutes until I can call the hospital and find out finally that my Mack truck kid nicknamed, *Magilla Gorilla* after the popular kiddie cartoon has survived the ordeal.

I collapse into my chair moaning, thank God, thank God, thank God, between sobs and gasps of joy and laughter. Thank God. And race back to the hospital as soon as I can to scoop him up in my arms and hold him tight, take him home and rock him back and forth the way I always do in the big Eames chair in the den and soon I have soaked his sweaty little boy hair with my salty tears.

CHAPTER 35

When the metaphorical dust settles, Andrew is fine. Life has settled back into its normal rhythms. Everything is back to normal whatever that means. I gird myself for the usual, expect the worst; I am not very surprised. There is nothing that surprises me anymore.

Look at you, sneers Steve with disgust. If I didn't know better, I'd say you LIKE being pregnant. God, that's disgusting. You've been fat forever.

I am assailed by a momentary pang of guilt aware of the planning that has gone into some of these pregnancies but it is only momentary because it is the smartest thing I have ever done, given the circumstances of my life. So I have my answer ready. I do like being pregnant if you'd ever take the trouble to listen to me you'd know that. I like being pregnant, I like giving birth, and I love my babies. I am speaking to myself, why bother to say it out loud. It never occurs to me that my stretched and bloated body might be repugnant him.

You've got a crush on that obstetrician, that's what it is. This way you get to screw around officially. I'll bet you can't wait to go for your next checkup so you can get fingered by your boyfriend the doctor, he sneers his words dripping sarcasm.

At least he talks to me I murmur in a low voice. The truth is I do have a little crush on the doctor, little fantasies going on when I need a place to escape to which is often. He is caring and solicitous where Steve is not. His touch is gentle where Steve's is nonexistent. I do it is true look forward to my monthly visits to his office. The fact is, there are no internal exams at this point in the pregnancy.

What did you say?

Nothing.

I have learned the hard way that it is better to withdraw than to continue the mindless futile battle. My old childhood habit of hiding behind passivity, of non-response is back.

What are you watching on the TV, chubby, the one about that guy that's always running all over the place?

The Fugitive, you know damned well what I'm watching. It is my favorite program this year. I gird myself for the next familiar gambit. Steve is nothing if not predictable. I close my eyes tightly and mouth internally his familiar words having already memorized his script my familiar canned answers on the tip of my tongue.

Oh, time for your weekly internal?

He is a pediatrician you jerk and that's not very funny. Why do you have to be so nasty?

Once a nympho always a nympho; he is not even looking at me already outside this conversation.

A woman who needs to be loved and likes sex, is automatically a nymphomaniac in Steve's lexicon. I dare to look back at our early days together. Who is this man and what did you do with my Stevie, I ask the invisible powers that be, silently? *On a picnic morning, without a warning...that-moon-glow-brought-me-you...*

My intestines shrinking into little rubber bands of tension I move over on the sofa as far as I can get away from him and try to watch the show. Fat tears slide from beneath my eyelids and wash my face and I don't even try to wipe them away. I am caught in this trap, caught, and there is no way to get out. It is the same as though he is murdering me, strangling me. I will die with my spirit instead of my neck broken. And then Steve will be happy. Why is he doing this? How have I failed him? I cannot believe that he is so distraught over the size of his family; he professes to adore his children.

We can't go on like this, Steve, I say between clenched teeth, barely able to get the words out. We've got to get some help.

Go on like what?

Don't you see? There is nothing left between us but anger. We're not communicating, we have no common goals; we are so far apart...all we ever do is carp at each other, criticize and complain. We never talk about anything important. There's no closeness anymore, I can't even remember when there ever was.

I don't know what your problem is, as for me, I'm perfectly happy. If you're not, then YOU go get help. I've always told you that you were crazy just like your mother and your nutty aunt. I still say it. You need a shrink, not me.

We have to get some help, I say softly, or there's going to be nothing left. It's not good for the children. If you don't agree to see a marriage counselor I'm going to get a divorce. I nearly choke on these words. They are against everything I believe in. Divorce is not what I want.

Divorce? Don't be absurd. If you want to go then go. Leave. Get out of here.

Are *you* crazy? You mean leave my children? With you? Forget it. He now wants the children whom he professes to love while pretending to resent, claims to never have wanted, never helps or plays with. He will keep them just to hurt me and because they are his belongings.

Well go or stay or whatever you want. Go see a shrink, it'll do you good. But for now go do some chores if you have nothing better to do but complain and let me read the paper in peace. I don't want to talk about it.

My stomach gives a giant lurch for the answers are painfully clear to me. There is no way that he is ever going to cooperate on this for this is an old by now discussion. I am going to have to think it all out and come up with a plan, a program that will work; for my own survival and for the happiness and stability of the children. They deserve more from life than this. I know all this from firsthand experience. I do not want my children to grow up with the fear and coldness and battles that were the bane of my own existence. I don't want their futures to be haunted by futile wishful dreams and horrid nightmares like my own.

I watch for the old relic of a Chevy, watch for it to turn the wooded corner of the cul-de-sac its familiar leering face the preface to yet another rerun of the familiar torture sequence that has become my only reality. Fascinated, mesmerized, ever optimistic, I stand at the living room window rigid with hope. (This time will be different.) Steve is home! I glance into the hall mirror to check myself. All systems go. I rearrange several hairs, check the contours of my lips, run my tongue seductively over their outline and seductively lower my eyelids for my audience, the mirror, adjust my sweater for maximum breast allure and feel the old familiar excitement rise in my gut. My husband is home, my handsome, sweet, warm, understanding, compassionate, darling husband. I pose at the kitchen end of the long front hall, my lovely young silhouette a sensuous invitation and wait, timing the moment when my straining ears become aware of the softly clicking tumblers tickled by the key in the lock. As he opens the door I will rush to him and throw my arms around him. He will hold me very tight, kissing my face, my neck…running his hands over my back, I'm so glad to be home darling, he will say, I've missed you, I've thought about you all day. I love you. The familiar feelings of peace and joy flood through me.

I walk over to my station on the kitchen end of the front hall, check my hair and sweater yet again, and wait, the familiar knot beginning to form in my belly. I feel the sweat beginning to form in tiny rivulets and run down my palms knowingly. The tension rises like minute electric currents, in ever expanding waves, from my soles upward, upward through my groin and into my chest where they take occupation like an invading army squadron and settle into straining cutting cords binding my chest until if you look down you can see the ridges of squeezed and tormented flesh. And suddenly he is inside the house standing in the front hall.

I turn to him fully and throw my arms up to slip them around his neck and turn my face upward for a welcome kiss but as usual before I can gather my composure he has side stepped my embrace neatly and is hanging his coat away in the hall closet first hanger on the left. I follow his long strides into the kitchen the familiar sinking sense in my intestines the trembling of my hands a sickening warning of the sameness of the scene, of the rest of the nightmare scenario yet to be played out in chilling, monotonous totality.

Barney, he says with that sardonic edge. Barney Oldsfield. Where did you go today, Barney, when you were supposed to be doing chores? Chores. CHORES. His favorite word. I flinch. You put exactly seven and three quarters miles on this car, LYNNE, he says in the usual testy manner accentuating the double "n" as though it is some prurient epithet. Where were you? I want to know exactly the correct sequence; do not leave out ONE stop. I want to know exactly how you were wasting my gas, my car, and time that you are supposed to be spending on your (I flinch) CHORES.

He looms over me, his huge six-foot frame dwarfing me. I can feel myself shrinking like Alice as his eyes bore into me. Please don't do this to me anymore, Steve, I think pitifully, please love me. Please.

I am very small and young and paralyzed with fright. My father stands before me looming immensely six feet tall. He is wearing his captain's uniform its brass buttons and medals gleaming evilly, ominously in the late afternoon sunlight. His captain's hat is tilted at a rakish angle and his stern tight lips beneath the dapper pencil line mustache do not have their occasional charmingly sardonic twist of a grin. Do as I say not as I do, he intones sternly as I quiver. Suddenly he is grinning, Cheshire-like, standing in front of me yet in his T-shirt and shorts. But the grin changes chameleonesque and quickly to grand annoyance. Is that how you go to school, in an outfit like that (uniform like that is what I hear, in his army sergeant voice) with your hair cut like a boy? What's the matter with you? Go to your room and do your homework. Here, he says, handing me back my test paper. What do you mean you only got 99%? What happened to the other one per cent? He roars, a great grizzly bear roar from his impressive bay window gut. I try to move towards my room but fear roots me to the floor. I wait for some directive fearful of making the wrong move, decision. Go to your room, he says, the anger abated, and moves back to his station across from the television. He sits amongst the ruins of grape rinds and apple cores and stinking rancid cigar butts one baseball game before him and another on the portable radio at his side giving their simultaneous blow by blows. I wonder why he isn't in some office doing some monumental or even ordinary things like the fathers of all my friends and acquaintances seem to be and I gather up my courage to begin the ten-foot trek across the living room to my bedroom fortress and safety.

That's why I am unprepared for the massive roar behind me, and jumping back I turn to see that gigantic roaring grizzly bear ludicrously wearing a T-shirt and shorts and waving his arms as he roars. Sonofabitch, don't you know any better than to walk in front of a set when ballplayercenterumpirefield is happening? He shrieks. GET OUT OF THE WAY...I run this time, race, tears stinging my eyes and cheeks, the familiar lump in my throat.

I finally reach the safety of my room and silently lock the door behind myself. I place my schoolbooks carefully on a corner of the desk all edges neatly lined up and mindful of the tremendous amount of work that lies before me and the punishment for imperfect grades I feel myself moving almost mindlessly toward the table before the window on which are spread out all my paints and brushes and other paraphernalia and resolve to add only one or two brush strokes to my current chef d'œuvre *before attacking the mountain of papers and boredom. Soon, I am lost in the myriad world of color on color, tone next to tone, emerging images...nirvana. I fall into this state of joyful hypnosis and allow the flow to carry me cleansing my flesh and organs of all poisons and pain. I float in caressing buoyancy and only the sudden raucous banging on my door jolts me back to reality and the gnawing creeping tightens in my gut. Coming. I reluctantly open the door, expecting to see my mother impatiently calling me to another choking dinner.*

What have you been doing all day, asks Steve, annoyance and disgust painted all over his face by a master's hand. I'll bet you were painting. I smell that stinking paint again. He moves around the room sniffing at the air, at the corners, like a starving Doberman sensing the proximity of a rabbit. I thought I made it clear to you that there was to be no more painting, no more time wasting. Why can't you be like other women and be content to be a woman! Wash floors, do laundry; look after your children! Where are your children right now, MOTHER OF THE YEAR? What did you do with THEM, while you were PAINTING? MOTHER...

CHAPTER 36

The move to East Northport should have tamed some of that art lust in me especially now that I also have Andrew nearly two, and number five on the way but spurred by the growing estrangement from Steve and the resultant frustrations thereof and no longer find nest making and decorating and gardening...which I keep involved with every waking moment...to be satisfying. I obey the beckoning of the ever taunting muse and now that I have been lured and seduced by the charms of the medium of the masters, oils, I find the odorless caseins that I have adopted of late in efforts to avoid Steve's discovery of and wrath at my painting flat and difficult to manipulate and long to follow through with the oils. Ultimately I throw caution to the wind and openly defy Steve whose fury knows no bounds although it is kept tightly bound up within him only showing up through added tightness, stinginess, and coldness, which is by now nothing new. I am quite used to it. Painting is the only thing that saves my sanity, feeds my soul, except for my children.

I am peripherally distracted by the buzz filtering from radio and television about the awesome Freedom Walk in early March from Selma to Montgomery in Alabama. On the seventh which came to be known as Bloody Sunday marchers were attacked with Billy Clubs and tear gas and fought back the following week by crossing the Edmund Pettus Bridge; on the sixteenth they were taunted and harassed by the National Guard, the FBI, and federal marshals as they traversed the Jefferson Davis Highway, this entire route memorialized as the United States National Historic Trail. People are fighting for their civil rights. I yearn for and fantasize longingly of a freedom walk of my own.

Finally, on March 26, 1965, the latest baby, Kevin, arrives. I have acquired a false sense of security comprised of unfounded expectations after Andrew's rapid birth but to my surprise and chagrin the fifth takes longer. After many hours of excruciation a spinal is administered and legs askew in stirrups, sheet draped, I become the lunchtime class for sandwich munching voyeur interns. *She is immune to shame or self-consciousness because she has already given birth to four other babies.* That's their version of logic. But soon Kevin has arrived. No visitors because of another late winter snow storm. Once more there is the usual battle over his name. Despite being number five with all of the obvious limitations that would appear to suggest Kevin turns out to be the most focused, must be Steve's kid. When Kevin is just two days old and I am still in the hospital I am

241

awarded my reward for service above and beyond... With a huge flourish on his part I get a new car of Steve's choice for a gift; a white Dodge Dart, no wood sides which appear on all of my dream cars, blue upholstery, which would be my last choice.

In two days I return home to my family, Shelly's baby appears soon afterward. The latest news is that with total lack of foresight or compassion the U.S. has bombed Nam with napalm. I absorb this horrific knowledge silently thinking about maimed babies and agonized mothers, keep it to myself as Shelly and I walk soundlessly together in the early spring sun and delight in our perfect children as the awakening season and the refreshing smells wafting across the pastoral countryside, two ex-patriot city girls in heaven. We have nothing to talk about that is of mutual interest. The other homes are slowly one by one reaching completion and new people are appearing daily. A feeling of excitement and expectation fills the air along with that sweet promise of spring.

As usual I alternate my days between great exuberant highs and wells of profound and desperate depression. I watch with awe the queenly honor and homage that is paid my friend by her family especially her husband and the hopelessness of my own situation plunges me even more deeply into an abyss of misery. I confide my hopelessness and desperation to Shelly who offers unrealistic platitudes of advice unable to conceive of my predicament within her own frame of reference. Why don't you go out and get your hair done, your nails? Buy yourself a new dress? My depression manifests itself in distraction and forgetfulness.

I have dressed all four kids, trundled them all into the car, headed out for the market, forgotten Kevin so new to my agendas, left him on the bed all bundled up. Barney Oldsfield is out and running, the mother of the year has left her baby alone in the house. Of course in moments I have returned and collected him, never even reached the driveways end, no harm no foul. But there it sits in my heart and mind; Steve is right, I am a hopeless failure as a mother; as a mother and especially as a woman. My self-esteem plummets even lower. I find some small consolation in my love of the outdoors, and interest in my garden escalates in proportion to my marginalization and loneliness.

I move back and forth among my chores and hobbies and escapes in silent forlorn desolation bearing now a far heavier burden on my chest than a gestating child and see less and less exit in the gray walls that surround me. Eventually I begin to not see as much of Shelly for I discover that she and hers depress me even more than is my natural predilection without any instigation at all. I find myself back in my private insular world of art.

Sunrise, sunset, swiftly go the years...a long time ago I made that choice to avoid competition out of fear of failure. There were paths to take and I chose the easy one, fell into the welcoming arms of a fantasy which had been programmed into my head and mind since early childhood although I was terribly confused by the mixed messages received from my parents about the status and place of females. There is an entire other world out there, a world of art, operating on another plane of existence as I bathe babies, find and lose love, seek security, drown in lost days and years, sink further and further into depression, lose more and more of the tiny fragments remaining of my self.

Artists are striving, achieving goals and successes, creating masses of wonder in a bustling teaming world of art that exists for me far far away in that other place of existence so distant that it is almost imaginary, floating out of reach, disappearing for long periods of time buried under the detritus of my deliberate escape into nowhere. Soundless internal voices shriek and mumble constant warnings and admonitions of the relentless passing of time, wasting of assets, lost in the roar of daily responsibility, filled with mundane pursuits. I make doomed half hearted futile attempts to rise to the surface of this miasma of loss, loss of my own unrealized destiny but they translate into impotent gasps. Steve is a looming impediment to anything regarding my self or its realization, wishes to annihilate any attempt at resurrection of my moribund art, my feeble attempts at self resuscitation. There were those four flat landscapes, the painted mosaics, the landscapes and still lifes and florals and nudes that I executed at those classes with Paul Puzinis whom I found at the gallery downstairs.

In the periphery of my sad ordinary sphere I am aware marginally of the real art world, secretly envy these struggling, pushing, artists, their social networks and gallery connection, their blatant hard earned successes full of envy, sensing that I was meant to be part of that world but have lost my destiny by deliberately losing myself in this one surviving barely between two parallel planes.

I do my painting now in secrecy anyway for I find it more politically correct to avoid open conflict. Since Steve is rarely home at night anymore but arrives at ten or eleven I have plenty of time to work and to clean up and store my supplies. Ultimately needing money both to support my habit, my addiction to art supplies, and moreover to purchase the necessary extras for the children that Steve denies and forbids me as well as to build some sort of security for the future, and having few wedding and confirmation photo establishments handy as I had in Queens to do the tedious hand coloring of portraits that had brought me added income, the only direction open to me is to teach.

Do I have the nerve to hold myself as an authority? My mother has always hoped that I would take after her and teach, though what she means is to teach for a school system. Maybe this is my moment to follow in her footsteps.

I am anxious to tell her my plan the next time she visits, but something is up. Mom arrives at the house after her school day as usual, except for her demeanor; she is unusually quiet and serious. I wonder now if she has been to any more luncheons or heard some sort of new imaginary story from Rose or even someone else. She is at the house by four o'clock and Steve is not expected home for several hours. I am apprehensive, fidgety, can't figure out what is happening, waiting for her to begin. Finally, she clears her throat and sits down, handing me a manila envelope. So and so private detective is the name on the return address which is somewhere in Queens.

I look up at her, all kinds of questions on the tip of my tongue, yet speechless, not knowing where to begin. Open it, she says, quietly. Just open it. Read it.

My hand shaking I remove the stapled papers from the envelope and begin to read. It is about Steve. Steve and some woman, a client of his. A client and something more; Steve has been seeing this woman for a while. *Seeing* is a euphemism for sleeping with her. There is documentation of their assignations, days, and many of those evenings that he has supposedly been working late, going to his interminable meetings. He has not been home most evenings for a long time, I have been aware of that. I knew this even before Mom handed me this information. When I have asked him on occasion why this is he retorts that someone needs to make a living to support *me* and *my* kids. Still, I am beyond stunned; this is so out of character. Who is this man that I am married to? How has this happened and what have I done to make it happen? It's the babies, it must be the babies that he never wanted, that he is jealous of. But they are all that I have. What do I do now? What has become of my carefully planned life? Isn't his treatment of me bad enough? This is way beyond that. How do I deal with this? Will it pass? Can I continue as though nothing has happened? What about the children? What can I do that will not spoil their lives? My mind is filled with swirling battling thoughts. Maybe if I don't say anything, it will all go away.

CHAPTER 37

The car pulls into the driveway and once again I am assailed with the usual panic, anxiety, trepidation. I refuse to think about familiar nightmares and try to ignore the feelings, to go about my chores of readying dinner with an aplomb that I don't feel. I want to spare the children knowledge of what is happening, save them from the terror and anxiety that I myself lived through in my own childhood. God, if there is nothing else I want them to have better than that. I glance over at them playing quietly in the den, watching cartoons, murmuring amongst themselves, innocent, precious; their entire lives before them.

I go through the motions of setting the table, moving dishes and pots from one place to another, feeling the mounting terror, china slipping through trembling fingers to smash on the cold tile floor. Something has to be done; this horror has to be resolved while I still have my sanity and my self. There is no more escape; it has to be resolved. I wait until we are all seated at the table which is the only time I have him in any sense of captivity where there is a possibility he might be made to listen to me and broach the subject once again, Steve, we have to get some help with our marriage. There are special therapists…I am trembling so hard that I am barely able to speak. I'm afraid of my own husband for God's sake how can that be? The children look from one of us to the other sensing something bad, my heart thumps in my throat feeling their discomfort; exactly what I am attempting to save them from. What have I started? I remember that choking sensation tears welling up and overflowing, that helplessness. I'll stop it here and now. Steve, I begin…

A shrink, he asks, incredulous? I've told you if you're unhappy *you* see a shrink. I am perfectly happy. There is nothing that couldn't be improved if you were a better housekeeper and mother. There is nothing to discuss. Case closed.

His case is always closed. But Steve…

I have nothing further to say on the matter. If you have nothing better to do why don't you go and fold some more laundry? Something takes over me, Bigfoot living deep in the recesses of my inner being. Too late…

What is wrong with you, I scream! And now that I am already in trouble for opening my big mouth, now that I have managed to lance the boil I continue blindly onward all thoughts of the children forgotten. What about your girlfriend? I know all about her. How is that supposed to make me feel? That's a big problem. How could you do this to me? Why have you done this? Don't you have any feelings for me at all? I pause a moment but in for a penny in for a pound … I cannot control myself anymore. You sonofabitch, I shriek, a venomous abscess of pain pierced finally and without warning by his barbed tone. Did I just say that out loud? I have now committed the unthinkable, the absolute verboten; I have cursed and even worse I have spoken back to my lord and master.

What did you call me? His face blanches and he grabs me by the arm and drags me into the bathroom where not for the first time he forces the grubby bar of soap into my mouth, holding my head still by clutching my hair. You know I don't permit obscene language in my home, he murmurs reasonably, though sternly, the teacher directing his inferior pupil, to say nothing of your lack of respect for me. In case you have forgotten I am your husband. I am your provider; I am in charge of this household. I guess this means that he can do whatever he wants to do.

I have become so immersed in my feelings of the moment and my concern for the entire future that I have unconsciously ignored that which is forbidden. The matter of his illicit liaison is nearly forgotten for the moment, his defense has taken precedence. I need to remind him of that. And what about your girlfriend? I ask him again. How could you do that? I sputter. I am ignored, as he continues to stuff soap into my mouth, no more than a second's missed beat. The children hover in the periphery silent and stunned.

It hasn't happened frequently during the years, the soap thing, but it has happened with sufficient regularity along with other proscribed punishments to have left a lasting impression, to have taught me well, to have programmed me into an obedient beast of burden. The fury growing in me, the persistent ghost of my love for him, my bondage to the archaic vestiges of matrimony, my concern for the family unit all combines in one flood to ultimately douse the inferno of fury and despair.

My punishment is not complete. Steve doesn't speak to me for weeks waiting for my apology. What is it about this silent treatment that reverberates, tattoos itself onto my soul for eternity; becomes my own personal Achilles heel? The rule is his rule is that infractions must be answered with abject apology or all privileges including conversation as well as love in any form are denied. Love. That would be sex. In my world, sex is love. Previously, I always capitulated for I could never bear to be rejected in any way and because I need so much any crumb of affection or closeness that is to be tossed cavalierly my way that I am willing to pay any price. Strangely enough girlfriend of not there has always been some amount of sexual contact. My head is swirling with the inconsistency of it all. Somehow this time I am unable to obey; something makes me mute, and rigid with the inability to comply. The matter of the girlfriend is never addressed again. I fear to bring it up again, my bravado exhausted; Steve goes his merry way as though nothing at all is out of sync merely ignoring me totally as if I have ceased to exist. How have I become the wrong one, he the wronged? I am afraid to bring this up. Afraid to shake the boat any more that it already has been.

My over burdened brain becomes strained beyond its limits in my anxiety to find a solution. No Exit. Finally I remember the Bar Association seminar or conference or whatever that he is scheduled to attend the following week at Grossingers upstate in the Catskills and after making sure that my mother will stay with the children broach the subject to him. Tremulously.

Stevie, please let me go with you on the weekend?

I wasn't under the impression that we were speaking, he answers in a very reasonable tone, bending his *Times*, talking over the top of it. However you can apologize and then we can discuss the matter.

I can't do it. The words stick in my throat like chicken bones. Please Stevie, is my pleading response, if you love me at all. We have to get away from all these problems, from the kids, spend some time together alone. Reconnect. I'm falling apart.

Am I to understand that you are apologizing to me for using foul language, for calling me that name, for your disrespect?

I look at him mutely longing all over my face, pleading with him for clemency but unable to utter a word. I don't dare mention his girlfriend again.

Well, he says curtly, I haven't got all night, either say it or let's end this time wasting. You could be doing something worthwhile instead of standing around looking like a spaniel that has just been kicked. He clucks his teeth together after another mute moment and turning on his heel strides away to the television. He knows that I have reached a point where I will not respond, capitulate.

Again, morning breaks with all of the joyous late winter sounds and smells and an almost warm sweet musky breeze floats in through the bedroom window that I have just opened. Should I apologize to him? Should I knuckle under once more? I almost want to, almost am able to, but not really. Somehow, I can't do it.

What about time away together? A brief memory of those weekends in New Hampshire flickers across my thoughts. I take a deep breath, and summon up courage from somewhere deep inside of myself. I will try again. He comes out of the bathroom, beginning to dress, puts on his business clothes, not really acknowledging my existence. You can see that he is still waiting for my words knowing that I am not far from capitulation, smug in the knowledge that ultimately I will weaken, willing to forgo his own needs and pleasures in exchange for this major victory but the cat has gotten my tongue. Well, he has someone else for that, no wonder he is so strong. Not like the old days. In the end my resolve disappears and I still cannot do what he expects, demands. The previously soft and willing compliant part of my heart has petrified, turned to some form of non-pliable stone.

I watch him dress and put himself together each movement the same as every previous day of his life. It fascinates me how he can be so enslaved to this personal rote. It horrifies me that I myself can be so enslaved to his whim. I wait with bated breath hoping against desperate hope that this time he might make one small deviation from form thereby showing that he is indeed a human and not merely some mutant robot from another world. As he finishes true to form I expel the forgotten breath harshly causing him to look up. Still not ready to apologize, hey? He smirks. It is getting to be an enjoyable game for him now waiting for the inevitable, your horse in a fixed race to cross the line. He grins at me. I am frozen into speechlessness. He grabs his suitcase that he has packed the evening before, always carefully planning, always prepared.

He starts down the stairs and out of the door at his usual brisk and businesslike pace. Suddenly unbidden surges of deeply suppressed emotion, fear and pain and loneliness force their way up into my chest and seem to push themselves like a geyser right out the top of my head. I am unaware of my action. Wait, I cry out running to the window, thrusting it open, shouting, Stevie, wait, I *will* apologize, I'm sorry, I didn't mean it. The desperation in my voice is palpable, strident. I shouldn't have said that to you...please wait.

He barely turns his head and murmurs over his shoulder, it's too late now. I have to leave for work. I need to get a full day in before leaving for the weekend. Why is your timing always so inopportune?

But Stevie, the weekend, can I go? I can meet you...Should I tell my mother to come?

No, you waited too long, now you can't go; it's too late to make arrangements. I might have changed my mind sooner, he adds reasonably.

Stevie, wait, I cry out the window not caring if all the neighbors hear, I'm coming down, please just kiss me goodbye. I ache all over. Ache to feel wanted. Ache to feel loved and needed, to feel valuable. There is a screech of tires as he pulls out of the driveway just as I reach the spot where he has been parked mere moments before. I stand mutely for a moment clutching my faded chenille robe around myself and feeling all hope sink from the massive lump in my chest to the screaming agony in my groin to settle in the heavy stumps of my legs. Somewhere far away Frank Sinatra sings, *you vowed your love from here to eternity,* and a vision flits across my mind of Deborah Kerr and Burt Lancaster writhing in romantic ecstasy in the surf, the sky aflame as Pearl Harbor explodes and burns in the background...

I stumble up to my room and throw myself onto our bed, limp with the fatigue of utter defeat. I am unprepared for the wail of agony that rises out of the tips of my toes and becomes a deafening unending shriek of pain that continues for what seems like hours in a vacuum of timelessness and doesn't end until all of the pain is gone, erupted like Vesuvius and run down over the top of me in ribbons of steaming lava. When it is over and I have slept for a while I get up to wash my streaked and tear-caked face and find with surprise that I no longer have any feelings at all. No pain, no discomfort, and no love either. Nothing; all of that, and now it is all over. I dress myself woodenly, and retrieve the children from their cribs and bring them down for breakfast and to begin our day.

Book I

Part III

Falls

CHAPTER 38

The present day, 2009

The minutes and hours are passing, the afternoon and my hopeful birthday expectations along with it is slowly being eaten away and I am still looking for ways to fill the time, make the day disappear, the tension to disperse along with it. I have hit a proverbial wall. Nothing is coming out right. It is one of those times when it is necessary to leave the studio, take a cleansing break; give creativity a rest. This intense concentration on writing provokes the escalation of memories, unwelcome emotions, and I feel myself falling helplessly, gratefully into self-protective mode. Now, I feel a revving of internal engines; I am entering that safe place where reality does not intrude. I know that I am about to become that familiar vehicle that Sorcerer's Apprentice of art production that is my familiar alter ego. My thoughts move faster and faster tripping over one another...Writing is usurped by uncontrollable urges that cannot be ignored, the world of three dimension calls out to me. It is time to take an intermission from my writing.

It is this overwhelming thirst to create. Anything. Well, not just *anything*. I have gone to the welding studio of James de Martis and cut out pieces from my old stash of rusted steel. Maybe this time I'll combine them with chunks of aged wood, spindles, farm implements and wheels, ancient rusted tools that are right now filling and overflowing assorted receptacles on the south side of my barn. The choices are endless. I hear a siren call...

There are lamps, glass and ceramic and wood and brass; I have collected thirty or forty this past winter and they have been disassembled so that they are now simple globes, in various shapes, colors and textures waiting to be threaded onto six-foot-high half-inch pipe set into heavy metal bases in assorted juxtapositions to form sparkling garden monoliths. There will be more than ten when I am done. I always produce my work in multiples, suites, series, which is why I am surrounded by so much art. It is a result of my years of forced production a habit impossible to change. Even those paintings that illustrate my life that I hope to make a part of this story are a series. A large series. This mass production *modus operandi* is how I was able to accumulate so much art, stock my gallery in the old days. My studio is so full of works in progress that there is little space left to work and I am forced to move out into the garden. This is one of the joys of spring, the promise of possibilities to work outside in good weather.

Maybe next summer I will construct a deck and lanai in which to continue this work in comfortable shade; an umbrella doesn't do enough. There are precious few architectural projects to address in this home anymore; I have fulfilled all my plans and expectations. In other times and places, this would signal the time to move on, to sell and to build yet again. I have this great need to build houses. The planning and construction of homes is the plus ultimate of creativity, the quintessence of art forms, as the designing and filling of the interior is equal to the construction of the most intricate and meaningful of assemblages in the tradition of Joseph Cornell, Louise Nevelson, Robert Rauschenberg, Alphonso Ossario; my most favorite media on a very grand scale of course. Although now that I am older I need to be content to enjoy what I have created, there is no longer time or energy for new construction and relocation. What is it about the process of home construction that excites?

Massive thrills of adventure and expectation, tingles and shivers invade my limbs, my chest, my fingers, my being with each visit to the freshly cleared building envelope in the midst of these oak woods, newly excavated, then poured foundation, then partially and fully framed beginnings of the first house I ever build, or rather at that time am a part of building back in 1963 when we have just the four babies; another obsessively addictive activity. A two-story colonial nestled in the woods of East Northport a suburb of Huntington Town in Suffolk County. Soon the two more babies join the family. I wander in the middle of the site, the house to be, surrounded by walls of lumber, two by four, two by six, delineating rooms. I imagine my future home, this is the living room, the kitchen will be right here; this is where I will stand while I am washing the dishes, looking out this window at my future garden. The play gym will be right there, and the roses will be there, and the forsythia will be there. There are no words to express the feelings that overcome me at such a time as this that can equal the sense of joy and anticipation. There is no other occupation that comes close to this sensation except gestation and birth. It is the same thing, I am gestating a home, a sculpture to live in and I await its birth.

I still cannot resist turning down that street when I am in the area and I am still amazed to see every single thing in the same place as though the mere act of my leaving would have negated their existence. I swallow and fight back old memories, my stomach jumping and churning. The homes are a little stiffer with their layers of paint, their weight of years, and a little prouder with their re-done and re-lifted faces and a little more crowded nestled amongst their overgrown foundation plantings. I steel myself as I turn into Arleigh Court slowing before that familiar driveway aware of the house, sharing an intimate glance with its familiar face and lock eyes with its windowed stare. I look away a guilty secret apparent; time has indeed passed by. Once golden glowing cedar shingles are grey and discolored by weather, antique brick facing has finally outlived its novelty now looking like bland and ordinary masonry. The front door is no longer geranium red. A simple foundation planting has morphed into a pine and rhododendron forest. My cherry tree is as large as an ancient oak or maple. My roses are gone, the forsythia are sparse and raggedy. My white picket fence has disappeared replaced by plastic. I feel time and alienation slipping over me, suffocating me. There are no bicycles and wagons and other marks of children in residence lying here and there marking territory. The old play gym also, is long gone.

Yes. It is all gone, all long gone. My eyes are closed tightly warding off threatening tears; sounds and sights and scents come barreling back. Small children are scampering all over shouting and yelling. Dogs are barking, bicycle horns and bells are honking and jingling. The odors of privet and honeysuckle and lilac mix with pot roast and hamburger, cigar and cigarette, coffee and apple pie. I inhale it all, absorb the sounds and smells, and yet I stare, helpless, mindless, as though critiquing an ordinary painting of a generic rural scene perhaps in my old studio. It is a quaint period movie short accompanied by nostalgic melody and words...are you going to Scarborough Fair? Parsley, sage, rosemary and thyme, remember me to one who lives there, he was once a true love of mine...

CHAPTER 39

1965

Into the sad and baneful vacuum of my life flounces Eileen Corby one sunny afternoon her perfume arriving before her in a cloud, her mischievous blue eyes twinkling and sparkling, her blond hair bouncing. She plops into a chair at the kitchen table and lights a cigarette. I'm glad you called, she says, I always like to get to know the mothers of the kids my own are playing with. Her son is one of Bruce's new playmates from his class in school. They are our newest neighbors just moved into their home. I am making my best effort to be the good mother I am convinced I am not. Steve has made certain to reinforce this belief. Eileen has arrived at my doorstep in answer to my smugly overly responsible note inviting her for coffee. I have had that same instinct that she has just mentioned. What a relief, she says, to finally be in that house...l thought it would never be ready. Yes, she adds, milk and sugar... I am also relieved. In secret I have dreaded the appearance of yet another Shelly Moskowitz my first acquaintance in this new home. I need not have feared.

The kids are all outside playing in the yard and the cul de sac. Busy with bikes and balls and dolls and swings and sandboxes.

Eileen has been sitting at my kitchen table for just a few minutes and already she has gone through several cups of coffee and several packs of cigarettes. Their broken remains now lay haphazardly piled in her saucer having been viciously stamped out either to emphasize some point or in answer to some silent hidden hostility deep within; we sit in a hazy, murky intolerable gray cloud of cigarette smoke residue. I am entranced by her liveliness, her slickly coiffed platinum blond bob, her careful makeup, her twinkling blue eyes. I have only known her for a short time but still I think I know her very well. In actuality I've barely touched the surface for beneath that charming expansive exterior are layers and layers of person and pain that are all but unfathomable to anyone who doesn't know her extremely well. I am not alarmed by this alien lifestyle that she drapes around her like a Joseph's cloak; it so fascinates and captivates me that I allow no will myself to become sucked into her vortex. I am a speck of dust and she a vacuum cleaner.

My life takes on a new meaning and direction from that day. I am inexorably propelled into the midst of an unending cyclone. I am expanding the parameters of my experience and we become inseparable that is to say we drink untold cups of coffee and I empty interminable ashtrays. Our relationship lives within the confines of my kitchen table. I am mesmerized, fascinated by the unending stream of patter and shtick, stories and tales that pour forth from Eileen's never sentient lips. It begins with the rather innocuous three nuns or the quintessential rabbi, priest and minister going into a bar, and escalates. Between choked gurgles of laughter she puffs out the punch line to a rather salacious story that I in my shocked stupor have not even heard... *with such bad gums, who could have teeth?* I may not understand completely, but I cannot help but respond with laughter, feeling an immediate relief from my sad colorless days. We become inseparable that is save for those mysterious afternoons when she disappears from our neat suburban lives for long and unaccountable hours and survives and recharges in that as yet unmentionable world of hers designated by a nebulous wave of the arm that exists somewhere vaguely in the direction of Babylon where she previously lived on the south shore of Long Island. Alas! I always think when I hear that name. Alas, Babylon.

I await these hours spent together with the same joy and expectation once felt while awaiting a new date. Our time is full of that never ending current of spicy anecdotes. Did you hear the one about Razmus, she asks (she seems to have a penchant for stereotypical black characters and ethnic speech)? Well, he's walking down the street in Harlem, you know, and he sees his friend Leroy hanging out the window...what you doing, Leroy, asks Razmus and Razmus answers, layin' linoleum, and Leroy answers, stupendous, do she have a sister...

and Eileen collapses in paroxysms of laughter, and I join in somewhat tentatively, again...

Catch this one, she gasps after she has caught her breath...this big black buck walks into a bar followed by two sweet young things. They look him up and down and one says to the other, you ask him, and the second answers, no you ask him...(I'm supposed to drag this out, but I'll spare you)...and finally he answers, two inches honey, two inches, and one girl asks, by the tape, and he answers, no, honey, from the floor... and once again she is convulsed.

I am not certain what I have just heard, how to react, know somehow that excited laughter is required; I have heard my share of off color stories, but this is an entirely new level for me...but I am a quick learner.

She appears to me to be a raconteur *par excellence,* salacious stories flowing like a torrent until laughter and outraged guffaws purge us both of pain at least for a moment as we mop up tears that have flooded our faces. The sole remaining sensation is abdominal muscle fatigue due to the paroxysms of laughter that consume us for that moment at least. Soon, I am able to commit to memory and recite great cascading series of these anecdotes with almost the aplomb of my tutor. There is one exception. Eileen is the master of dialect which eludes me. We begin gradually, tentatively, to confide in each other as the protective shell that we each wear so gingerly becomes slowly breached. I learn, finally that her husband Patrick, tall and well built and successful, full of blarney and irresistible Irish charm whom until now I have seen as some sort of paragon of husbandly virtue and perfection and envied her, is not whom he appears to be.

But Eileen speaks in code, in carefully protected and masked innuendo. I am never certain what she is saying. Everything she says must be examined, interpreted. She wears a suit of armor, a thick coat of pride, her history and her feelings are deeply hidden in an invisible mysterious vault. She has a very healthy respect for what the inexorable *they*, the rest of the world; thinks of her image, her comings and goings. Intriguing, because their very surreptitious and shady nature would give anyone cause to raise an eyebrow or two. Above all it appears to me she must protect her own toughly vulnerable hide. To this end, she takes care to cover her tracks in advance given the uncertainty of whether or how far she can trust an non-initiate like me with her cynical secrets.

Well, I'm off to the wars, Eileen calls out gaily from my front door, going shopping, do you want to come? I don't have a sitter, and I don't have any money, anyway, I answer. Don't you get a weekly allowance, she asks, for food, for the kids, for clothing and stuff, and I tell her, yeah, but it's barely enough for food, I sew most of their clothing and my mother buys a lot of stuff...I color-tint confirmation pictures for a local photographer but it doesn't pay that much...I tell her to have fun and she assures me that she will.

For a long time she appears to question the advent of my potential treachery in our budding relationship; there is an air that surrounds me like my own impenetrable cloak of sanctimonious innocence. Finally she begins to trust me a little, takes a leap of faith. I begin to receive invitations to *go shopping* with her and have trouble understanding her impatience at the stores since she after all, is the one who has invited me. I can see an immense internal battle raging. Ultimately she summons the courage to suggest tentatively that we stop for a while at a local pub she knows of for a tiny drink or two just to pass the time of course purely innocent. I am shocked and titillated; the thought of such naughtiness tickles me, instigates and feeds a growing need for rebellion. I am tired of being virtually incarcerated, of being perpetually angry with Steve. This sounds like a novel way to both pass the time and rebel. No one will ever know. Here is a way to act on my desire to revolt against the arbitrary restrictions that he has imposed upon me, at the secret knowledge that I keep well hidden about him. I surprise myself at just how quickly I agree. I have no clue as to the depth or complexity of the world I am entering into. My naïveté and innocence are laughable yet no one is laughing.

How intensely, spicily enticing this all is to me. To visit an establishment as disreputable as a *Gin Mill* for any reason is not only an act totally alien to anything in my own experience and life style, but would shock Steve into cardiac arrest in a moment, should he ever find out. I don't know what to expect, have never been inside one of these places. The very word encompassed by its alien feel, gin mill, rolls around in my mouth with titillating discomfort.

Shivers of apprehension race through me. The very thought provokes paroxysms of nervous giggles. I can accomplish the virtual emotional murder of my abuser by merely partaking of a forbidden cocktail in a disreputable bar. Especially since lately I have been fantasizing long and gory incidents of his accidental demise, even murder. I awaken sweating profusely with a bloody knife in my hand that dissolves into a clump of blanket as my eyes clear; Steve is quite alive, snoring blissfully. I have also visited the possibility of ending my own life, saying goodbye to all of my agony and frustration. But the thought alone is another act of futility; I cannot envision abandoning my children.

Now my new friend offers me a potential exit from my Hell. Steve only allows me to have a cocktail on a special occasion like a birthday or anniversary. He warns me quite sternly, prohibits me from accepting such tabooed libations at social occasions where they are readily available. At the top of his list are those innocent and festive looking scotch or whiskey *sours* that flow so freely at the numerous Kiwanis and Bar Association dinners which we constantly attend; those same affairs where I am sternly forbidden to speak especially on matters having to do with world events or politics. I have been deemed too stupid, ignorant, uneducated to be permitted to voice my ideas. The mere suggestion, mention of sitting at a bar, even a woman who is accompanied by her very own husband invites invective that never fails to bring the blood rushing to my face. At crowded restaurants of those rare occasions that we indulge in dinner out we await our table in the vestibule.

I join Eileen that first afternoon tingling with apprehension of action alien and forbidden, nursing my one delightful and forbidden whiskey sour with joy, watching with growing shock and awe as she consumes five or six gin and whatever or some other nameless concoctions. She grows more and more voluble and volatile by the moment and the quantity of drinks consumed and she performs her endless repertory in a torrential sluice of words…listen to this…*a giant ship runs aground on an reef somewhere in the south seas and the only survivor is a tiny baby who washes up on the shore, and is cared for by the animals who are the only inhabitants of this island. He survives by eating berries and other fruit and digging for clams. One day when he had become a young man he hears a horrid crash and going to investigate finds a beautiful young woman lying on the beach. Things happen and later she rolls over and looks into his eyes and asks* (Eileen effects a deep sultry voice) *how it was, and he responds, great, but look what you did to my clam digger*…and it goes on and on. Rapidly the admiring amused crowd of after-hours businessmen and construction workers are convulsed with laughter from her brittle and acerbic wit. One by one the customers sidle, walk, stride over to the scene of the hubbub, where we sit. Soon we are surrounded. It is raining men. The convocation of testosterone becomes intoxicating in itself with all of its unspoken implications. I feel a bit uncomfortable at first and as guilty as if I had broken some actual or imponderable commandment but I am surrounded by a feeling of good will. I am studied from head to toe, glanced at with unabashed admiration, with tacit approval. I am accepted with no dissenters as one of the group. Suddenly and unexpectedly I feel valuable. The heady response I have to feeling desirable and attractive proves an opiate impossible to resist. Yet I have no desire to become involved with any of these men attractive as some of them may be. The thought barely crosses my mind is instantly dismissed.

Guilt is my companion as I return stealthily home. My heightened senses foretell of an ineffable fear for what may be waiting beyond the horizon. I feel suddenly a great surge of affection born maybe of that truly undeserved guilt, for Steve, and force myself to fuss over him flirt with him try to attract him anew to give him an opportunity to fill the yawning void in our lives together. To give him some reason to end his liaison with the unimaginable mistress. I have no idea who she is, what she looks like, what her attraction may be, just what I am up against. My efforts are met with not only rejection but with a stern admonition that my behavior is unladylike, too forward, an indication of my degraded moral state. I blush thinking about the drinks at the bar, the men surrounding me, the surge of wellbeing that has been engendered, Eileen's other mysterious activities. I am wondering why I am so unattractive to my husband and so appealing to so many strangers none of whom I want. But innocent of these facts he accuses me once again of being a nymphomaniac. Groundless guilt and general fear silence me. Disgusted by my offers of and need for affection he drifts back to the inexorable television set once again. He goes even further, forbidding me to watch with him. I distract his attention, he says, thereby ruining the show for him. This applies even to commercials it seems for even when they are on and I sit down near him silently in mute agony unable to force the words from my mouth to express my growing desperation he orders me from the room.

Is it any wonder that I begin to join Eileen more and more on her *shopping trips* even though I still experience great guilt from merely partaking of the drink and the company? Sometimes an acute discomfort as she disappears for several hours laughing raucously as she leaves on the arm of some new admirer feeling no shame to be abandoning me albeit for a short time emboldened greatly by the huge amounts of gin that she has consumed and the tremendous need to be touched in a cold and un-tactile uncompassionate world. I wonder sometimes whether Steve ever feels any guilt for his own actions; he certainly doesn't show it. As I become braver, more confident of the quantities of whiskey sours I can handle in direct proportion to the consoling and soporific qualities that they induce I begin to relax, and become more and one with the soothing darkened atmosphere with the hypnotic strains of never-ending pop and country ballad recordings. I have reached the ability to tolerate two and learned how to pace myself so that I rarely have more than that two and play for a while at pretending to drink a third. The music becomes one with the entire feeling of rocking in an embrace of good will and warmth. *Make the world go away, get it off of my shoulders...*

CHAPTER 40

Eileen likes flyers or people who can afford to fly planes or to own them; this is why the Sky Lounge in Deer Park is a favorite haunt of hers. I move into her province like an unwilling unknowing shadow in a fuzzy daze. Yet in these lonely hopeless days with no other answer to the dilemma of my life than escape it becomes a haven to which I begin to gravitate. It has become more familiar, more comforting, than my own living room. I sit in the bar alone many nights after the children are in bed and when Eileen is occupied with the other pursuits and activities of her complicated social venue, safe in the continuity and familiarity of the only facet of my life that doesn't make demands on me but instead wraps protective enfolding arms around me and cradles me in its edge softening forgetfulness. The place itself is narcotic, addictive, a sense created by the mood of soporific ease that it induces. The lights are very dim, and the only glow comes from hidden bulbs set behind the richly tinted bottles. There is a certain atmosphere created by these dim and fragmented rays, the raucous background music of the juke box, the rise and fall of easy relaxed bar chatter, the camaraderie of strangers thrown together fractiously in an accidental vacuum of time and space. *All the lonely people, where do they all come from?* You can join in the silly unobtrusive banter or keep unmolested to yourself, as you wish.

The safe dark corner around the curve is where I go promptly to the same seat at the far end of the bar where I sip my whiskey sour slowly feeling the peace and anesthesia begin to seep through my body and the pressing discomfort that is my constant companion, disappear. I then begin to let my thoughts go inward in babbling confusion until finally from the murky fuzz of the drink and my relaxation emerge all manner of truths and realizations that have until now been tantalizingly out of reach. It doesn't seem to matter that most of these gems of truth are never remembered on the following day, for in the moment they cause respite from the haunting demons that hold me captive all through my waking hours. I sit there one night, particularly immersed in the extremities of agony that torment me on that particular day beyond the normal pale, the usual pain. Steve has been particularly ugly to me and has been out quite late for several nights in a row. In my anxiety, I have consumed three maybe four whiskey sours before I even realize it. After a while I make my way carefully out with great care, giggling a little at my state and commence the fuzzy trip homeward.

Some days are worse than others; when the realization of my aloneness and misdirection and hopelessness become the most strikingly apparent, my mood swings even lower than ever and the inclination to escape even further becomes the more insistent. Then, I partake of more than the usual amount of sours without even realizing what I am doing in a steady and relentless determination to blur all the edges as quickly as possible and with the solicitous help of the bartender and one or two regulars achieve my goal of self-anesthetization in record time and beyond. Finally slipping off my bar stool to head for the parking lot; I encounter a patrolman, a regular here with whom I am acquainted, accustomed to seeing, comfortable with. We were introduced by Eileen one time and I've seen him almost nightly when he stops by for his evening nightcap after getting off duty. He has always been courteous and respectful.

Somewhat wobbly with the quantity of liquor that I have consumed I gratefully acquiesce when he offers to walk me to my car blessing my luck that an officer of the law oh sacred vocation is available just when I am in need of a trustworthy elbow. I stumble out to the car, his strong arm guiding me and throw him a grateful look. He takes my key and opens the car door expressing concern for my condition suggesting that we go somewhere for coffee, but I am loathe to spend the time and fervently wished now to get home to the non-swirling steady peacefulness of my warm bed.

I move smoothly into the driver's seat and before I have a chance to be aware of any motion at all he slides in behind me and pushes me deftly over to the passenger side. Suddenly he is reaching, groping, pushing me backward, downward on the seat ripping my trousers off and unbuttoning his own with an urgency that all but freezes my blood. I talk quickly, trying to rationalize to talk him out of his obviously intended action. I try to apologize if I have allowed him to get the wrong message by walking me out to the car but he is single minded in his concentration and his goal. And he is no Joe College. I am figuring out fuzzily that I am out of my league. He becomes more and more determined in direct relation to the degree of struggle I put up. The spurt of adrenaline that is surging to my brain seems to have cleared my reflexes at least and I begin to think a little more clearly. I reach back and open the door behind my head, planning to either scream or begin wriggling backward whatever works best as soon as opportunity permits.

A glancing backhand blow of his navy clad right arm catches me off guard. As tears sting my eyelids and I react to the suddenness and sharpness of the blow he stands half up for a moment and begins to slip down his pants exposing what I guess he considers to be a weapon of considerable magnitude and force. As I see his huge looming body preparing to attack a sudden inspiration of enchanting proportions leaps into my mind and I give in to my last opportunity. It is my only chance but I know it will work. I force myself to think about Eileen's best stories and I begin to laugh. I laugh and laugh and laugh until the tears run down my cheeks. The laughter borders on the edge of the hysteria that I am feeling underneath but he can't see this, can't have known. Quickly unarmed by my derision he blushes a crimson red due at least as much to mortification as to the fury that he feels. I am sensing that he would very much like to murder me. Some innate sense of responsibility surges to the fore in direct answer to his shriveling manhood. In fear of doing something that might severely alter his comfortable life he replaces his clothing and zipping and buckling as he leaves, curses me under his breath and slinks away. I close and lock all of the car doors as quickly as I am able, rearrange my clothing and repair my face, but I cannot control the shuddering and shaking of my body for a long while. Once again, I appear to have thwarted an imminent attack diverted another potential rape this time perhaps not so small.

Shivering with rage and relief I drive quickly as I am able out of the area before some awful sequel presents itself. I am barely able to see the road and heedless of the jolting of the wheels as I hit rut after rut and swerve back and forth across the white median line, in and out of the ditches at the side of the road. I continue to sob and shudder as I charge relentlessly toward home, my mind a mass of confusing feelings and thoughts and some ever escalating destructive force bidding me agonizingly onward. A woman who drinks alone in a bar is asking for it, he has yelled at me over his shoulder as he left although I find all this difficult to comprehend. Separate and unequal, that's men and women. I never go back to the Sky Lounge ever, even when Eileen hearing my story roars with laughter remembering the cop in question and hilarious at my yet subsisting naiveté. Cops, she exclaims, tears of mirth rolling down her cheeks, you what? You trusted him? Her voice is overflowing with disbelief. Cops are the very worst. How you can still believe that they are some higher life form is beyond me. But you weren't there to guide me, this is not my bailiwick, not my comfort zone, I want to tell her, but hold my tongue fearful of losing the only relief from life that I now have. And she roars and laughs again. I imagine you believe there is such a thing as justice also, she smirks.

It is a stunning revelation; one by one my long held inviolate beliefs are being stripped away. Now it is cops. First is love and marriage then the sanctity of elevators then carpenters now cops. What will be next? I still believe in justice she can't take that away from me. And somewhere out there is love. Dean Martin says so, sings it in that deep sultry seductive baritone; *everybody loves somebody sometime...*

CHAPTER 41

The morning awakens bright and promising with just a touch of the soon to be extinct chill still clinging with stubborn tenacity to the edges of everything. There is a promise made by the gently warming sun and the cool yet crumbling and no longer sodden earth that inspires in me hungry thoughts and compulsive desires to scour nurseries for early season specials. This first spring in our new home it seems to be an impossible task to find sufficient quantities of plants, thick contrasting tones and textures, combinations of greenery and varied continuing bloom to inhabit this vast barren half acre. My imagination has been tweaked, tantalized by home magazines. It is early in the season yet, bulbs and early perennials that I planted last season are still only the bravest of thrusting pale spikes and my one forsythia moved from our old home splendid in her golden yellow raiment is alone and solitary needing company. I envision an entire row of them, staggered, bordering the property line. However, it is early, and there is little to do except attempt surveillance of the suddenly restocked and bustling nurseries previewing selections and prices scouting for the locations of those most varied and reasonably priced. Really it will be an excursion of the soul, more of esthetic rejuvenation than of practical purpose.

Mildred is my newest neighbor just across the *cul de sac* who doesn't drive and whom I know only from our brief but intense neighborly conversations mostly of trivia at her mailbox. She is a lot older than me, neat and organized, wears painfully constraining garments which typify her rigid nature. Her precisely colored and tightly coifed hairdo is always perfectly in place. What I have discovered about her, though, is that she is also an ardent gardener which Eileen is not, Eileen's interests being of a more venal nature. Do you want to go for a ride to check out local nurseries, I ask, repressing my excitement? The answer is a friendly enthusiastic yes. While Mildred readies herself for this excursion that promises untold measures of delight, I busy myself with bundling the hoards including my newest Kevin mere weeks old. It is a task that is Herculean in scope, considering the ages and predilections of the group. Snowsuits and scarves, over sweaters, hats and boots and mittens on strings, when I am through they resemble a pile of well decorated, colorful, filled and wrapped pastries. Ultimately we are ready, dressed and bundled and stuffed as well into the white Dodge Dart station wagon. The car is Steve's gift to me celebrating Kevin's birth and the weary and silent demise of the old '56 Chevy or rather not for me but for the children. Although it is delivered with much fanfare and flourish it remains in his name. I have not been consulted on any of the choices implicit in the purchase of a vehicle type, color, or style therefore it is the antithesis of any automobile I might have desired had I even been consulted. In addition like everything else in my life, in our marriage, it is owned by Steve; I am just permitted to exist within its perimeter or to use it as the case may be.

Use it I will. In the spirit of the occasion I honk vociferously for Mildred, she quickly and happily joins us in the car and we drive off into the wild blue yonder making the joyous rounds of every nursery within a ten-mile radius. We are explorers in a new world both new to the area, recent inhabitants of this brand new housing development. Spring has awakened the gardener in us and we have answered the call of our muse.

Now somewhat disheveled after our productive morning the children are beginning to wilt having exhausted themselves running through each and every nursery full of spring abandon, in and out of rows of plants, around and around tables of flats and pots. It is time to aim for home. We turn tentatively at an unexpected road, Stoothoff, it says, that promises to lead more quickly to the development passing pungent cabbage farms and picturesque old farmhouses and barns, following winding curves. It appears unexpectedly out of nowhere, a tiny unheralded and barely commercialized nursery its shabby ancient sign so unspectacular as to be nearly unnoticeable. What draws us is a sea of yellow, an immense wide golden mass of balled and burlapped heavily blossomed forsythia that line the rutted driveway and parking area with their raucous allure. Something here is different from the other nurseries we have visited. This time there is a grand invitation expressed by the joyous yellow masses.

Look Mildred, forsythia, exactly what I have been talking about. Maybe between the two of us if we buy a bunch of them we can make some sort of deal here, both save some money. Just mere moments before we have been discussing the idea of bordering our properties with these flashy spreading bushes even more enticing for their relative lack of expense. Better than privet because they bloom in early spring. Anything that blooms is better than anything that doesn't; this is my new philosophy. I have not yet been introduced to the bloom of the fragrant privet certainly less showy than flamboyant forsythia. There is a man who appears to be in charge stooping over his back to us, tying up the burlap on those plants, I think.

Hey, how much will you charge for say, forty of these forsythia, I shout. We both...He turns around, still crouching. A lightning bolt comes out of nowhere and travels through me. What is happening? I...We...Mildred, I begin, looking first one way then another, attempting speech, trembling, feel totally confused. Again, I try to speak, but the words are not there. I fumble for control, equilibrium... words. I can use about...how about...they're really nice...

I've dug these for someone else, he answers, rank cigar stuck in the corner of his mouth bobbing as he speaks. Why am I not repelled? The odor of it wafts in front of me mixing with a whiff of Old Spice. A brief thought of Daddy crosses my mind except that he resembles a sort of young Richard Burton with a little bit Cary Grant, a hint of Robert Redford, a dash of James Dean in chinos and flannel which is almost a complex oxymoron if you think of it. He doesn't appear to have noticed my discomfort; I can see nothing but the compelling blue of his eyes, the radiance of his smile. Our eyes meet and lock in some bone chilling atavistic gear, a magnet of mammoth animal propensities draining my senses at least of consciousness so that I can barely speak. He seems to be frozen in the same time warp that I suddenly inhabit. Probably it is just in my mind. I feel the heat rising to my face in embarrassment and wonder if staid and proper Mildred has noticed my demoralizing stumble. I am afraid to turn and check indeed too paralyzed to move. I wrench my eyes away. This has never before happened to me in my life. It is the very essence of all that is lacking in my existence. Everything that has always been missing, it would seem. Most especially right now. I look at the screaming yellow masses of flowering shrubs. My imagination is working overtime, it's just the combination of spring and hormones I tell myself.

Well, you've got a lot more, how much are you getting for them? It is easier to speak, not looking.

Three dollars each, will you want them delivered, planted?

I scan my brain desperately seeking a way to prolong the association. I can't leave yet. Maybe...And Magnolia, I say, I have decided that I simply must have one, do you have any...Magnolia? And a Pink Dogwood, I am rambling and oh look, my consciousness returns and I begin to see the other varieties of plants that seemed to glow with care, with lushness, health. These plants are well tended. Oh look, I rhapsodize my voice beginning to squeak, Rhodies, Azaleas? Do you carry peat moss? I am talking too much, babbling with self-consciousness, confusion. Have no idea what I am saying, doing, what to do or say next. Where will I get the money? I'll ask Mom.

I guess you have a new house. You probably need a whole bunch of stuff. He smiles that mesmerizing smile again. Why don't I come over to your place and see what you need?

Oh yes I think my knees as loose as gelatin something strange rising from my stomach into my throat! When? I ask. I don't even know what I am thinking, what I am hoping...

Soon, he says, looking around thoughtfully at his stock, maybe I'll stop by this afternoon. God, I muse, he really does exist, someone who engenders that incredible ineffable, untenable feeling. I have lost all touch with reality, my true existence. And I wasn't even looking this time. I have forgotten to look as I used to do in earlier empty days so immersed am I in my preoccupation with the new baby, with spring and planting. I am reeling with this unexpected sense of shock. I feel a great need to grab hold of something. I fear I may fall down if I don't. My chest is tight and heavy, my breathing rapid and I choke on every breath. Some enchanted evening, you will meet a stranger...strangers in the night... old memories of the familiar music and words of Ezio Pinza and Tony Bennett are creating a cacophony of promise and precognition in the turmoil of my mind. I feel suddenly awkward; wonder with no connection to reality how I look. Is this position I am standing in suddenly stiff and awkward and ungainly as ungraceful as it suddenly feels? Wouldn't you know I'd wear these old pants and ugly shirt today? *Someday this man will mean everything to me*...the thought flashes like a brilliant neon sign in my head followed by a sense of pure terror all at once overruled by shame and guilt. How can this be happening?

I find myself in the center of an insoluble conundrum; what can I do? Where were you eight years ago when all my life was ahead of me, uncomplicated, no issues of fidelity, loyalty? Why did I jump so fast to marry why didn't I wait? Just the briefest glimpse, images of Steve and his mistress flit across my mind lost in the massive emotion of the moment. Just because he is doing it doesn't mean that I should…Again my chest and throat constrict. I feel hot tears rising from my belly to squeeze from full eyes. Why do I feel nothing but grief? How can this be happening? I have a husband, five kids, a life empty though it feels and you must also have a wife and kids I say silently in my head. I wonder what kind and how many and stifle an inward giggle at this non sequitur. Maybe you are one of those serial cheaters. I don't want to believe that. Like the *friends* that Eileen has at the *Sky Lounge*. Like those men who are so ready to make passes or attack. Like that carpenter and that cop. Like Steve. I doubt that, I can see too much *soul* in your eyes. I can see right through the depths of you and I see a flashing image of us together. I am the queen of wishful thinking. Where have you been hiding, and what do I do now? What am I even thinking? I am not certain that I have sufficient self-control to do battle with these feelings. How can I reconcile my actions with this moral code to which I am shackled? Thou shall not be promiscuous. Drinking in bars is bad enough. Thou shall certainly never commit adultery. At least I shall not. This is a question with only one answer. My first joy at my discovery is destroyed by this certain knowledge.

I will never have a chance to feel alive again, to feel true passion, real love. This can never happen, I think sadly. But what about Steve, I ask myself? And then, I've waited so damned long to be loved, I think, arguing *ad nauseum* with my better self. Emotions are doing battle inside me. Who will win? O GOD PLEASE, oh please, I think slipping past that rigid moral barrier for a moment of self indulgence, let this man love me. Reason is deserting me. I am asking the moral *leader* to break his own laws. All right, I'll make a deal. I'll give up anything, take half my life. Just let him want me. I think I am entitled to at least that. Let him touch me just once; love me once, HE MUST. How will I live without him now that I have found him? He must feel the same; I see something in his eyes. What will he do? Is it all in my mind? I am too much of a romantic, too desperate, too self-indulgent. I am a prisoner in a seriously diabolical Oriental torture trap.

My thoughts continue to surge onward, the argument continues internally. I need to discard all my old mores and rules, need to adapt to this new world, this strange new world. The world I have discovered with Eileen's sad joyous guidance. That has presented me with an entire new set of permissions. The only other choice is to drown in the otherwise inevitable misery that drags me downward daily. I will do whatever it takes. All the men out here are unfaithful, it is a cultural phenomenon of the suburbs, common knowledge whispered at beauty parlors and super markets and coffee klatches. I need to adapt to this new mindset, send out silent signals, let him know I'm available. There is a good chance, I think, that he will take the bait. My thoughts are rocketing, swirling. I wonder which gin mill he hangs out at after work to drink when he probably should be home with his family like all the rest of them. If I knew I'd just walk in casually, *Why, what a coincidence, imagine meeting you here...just stopped in for a little drink.* I could show him that I am intelligent, aware, contrary to my alleged reputation, make conversation, *did you know that Washington is reporting that Castro's sister has been a CIA spy for four years?* What is this new bravado, and where has it come from? Who am I? Who am I becoming? Who are you and what have you done with Lynne? I am becoming Eileen. Terror overcomes me mixing with need and desire.

I return to the car and the waiting children and sink gratefully into the seat thankful for the just in time support for my wavering knees. I drive homeward oblivious to the whining and prattle of the tiring and hungry kids. I smile absently at Mildred's innocent conversation having to do with the planning of landscaping of her property and the care and feeding of respective plants that we have seen. The car radio supplies the background music...*I'll remember April, and I'll smile...*But it is Mildred who smiles happily back at me innocent of the thoughts that roil in my head. I allow my teeming thoughts to finally encompass my mind. Somehow I manage to get us all home intact, a great feat of concentration. And just in time the Beatles release *Hard Day's Night.* Yeah, I think.

I doodle his name absently on my grocery pad.

Oh...Steve...I feign disinterest, feeling my ears burning, turning red, no, nothing, just a grocery list. You know my lousy memory (nervous laugh) must write it all down or I'll forget half the stuff when I go shopping. Am I convincing him? Just who am I fooling? Should I care? My ears, my face, are blazing. Did you know that that new Medicare bill has been signed into law by Johnson in the Truman Library? He gives that look; you're nuts, and turns away.

I determine that these thoughts have to end. I have to be strong. This is not going to happen. I seek moral support and affirmation from a strange source, maybe not so strange at all, as our regular coffee klatches continue when the last of the children have mounted the school bus. We avoid the elephant in the room, revert to banter both neutral and banal.

Hi Eileen, coffee?
Yeah, where the hell do you keep your ashtrays these days?

Well another day in the old rat race, huh?
Yeah, wouldn't mind the diapers, dishes, etc., if it weren't for...
What's today, Thursday? I'm going out tonight.
Where?
Don't know, couple of drinks somewhere. Want to come along?
Another time, maybe.
...Well?
That S.O.B., know what he did? did did did...

And the daydreams and fantasies flourish as life goes on as usual. I am as circumspect about confiding my desires to Eileen as she is to me. But I can dream, can't I? Lalalalala.

❧◦❦

Food is piled high on the table from one end to the other; we are having dinner with Mom and Daddy, all of us, Steve and me and the kids. Talk has turned to the topic of the day. The newspapers are full of the Crimmons kidnapping and murder of two children in Kew Gardens Hills just over the Jewel Avenue bridge near where Mom and Daddy live. They have been carried through an open window and disappeared, small destroyed bodies found in local empty lots after a long search. It is reminiscent of the Lindburgh tragedy says Mom sadly looking somewhere inward. Lindburgh was a Nazi sympathizer, says Daddy with venom, and so was his good buddy Henry Ford. We had been talking about our new car, the white Dodge Dart that Steve purchased after Kevin's birth; I am bemoaning the fact that I never get to choose anything, to take part in decisions, whining petulantly that he knew I had been fantasizing about that Ford station wagon with those imitation wood sides and oblivious to some of these details of War and Holocaust logistics I mindlessly prattle on. Mom and Daddy hit the roof, their aversion to Ford and Lindbergh is rapacious although Mom has mixed feelings about the kidnapping, no matter what, no one should ever take children from a mother, she insists, can't encompass the fact that Alice Crimmins has been accused of murdering her own children in the midst of controversy about the dearth of evidence. How can you accuse someone of something so heinous without proof? But the media grabs the ball and runs with it, and she receives her own personal scarlet letter, **M**, carved into her forehead for eternity, for Medea, *The Medea of Kew Gardens,* they call her. Who would be so cruel, asks Mom.

CHAPTER 42

Bye, bye Miss American Pie, drove the Chevy to the levy but the levy was dry... the kids, hers and mine are singing at the top of their lungs, accompanying the car radio which plays at its highest decibel. By the middle of summer, Eileen and I now inseparable spend the long hot summer afternoon with our nine cumulative bleached blond kids baking on Crab Meadow Beach. Our summer discussions are interrupted by the throngs of demanding little people who have spent the afternoon in the water or building sand structures, arguing and running and jumping; concentrating on their busywork, carrying pails of water, filling them with sand and making mounds and turrets, scooping and piling and patting. Mommy, Mommy, Mom, Mom...*he* did this, *she* did that, mom, mom, he's looking at me, he touched me, and on and on, calling out, whining, demanding; we ignore them, smile, issue platitudes and demands for obedience and silence. Our discussion continues unabated during both travels, activities, and the short drive home from the beach. I've been numb till now, Eileen, I say, but I don't know...I'm so damned tired of filling the hours with stupid projects...how many shrubs and trees and flowers can I buy for Godssake? I cannot stop thinking about this man. Every time he delivers something I have bought, every time I watch him plant the stuff I feel worse instead of better, my thoughts go wild. Even though just being around him, talking to him is so sweet.

My thoughts swirl around in my head. I've always been a real prude, you know? Mocking these miserable people who have no more morals or self-control than rabbits; how smug and insensitive I am. Open mouth insert foot. Poor Eileen, tact was never one of my strong points. Any marriage can succeed with a little effort. What bull crap. But something is changing. After all I have Eileen to admire and emulate. *She* seems to have found solutions to a miserable existence! And Steve is *already* breaking our solemn vows. Love? I've learned all about true love. But maybe I haven't, maybe I am foregoing the last opportunity I will ever have to find out. How will I ever know if I don't try?

Race riots are proliferating in Watts in August and fifty thousand more troops are being sent to Nam. A sense of thrill is circulating in the buzz around our friends and acquaintances because UFOs have been seen in four states and all I can think about is that my life is so empty, Steve is so not there, I whine, continuing my soliloquy. *I'm 'Enery the Eighth I am, ' Enery the Eighth I am I am, I got married to the widda next door, she's been married seven times before...* the shriek and volume of their voices nearly drown out our conversation, but they can't hear us either. Damn, I say to Eileen, you only live once, one little short life...do you realize I don't even know what it would be like to be with another man. Steve is the only man I have ever known. Who knows? Maybe I'm lucky; maybe I don't know when I'm well off. One of these days, I say with rising bravado, speaking a little louder with it, the opportunity will present itself and boy, am I'm gonna find out what I'm missing. If Steve can do it, why can't I?

Seen one, seen them all, murmurs Eileen, dripping cynicism like paint off a roller finally getting a word in edgewise. Anyone particular in mind Eileen asks already knowing the answer. How could she not? I have been rhapsodizing about him since April, the words pop into my mind, *I'll remember April and I'll smile...*

Well, Cliff, maybe. I don't understand it, but I feel a strong connection to him. When our eyes meet, I melt from head to toe. I hope it's him. The words surprise me as they slip from my mouth. I had believed that I had successfully avoided that pitfall. Eileen shudders when I speak; it is all too sweet and trite for her. There he is, see? Putting in that sod lawn, the guy over there, with the gray chinos and no shirt; this is the first time Eileen has come face to face with him. Do I dare take a chance that he will be captivated by her blond seductress charms? Should I stop and say hello? I better not...but in a moment I am leaning out the car window. Hiya Cliff, HOWZITGOING? My mouth moves independent of my brain.

He smiles that glorious smile at me and I feel that by now familiar warmth creeping through my body. For God's sake, slow down. Did I speak out loud? Eileen looks at me strangely.

I pull over to the side of the road doing facial exercises, freezing my face muscles into an expression of ennui, trying to get control of myself hoping also to prolong the intense thrill of this moment. Tremors of anxiety rush through me.

Could you possibly deliver a couple of bags of peat moss if you have the chance? I ask him ingenuously my eyes huge and innocent recovering my composure inventing cover my jaw stiff with forced control.

Sure, see ya later. Very circumspect... no frills, no warm open inviting smiles. There is a stranger in the car and we are both married. He has no idea who Eileen is.

You see, you see, I cry with unabashed and irrational enthusiasm obviously out of proportion to the moment, he came right over to the car. Did you see his face light up...he didn't have to come right over and smile like that... Isn't he special? How could she possibly know, all she sees is a gardener without a shirt, planting grass. He is not her type, she prefers businessmen with expensive suits and fat wallets. He seems interested doesn't he? You can tell. Do I look all right? Lucky thing I wore this bathing suit, it's my best one. It is a tiny bikini thing covering very little; we have not bothered to dress for this short trip home along quiet country roads. I blush. You can tell, can't you? I hope to God he…I wish…The more I talk the less I believe. My self-confidence never strong, plummets. I don't know, Eileen, he would never want me, could never love me even if I were available. No matter what I might do to try and entice him he would never even approach me…I'm afraid I'd never even have a chance…

Who said anything about love, she answers; *love* is just a four-letter word. She laughs, caustically. He'll come around, they always do, she says, matter of factly. There never was a man who didn't take up an invitation. Take my word for it, she says with some disdain, you only need to be patient. But never never think of love. Love is not the issue. Love is for losers. Her disgust is palpable. She is an amalgam of every cynicism ever invented.

She is preaching to the wrong choir. Love is what it is all about always for me. As for her pessimistic premise concerning men and invitation I am not convinced, I have that little faith in myself, in my allure. Steve has fixed that. I am overcome with despair, feel hope sinking in my stomach like a hot brick. He's got to, I whine, emptiness enveloping me anew. Life is too painful, too meaninglessness, it looms ahead forever, empty and lonely. Steve has his comfort. Of course, Love is what I am looking for. The rest? What goes with it.

Just give it time, Eileen sighs, losing interest in my pseudo-melodrama. She is thinking no doubt of her next venture in search of everlasting fun, of the acquisition of material reward.

I know he's interested, I can tell, desperately, a woman can tell. Is this a statement or a question? Suddenly I am full to bursting with a hidden source of insipient female wisdom. I babble on and on. What will I do if he never even tries? What if I find out where he hangs out and suddenly appear there? I try out my casual sophisticated club voice, *Oh, hi Cliff! What a coincidence! Buy me a cup of coffee or a drink?* Would he laugh at me? Be kind, at least? Maybe, maybe accept the invitation. I have a new parameter, the gin mill, previously, pre-Eileen, an unknown entity for me. If only I knew where to look for him. Who is this woman living in my head? I can't even recognize myself anymore.

Now I have a new worry to stuff into my gunny sack of woes; I am truly turning into Eileen. Talking like her, acting like her, thinking like her. Except that I am focusing on love and she on the game. Where will this end? But I have never felt like this before and it's good to be feeling alive and hopeful again. I am teetering on the edge of an abyss. What will happen?

Maybe there will be some sort of sign so I know what I am destined to do. Maybe something good will happen and I will be saved from the ramifications of a bad decision. I guess I need to be strong, here. I have to do the right thing. I need to try hard, even harder. I did love Steve for so long, and he is the father of my children; that old chestnut that I am tired of hearing, of repeating.

But there is the question of those late nights at the office, or wherever he goes, that woman he is seeing; Mom's detective report, the story Lenore Namm told me in the ladies' room at that last Bar Association dinner that affirms Mom's report, of some woman, a client, that he is seeing. There was Lenore's husband, Stu, our friend, Steve's Brooklyn Law School buddy taking me aside and suggesting that I consider divorce but refusing to tell me why. I can't tell him that I already know, it is too humiliating, I haven't the nerve to bring it up. I am too proud to tell them what was in the contents of my mother's manila envelope, do not know if he knows that his wife has told me about it all. So here is yet another burning stone to sit with all the others in the pit of my stomach. Here is yet another reason for me to rationalize, to not feel too much guilt for my feelings for Cliff. I have not yet addressed in my mind any thoughts I may have about Cliff's wife. I put her out of my mind. I can't see her, don't know her, therefore she does not exist. I cannot afford emotionally to let her exist. I do not want to be her version of Steve's mistress. I care only to discover and enjoy my place in the sun, and I shudder for one terrible moment as I feel myself, a lovely innocent Elizabeth Taylor teetering in a fragile rowboat in unstable waters, but the sensation quickly passes overwhelmed by a dreadfully fantastic unjustifiable sense of hope and expectation.

CHAPTER 43

There are a plethora of questions hanging in the atmosphere waiting to be answered with no resolution in sight. The words and melody of Bob Dylan wafts across the airwaves...*The times they are a changing*...and...*the answers my friend are blowing in the wind,* but what are the questions? There are draft card burnings and self-immolations in protest of the war. New permissions are presenting themselves. Where will it all end and how will this all affect me? Where am I going and where will I end up?

I find that in these weird and limbo days of darkness Daddy and I become closer than we had ever been. Perhaps I can be less critical of his own shortcomings and seeming failures and inability to grasp a firm hold on life in view of my own late situation of disorder. At any rate since the day I ordered him out of my home at the inception of one of his screaming temper tantrums directed at and once again innocently goaded by my mother's bad timing and obtuseness, refusing at long last to be victim any longer of these childish scenes he accepts me as an adult even a friend and we are able to enjoy each other as individuals. In my present situation given the guilt I carry for my recent defiance and imagined transgressions and given the reasons I begin to understand Daddy more than I ever have. Needless to say, I can identify even more with certain other of his essences in that I bear the same genes and more and more see my father in myself and vice versa where previously I had been the spitting image of my mother, according to everyone.

We meet occasionally at a nearby diner for breakfast as he makes his way out to the office from which at this time he is selling homes or condominiums or whatever and in those brief minutes cover matters of both minor and major issues joke around a little and touch base some. I remember the day I try out the idea of divorce on him knowing all about his misery with my mother (and vice versa), their intense love/hate relationship and the desire and inability that each has had for so long to dissolve this unhappy union, or not and wait for his sage opinion trusting him above all others for some god-forsaken reason feeling at this time of my life that of our spiritual kinship he is perhaps the only creature in the world, black sheep that he is indeed who is able to see into the black scum of a cloud that surrounds me and give me the most objective advice.

If you are unhappy divorce is never the answer, he says, raising mustache and lip alike in that familiar Flynnish grin, too complicated and too costly. Find yourself some new friends to fill the void. If you fool around be discreet, and if you drink always drink scotch. With these final words, he jumps quickly to his feet in the same rapid motion with which he does everything and paying the bill with the same dispatch, gives me a peck on the cheek and strides rapidly out the door. He leaps into his car and waves at me quixotically whipping out of the parking lot of the diner with a squealing of brakes and a scraping of tires before I have even reached my own car. I shake my head with amusement and smiling for the first time in a long while think to myself that he is indeed an atypical individual, and like it or not, I seem to be my father's daughter. So I change from whiskey sours to scotch sours when I go out. That should do it and think no further than that.

Suddenly I understand all those surreptitious phone calls, the sudden disappearances and late returns, the phone calls where there is no one there. Suddenly I know why Mom is acquainted with a private detective, why she has been inspired to pursue the unthinkable, the impossible.

Ghouls and witches and cowboys, cowgirls and ghosts and Frankenstein monsters, milk maids and gypsies and...all carrying shopping bags, some accompanied by a parent, all on a mission, a mission to reign supreme amongst their peers, he who has accumulated the most candy. Neither my fondest holiday nor my favorite occupation just not my thing, yet I have helped my own children with their costumes, whatever they want, the more creative the better. The older of my children are out there with their friends, Eileen is the willing chaperone of choice, I am gratefully home with the babies too young for this activity.

With the streets filled with mobs and troops of costumed children great unimaginable masses of them marching together on their mission he comes to the house on Halloween to deliver mulch. It is as good of a reason as any. Cliff's old beat up pick up of nondescript color the name of the nursery on its door arrives in my driveway. We talk for a moment and I unconsciously put my hand on the open window frame, the sill of the truck and he covers my cold trembling hand with his large callused warm one; he touches me and nothing ever is the same. I hear it in a pop song, Barbara Streisand sings it and that song becomes my mantra. When I hear it played that means I will soon see Cliff. That is precisely what happens most times. Scary. Happenstance. I find it on my Streisand album and play it over and over again so that he will always be with me, so that I will always be about to see him. Did it really happen? Did he touch me? Does it mean what I hope it means, portends? I am more confused, more distressed than before. I don't know where I am in this story. I don't know how to bring the disparate parts of my present life, of all that is happening, swirling around me, into some kind of readable comprehensible focus. Something I do know is that I relive that moment, the one of the magical touch over and over again in gory detail, savoring every delicious memory.

Nothing is ever said about the electricity, the magnetism, this entire summer, my manner of dress or undress, transparent shifts and varieties of bikinis, about my obvious attempt at seduction, about what is happening between us. I can see that I am affecting him, by his eyes, his demeanor. But we are mute on the subject. He has been stopping by for coffee every morning for the entire summer and I welcome him, welcome these close intimate moments. He praises my coffee; I watch carefully but he doesn't bat an eyelash when I fill the cup to the top, stir it, watch it overflow, and drink half, laughs disdaining when I tell him about Steve and the coffee. He raises an eyebrow in mock contempt when I tell him about ironing washcloths and socks, about being called mother of the year and Barney Oldsfield, and moves his hand closer and closer to me, as though he wants to cover my hand with his comfortingly but he stops short of touching me. My hand screams out to his, touch me, touch me, and shockwaves bounce and vibrate across the table. We can talk about anything, everything, it seems. I tell him about our dynamic,

Steve and me, of my rejection, of being compartmentalized and ignored; somehow I know he will understand. He understands everything else, he listens, he cares. He tells me about his marriage, how it was a shotgun thing while he was in the army when a one-night stand resulted in a pregnancy, how there is little between them, how she pushes him away constantly, how lonely he is. I can see all that, find it easy to believe him, sigh with relief as guilt is replaced with permission, only want to see him smile, be happy. I have never known this closeness, never felt so safe, so cared for. I am teasing him, tantalizing him, with everything I have or know, using the only language I know of love, sex, and still he stays behind that façade of friendship, while we both feel the tension and attraction; we are both aware of the elephant in the room, that nameless need. For some reason I do not see his distance as rejection, even though Steve's dismissal of me lives inside of me like a pulsing creature. Somehow, I do not feel unwanted, only in comfortable holding pattern. In some way, I am relieved not to be faced with a moral decision. It is obvious that to go further would be wrong. It is a line over which once you cross, you can never go back. And then he touches me.

ৎৡ৶৻

The late afternoon grayness begins creeping on little cat feet into the corners of the house and glancing at the clock I realize that it is time to begin cleaning up my project. Scraps of multicolored fabrics are scattered all over the kitchen as I race to complete some new outfits for the children or they will have nothing to wear this summer. Steve is his usual tight self when it comes to doling out the dollars even for the clothing of his babies. I think I will send for a Sears catalogue and open a charge account because this is getting to be a losing battle, keeping up with their incredible growth. That will be a great convenience.

I finish tidying up and begin dinner the first nagging sensations of uneasiness beginning to tickle my intestines. As the minutes pass by slowly each tick of the clock is a reminder that the quiet of my day and the peace of my privacy are coming quickly to an end. Soon as usual my hands began their icy trembling. Holding off for as long as I can I finally succumb to the need and reaching into the depths of the pot storage cabinet bring out my private bottle of scotch. I have graduated from whiskey sours at a bar to a hidden bottle of scotch in the kitchen in a few short months. I pour a half inch or so into the bottom of a coffee mug and take increasingly larger sips the warmth of the liquor beginning to soothe the jolting queasiness of my stomach and the jumpiness in my chest. I keep one ear perked for the sound of the car in the driveway, and steel myself for the daily horror hour soon to be.

Soon calm and anesthetized by the few sips of scotch moving as if in a dream I smile to myself knowing that tonight at least Steve will not be able to reach me. Soon, he has arrived home, hung his coat. I know without even bothering to look, that it hangs on the same hangar in the closet as always. He starts his daily route pacing through the kitchen, the living room, the dining room and back again through the kitchen...and round and round belting out his usual questions in rapid succession in the usual order: How are the children? What did you do today? What are we having for dinner? Did you do all your chores? Who called? Around and around and around he continues the same questions and the same obsessive, compulsive pacing.

Sometimes he asks me with that edge to his voice, Barney, Barney Oldsfield, where did you take my car today that you put seven miles on it? If all my chores are not done, he asks me, Mother of the Year, why aren't your chores done? If anyone has a cold or cough or a scraped knee he accuses me, Mother of the Year, of trying to kill his children.

Usually by this time I am a bundle of nerves but medically reinforced as I am I let the whole scene roll right off me. He keeps at me though, criticizing everything from the way the kids are dressed to the way the house looks, my failings as a laundress and a cook, the incompleteness of my list of required chores and my general stupidity and inadequacy. As the mealtime wears on, my reinforcement begins to wear off and I begin to feel the same old twitch begin to start in my eye and the jerkiness begins once again in my stomach. Once again, as has become my habit of late I begin to plan my escape. I can't stay five minutes longer in this house, in this prison. I move into the inner recesses of my mind almost able to tune out the carping, rasping nagging sound of his continual litany focusing on the escape however temporary that will be accomplished in the coming evening. I think for a moment of taking another dose of my nerve tonic but can't figure how to do it with Steve right there in the room. I cannot keep my eyes off the guilty cabinet, certain that Steve will sense my preoccupation and ask me why I am staring so and discover my guilty secret.

I resolve that I will find a way to be free of him. I know what I need to do.

CHAPTER 44

I feel as though the minutes will never pass. Time stretches out before me into infinity. It is about eight o'clock and the children finally abed I mumble something to Steve about shopping to do and drive to Klein's Department Store in Commack to see if I can find anything interesting or useful tonight. Mostly, I am just looking. I have no extra money to buy anything; every extra nickel I can put together from my meager earnings tinting photos to contributions by Mom, have gone to clothing and shoes for the kids and for nursery stock, a handful of loose change put aside for that occasional drink while out. But this is as good a reason as any to get away from Steve and torture, my prison. I don't want to go out drinking, even the thought of sitting in a gin mill is turning my stomach lately, buying that first cocktail or when broke that Club Soda, twist of lemon, waiting for someone to buy me a drink. Having exhausted the entertainment value of shopping, forced myself, pretended that I am interested, I drive and drive and drive, up and down local parkways and my favorite areas of the countryside Route 25A in Fort Salonga hills and curving roadway lined by undulating spreads of tall oak, pine, mountain laurel and rhododendron but everything keeps blurring before my tears and the queasiness in my stomach refuses to cease.

Finally, desperately, I stop before a phone booth in the darkened corner of a disreputable looking service station and dial one friend after another, Eileen, even Shelly Moskowitz, hoping to find someone home so I won't have to return to Steve and the twin sinking feelings of entrapment, desperation. I fight the rising impulses but find myself unable to resist. Hand trembling, fantasy mixing with reality in my mind, I dial the familiar number that is by now firmly engraved in my mind. What am I thinking? Thinking, thinking, thinking, I try to dream up an excuse for the call, and when a child answers, hello, this is Scotty, suddenly suffocating with guilt ask for Cliff, planning with sudden relief at a brainstorm, to pay for some shrubs before I spend the money, ha ha. No matter, after all, he isn't home he is at the firehouse, why don't I drop it off? Well maybe later, ha ha, well, thanks.

Mortified, terrified, despairing, I drive and drive again through a sudden rainstorm my window open the rain mixing with my tears of fear and exasperation nervous and unsure of the madness I am about to commit. He has a child. I knew he had children. I knew he had a wife. What was I thinking, what am I thinking? Still, I am focused on my cause determined one way or another to do something. Sins of commission, I think, remembering. If I don't do something, I will lose my mind. Or worse. I am shaking badly now and I feel this immense need to reach out to someone. I don't think I can hang on without some comfort, a connection. I have always feared death so deeply but now the thought of release beckons to me and I give that solution some consideration I must admit for it seems sometimes that there is no other way out. But I am a coward. Not coward enough to avoid this next move.

But what does it mean, the way he touched my hand, those daily cups of coffee, all that conversation and compassion? Those smiles, those looks...What if he meant...what if he didn't? Finally in the center of town, I drive right up to the firehouse acting with a combination of incredible innocence and classic stupidity and ringing the bell at the door I ask the rough and super masculine swaggering volunteer firefighter who throws open the wide double door, for Cliff, and learn that he has left. I am devastated, incredibly disappointed. This is the letdown of all time. He is grinning at me knowingly. He is mentally reviewing the punch line of a dirty joke, of an entire library of dirty jokes. Flushing profusely, I am suddenly aware that I have committed some major social gaffe but I am too new at this cheating game to know quite what the rules are. I note his leering grin and wonder what he is thinking of me and whom they will tell of my visit after the story has entertained the rest of them, and they have had the opportunity to make all their stupid dirty jokes. I will be the new one. I walk quickly and self-consciously back to my car and leave as quickly as possible. God, what nerve...go home, I command myself sternly...crying at the humiliation, the futility of it all. Praying that there will not be hideous repercussions for my stupidity. The very thought, the possibilities...

What kind of trouble have I gotten myself into now? What will happen when they tell him that some woman was looking for him...would he realize that it was me? Will he laugh about it with his wife, call Steve and inform him of my perfidy? How will I ever face him again? Will every volunteer fireman in the world leer at me knowingly and pursue his own opportunity to bed the town slut? Does this mean that my foolishness has precluded my ever being in the presence of the one human in the world who gives me solace by merely being? Will he treat me with anger, condescension, solicitude, or will he even ever speak to me again even on business? I die a thousand deaths.

≈❦≈

Saturday morning. Another beauteous morning and even though Steve is home nothing he does can dim its glory. The world appears less threatening after a good night's sleep. I feel less angst, less guilt. I take the station wagon and head for town deciding to stop and offer to pay Cliff for the nursery stock, give credence for my improbable call. Play dumb, pretend that this was maybe all a misunderstanding. I will remark quite innocently that that was why I had been looking for him the night before. Right.

It is a truly gorgeous autumn day; clear, blue skies and bright yellow sun, sweet breezes and warm caressing air currents. Spirits high with definite goal in mind especially in contrast to the depression of the night before I accelerate the car and feel the surge of power go through the engine, throughout my body, and rise singing through my ears. I am going to see Cliff for a moment at least however brief. I try not to imagine that this may indeed be the very last time. I fix my mind on that incredible smile, those blue, blue eyes. I take those hairpin turns ZIP, and pull in at the sign (uh oh, slow down), fear is a coiled snake in the deepest pit of my stomach...and expectancy. I am an addict seeking a fix.

He is there, he is busy…he is walking over…that plodding weary walk, power in check behind it, a young tree, a strong trunk up–rooted with each step. NOW. That smile. How are ya?

I look down feeling the red of humiliation spreading across my face. I fumble for words; attempt to force them through mouth of cotton. Hi, I want to pay my bill, and I want a red maple, can you…my words trail off lost in the spreading ray of his broadest most beaming smile ever. Thanks, and yes, and sure, I can…by the way, was that you? Up at the firehouse last night asking for me? Is he toying with me now? Of course he knows it was me, who else could it have been? Indeed. Who else could it have been, he asks me. They said a beautiful red head and I figured it as you. I was downstairs at the bar but those SOBs never even told me…I would have been upstairs in a minute with bells on. That was their idea of a joke. Some joke. He smiles again and the entire world is inundated with light.

I blush crimson on top of crimson. I am not certain if anyone has ever died from mortification but if not I may be the first. I wait but nothing happens to me. I was just…I thought…maybe we could have (I take a deep breath and go for it) gotten together…or something. I was so lonely and I thought we could… just talk…like we do in the morning I rush to add. There. It was all out. I sigh; relief and humiliation. I look at my shoes, crusts of drying mud forming around their edges, study them in detail fearing to look up.

Yeah, I was kicking myself, I didn't even know…I have wanted, you know, to…he pauses…(I can't believe my ears, glance up at him)…I'm really happy that you…again…(he is as nervous and nonplussed as I am) I've wanted to…for a long time, but I couldn't get up the courage, kind of thought that you might be…interested…but it's a touchy business, I didn't want you to misunderstand me (he has recovered his composure)…I thought, but I wasn't sure…You know. I really like being with you. You've been on my mind a lot. I love having coffee with you in the morning, talking to you, being with you, he says again. It makes my day. So simple, an innocent cup of coffee is all he wants, but…

After the trip to the firehouse, everything changes.

☙❧

The three oldest kids are in school, Andrew and baby Kevin, asleep in their cribs. There is no question of any thought of Steve being on my mind, he has ceased to matter to me; my only thoughts are of Cliff. I have grown tired of, frustrated with coffee klatches; I am needing more. I am bored with this charade, answering the door after showering so that I am fresh and clean and ready for anything, wearing a lightweight cotton shift, sunlit from behind. Sweat dripping down the sides of my body, nervous, meticulously made up, my hair carefully arranged, smiling my welcome, shaking inside, extreme sensation, throbbing focused nerve endings. Talking and drinking coffee fingers barely touching across the wide kitchen table, fingertips tingling, burning.

This time he comes to the back door, the laundry room. The sun flaunts its false promise of warmth, autumn has already fallen to winter's force the trees are nearly bare. I am wearing a loose thin cotton shirtwaist falling just above my knees. He bursts into that awesome smile as I open the door taking in my nearly transparent garb blue eyes examining, caressing my body with tacit approval. He stumbles inside clumsily closing the door behind him letting in a brief frigid breeze never removing his eyes from me. I am staring at that smile, quivering with anxiety, expectation... I didn't make coffee, I say, yeah, okay, he answers, I had some already, he says staring intensely into my own eyes. He puts out his arms and welcomes me into the warmth and wanting, kisses me gently, holds me close in his cozy bear hug. Heat is flowing through me, hot oil in my veins, a sensation like burning liquor running through my stomach reaching all of my extremities. I am home. Finally, I am home. I feel safe and wanted for the first time in a long while. My heart is full.

We are suddenly aware of our location, our situation suddenly strange and self-conscious, can I get some coffee now, he asks, and I smile back and say, yeah, of course, grinning inside and out very pleased with myself feeling happier than I have in a long time actually in forever. Perfect harmony, soul connection. There do not seem to be words enough or necessity for allusion to what we have just shared indeed there appears no reason to even speak about it. We walk hand and hand self-consciously again into the kitchen and I look at him and wonder what is happening, what I have done, what I have allowed to happen; why I do not feel any guilt or remorse, just joy.

We sit at the kitchen table for a while sipping coffee saying nothing and he opens his mouth but nothing comes out. Finally he speaks. This is not what you think, he says, not something casual, just because...I interrupt him, don't, I say, you don't have to...no, he says. This is very special; I just wanted you to know it's more than just...feelings come surging up into my chest, my heart, my head, and all I can do, is sigh like Deborah Kerr says about Cary Grant that all she could do was say hello.

☙❧

The mornings become even more than before a daily ritual of coffee mere moments after Steve turns the corner. We cling together for warmth and sustenance, members of alien worlds come together for a split second in time with no hope of seeing the future together even though he keeps reminding me

that the children will not be young forever; in a few years we can make plans...
The only thing that we can do for each other is to provide an ear for both the real
and imagined abuses, add enough intimacy and joyfulness to provide a reason to
go on living and touch each other with the warmth that living creatures need to
survive. I spend long hours listening to love songs and ballads on my old portable
phonograph and either smile a lot or cry a lot. Futility joins hands with guilt
and begins to tear me apart. It doesn't really matter what Steve is doing I feel
guilty anyway. I wait for the phone to ring in case Cliff manages to find a space
in his work day where we can meet or even let me hear his voice for reassurance.
When it doesn't ring I divide the time between staring at the ceiling above the
sofa where I lie prostrate daydreaming of him and reliving our latest moments
together or crying quietly and hopelessly knowing that there is no salvation. I
listen to Vicki Carr wail and keen about waiting for a call and feel my chest and
bowels tighten up with combined apprehension and hope whenever the ringing
begins and with desolation when it isn't him. Barbara Streisand sings *he touched
me, he put his arms around me and he touched me...* and I remember and chills go
through me. I think a lot about the shadow of his smile that haunts me always
with me. *Oh my love my darling, I've hungered for your touch...*

Soon I begin driving around town hoping to spot his truck so that having
only casually bumped into him we might chat for a while. Perhaps I might
lure him into buying me a drink in some dark and cozy gin mill where once
he has partaken of a few I know he is good for a long warm satisfying respite
albeit in an alcoholic haze mindless of responsibilities that beckon from the real
world. I feel some small guilt about this but need his company too much to
pay much attention to the warning noises in my head. Of course, these jaunts
have to be carefully planned around the school schedules of the children and the
availability of babysitters. Thus they are not that frequent.

I begin to develop a sort of sixth sense about where to find him...and start
wondering about extra sensory perception for sometimes I astound myself with
my incisiveness. It can't be coincidence, I say, there has to be something more
going on. The eternally playing radio guides me the rest of the way; a series of
popular songs magically become foresight unfolding imminent situation. But it
works. I live on a razor's edge of expectation and disappointment bolstered only
by the now frequently replaced scotch bottle in the pot cabinet. I balance on the
edge of sanity.

At night unable to face Steve with my guilt, fearful to confront him with his
or to spend time encapsulated with him in the same stifling area imprisoned and
restrained, I take to running as frequently as is viable to one or another of pubs
that Eileen has introduced me to. I feel very little guilt to leave him to supervise
sleeping children especially when he does so little for them in any circumstance.
Once sitting at the bar I feel relatively safe for the bartenders know me as a quiet

patron who doesn't want to be bothered most especially by the men who frequent the place looking for some quick action. I become quite adept at fending them off for myself and out of mere boredom become an avid conversationalist my specialty being the sympathetic ear to some disgruntled husband. I am a chameleon. It is very easy to be understanding to somebody else's miserable creep when you don't have to go home with him or to him. It is almost satisfying to be able to talk to someone, to listen to his story, his dreams, his problems, play the part of his perfect woman. I have only had that with Cliff, have never had it with Steve. He has never talked to me, listened to me, confided in me. With Cliff unavailable I will listen to anyone else but there is never anyone who touches me as Cliff does. There is only Cliff. I sip slowly drinking very little enjoying the anonymity and escape. Always leave alone by choice.

Somehow I know though that Cliff is different, the problem is that we are unable to connect in the evening when I am feeling the most trapped when Steve is home. I escape to my role as compassionate mistress geisha. Sitting in those places night after night, hoping that there might be a fire call from the firehouse, an opportunity to connect with him, afterwards. On nights that I stay home I go about my business with my ears sharply perked in order to hear any possible siren. At such a fortuitous time I discover a sudden need for ice cream or Kotex or some other necessity and run for the car heading immediately for the firehouse like some silly schoolgirl. Once there I circle casually and tensely, rivulets of nervous sweat forming and running down my body.

Ultimately we meet. Maybe it is an evening, maybe it is enchanted; perhaps it is by accident, not really by chance and race immediately for some quiet spot where we hold each other tight and talk for hours until with sad and guilty grimaces we tear ourselves apart and rush painfully home.

After a while the tension begins to tell. There is the ever looming fear of being discovered, there are the complicated dynamics of continuing; planning meetings and phone calls, inventing excuses. There is the overwhelming sense of guilt that we each bear. We spend an inordinate amount of our precious time together staring mutely, desperately, hopelessly into each other's eyes. It's no good. The beauty and wonder of our feelings for each other are ruined by all of this. On several occasions, we attempt to find a way to end it but we are marionettes guided by an insurmountable magnetic force, part with great sadness and grave recriminations and find ourselves uncontrollably thrust back together. Still we try to do what we perceive, know to be the right thing and our meetings have become strained and sporadic indeed. Our phone conversations have become stilted with long drawn out silences; our plans are stiff and tentative and more difficult to coordinate. There is a lump in my throat when he walks toward me at some assignation that guilt stricken miserable expression on his face; guilt and futility grip me as well in a forbidding steely embrace. He

love once and I can find it again I tell myself between bouts of heavy sobbing, maybe without this pain and certainly without guilt. Now there remains only one possible solution to the horror that my life has become; create a plan for escape. The optimist in me rallies my inner forces. Survival is the only possible direction to take.

It promises to be a good year. It is only January and a woman, Indira Gandhi is premier of India. We women are gaining ground, there is opportunity ahead; the times they really are a changing. In March General Motors apologizes to a young Ralph Nader after his book criticizing the company, also knocking Rolls Royces, *Unsafe at Any Speed* is published but he is hammered by Henry Ford. I am incensed recalling Mom's and Daddy's remarks about Ford, their contempt. In the beginning of May Mao has launched a cultural revolution in China. What is next? It is possible to criticize bullies; that is the lesson to be learned. Revolutions are on the horizon, women are gaining ground. There is room for me in the future. I *have* a future.

I am going to stay married to Steve for a little longer though, go through the motions until I am able to support myself and it is a sad truth that old habits and needs still exist, things happen. It is also true that no matter how much I adore my kids and love being pregnant there is no way I want to be pregnant now. Not with my plans going so well for freedom. With the same passion and focus that I planned and maneuvered the other pregnancies I guard my single state and trim figure now with a sense of responsibility that belies my reputation in the family for being a bubblehead. Five kids are enough. Soon I will be a single mother if all goes according to plan.

❧❧

The Beach Boys are harmonizing at an ear-splitting decibel about surfing safaris and the sloop John B on the radio, the carload of kids joining in at the top of their lungs once again and Eileen and I can't help singing along and when the news report chimes in we find out that a joyous Frank Sinatra has married Mia Farrow. Tsk, tsk, we think out loud together, he's robbing the cradle how obscene, both a little jealous. It was bad enough when Eddie Fisher wed Debbie Reynolds then left her for Liz Taylor. Then it is hollering about Eleanor Rigby with her face in a jar by the door at an unholy decibel. In July, we are shocked to hear about a grisly discovery of the bodies of eight nurses that have been murdered by a psychopathic serial killer named Richard Specks and several days later one of my favorite actors Monty Clift whose best friend is Liz Taylor, has died. A sense of mortality hovers in the ether, unable to be collated in our youth. It is all so abstract. Why would anyone murder eight nurses? What is going on with the world? Why do we seem to be surrounded with death?

The scare about The Pill, blood clots and potential cancers has been gathering momentum and my own discomfort from its ingestion has become untenable especially given the infrequency and lack of inspiration of my physical relationship with Steve albeit all that I now have so I bravely move on where some the less intrepid and more conservative fear to tread. I insist that my doctor fit me with one of those new intrauterine devices, IUDs as they are called. I make this decision in deference to his insistence that they are foolproof and the most effectual answer to the time old problem of unwanted pregnancy that man has yet to devise—man. Another pregnancy believe it or not is not what I want right now.

I brave the discomfort and embarrassment of its insertion with the same stoic patience with which I have survived the pregnancies and births that precede it. I leave the doctor's office for home a feeling of optimism encompassing me for now I feel the issue of pregnancy will be ended. Oh, I expect a short period of slight discomfort, even staining as I have been warned but poof that will be the end of it. I rejoice in my new freedom. I want to be prepared for the infrequent and uninspired attentions of my husband. For as long as he is my husband, I still have infrequent urges as does he. Less and less frequent. How much of that is hormones and need? He is now my only choice. I wonder sometimes how I fit into his life, why I am willing to share him with his girlfriend, why I even care. It makes me feel a tremendous amount of guilt over what I have done to Cliff's wife causing all kinds of livid and confusing images to torment me.

About a month later the early May sunlight is dancing among the tender newly emerging leaves, tulips and daffodils and forsythia and azaleas are shouting out joyfully that spring is here again. I am especially missing Cliff and trying not to think about him. All at once my attention is diverted to the somewhat light and sporadic staining that I experience at reception of the IUD. It has become a full-blown bleeding. I make numerous phone calls of accelerating intensity and fear to my doctor who blandly reassures me and admonishes me, mother of five, teacher, housekeeper, to stay off my feet.

By Sunday morning, the golfers are on the ready all lined up and raring to go at all their various courses and the baseball commentators are readying their *schpiels*. I am silently and frantically mopping up bloody, literally scarlet floods, and using Kotex pads by the threes. Nothing will stop the outpouring of what only appear to be tomatoes. I am truly really frightened. I call the doctor and I'm told yet again quite pedantically to stay off my feet. I can just see him glancing at his watch and keeping one eye on the first hole tee while we speak. He tells me he will check in with me later on that day and perhaps impatient not to be disturbed on his one day of rest hangs up.

By noon I know that am in serious trouble. I call the doctor's service and tell them of the predicament and inform them that I am heading for the hospital. I don't want to go to nearby Huntington Hospital because my doctor knows me having delivered all five of my babies and in my panic I need the security of familiarity. I tell Steve that we have to go to the hospital. His answer does not surprise me; if I feel the need to go, insist on drawing attention to myself, indulge in my usual self coddling selfishness I can go but he certainly isn't going to miss one of the opening games of the season for so ridiculous a reason. This is my problem.

Why can't you get sick on weekdays when I'm not around to annoy like a normal woman? What did you do, plan this just to annoy me? You know that I always watch the ball game on Sunday, he says with matter of fact disdain.

Please, I plead, feeling the flow of blood as if it comes through an opened faucet.

If you're looking for yet another excuse to play hooky, to desert your children mother of the year then go right ahead. But be sure to get home in time to cook us dinner, you're not going to work this into some kind of free mileage for pizza or something so get that right off your mind.

I move slowly to the car aware not only of the flow but of the stabbing gripping pain that runs through my middle and feeling quite weak and dizzy drive somewhat slowly though steadily to New Hyde Park some distance away. I want to be treated by my regular doctor not some stranger in our nearby hospital. I waste more precious minutes once there looking for a parking spot, for the sign in front of the emergency entrance was marked *authorized vehicles only* and it never occurs to me to consider myself important enough to be included in such a designation. I lock the car and begin walking toward the door not realizing that my Bermuda shorts, originally white, and my white shirt are now completely blood red to my armpits. As I walk, I am aware that lumpy red clots are sliding down my leg and landing with a splat on the parking lot leaving a trail behind me. For a moment I feel a twinge of guilt that I have left a mess but I am too weak to care anymore, and force all my attention to the task of getting myself to the door, in the door, and up to the desk.

I quickly lose consciousness as soon as I am placed in the bed they have brought me to. A beauteous early spring Sunday morning and they are greatly understaffed for nobody but the lowest of the pecking order can be coerced to work. I try to insist that no one touch me until my doctor gets there but I drift in and out of consciousness and before I know what is happening an intern informs me that he has removed the guilty IUD and I will be all right. I am given infusions of blood. Either they weren't able to reach my doctor or he didn't wish to be reached. Either way, the thing is gone now, and so according to my young intern is the tiny embryo et al. that had been clinging frantically to life. Didn't I know? The manner in which this device operates is to cause a mini-miscarriage for every tiny conception that occurs. This is what it is all about.

I am nauseated and repelled at the same time and fearful of what damage can possibly have been done by this youngster probably gravely inexperienced and certainly unfamiliar with the mysterious and cavernous depths of me. When my very own doctor arrives at six to check the damage his new tan glistening handsomely beneath the examining light he puts my mind at ease. Everything is all right, he says with authority, he did as good a job as I would have done. Stay off your feet for a while and relax, you'll soon be as good as new. You'll get a normal period in a month and everything will be the same as usual. Don't forget to take your pills now, he wags his finger playfully at me. With a pat on the shoulder he turns and is gone. He must continue with his weekend social plans.

Someone has found clean clothes for me in the gift shop. I phone Elaine hoping for some kind of help or empathy from my sister-in-law, but she has other plans. I drive weakly home no one else available for the job putting my full concentration on the road oblivious to the delicately opening dogwoods and the glowing willows and proudly thrusting delicate birches. I arrive to find the children squabbling among themselves and lights all out save for the glow that emanates eerily from the television. When the first commercial comes on and Steve glances up to see me standing there he testily reminds me that the children have not yet eaten which is obviously my fault and asks me snidely if I can possibly whip something up, *Mother of the Year*, he repeats with dripping sarcasm.

I quickly throw together some pancakes, tickle the kids by topping the cakes with ice cream and strawberries, and leaving them all eating gratefully sink down on the bed too exhausted and empty even to cry.

Now there is no going back at all even if there had been. I can never forgive Steve for refusing to help me when I needed him this last time. The fact that I have lost a child, his child, no matter how early in its embryonic growth is of no concern to him. Especially since he already has five, as if this lost one is without worth. The emptiness of life without love is overwhelming especially now that I have known the real thing. The vacuum caused by a total lack of compassion or affection is a chasm that has swallowed me completely. I silently immerse myself once again in my garden finding some solace in the rich warming earth that peacefully demands no more than to surround and give succor to the joyfully renaissant shrubs and flowers. When I exhaust my energy and garden chores or the early spring air becomes too raw to continue I retreat to the worlds of Agatha Christie and other kindred spirits eager to lose myself in the problems, horrors of others, fictitious others. I fill the unencumbered hours with escapes into fantasy. I survive barely, in a fuzzy state of near catatonia going about my business only just, while my mind tunnels deeper and deeper into itself seeking solutions to this endless miasma.

❧❧

One solution hovering in my subconscious seems to rise head and shoulders above the rest. I decide that I certainly can teach beginners the rudiments of painting. I tentatively begin this experiment when Steve is at work. After simply placing a small ad in the Pennysaver I am astonished to receive several responses, which escalate into several classes.

I love those Wednesday morning classes and enjoy the challenge that teaching presents and the sense of achievement from helping someone. My prize student is our rabbi who has his lessons on Wednesday mornings, promises not to tell Steve about my clandestine classes unless he asks and counsels me with grave Talmudic wisdom about the dynamics of marriage that encompasses very little more than obedience and humility. I am adamant about my plan though, determined to become financially independent so that I can deal with the matter of divorce which hovers like a rapacious phantom over me all the time. The rabbi is having difficulty with his painting of a religious Jewish gentleman in his yarmulke and prayer shawl an ancient rabbi no doubt so I help him and end up doing most of the painting myself little by little in answer to his pleas. My student full of rabbinical integrity claims the painting with great pride as his own. This doesn't give me a whole lot of confidence in his intensely offered advice about my marital problems.

Ultimately, on a momentary whim impressed by my success to date and with thoughts of divorce and survival uppermost in my mind I throw caution to the wind and apply for a position teaching painting in two local adult education systems, Northport and Commack. I use as credentials several of my more successful paintings executed in the fourth year of my marriage just after Caryn's birth when I dared to defy Steve and took painting classes with Paul Puzinis. It turns out that I excel as a teacher of painting.

The transition from adult education classes to North Shore Art Studio is relatively simple; that's the name I give the school that I am opening. Once I realize my success as a teacher and acquire an insistent following of students who encourage me it is a simple matter to branch out and start my own school. It is true to be sure, I never can earn enough part time with only adult ed to support myself and my children and the desire to be free of Steve's iron rule and demonic possession has culminated in serious fantasies of escape. These classes are underwriting the costs of my new venture and private classes enhance my profit margin. The school will also pay for an occasional housekeeper so that I will be freed from the tyranny of housework. It will enable me technically to keep experimenting until I am able to develop skills sufficient to earn a living by moving out into the marketplace, selling sufficient quantities of art to become independent, to implement my five-year plan so called, to gain my freedom from tyranny and oppression.

It isn't even a choice for there is none to be made. The only things I have been able to do thus far are have babies, care for a house, and paint pictures. This is aside from the fact that I truly care to do nothing else. Paramount in my thoughts is giving my children a better home life, a happier and more secure childhood than the one I myself knew. For the present I will schedule my classes while the older ones are at school, the littler ones at nursery school.

My carefully conceived plan is right on schedule At this point I ignore Steve's criticisms, admonitions, and dire warnings, and damn the torpedoes. I am moving full speed ahead.

I am a success as a teacher but the real rewards come when I indeed create a viable product and begin to exhibit in the popular series of outdoor shows and I am ultimately discovered by an art gallery agent. At the time this is not only financial salvation but ultimately a voyage into a kind of subservient Hell that not only enslaves me but stifles my creativity for years to come. The catch-22 is that the more it pays for the survival of my family the more it destroys me. Only a certain string of ill-fated incidents or perhaps in some ways a force of destiny breaks the pattern and allows me to begin to think of my true direction and compensation for the lost years.

My only real consolation for the angst of those years is that as I hack away desperately seeking innovative artistic concepts to keep sales flowing and the gorgon-headed monster fed and clothed I develop many more exciting techniques and media than I ever dreamed existed.

On a lighter note I now have a new controversy to address as the miniskirt has arrived in the fashion world shocking society as well as Steve who forbids me to wear one, and even more compelling, both Margaret Sanger the birth control advocate and Walt Disney who have both played such important roles in my evolution have died.

こ๛๑

There is a new art form taking over the communications wavelengths, creating a buzz; artists are digging holes and shapes in the ground making something named provocatively Earth Sculpture. Christos drapes everything with cloth, buildings and canyons and anything large that is nailed down. The beat generation is taking over our culture, we are surrounded by *happenings* and *funk.* Although Jesus Christ Superstar is the latest hero of note Zen Buddhism is the faith of choice... *the value of art is in the making not in the intrinsic worth of the materials,* a spokesperson for the movement says. I am completely involved in the making of art, really truly involved in making art...but what's wrong with selling what one has made I wonder, especially if it helps you survive to make more?

This is the impetus of the creation of the North Shore Art Studio in late fall of 1966. The impetus for the school probably comes from the added hormones surging through my system for here I am pregnant with number six only the third of all of the babies so far unplanned. Margaret Sanger where are now that I need you? This is due in some part at least to the incompetence or at least inexperience of the young intern at the hospital who ministered to me in my emergency that bright Sunday morning as well as to the grave allegiance of my obstetrician of his stern and demanding religion golf, which kept him from my side when he was so desperately needed. The initial blow that this pregnancy inflicts upon me on the eve of my escape from tyranny is a tough one to take. Abortion is not yet on the table and I am feeling the most obdurate of desperation. Somehow after the crying and chest beating is finished I am aware that it has served merely to galvanize me further, to guide me through those first deliberate moves to create my own school. Just in case I am seeking further inspiration three books are published this year that stand out for their pertinence to my existence: *In Cold Blood, The Fixer,* and *Valley of the Dolls.* Is there a series of hidden or not so hidden messages there portending evil, degradation and conspiracy yet to come?

CHAPTER 46

I do not want to do this, do not want to go anywhere be with anyone speak with anyone. It is a command performance. I especially do not want to be thrust into the company of Steve's sister Elaine, I don't want to face the family, not this family that is not my family, don't want to be anywhere with Steve who is my husband and yet, not my husband. I don't know what Steve has said to her about me, about us but things are tense and I am not comfortable. I remember the fabricated story about me and the carpenter and that was nothing. I still haven't forgiven her for that one if you must know or for keeping me at arm's length all these years as if she is too good for me. If she does know anything, if she says anything, I will pass out from shock and terror. How can she possibly know where I have been going, what I have been doing? I don't even know. I don't even know what is happening to me or where it will end. I only know that I am spinning on a carousel that never stops and it is making me dizzy. On top of everything else California has elected Ronald Reagan governor. He has *won one for the Gipper*. Where is he going from there? I ask myself. How will California survive with an actor for a political leader? I want to talk about it with Steve but I know better than to even try.

So it is another Thanksgiving rolls around and we are going to a family affair; Steve's family for a change. Preparing the now five children for any occasion, especially a dress up visit to someone's home is a chore to end all chores. That is, to visit *anyone*. To visit Aunt Elaine means a spit and polish job beyond the pale and the exquisitely careful selection of each facet of every outfit, the coordination *en toto* of each of the boys and each of the girls and the melding together of an entire theme...Aunt Elaine has perfect taste. Her own life is designed and tailored with complete and total impeccability and she holds nothing but scorn for those of us poor unworthy plebeians who are unable to live up to her fine standards. But *noblesse oblige*. Elaine tolerates us. She finds this a trying situation but she does her very best as usual. She even manages to affect a hearty *hale fellow well met* attitude when she is forced into our company and treats us to yet another dose of generous condescension. After all it is only once or twice a year!

This particular Thanksgiving is indeed to be a very noble and magnanimous gift to her brother's difficult and unwieldy family, more like a sacrifice. How embarrassed that makes me feel. However it is a command performance by other members of the family who desire to see *Stevie's* children. They are not my children, not even then. I am just the nanny, the caretaker, non-paid hired help. There simply is no way to escape this dreaded and distasteful chore.

We arrive at the lovely and gracious home in the posh hills of manicured Woodbury and disembarking from the station wagon we descend upon our warm and beaming hostess; we are immediately escorted (warmly) to the basement playroom where we are gently and graciously (and firmly) advised to remain. Elaine's polished antique fruitwood and silk and damask and thick plush carpets are not to be molested by creatures newly captured from the wilds. We eat our dinner on a paper cloth covered sheet of plywood thrown over the pool table and feeling even less welcome than had indeed been intended leave early.

This is more or less the extent of my relationship with my sister-in-law, her interaction with my children. It is strange because when we first started out I had been so excited to have a sister, to have a niece and nephew. I babysit for little Amy at the beginning when things are fresh and new and friendly.

I love you, Lynne, warbles little Amy hugging her soft plump arms around me. Are you going to marry Uncle Stevie and be my aunt, my very own aunt? I guess so, honey,

I answer, giving her a little squeeze. Elaine returns from shopping and places her large bundles on the kitchen table. Thanks for sitting, she says, it's really a big help in this weather when she's feeling sick. I miss my mother more than ever when I'm stuck like this. She smiles and I feel good and warm to know that soon I will have my own sister, finally. Amy gets up and starts to dance around, asking what she has been brought, dancing and getting excited just thinking about what might be in the packages for her. Suddenly her little face flushed from the excitement she gags a little on whatever she has popped into her rosebud mouth and everything happens too fast almost for recollection...First Amy dances on the lovely beige plush carpet, then she gags and both Elaine and I spin around, then Amy begins to vomit and then in a flash Elaine has clamped the first thing that comes to hand, a filthy dishrag, over Amy's sweet mouth. Not on my carpet, she shrieks in horror as I merely stand by stunned and disbelieving. The child heaves and gags and chokes but still the ugly cloth is held tightly over her mouth.

Finally her mother lifts her right up off the floor one hand on her soft bottom and the other still clutching the rag—over her mouth—literally carrying her to the bathroom. Not a drop is spilled. Oh, she's always throwing up, said Elaine a little sheepishly now but still the bustling confident matron.

Dear God, I think to myself. Please never let anything ever make me treat a child of mine like that.

Things are never the same between us, after that and I can't recall seeing Amy again except at my wedding when she is a well dressed well coifed flower girl.

My expectations are stunned, my sensibilities are numbed by experiencing the inexplicable, the inexcusable and I am no longer able to be shocked when the U.S. admits to killing civilians in Nam.

CHAPTER 47

1967

Winter sunlight floods this vast loft space through a bank of picture windows that spread across the back wall corner to corner joined by the extra light source created by the eight fluorescent fixtures that I have installed as part of my agreement with the management that rents for the most part to the Big Apple supermarket that sits directly beneath us. I am to pay them a minimal sum, $100 per month for a year as a trial, and put in the lights. The huge loft is otherwise empty and doing nothing for them. It is perfect for my school. I have convinced the respective school systems that my new premises will allow for Adult Education day classes, something that is not available to these people during school hours. They are intrigued, and agree to give me a chance given my popularity as an art teacher, are thrilled to be able to satisfy the great demand for these classes. My new private students along with sales I make at the outdoor shows give me the profit. The unexpected bonus is that I meet so many people. Dorothy Walmsley becomes a buddy; I am close to Diane Oliva, Connie Scott, and Anne Donnelly, who is determined to be the next William Blake for a long time. The second bonus is that they all think that I am wonderful. What a surprise. I enjoy meeting all these new people, making several lifelong friends and bask in the new glory of their adulation and my unmistakable successes. This is a heady although unexpected success for me.

The best of my most recent attempts at painting hang on the remaining walls, the ones without windows including those spectacular nudes from the Tuesday night classes with Puzinis when Caryn was born and the painting of the rabbi that I actually painted in his name when Rabbi Wernick was my student. I am ecstatic. But my ebullient mood is dulled for a time when I discover that three astronauts have been killed in the flash fire that has engulfed the Apollo I spacecraft on the ground during a simulation. The very thought of this horrible incident haunts me, enhances those hovering feelings of mortality that are always with me, makes me wish to accelerate my plan, move ahead quickly; it appears to be a message that life is indeed short. This is a concept that I cannot usually embrace.

I make the rounds of the proliferation of trendy galleries that have sprung up in the new art awareness and resultant boom of the mid-1960s. My research provides me with knowledge of what is creating the success of the most popular of the current artists. I borrow generously and without shame from what has already proved itself worthy, and I build on it. Impasto techniques are popular, the clientele seem to love that palette knife approach. I am painting landscapes, seascapes, trees and flowers. Slowly but surely, concept and style begin to emerge. I enter several competitions, and find myself the recipient of a drawer full of ribbons to my great gratification and surprise. Still I sense a lack of something necessary for true commerce, can't seem to put my finger on what is missing.

My schedule is frantically full of running. I run to open the studio for a class, run home to wait for returning school busses; I race to pick up babysitters for an afternoon class or to finish some promising painting that is at best on the verge of greatness or at worst solution. Then I run back home in time to fix dinner for the crew. I then leave Steve to bathe them and put them to bed. Until this time he has had no contact to speak of with his children, never cared for them, maybe those sporadic baths when there were only three or maybe four like when he left Wendi to drown. I figured that not only is it important for him to be involved with them on some level but it is certainly only fair that following the years of his law school and my imprisonment, it is now my turn. I am becoming aware that women may have some claim to civil rights, also. He still comes home very late on certain weekday nights; I no longer need to know nor do I care any longer where he is spending this time. I continue to attend school conferences, Open School Nights, concerts, chorus and band performances by my budding musicians accompanied mostly by Mom because Steve is always occupied, never around.

Still I alternately beg him to go with me to see a marriage counselor and for a divorce. His response to the first request is that there is nothing wrong with us except for my inadequacies as a housekeeper and mother especially due to my despised and mostly disregarded *career* and to the second that if I am not happy, then I can leave *without my children*. He says it in a voice that fills me with an icy fear.

I place a few advertisements for classes in local periodicals, and begin to send out press releases with hopes of increasing my classes and The Long Island Press decides to write a story about me and my school, calling me the first Long Island Feminist when in answer to a question about why I opened the school I tell the reporter that it is part of my plan to escape my abusive marriage. A photo appears of me teaching a class dressed in my standard black sweat shirt and pants my gestating baby very obvious. My Puzinis paintings and the rabbi's rabbi painting can be seen on the walls in the background.

Each trip back and forth to the studio entails the racing up and flying down of a double set of marble stairs for the studio is located in a loft area above a shopping center. I gain less weight with this pregnancy than with of the others and ultimately give birth much sooner than is expected.

The very first morning of the spring season, my first class in the new studio, I welcome thirty-nine students to the large though now crowded room so far and wide has my reputation spread. I race up the stairs to open up and have to practically wiggle my way through the crowd that throngs in the hallway to reach the door. I thrill to the feeling of authority that envelopes me as I slip the key in the lock of my professional studio and school.

Once I am settled into the seat behind my desk the unwieldy group quiets down. I hand out a supply list and take their registration slips. I begin to discuss my goals for the class noticing that I feel a little strange. Throughout the duration of my administrative chores and class goal lecture I begin to feel little tightening spasms across my belly and remember telling myself how stupid this is for it is only February 3 and the baby isn't due until March 15. Never, never, has one of my babies been born early; this is obviously Braxton-Hicks, a magic-sounding group of letters put together that fail to delineate their meaning, still they are gaily and confidently repeated to explain a common phenomenon. *Oh, this is obviously*

Braxton-Hicks. I continue my talk uneasily all the time assuring the dubious group that my child's birth is six weeks away at best and that I have at worst a very quick recovery quotient.

This news reaches their disbelieving ears with a tinny false sound for they have all borne children and can remember their own confinements vividly. The clock finally reaches noon and I gratefully dismiss them, gaily calling out to them that I will see them the following week, bright and early Tuesday morning. I immediately call the doctor. It is no surprise when he reassures me that it can't possibly be time but that if I care to drive to the hospital he will take a look. I quickly call Steve and tell him that I have to go to the hospital and he informs me that my timing is inconvenient as usual and this will have to wait until he returns home from work. Feeling the contractions grip me more intensely I tearfully plead with him but true to form, in the same way that he had reacted the spring before during my emergency he refuses to be moved.

So I arrange by phone for a sitter Dolores to be waiting at the house and drive myself once again to the hospital. By the time the doctor gets me to the examining table the pains seem to have stopped. I praise my good luck that I have not insisted that Steve leave work early to drive me here. The doctor smiles sweetly and apologetically at me patting my head consolingly just a little condescending and sends me home with a shrug. By the time I am back on the road the pains have increased in intensity so that once having reached home I literally am compelled to crawl from the car to the house on my hands and knees. Frightened and apprehensive I ask the sitter to stay.

When Steve finally arrives home in due course soon thereafter I beg him in tears to take me back to the hospital and only after he has read the paper and had his dinner does he acquiesce. Somehow, I prepare dinner. It is of course my fault that he is missing his favorite program. I spend the evening at the hospital the contractions starting and stopping with the same regularity as the elevator that bore me back and forth to and from the maternity floor. The fatigued doctor who has already attended several deliveries this day and depends on his schedule of carefully planned inductive births begs me to go home again and I refuse fearing desperately to give birth in the car or worse even at home.

I know that this baby is coming. I don't know why the contractions keep stopping but I KNOW THIS BABY IS COMING. Finally deep into the night, with the janitors mopping the lobby around me obediently lifting my feet when they come near my seat and Steve threatening to leave me there alone and never come back, a sympathetic and rather desperate and rattled desk nurse calls my doctor comfortably ensconced at home by now and they sign me in at least for the night. With the sedative that they administer intravenously all night albeit with some reluctance and disdain I manage to get a good night's sleep. The contractions however stopped temporarily by the medication begin again in the morning the minute I am disconnected from the intravenous line. The doctor comes in for his morning rounds, gives me one of those hearty *how are you today* routines and after examining me tells me to get dressed for he is signing me out. The bed is needed for someone with a real situation.

Somehow as I gingerly get out of bed and stand up a flood of water runs out of me covering the floor and now my doctor whom I have sarcastically named *Dr. No* is obliged to keep me there and see what he can do to hurry the birth. The last terse words that I hear as the icy sleep-inducing liquids seep from the tube into my arm and fuzziness soothes me into sleep are the doctor's admonitions to Steve to go home. This might be forty-eight hours at least, he says caustically, and he isn't even sure at this point if he can save either one of us, me or the baby, it is way too soon for this to be happening. He is annoyed. He administers the dose of Pitocin which induces labor and twenty minutes later Tracy, five pounds, is born. We are both fine and I am exultant. She is tiny but has exactly the same precious face as her five siblings. Steve arrives home, receives a message that his sixth child has arrived and turns around and goes back to the hospital. You could have planned this better, he tells me dryly.

In three days I return to my classes in my new painting school, baby and her paraphernalia under my arm. Classes continue, to the shock of my students. I am almost able to live with the vacuum created by the absence of Cliff in my life for teaching and working both are so all-encompassing that there is little time or energy left for either self-pity or the logistics and planning of infidelity, for fruitless and futureless efforts. Still I have my moments usually late at night when exhausted by a long and satisfying work day there arises a need to cuddle in someone's arms and repeat the successes and failures of the day to a caring ear. There is so much to talk about, and no one with whom to talk. I am alone with no one to confide in. At these times I run to some pub and down scotch sours until all need as well as pain fades along with most of consciousness and stumble home to fall dead asleep only to face another day like the last. Soon it will be over, I am attempting to convince Steve that we need at least a trial separation with not very much success and yet I push onward.

৵৵

We look like just any other couple out for Friday night dinner kids probably left with a babysitter. In reality we are two armed camps, clenched teeth and barely spoken words. My stomach is sinking, my gait is stiff. Steve is a zombie unable to make the simplest move. He is stricken, sunken into himself so helpless that my heart goes out to him for a moment. I have gotten what I want. I have gained a measure of control, have seen him suffer as I have. The first heart transplant has taken place but the pain in my own heart is indefatigable. I have persevered; I have convinced him finally to leave so that we may at least have a trial separation. He is not happy. I am not happy but I feel freedom in the wings awaiting the stage, sense the faint possibility of future happiness.

So here we are at yet another Chinese restaurant ordering dinner. I am filled with a combination of rage and compassion, desperation and hope. I have never been so conflicted in my life. I must hold onto the fact that I have made a plan to escape bondage and misery and I have fulfilled my goal for the most part. It may be painful but like any other birth the pain will be worthwhile. And yet there is the awareness of death, something once precious has died, an irreversible end has been reached.

Chicken chow mein, wonton soup, eggroll…again and again. It's the same old same old déjà vu all over again. Can't we ever try something different? I am impatient and irritable. What is this revulsion for variety? There are so many tantalizing choices in the menu. This sameness, the rote of every facet of our life drums away at my brain like the incessant swinging prodding elements of a well programmed industrial machine that until recently has governed the reality of our existence; it emphasizes the futility of it all, emphasizes the exquisitely painful contrast of the persistent turmoil of indecision and the unknown future.

The daydreams and fantasies flourish as life goes on as usual. I can feel a familiar small tic beginning to throb at the corner of my mouth. Again. It isn't the dinner, I think, it is everything. It is the exploding fragmenting particles of dreams and the essences of life's elements. At least here at this restaurant there is no question of the usual hassle concerning shrimp and dessert that is our companion at every dinner out; here we are safely entombed with the improbable temptations of rice and tea serving as the ultimate of inspirations. I attempt lackadaisically to control a streak of nasty cantankerous viciousness born of an entire decade of frustration which taunts me to be let loose.

Steve bites into his wonton and expertly maneuvers several stringy slivers of meat onto his spoon enveloping them with his lips quite characteristically efficient. We have eaten this same uninspiring Chinese meal for many years. I watch him fascinated, and before I can control the impulse say quite conversationally, do you know that those strips floating in the soup are pork?

Before the words are completely out of my mouth the mouthful of soup is out of his.

What did you say, he sputters. I said, I repeat quite calmly entranced by the unaccustomed feeling of power that infuses me, that is PORK that you are eating, *Yeshiva Bucha*. The devil has made me do it.

He turns a lighter shade of pale and draws back into the plastic softness of the booth. But it can't be. That's CHICKEN. Chicken is kosher.

No sir it's pork, all right. And even if it were chicken it wouldn't be kosher anyway since it's cooked in the kitchen *with the pork*. My voice has become tense and a little louder. Do you think they have a separate set of pots for everything porkless, especially for clientele who worship at the shrine of hypocrisy? Some Jew you are! It kind of encompasses everything I am feeling about my husband and my recent religious experiences as well.

Anyway chicken isn't meat, he answers petulantly wiping at his mouth, and only meat applies to that law. Why didn't you tell me sooner? He is growing paler by the moment. *Because I loved you and I didn't want to hurt you, you ass.* And in that moment, I realize that despite everything I do still love him. Why I can't quite figure out. But what is love anyway, and what does that have to do with happiness or even survival?

I think I'd like a shrimp cocktail, I say sweetly, throwing caution to the winds. What can he do to me now that he hasn't already done? What do I have to lose anymore?

Book I
Part IV
Salvation

CHAPTER 48

Today, Spring 2009

I have hit the familiar proverbial wall. Nothing is coming out right. It is one of those times when it is necessary to leave the studio, take a cleansing break; give creativity a rest. The minutes and hours are passing, the afternoon and expectation along with it is slowly being eaten away and I am still looking for ways to fill the time, make the day disappear, the tension to disperse along with it. I look around, and notice that now with an absence of rain infant leaves are drooping quickly, it seems, the earth is looking dry and crumbly.

If I can successfully nurture my garden, my substitute family maybe I can find a way to nurture my children, bring them home. I cut branches of forsythia, a tradition, to force indoors and soon inside and out they will be screaming their yellow song. I fear for my border of hostas which last year were dragged underground by unseen creatures and replanted helter skelter in strange places where they dutifully reappeared finally to gamely wave their mauve and orchid flags. This year there are no signs of them at all. Anger and frustration living deep in my memory and my soul regenerate and come over me as I realize that once again the moles and voles have decimated my tulips and crocuses. Anger and frustration have become my most loyal companions...

Spring once again hovers impatiently in the wings as I work day and night to complete my story inspired by a deluge of memories and our weekly workshop spurred onward by the enthusiasm of my buddies, my partners in crime...Maybe it's good enough, has enough appeal to be purchased by a real publisher. I am thinking, thinking, wondering...the first step is to find an editor; I begin a fevered search...

Eileen, a new Eileen from the writing workshop; she is Eileen Moskowitz which tickles me encourages my tendency to magical thinking; she is a bizarre coincidental combination of Shelley Moskowitz and Eileen Corby from the old days in East Northport that cannot merely be a random act of happenstance, must have some metaphysical meaning in the greater picture, has a friend, an editor on the west coast who agrees to read my manuscript. She says she is impressed with it so far but she is closing the agency and she wishes me luck. After this positive response from Eileen's friend although a little disappointed that it has come to naught I am motivated to find another editor who is willing and able to edit my story. I continue searching, researching, talking to friends and I find an editor who has wonderful references, someone who belongs to Pat's dojo and has an impressive web site and a resume describing major accomplishments. She reads the first fifty pages and her response is also positive; she suggests a few changes. She will be thrilled to work with me but the cost is incredibly high. Should I do it, go for broke? Pat is going to Tibet; Christine is getting lipo, Botox treatments and facelifts, which all cost a fortune. Should I spring for the edit, use my savings; put it on a credit card? It is a lot to think about. But I am distracted, spring is hovering, taunting with the usual promises and distractions.

I am as ever totally occupied moving everywhere at once aware that time is passing quickly. I multitask flitting between all of my different interests and responsibilities as ever leaving my art, my writing behind me for a moment to water flower beds and some new shrubs and perennials and find this to be as soothing and satisfying as it ever has been. Standing there hose in hand pointing and spraying. I am consumed with my love of art and garden unabashedly not only for escape, for protection but to feel alive. Always hovering in the background is the awareness of my story, of the need to complete it, to explore its potential. I am as usual writing chapters in my head, saving them to record later. But for the moment I focus on the promise of life and color which is everywhere. I need to remember however that it is merely a promise and I have learned from life over and over again that promises are easily broken.

I understand the seasons and their changes; I am attuned to nature and her vagaries. I am one with the ebb and flow of time and weather. But the motives and actions of people elude my best and finest perception. I am back in the awful past.

But for one shocking moment I am in the midst of an old nightmare from those troubled and arduous years before I lost the children and I shudder with the memory, my extremities becoming ice.

I am pushing a baby carriage, a weighty burden almost an impossibility, it is so heavy. My stomach sinks heavily into my lower abdomen shrinking and twisting as I summon up the courage to ask their father for help and he whines and carps and complains finally ripping the cold hard handle of the carriage from my hands, assuming control. I feel the hot churning force of anger beginning to take over my body losing itself in sinking frustration and helplessness. Why can't you just help? I plead silently. At first I follow several paces behind shackled by frustration feet encumbered as though embedded in wet cement or sucking quicksand. I struggle to move forward to see the children, to touch them, to reassure them that Mommy is still there for them, struggle with my immobile mouth, my locked jaw. Father laughs loudly, raucously, diabolically, raising an arm between me and the carriage, impeding any contact. I will make sure that you will never see my children again, he says firmly, icicles dripping from his voice. I will make you disappear. I assure you, you will cease to exist. That is a promise. He and the carriage get dimmer and dimmer as they disappear down the street and are lost in a swirling burgeoning mist, the echoes of his laughter continue jubilantly in the emptiness.

Old tears are streaming down my face. Stop, I scream in my head. I clasp my hands over my ears, as if to stave off outspoken thought. I will not play this game.

I return to my safe havens, my saving graces, my art, my garden. I am studiously refusing to address either teeming thought or the still silent phone.

CHAPTER 49

1967

Time passes quickly, and then it is summer and the adult education season temporarily ends. At the end of June Israel smashes the Arabs in a six-day war as the Monterey Pop Festival draws fifty thousand kids. At the end of August Thurgood Marshall is stunningly the first black justice on the Supreme Court. Minorities are beginning to make progress; what does that mean for women's rights and Feminism? Steve sees my new independence and self-sufficiency, senses my resolve and is suddenly desperate to fix things. Why? I ask myself. But he decides that a vacation will be the healing balm, give us time together to work things out. Why does this sound familiar? Oh yeah, that was what I pleaded for not so long ago; now it has become *too* long ago. I am not convinced, I do not trust him, or his motives, I cannot even bear to be in the same room with him never mind on some island in a hotel room. The Caribbean? Shades of Bermuda. That's when I should have nipped this thing in the bud, left him, right after our honeymoon. But then, the thought assails me, I would not have my precious children.

We deplane in tropical paradise for the second time in less than ten years. Jamaica is a more pungent colorful lively tropical island than Bermuda, unrestrained by confining staid British traditions and mores, filled with a unique more rhythmic movement, accompanied by a cacophony of more mellifluous as well as dissonant joyous sounds of commerce, music and voice. The last time was our honeymoon which was filled with joy, expectation and hopefulness. This time there is a palpable absence of optimism or anticipation, rather, we progress heavily through all of the necessary and proscribed rites of travel surrounded by friendly Caribbean exotica yet impervious to the efforts of our hosts to make the experience brighter and breezier.

Steve and I proceed as insensate non beings going through traditional rote, moving through tepid steamy air as though it is a translucent solid mass comprised of weighted amorphic crystals and I am feeling nothing, less than nothing; the sun reflects happily from never still multi colored surfaces as wild cacophonies of reggae and the lilting patois of island chatter are cloaked and muffled by the invisible barricades of our morose diffidence. Steve is tentative, suddenly hopeful, wanting this magical trip to a magical place to solve all our problems and be our fantastical mulligan. I am feeling overpowered by hopelessness and despair, faced with ten days of this weighty overbearing aura of tedium that stretches out before me like an unending inescapable program [zeitgeist] of ubiquitous torture. Despite his hopefulness that he wears as heavily as one of the omnipresent exotic floral printed native shirts that pervade this island I am certain that Steve is sorry that it is I who am accompanying him here when he I am certain wishes is was Pearl, just as I am lamenting the fact that Steve is not Cliff.

There is a strange uncomfortable sensation of tiny invisible ants creeping up my legs as I stand with Steve before the registration counter and he signs us in, receives our keys and waves them gaily at me with a wistful crooked smile that I cannot bear to look at, and so I look away. What is this all about? I am finding it difficult to believe that Steve suddenly wants me again, finding it impossible to allow myself to move past the barrier that I have so painfully constructed over the years to protect myself from his barbed criticism and neglect. We move ahead to settle into this alien room in an unfamiliar place to attempt to accomplish the impossible. There is a momentary flash of memory, the hotel room at Idlewild (now Kennedy) Airport on our wedding night. My feet are iron weights that refuse to lift from the ground.

Now we tentatively enter this awesome place that promises so much unachievable joy just by its existence; the turquoise ocean casts its fierce waters onto the sparkling white crystal sands just beyond the glass wall that frames the panorama. Lush carpet and flocked wallpaper are the background for assorted color coordinated brocades, full pleated drape and flowing bed spread; gay tributes to Caribbea, local markets showing smiling brown natives in typical island dress and assortments of lush fruit and vegetable, ocean views with wicker furniture and colorfully printed cushions are protectively framed behind glass and welded to the wall. Live it up, the room screams to us, and we answer by withdrawing more deeply into ourselves.

But we continue by rote to follow the prescribed list of activities, and after the automatic change into swim suits, reluctant trudge across hot glistening sand and obligatory swim we shower and dress for dinner. Thoughts of fresher than fresh lobster, crayfish and shrimp, pineapple and cantaloupe, and enticingly described side dishes filled with ginger and other exotic spices, blackened swordfish and steak fail to inspire; we attempt to wash down insurmountable lumps invading mutual throats with excesses of Planter's Punch. We smile at each other with guilty despair and go through the motions of dancing to the charmingly enticing music, but we remain strangers, strangers of lengthy relationship and lost intimacy. I am dreading that moment back at our room when the attempt will indubitably be made to regain that intimacy. The promise of failure is easily fulfilled.

Steve rushes out first thing the next morning to rent a car so that we may, as planned, explore the island. He has already made reservations at certain bed and breakfasts around the island. It is what we never got to do in Bermuda, despite my then desire to do so. I am being suddenly solicited to, fawned over, catered to, but it is too little too late. I simply cannot, or maybe will not allow any of this to reach beyond the armor that surrounds my being. We begin our voyage around the island in our leased car ensconced in freshly scoured upholstery enveloped in the fragrance of newness; to gild the lily, a pine air freshener hangs gaily, aloof from the rear view mirror.

We pass through the noisy traffic of Kingston, the crowded colorful market, the bustling wharf and slowly find our way out into the countryside; we move through silent dirt roads through sugar cane fields with mansions growing mightily from the waving stalks in the distance, workers in colorful garb walking along the road, wagons filled with them. Smiling barefoot black women in bright blouses and printed skirts balance huge baskets on their heads pass us and wave.

Then we are driving along the coast, feet away from rocky shores, waves crashing, creating spumes of salty spray that threaten to fly between the rickety wooden shacks that abound and soak us through our open windows. We pass a family of eight, mom and dad and bevy of ragged urchins, six dark children with wild sun bleached blond curly hair indicative of their mixed parentage who all wave gaily and joyfully and continue onward along the coast to Dunne's Falls. Here is that mountain of rocks rising nearly straight up to a disappearing precipice, tons of water sluicing over and downward over caves and crevices, landing in this ovalesque swimming hole that is mobbed with laughing screaming splashing cavorting families and a smattering of cautious tourists. We join them silently with tentative grins, swimming, attempting to adopt the lilting sense of fun, the buoyancy of spirit that surrounds us but we remain in our silent sad insensate bubble of gloom and submission.

Around the far side of the island through dark menacing woods of alien looking gnarled tree trunks, thick masses leaf structures and assorted waving fronds there is a sudden rhythmic pop, pop sound like gunfire and terror grips us both all at once. When silence slowly envelops us and an implication of safety begins to sooth us, Steve unlocks his door and bravely ventures outside to reconnoiter. It doesn't take long for him to discover a flat tire, and then another, and that there is a strange assortment of wood planks sporting ominous steel spikes strewn across the road. In moments, before we are able to draw any conclusions four men pull up behind us and offer help, their speech that lilting unintelligible patois and their manner menacing, and we freeze. Hey, mon, it seems you've got yourself into some trouble, says one... Yah, mon, you'll be wantin' to get some help wit that, and they grin, maybe leer, showing glistening white teeth. We'll be pleased to help you wit yore problem, says the one presumed to be the leader because of his position in the group and his sense of authority, for a tiny consideration. And they all grin again, slouching against nearby trees, so we smile back feebly and shake our heads yes, of course, why not, and they go immediately and fetch help for our two flats, one spare, while we are left to surmise about our impending murder and dismemberment, terrified of the rumors and anecdote rampant about this island miasma of spells and voodoo. They fix both tires with well practiced dispatch, accept exorbitant payment from trembling hands as we make the required contribution to this healthy cottage industry and leave as rapidly as is possible, happy to be intact and yet alive. As we roar and bounce post haste away from our recent ordeal we glance surreptitiously over our respective shoulders to see the group rejoicing, laughing uproariously, slapping their knees and each other's backs at our obedience perfectly aware that we have never been in any danger at all but have fallen victim of nothing more than fiction and prejudice.

We arrive at our next scheduled destination limp with spent terror and faintly furious at having been taken. So we are spending the night at a bed and breakfast cottage typically already reserved, making obligatory hopeful uninspired love, lying there wondering why we are here and how soon it will all be over, and I am noticing those little black marks on his belly that look like bits of mud or seaweed, curious, reaching over to scrape one off...noticing how many there are, and that they are also all over the sheets...we have fallen into a nest of crabs, not the large orange edible ones. It is the one laugh we have all week, and an insipid one at that, is not the kind of travel anecdote one brings home to pass around among friends and associates at friendly gatherings, but it is sadly, all we've got.

We arriving finally and gratefully back at the hotel on the beach and partake of that last wistful, soulful night of elegant dinner and consciously romantic dancing and I feel the absence of Cliff as a dense and palpable chimera.

And all at once we are back home eager to be free from enforced confinement and artificial camaraderie, and to check on our renovation, the addition of a bedroom wing to which Steve has acquiesced in his new desire to please me, for what reason I have yet to discern. I am sublimating misery and hopelessness in creation. It is a large trapezoid attached to the dining room, divided so that one end is an office for Steve so that he may be home more, which is a mixed blessing, at least partly curse. Two walk in closets and a custom bath with wall to wall walk in shower that promises something erotic although I am having trouble grasping its ramifications in full, ignoring deliberately its romantic and salacious promise. The wall that faces the back yard is complete glass including several eight foot patio doors and the continuation of the old deck now wrapped around the entire back of the house. The job is being completed by Mickey MacDonald, the former fire chief who was recommended by Cliff. I am not certain if Steve is aware of the connection. Mickey keeps looking knowingly at me and I refuse to meet his eyes with my glance.

☙❧

Jamaica has done little to make me want to renew the marriage; if anything it has strengthened my resolve to get the divorce. I am still trapped though caught between doubt and indecision. I begin taking long drives to Fire Island and the East End to study the farmlands, the flatlands, the ocean, the sunsets, driven by a restlessness that cannot be ignore or controlled. Babysitters are a dime a dozen in summer time; the kids are well cared for. Time spent at the house has become utter agony, a tight balance between screaming sarcastic donnybrooks horribly reminiscent of Mom and Dad and gut-churning physical unease...my usually voracious appetite has vanished, drowned somewhere between liquor and hangovers and wrenching malaise of acute misery and I am thinner than I can ever remember being since the age of twelve. It fit right into the *poor boy* image that the media and Seventh Avenue are selling to a willing public so I cut my hair in a short shaggy little style and follow the hype, ribbed T-shirts and hip-hugger jeans.

I head for the Sagtikos Parkway, usually empty of traffic, the South Shore, and Robert Moses State Park impatiently parking quickly, walking a bit, sitting on the dunes, staring at the ocean, the vast sky, finding a measure of peace. I remove my paints and easel from the car and set up on the edge of the dunes. I lose track of time, stay late to paint the ocean sunsets, fighting the quickly passing minutes and hours to capture the rapidly changing colors. Finally I return home a bit calmer, more in control. Now I can deal with reality, my present life at least for a while until the next crisis.

∂∘๕

Twenty five hundred dissenting Women Against War storm the Pentagon while the biggest assault of the Viet Nam war is being implemented; I could be one of them if I wanted to be. Women can have power; they only need to grab it. Stalin's daughter is defecting to the U.S. There is a new attitude growing, a new lifestyle is emerging; ten thousand hippies are rallying in New York. I wonder what that means to life as I know it.

I see bits and pieces of this new lifestyle as I attend the various street art shows around the area but here they are artists and wear this attitude naturally. I have been working all winter, have created a new form of leaf colored textures semi abstract that I have high hopes for and I have my artwork set up on another Main Street this time in the town of Smithtown not that far from home. Mom has come out to stay with the kids so that I may attempt to sell some of my work. *Please come to Smithtown in the springtime, you can sell your paintings on the sidewalk...* I sit on my wood and canvas deck chair reading my current mystery thriller in the shade of a leafy maple thankful that I have landed this protected spot away from the unexpected intense heat of this spring day. I have one ear perked like an antenna for comments about this new painting, yellow and gold and pale green, loads of impasto, globs of paint, swaths of thick white in the background and foreground, light and air and sky.

My book momentarily grabs my attention, I am fully and deeply involved in Tom Clancy's intrigue the sound of a throat being cleared deliberately several times finally invades my periphery and I am surprised to see a man staring at me, notice the woman standing at his side. He clears his throat again and smiles, and says that he would like the price of the Birch Tree piece. Birch tree, I wonder, I don't actually have a birch tree piece, and he points at the new abstract and sure enough there are suddenly birch trees in it. Delicate impasto lines of black and white grow from the bottom of the canvas branching out as they rise. Nice, I think to myself, wonder who did that and why didn't I think of it? I tell him two hundred and fifty my hand in front of my mouth to keep from laughing out loud because I have suddenly realized where the birch trees came from. Yeah, he answers, okay, we'll take it, but it's too big for our car, can you deliver it? Of course I say, and accept his payment and directions to his home. After this couple leaves two more couples come by and ask the price, and I sell it two more times. Then of course I need to race home and paint two more, deliver them as soon as they dry. Of course I need to adopt the technique of the *birds* who are responsible for my success. What if I had not been assigned to that shady part of the street? A $750 bonanza for me and the beginning of an entire theme! The following week I am back with spring birch trees adorned by daisies in the foreground, the following week I bravely add day lilies and I am off and running. Soon Queen Anne's Lace, black eyed susans and wild blue chicory have happily joined the lilies. Birch tree scenes in all seasons and color combinations have become my insignia and my failsafe.

We are minding our exhibits on Main Street in Westhampton Beach this summer day, sitting on our folding chairs chatting and passing the time of day waiting for customers as the warm salty breezes float over us. This summer reverie is broken by the news on August 1 that a sniper in the tower at the University of Texas at Austin has terrorized the campus and killed twelve, some parents' children. Shivers of shock go through me; I am overcome by the evil in the world, the hovering awareness of the relentlessness of fate.

Summer turns into autumn. Now the trees have changed their dress to autumn tones. But I need more than just this narrow new subject if I am to survive, support my own children alone.

CHAPTER 50

I hear the call of the studio this evening after dinner is completed and the children are ready for bed. I have been home for several hours, done the marketing and cooked dinner, looked over homework and read stories. Already, the television is blaring and I am alone in the patently empty and dreary kitchen. I have no doubt that Steve has very little interest in whether or not I am in the house, and I have long since disavowed myself that there is any point in pretending at camaraderie. I am compelled to return to work on a painting that promises success, puts me on the verge of a major breakthrough. In general, I am happy with the direction my painting is going. I am trying new things, lots of palette knife details, texture and vignettes against white impasto backgrounds. I am using some of Paul Puzinis' classic old world techniques in a totally different manner. It is still a struggle, I am floundering in the dark uncertain where I am going, what I am looking for.

I am worrying over an elusive glaze when the phone rings breaking my reverie. It is one of Cliff's friends, Phil. Phil and his wife Gerry are new friends whose children are in school with mine. Gerry poses for my figure drawing and portrait classes. They are fond of me and worry at the pace that I follow and at the futility and pain that is my unwelcome burden since the end of my thing with Cliff. They sympathize with the pain we are each experiencing at the end of our relationship, at the futility of it all.

Phil has a friend he tells me who has recently moved to New York after living in Chicago for several years since his divorce and now having relocated on Long Island, knows no one. He is a nice guy insists Phil. Would I just meet him for a drink or two as he's somewhat shy and hasn't had a chance to meet anyone? I don't need or want to meet anyone, I don't care if he's shy or lonely or what. My head is not into meeting anyone new. After all, I say to myself, I am still married even if my plan for divorce is well under way and I no longer consider myself connected emotionally to Steve. But I certainly am not seeking another painfully impossible liaison to suffer through. This is something I do not wish to deal with at this time. But you're going to get a divorce, aren't you, isn't that what you have told us? Just meet him, he says, there's no obligation to meeting him! How much trust can I put into a man who advertises his cesspool cleaning service by putting a sign on his truck that says, *your shit is our bread and butter?*

I tell him no but later on when dusk falls and I am enveloped by the usual malaise of loneliness and hopelessness I have second thoughts. After all this will not be like some casual pickup. I will not have to deal with dueling over unwanted advances wrapping my head around loaded conversation that goes nowhere, the courting dance leading to ultimate acceptance of unwanted meaningless sexual connection, but perhaps just another solitary soul seeking to touch base with a similarly needful creature. Maybe I will make a new friend.

Arrangements are made, an assignation is planned with this Richie at the Sit and Sip Inn in Smithtown, my latest sometimes haunt. Larry, a good friend and former associate (though not a great fan) of Steve, is now bartender here. He has left the pressures of the insurance game to founder in the downward spiral created by a host of business and personal failures. I know that I am safe here in case this new guy turns out to be a jerk.

Surrounded by the usual and accustomed ambiance of darkness and glistening bottles and glasses, ongoing soft pop music of a juke box, I sit awkwardly on my barstool for a while not knowing which of this motley crew of customers is waiting for me. Dean Martin sings again seductively that everybody loves somebody sometime. It is difficult to appear nonchalant and sophisticated, in this position. I practice various attitudes, arm and hand placements and wish I were a smoker so that I could at least appear occupied, elegant, blasé, and have that very convenient prop to use. In a sweat of apprehension I almost get up to leave several times except that I am not inclined to disappoint Phil by breaking my promise to him. After all before I opened the art school he did sort of save my life that time when I consumed a bottle of aspirin having just discovered the new pregnancy roadblock in my escape route. I had chosen to end it all by a futile attempt at overdosing with aspirin. Luckily Phil, also a volunteer fireman knew what to do, called an ambulance to my embarrassment and chagrin.

I sit at the bar feeling generally comfortable on my own turf, so to speak. This is a place to which I escape on many occasions. I feel safe here, and I am able to hide in the shadows, sip a drink, chat with Larry or someone at the bar nothing more no complications. Larry, slightly shopworn once handsome and Italian is dispensing booze from behind the bar with his usual deadpan ennui, keeping one eye out for predators and signs of distress. The only man at the bar who even vaguely qualifies to be Phil's friend is another dark skinny Italian, well dressed but having a little of that *wiseguy* thing going; a combination of Sal Mineo and Montgomery Clift and I don't know why but a hint of Bill Cosby. Not really my cup of tea. This disappoints me and makes me want to laugh and run at the same time. There seems to be an excess of this Italian influence going on. *O Solo Mio, Be Mine Tonight*...He glances at me surreptitiously from time to time over the top of a newspaper that he sports as an obvious prop, a strange one for a bar where it is too dark to read. I watch as the rest of the motley and unworthy patrons leave one by one.

Finally as the bar empties leaving fewer and fewer choices I am tiring of the cat and mouse game, feeling self-conscious and vulnerable by the failure of this paragon to approach me. What is he finding wrong with me? Too bad if I'm not good enough for him, what do I care? Who needs him, anyway? I am bored with agonizing over the question of whether or not to approach this guy and decide to just go home. As I am preparing to get up and leave in disgust he appears suddenly to have recovered his own courage and walks a little tentatively toward the barstool next to mine. Are you Lynne, he queries, seeming unsure as would be expected but not too terribly unhappy. Too late, I think to myself, now I'm stuck.

You must be Richard then I simper nervously disgusted at my own triteness and the pitiful impression I must be making. I don't care anyway because I have already decided that he isn't my type. I'll do my best to weasel out of this whole thing as soon as possible, I tell myself. I want to go home. Richie, he says, Richie is what they call me. I am staring at him wondering what he is thinking, my imagination is working overtime...

I have to get her out of here, Richie is thinking to himself, because with that bartender hovering like a protective mother hen I won't even be able to make even the most halfhearted attempt at conversation. I hate to hurt Phil but it's going to be difficult enough to get through even the tiniest period of time with another one of these castrating tramps. He sighs, furious for permitting himself to get into another one of these obligatory situations, and curses his own vulnerability and loneliness that has allowed him to be so weak as to fall into this trap. Now he is forced to follow through, at least, to go through the motions, for a while. But a promise is a promise and he prides himself in his great integrity.

So you're an artist, Richie says halfheartedly. *This will never do, is what he appears to tell himself.* What do you do? he asks blandly.

I'm still struggling to find my artistic voice, I answer tentatively, uncertain how much he really wishes to know. I have my own school, which pays the way for me to do some experimental work and care for my kids. I pause, and sort of ask him, I understand that you're a pilot? I try to work up the expected sense of enthrallment that should probably go with the whole ambiance of flying, remembering Eileen's thrall in those Sky Lounge days, try to open some sort of door for conversation, sensing a sort of vulnerability and pain in him on second glance that forbids me to cut and run. Suddenly I want to see that pain in his deep brown eyes washed away and replaced with the glimmer of naughty humor that I can sense is threatening to surface.

A moment later, I realize that he is feeling just as trapped, feeling that same sense of disapproving impatience that I am and suddenly I burst out laughing, the devil makes me do it and need immediately to qualify my mirth by explaining my thoughts to him lest he feel that I am actually laughing *at* him, the look on his face says that that is exactly what is happening .

I can actually see it as I laugh. He is resisting the impulse to turn his back and disappear unable to take any more humiliation at this time, unwilling to make any attempt to fight the overwhelming feelings of anger that flood through him. His feelings are written all over his face: She's feeling exactly the same way I am, he is thinking wonderingly to himself, and she at least has some weird sort of sense of humor...maybe I misjudged her...

He breaks into a smile that changes his countenance from sullen and a trifle gross to vibrant and almost handsome. As a matter of fact a new animation suddenly lights up his features. I smile. Let's get out of here, he suggests intently, I know a nice place nearby. Warning lights blare and sirens go off. I glance at Larry who winks at me and surprisingly nods his approval and we sidle clumsily out in self conscious newness.

The Cavalier Club off the service road on the west side of Sunrise Highway is one of those jock places where macho types gather to compete and develop their various skills and muscles in boisterous locker room sociability. They stop by the club after their hearty physical ministrations to guzzle booze in an even greater spirit of competition and to compare experiences both sexual and financial. They revel in an excess of boasting and boozing that seems to enhance their faltering egos and desperate search to support their respective masculinity. But the place is carefully decorated and charming the ambiance soft and gentle, wood and beam work and leather, brocade and Tiffany lamps and I immediately feel at home in a comfortable armchair at our small table. Richie shrugs, and says that Phil and his brother have recommended it, he's new here.

It's a pleasant atmosphere. Richie explains that he has only recently relocated to Long Island, having lived in Chicago since his divorce which I already know and prior to that resided in Connecticut before his divorce. He winces when he mentions or makes references to his former marriage and I realize that there is a heavy layer of still raw scar tissue coating every surface of his being. It filters through what little real contact he makes and keeps anything of a potentially threatening nature from penetrating his surface. We sit quietly for a while each extracting facts here and there like fishermen in heavy rain gear and high boots casting out lines and sometimes reeling in a glistening fish. I fear that something I say will pierce the armor of his carefully stored memories and cause a massive explosion.

So…you're married, you have six children, you're planning to get a divorce, and you're unhappy; that I can see. What is the real problem, he inquires sardonically, a broken romance?

Phil must have told him about Cliff, I muse to myself. Maybe he's just comparing me to what his own wife did. *She has cheated on him, he says with some contempt and pain, lied.* I cannot help blushing. There is no way this can work, not with my baggage. Why did she *cheat,* though? I ask myself hating the word, this is something to consider. What is wrong with him? There must be something, you don't find someone else for no reason. But I must make him understand that I'm not like his wife. Am I? I have to make him understand my situation. But what did he do to make his wife cheat, leave him? Or what did she do to make him…whatever. This is too complicated; it is all making my head spin. But I look deep into those burning black coals that are his eyes and feel compelled to tell all. Not knowing how much he knows, I cannot under any circumstances lie. Not if I hope to see him again. And, I do. The effects of several sours do nothing to lessen the compulsion, my tongue flaps loosely in my mouth, everything is soon revealed. *I wish you bluebirds in the spring, a hand to hold, a song to sing…*burbles the juke box.

Why do you look so sad, he murmurs gently, are you thinking of someone? A fat tear trickles down my face.

The music changes to a loud wail…*let it please be him, please oh God…it must be him, it must be him, or I shall die…*

He puts his huge hand over mine and sighs, *I know,* he breathes, *the ever illusive LOVE.* There is a long silence. Is he sincere or is he mocking me? I cannot tell. *Since I was a small child all I have ever wanted was someone to love me. All I ask is for someone with whom to share my life,* I say, strangling on the choking lump in my throat, remembering, *all I ever asked for was to be loved. Is that so awful? I thought Steve was the one. I invested my entire being in my marriage and then I couldn't do it anymore.*

Love! He spits the word out. *Love is just another four letter word.* There is another long pause. I watch a series of emotions race across his face and think of Eileen Corby. He relaxes and begins again softly. *How do you define love,* he asks, somewhere between sarcasm and real need to know my answer, he waits. I am being tested. I have mixed feelings about this, like how dare he, and what's it to him? But in for a nickel...

I consider the question for a while sensing that our whole fledgling relationship, suddenly important to me, his entire acceptance or judgment of me depends on my answer. Quite I suddenly I care very much how he feels. I decide that I want to see more of this sensitive and intelligent man whose pain so similar in manifestation to my own cries out to be healed as does my own and who promises with his every essence to bear feelings of such depth and intensity that the very thought of this becomes a magnet drawing me closer and closer with every moment that we share. I want to make him believe in love again. *It's all right, it's all right with me. It's the wrong time, and the wrong place, though your lips are tempting they're the wrong lips...though your face...is charming, it's the wrong face.*

When she gets lonely, women do get lonely, wearing that same tired dress...(familiar words trickle across my mind). Tenderness, I remark lost in yearning and thought, *tenderness, consideration, compassion, tolerance.* I remember Steve's failings, his treatment of me, and shake my head to denote reaffirmation, yes, that's what it is all about. It is not like I haven't given this a lot of thought over the years. What I really want to say is *trust* but fear to bring up this touchy subject. After my maudlin story how could he ever trust me?

Tenderness, he muses, his eyes boring into me as if to see into the very depths of my soul, as if making some judgment of weighty import, weighing and deciding, and finally making a decision vital to the survival of his soul. He reaches out and puts his huge hands on either side of my face, cradling it, and continues to look through my eyes that have become the windows to my soul, and I am filled with that forever evasive sense of warmth and security. *And respect. And trust, I blurt out, there has to be trust.* Now I've done it, I think. He smiles. It's okay. I sigh with relief, smile back. Then a momentary thought crosses my mind and quickly disappears into the ether, how will he ever trust me when I am here out with him while my husband waits at home?

We dance our way through the rest of the night finding comfort in just being close and I let him guide me expertly and smoothly across the floor amazed at his dancing prowess yet unsurprised to learn that at one time he has been a professional dancer. He has a high school diploma he apologizes, but appears to be self-taught to a extent that goes beyond the normal education of most college graduates. I can tell. We discuss literature, history, politics, and art. He certainly seems to have more education, sensitivity and intellect than Steve who preens over, revels in his two degrees, Bachelor of Arts and Law, but lacks imagination or creativity. I wait for the expected comment about my ignorance and stupidity my body rigid with apprehension but he doesn't appear to have noticed, seems to accept me as an intellectual equal.

He also has I discover a severe and stringent moral code that makes me want to hold tightly to him, remain under his supervision, makes it imperative for me to gain his respect. Here is my opportunity to rebuild my character, cure my moral dissolution real or imagined. He has a formidable influence on my ugly fragmented existence, my downward spiraling guilt inspired self destruction. *Femina, duzina mala femina,* the jukebox burbles on, that's you, he smiles, a sweet naughty woman…I'm not certain how to take this.

꒰ঌৡ꒱

I expand the by now very successful school in late autumn moving to a new location on street level and perhaps get a little more exposure in a gallery setting hoping to sell some of the new and exciting pieces that are evolving, maybe that abstract autumn piece that won the prize at the annual Suffolk County Art League exhibit at Abraham and Strauss right after I added the birch trees to my abstract version of autumn. Maybe someday my name will be recognizable like DaVinci whose portrait of a prince has just sold for five million dollars. My involvement with my art…and the kids of course, along with the thought of my ultimate escape are the only things that get me through that painful time.

I remain focused on my plan and I fall into the next season grateful for the diversion that teaching, once again brings. I have moved my school with its accoutrements, easels, bar stools, tables, art supplies, to this storefront next door to a popular Northport restaurant. It is larger, and offers the added bonus of a plate glass window so while I teach in my school in the spacious back room I have the added benefit of a gallery showroom in front. My artwork is now officially on display for the public to admire perhaps purchase. I am on my way. The centerpiece of the display is a portrait of the children on a monkey bar, climbing and swinging and hanging upside down sky and clouds seen through the spaces.

Tracy's infant seat has long since changed to cavernous ancient baby carriage and finally to a playpen and she is the gurgling, chuckling dimpled star of everyone's day. She is the happy and welcoming recipient of dozens of donated donuts and cookies destined for coffee break time and soon her masses of ringlets cascade over rolls of plumpness and her cooing and dimpled smile enchants everyone. By now the three oldest are in school and the little boys are dropped daily by the nursery school bus right at the gallery and we hasten homeward in time to greet the others. It is a bizarre schedule to some but it works for us, at least for me. Frequently when they are in bed I hurry back again after dinner to teach another class or to work once again on new things that are beginning to approach the concept and quality that is my goal. I have again made the rounds of all the popular new galleries that now cater to that new American art market that has suddenly appeared spawning hoards of New Age circa 1965 artists and trends. I have viewed and studied and analyzed all the new media and concepts, wild and creative, harnessed only by the limits of a tentative market. If I can create some manner of art form that is ultimately salable in the current market I will be on my way to independence and thereby freedom. I can all but taste it. Freedom.

Meanwhile Richie and I are excitedly sharing knowledge and sources each hungry to learn what the other knows. I do a painting of Richie's nephew who has been killed in Nam; Richie gives me a copy of *Many Lives, Many Loves*, the autobiography of Edgar Cayce the prophet and a whole new world and direction opens up before me. I read the book and as many of its sequels and related subjects that I am able to find, voraciously. I am amazed to discover the concepts of reincarnation and Christianity and the wonders inherent in the belief that there could be another life beyond death. It gives me a solace greater than anything I have ever experienced. It also gives me comfort in the thought that even the most evil and guilt laden of beings is not evil into perpetuity but still has the right and the potential to change, to improve. He offers me a supplement to my formerly incomplete religious education and ultimately gives me hope. But that is for later. The simple fact is he is saving my life. I am beginning a new phase in my personal and spiritual development, have discovered a new form of flight. A new obsession. I want to delete the *mala* from my description. I don't want to be known as bad. I justify my interest in Christianity by acknowledging that Jesus was indeed a Jewish boy, a rabbi, and that it all seems to be a natural progression in religious development.

This is where I find myself escaping more and more frequently as life with Steve becomes even more and more intolerable as I wait for enough artistic stature and financial viability to force a divorce. Even at twenty-eight years of age I still seek a family to be a part of just as when I was a child, a teenager, and later betrothed!

I begin to spend a lot of time with Richie; I get a sitter evenings when the studio is shut down and the kids are asleep. He is struggling along as a flight instructor at a MacArthur Airport based flying school and he lives with an elderly woman, Louise who rents out rooms to flyers near the airport. She is related or connected in some obscure way through friendship to Phil. Richie arranges for me to paint a mural as a paid commission for Louise's son and his wife who live next door and I discover a warm old-fashioned Italian family into whose bosom I am welcomed. Here is a whole new world for me. I complete the painting of the mural and I am invited to stay for dinner. They are all so friendly and simpatico that I feel myself drawn into their fold; Louise's home becomes another in a long line of adopted havens. Her cooking, Northern Italian school, is exquisite, an art form in itself. Mealtime at her home engenders joy of such sensual propensities that it becomes yet another addiction along with the warmth and enveloping sense of family, the contrast with the chaos and coldness at my own home. The soft patter of spoken Italian and classic and pop Italian music, the loud loving family arguments are the background for interaction. They call me *La Belleza*, the beautiful one. We become close, and partly from an incipient need for camaraderie and partly pure unadulterated curiosity I accompany Louise and her daughter-in-law Fran on a few occasions to visit their favorite psychic, The Egg Lady. We are getting our fortunes predicted by an old lady who breaks an egg into a bowl and somehow reads the future in the patterns and images created by the egg white. Wow. In addition to Edgar Cayce this is another unexpected and foreign concept, more new people to hear and learn to understand, another strange new world activity for me to absorb. *O brave new world that has such people in't…* I join in cavalierly accepting with grave aplomb though patent wonder everything that happens as if I have been a part of it all of my life. My horizons are expanding. Sometimes after dinner when we sit around the kitchen table sipping espresso Louise brings out the Ouija board or the tarot cards and we play at telling each other's fortunes with casual laughter and specious taunts that hide our mutual sincere and serious intent. This is another first for me. It is intriguing and hints at the promise of something intangible and tantalizing but a little voice still murmurs of disdain and I am not really convinced that this is all real.

Now, my life evolves into a schizoid program of housekeeping, childcare, studio and teaching time, and what is left. Richie and I divide this remaining time, evenings, between lounge hopping, lighthearted bouts of drinking, dancing, and joking, and long serious discussions on the meanings of life and faith. He sinks from time to time into a state of melancholia so deep and forbidding that he closes me out for long stretches of incommunicado emptiness that serve mostly to make me only more determined to hang onto his friendship. He's Calabrese, says Louise with her Italian accent gesturing with her hands, shaking her head up and down, yes, as if this explains everything. They have hard heads, moody. You have to let them be when they are like that. It will pass. I am too young and foolish at this time to realize or accept that sometimes people need to be left alone. I persist in helping and soothing and pressing myself into him to a point where he can longer tolerate my presence. He takes me outside to Louise's lush verdant garden after dinner one night and tries to tell me gently that he no longer wishes to see me that way. A sliver of a wry smile crosses his mouth because we have discussed the possibility, made reference to that old song in passing usually with wry and playful humor. Now it is playing soundlessly in the background of this unacceptable moment. *How insensitive I must have seemed, when I told you it was over…* He can't mean it, he will change his mind, I just need to give him time and space. It is his friendship that I miss. But if not I will find someone else. Been there, done that, anyway, I can do it again.

CHAPTER 5 1

Every morning I get the kids off to their respective schools, straighten up, get in the car and drive the couple of miles to the studio. It is a good feeling to pull into the parking lot in the middle of this small suburban village, see my sign, open the door, and feel myself surrounded by my art, on display to the world at large in the small storefront blocked off from the classroom studio behind a temporary wall. This is my first gallery, my first real adventure into the world of business. Although sales are sporadic, the response of the community is warm. Still my income is derived from teaching. I continue private classes in the new studio and encounter new friends in this year's batch of students Connie and Diane, Eleanor, Dorothy. Anne, blond and confident and svelte has been with me since the beginning, in the original studio above the Big Apple. There is something warm and compassionate about Diane that draws me to her, invites confidence.

Well Diane, I've made up my mind. It's time to get off the fence. We sit at my desk in the darkened gallery the rest of the students gone for the evening cups of steaming coffee before us the winter chill permeating all. A storefront in a tightly closed up town on a cold rainy winter night is not a place of comfort in any circumstance. All manner of art surrounds us both completed, being displayed on the pegboard dividers and in the process of, leaning and stacked in every available space. The huge antique baby carriage sits in the middle, and a playpen Tracy's last half eaten donut lying on top of a pink blanket. This has been a fruitful day and I am tired with the fatigue that comes from being my most productive. I am very near the solution to the technique that has been eluding me for all this time and I feel close to some form of salable product. Success is tantalizing me hovering just out of sight. Close enough for me to have become a trifle over confident.

How are you going to handle that money thing? Diane asks with a wry grin scrinching up her pretty features in mock dismay. She is leaning against a bar stool in front of her painting, on its easel. We are surrounded by my new paintings, the walls are covered with them, experiments, successful and not. The comforting pleasant all-encompassing scent of turpentine and linseed oil, dammar varnish, combined, surround us.

I've told him to give me whatever he feels he wants to, for his kids. I feel guilty you know for forcing him to leave this way, for separating him from the children even though it's for their own good. The thing I want for the kids is a loving home; no fighting or tension, a fine example by a united parental unit. That is what I am leaving for, to find them that. I have learned the hard way that I have to be free before I can begin looking if I have any chance at all.

He'll see them on weekends won't he? That's probably more than he ever did. And it's not like he ever gives them any quality attention anyway. Why are you feeling guilty?

Well he's entitled to be able to start a fresh life without being tied down to payments that will make it difficult for him. After all I'm the one who wanted to be free.

Yeah free. Free from tyranny and abuse, free to have a real life. Listen to yourself, she scoffs. What are you thinking? If he had treated you right you wouldn't want to be free. You've grown so accustomed to the horrific way he treats you that you have no proper frame of reference if you ever did. I don't believe you have any idea of the way a husband is supposed to treat his wife or his children. What kind of example is he setting for them for their futures? She stops for a breath, inhales deeply. He's the dope, Diane continues, and then there's that girlfriend. That would be the coup de gras for me, she says, he would be finished. The less you take the more he has to spend on her. What are you thinking?

I am playing with a stubby pencil, rolling it back and forth between my fingers looking down. I know she is right but I am stubborn.

When are you going to realize that he's the one responsible for the whole thing? She continues her rant and I listen reluctantly. If he had been willing to get help, to try and change a little then he wouldn't be out in the cold. It doesn't mean that you have to let him get away with murder you know. He needs to know that it's his responsibility to take care of his children

Well it's not like I'm not working you know, I can support them, at least to some degree. I can certainly try my best. I have the income from classes; I have been selling my work, making some money. It will get better. I need to do this myself, need to be independent.

Independence is greatly overrated. This is a biggie anyway, the amount of money you will need. Do you have any idea what this amount is? For God's sake the effort to care for six children alone is a job and a half any way you look at it. The children's father should have to pay at least a fair amount for their upkeep. I'm not sure if you can depend on a steady income from art, either.

I'm not concerned, Diane, Steve is a person of honor and he loves his children very much. You'll see, he'll do right by them. I am speaking from the middle of a bubble of optimism and hope, have forgotten his awful threats over the years, already, forgotten his neglect of us all heady with the thoughts of freedom and the promises of the future.

Famous last words Baby, but I hope I'm wrong and you're right.

Finally that New Year's Eve an infant year waiting in the wings I realize that this double life, this meaningless emptiness and farce need to be over. I take a deep breath, reach down to my bootstraps, apply all of my available courage and insist that Steve leave at least for a while so that we can each continue with our lives, alone or perhaps after a break, together. I don't have any real thoughts or plans for together for my tolerance of Steve is worn sorely thin. I cannot see any changes in the near future that will permit a new start; he has not accepted any responsibility or blame for our rift, our failure, he does not believe there is anything wrong, except for me myself. I am the cause of everything wrong with our marriage. The memory of all that has happened over the years, the recollection of that last morning when I had released that primal scream and realized that it was all over were too intense to allow a change of heart. And Steve's girlfriend is still in the picture. But Steve's pleading is so suddenly pitiful that I have to leave an open door. Maybe we can work it all out.

When he is gone melodramatically out into the winter storm the swirling snow falling briskly and intently I call Eileen. She walks over to my house in the snow and we bring the New Year in in style with lots of champagne and more tears. Her esteemed husband Patrick is spending this year in jail in Riverhead for embezzling funds or extortion or something equally distasteful. The two of us have plenty to cry about between us, God only knows. I begin the New Year with earnest efforts to rebuild my bankrupt morale which is difficult enough considering my marital estrangement but even more complicated in terms of the logistical dynamics of economic survival and the emotional growth and healing involved. Steve sends me the agreed upon grandiforous sum of $50 a week which is supposed to cover all my expenses for a family of seven. I have to turn my efforts grimly to the acquisition of additional monies escalating my program, and I begin to attend the abundantly available shopping mall and outdoor street art fairs with a vengeance that defines my desperation. Somewhere on the edges of my consciousness I am aware that the Viet Nam reds have launched the so called Tet Offensive which has thankfully been blunted by U.S. troops. That Haight-Ashbury has become a hippie haven and that Dr. Spock has been indicted for giving anti-draft advice. News about Viet Nam is an ongoing melody hanging in the background, reminds me of my childhood during World War II, brings up ancient memories long forgotten especially of Daddy being gone.

I have a few doubts, recriminations but in my heart I feel I am doing the right thing. The kids ask where daddy is but without much interest; he has never been home much anyway and when he has been hasn't given them much attention. Even his visits although punctilious are short and without much contact or content. His help is not missed because it has never been there.

I am painting long hours, writing poetry, meditating and praying... to whom and for what? I am praying to a formless nameless faceless god for an end to loneliness, for resolutions to problems, for strength, for peace; for a real live Brady Bunch life. I fall into a deep sleep exhausted by my day's travails. I am in a deep dark place filled with swirling colors mostly blues and grays, touches of pink and peach like a bit of ambient sunset light on the underside of clouds. I am in a small plane and I think I am with Richie but I cannot see him and somehow I know it is not him. Suddenly the plane is out of control, tipping and swooping and jolting from one side to another and in moments it is falling, plummeting downward and I feel myself screaming, feel the terror rising from my stomach to my chest, hear an immense crash, and feel the flames around me, hear the screaming but it is not me and I wake up sweating my heart pumping much too quickly.

I am terrified, terrified and distraught. Has something happened? Has Richie been flying tonight? Is it any of my business? Should I call him or is this just another rationalization a new and pitiful excuse to call? So I pace and I wait, and I talk to myself and try to talk myself down and then, compelled by an unknown force still trembling with an unnamable terror I make the call even though it is very late. Richie is summoned from his bed and listens as I tell him hysterically about the crash, how I was worried about him, and his scorn is lividly apparent. Look. I'm okay, he says, if I weren't you would know it. Don't worry about me, don't call me, stop dreaming about me. I am using this horrible thing as an excuse to harass him, he says, leave him alone. I cry myself back to sleep, the dream was so real. The next morning the phone rings, it is Richie, his voice soft and stiff telling me gently about the crash at MacArthur that has happened, his friend has died...a little while after my call. He apologizes. He'll talk to me soon, he says.

I have been exonerated but still I am alone and now there are new questions like how could I have known about this and what does it all mean in the greater scheme of things? I content myself, although console would be a better way of expressing it, with reading the book on Edgar Cayce that he has given me, again and again as if to extricate every last bit of its essence, to bring me closer to him. I am hungry for answers, anxious for clues as to the meaning of life; desperate to know what awaits me in the future even if especially if it is not Richie. The Cayce book has opened up doors to the occult and worlds both spiritual and mystical that I have in my safe Jewish cocoon, in my entire existence never even known existed. It introduces me for the first time to the tenets and origins of Christianity formerly hidden behind a mask of threat and enmity. Entranced and intrigued with these new worlds I begin to explore with fervor born of desperation, to believe in the possibilities of immortality and in all of the avenues of Esoterica that I can discover in my desperate quest to know my future. A faint memory of that summer my beloved grandfather died flits across my consciousness, and I wonder for an instant whether my prescience at that time and now with my dream about the accident was no more or less than extra sensory perception, clairvoyance, what else could it have been?

In the midst of all this I continue writing poetry which consumes even more time. The words seem to come to me without conscious thought from somewhere deep inside me or somewhere else completely, but where? I am beginning to acquire a collection. Richie is the inspiration of many of the poems and of course Cliff; my search for true love, faith, and the meaning of life, and the future, my art, are the rest of it.

I run on an occasional evening to escape in camaraderie and gluttony at Louise's house unable to rid myself of my obsession with Richie and powerless to stop chasing after him always hoping that one day he will decide that he loves me. There is no amount of rejection that will deter me. In fact rejection seems to merely add fuel to the fire that propels me onward. Perhaps I am allowing myself to be punished for the various transgressions that haunt me with their heavy implications of guilt. Cliff. Forcing Steve to leave. There is no way that I will pursue the seemingly only other solution which is to ask Steve to come home. This thought is a enduring theme, running continually through my mind haunting my thoughts every moment. Finally Louise tells me that it is the six children that he is afraid of, he's not ready to father someone else's children, Six of them. He doesn't wish to be thrust in the middle of this family feud. This is the first time it has occurred to me that this is an issue. I put it right out of my mind, I'll think about it tomorrow.

I am barely drinking anymore not only have I lost interest in all that but there is simply no time in my busy schedule and I given up on trying to justify the need to mask the pain and loneliness that are my everyday companions. I must learn how to deal with all of this. There is a tantalizing essence lurking out of reach that might be the need to discover, adopt some sort of faith, something positive rather than negative. What I do is concentrate on my work and ability to care for my children. This compulsion is a force born of a need stronger than any other existent life force; the very pressing need to provide for my family. Spiritual strength and belief in any higher power dance just out of reach so an occasional drink in a social setting helps me to obtain a momentary respite from all of the other painful realities of my life like desperate loneliness and emotional bankruptcy and failure to come to grips with all of the old insecurities from earlier years. I tacitly avoid the old scars and emotional stresses and the sick mindsets that swirl about my world. Desperation not soothed by prophecy or platitude becomes more a way of life than any optimism for the future. The only reality that I can perceive of has to do with pain, rejection and struggle. Now, they call this depression. In 1967 we are unaware of this syndrome, of the widespread existence of it and certainly didn't have names for it. A name or rationale for the cumulative effects of year after year of post-partum depression with no treatment or comprehension does not even exist.

Richie and I have achieved a kind of détente that blossoms into friendship if a bit strained with occasional benefits, the sharp edges around him have softened since the plane crash and once again I find comfort at Louise's home respond to her invitations to join them for dinner. I will take whatever I can get. I take advantage of her invitations knowing that despite our new arrangement each time I arrive here I have put another nail in the coffin that contains any future for me and Richie. I am a prisoner of my obsession helpless to escape. I am helpless to keep distant even for a short while even with the vague promise of a future hanging in the air. I can get out of the house for an evening finally with a free mind. Now that my paintings are beginning to sell in the street show circuit as well as at the gallery I have some extra cash and hire a live in housekeeper, Helen, who loves the kids, handles them well. I have already helped them with their homework spent some time with them and they are content. So I am sitting around Louise's table with a gang of the boys from the flying school and Louise's son Joey one evening when someone gets the bright idea to invent a new drink. Richie is being kind but circumspect and I am ever hopeful. But this time I am caught up in their silliness and the spirit of camaraderie; in the effort to prove what a good sport I am. It is not difficult for me anyway to imbibe anything that will dull the edges of pain that are growing more insistent with every moment that Richie rejects me however innocuously and gently however innocently my dreams fade away; his failure to respond to me is an automatic rejection in my mind although he is merely trying not to encourage me. This is the same old dynamic, in my mind, that I shared with Steve that had been so destructive. The same thing I lived with and ran from in my parent's home. Why do I continue doing this? The more I am ignored the more freely I sample the noxious concoctions uncaring of the potential result, faced with my old *bete noire* rejection. There is a devil may care air in the room; they do not have to drive home or anywhere. I do.

Finally filled with the glowing high spirits that envelope me and very conscious of the lateness of the hour I start off for home. Yeah, I say, I'm okay, I'm fine. I am not really fine. As I drive along Vet's Highway a movie begins to play of the evening, of the last few weeks with Richie's rejection the main theme, of the slights both imagined and real that Richie has delivered this evening. It had grown all out of proportion. I begin to dwell on the desperate misery that I am feeling, blaming him, accepting no responsibility for my own actions, attitudes, reactions, firmly placing all liability and blame on the object of my desires.

The road winds round and round in murky desolation; it is deserted at this hour. It becomes a symbol of my entire life taunting me with my own solitude. I begin to cry in drunken self-pity and helplessness made even more emotional by the quantity of alcohol I have consumed. Where am I to go? How am I going to solve the problems that overwhelm me? What is left of my life and what good will it even do to fight any longer? An image flashes through my mind of an endless road that suddenly does end in mid air with water rushing far below, that old nightmare of my childhood, and sobbing freely now, I feel compelled to end the agony right now. I try to turn the wheel but it will not turn. Dispirited by yet another failure I sob quietly and continue along the route intently concentrating on the white line that marks the lanes. I am barely able to see between the drinks and the tears, totally exhausted by all of this turmoil. My mind drifts off to embrace Richie once more as my eyes cling to the wavering white line. Only by a fortuitous quirk of momentary focus do I realize that the line that I am following so intently announces by its gentle curve the upcoming turn lane which I easily slip into in my present state. At the speed that I am presently traveling I will soar over the rapidly approaching center divider taking with me two telephone poles and a giant green sign announcing the upcoming entrance to the LIE. I am aware suddenly of my situation. There is no chance that I will miss.

I reach down into the recesses of my strength made fuzzy and insensitive by my inebriated state for instincts of coordination that I hope will not fail me now. The wheel that I have attempted to turn gently and precisely spins around beneath my thick and uncooperative fingers and before I can identify my error I have to spin it in the opposite direction in order to avoid the fast approaching corner, electric line and more telephone poles. Hurtling through space in foggy incomprehension I whip the recalcitrant wheel to the left, too late realizing that I have again over steered and unable to correct my misjudgment, feel the entire car in an instant of supreme horror rolling over and over and over a mixed jumble of soda bottles long resident in the wagon's cargo area awaiting their delayed return for deposits; we are tumbling around like the contents of a washing machine with the motion of the car. I am somehow aware that I am listening to the tinkling of broken glass in an interminable concert. I feel my limp body bouncing loosely and flaccidly off the sides and top and windshield slack and ungovernable as the vehicle finally comes to rest upside down on the median.

I lie there on the ceiling encompassed by bottles and broken glass wanting to giggle at the weirdness of it but too conscious of the chill of the metal pressed against the cold damp ground to think of joking. I am aware of the eerie silence, stillness and aloneness that encompass me and somewhere niggling around the corners of my brain is the certain knowledge that the engine could explode at any moment. Sensing no pain or injury however I just wish to pull myself out of the vehicle but find myself shivering uncontrollably and unable to move. I allow the sensation of numbness to permeate me and concentrate on hoping that someone will come along and notify the authorities. I also think that now I am in real trouble and also carless. How will I deliver my paintings, shop for my children's meals, visit my friends?

It isn't very long before a flashing screaming police car pulls screeching onto the median and two officers appear immediately at my side. Get me out of here, hurry, I want to say but nothing comes out of my mouth.

Pull her out of there, shouts the officer in charge, before it blows.

What for, answers the other, lackadaisically, bored, she's already gone.

Don't be an ass, replies the first, *here, help me grab her, pull her shoulders...my God, it's just a young girl...here, throw this blanket over her.*

Hey, not so rough, that smarts, I want to complain, but again my mouth won't work but at least I am feeling no pain. I giggle but no sound emerges.

Not over her head, you moron, just cover her and then go get the smelling salts.

Jeez, why waste our time; you can see that she's gone.

I suddenly feel myself hovering over my body looking down at the tableau before me and want to give that idiot a kick in the ass, what do you mean, gone, I'm fine, what are you, crazy? I try to scream at him but hard as I try no one seems to hear me.

Get the goddamn salts, the first demands, and stop your goddamned insolence. He takes the sullenly proffered bottle from the younger officer and I watch with interest as he waves it back and forth a moment or two under my nose still trying to figure out this strange phenomenon of being a witness to my own situation. Suddenly there is a pop and I am no longer watching but moaning and moving my head from side to side to escape the acrid odor of the stuff, feeling the stiffness beginning to set in and very aware once again of the cold dampness of the muddy ground.

My God, gasps the second officer, you were right, OMIGOD!

Oblivious, numb, alone and very frightened I ask them in my desperation weakly to call Richie at Louise's, and never at his best when awakened suddenly he arrives grimly to pick me up and take me home. As I climb clumsily into his car, mortified I hear the first officer telling the other something about the miracle of my escaping without even a scratch. Thank God I am so anesthetized by our cocktail experiments that my body is too loose to break.

I am thinking of, wishing for Richie, but it is still Cliff that I am really wanting. Cliff has rushed over to the house as soon as the scuttlebutt has reached him to make sure that I am all right and both his presence and the warmth of his arms momentarily heal my aches and pains but nothing has changed and as soon as he leaves I realize that we are truly and finally broken and there is no use hoping for him now; I am still needing someone with whom to share my life. When the stiffness and hangover finally wear off I vow to change my life; so profoundly shaken am I by the entire experience that the shock actually blasts me right back into reality after all these years. Except my reality is now tinged with a sense that there is something beyond reality as I know it that is larger than life, greater than just being waiting to be discovered.

CHAPTER 52

Everyone, the country, the world at large, everyone I know is anxious to see beyond the barriers of reality. Or mortality. It is the subject on everybody's lips. Hey, have you ever tried, really reaching out to the other side…

We are all so aware of this thing called mortality, of the soft delicate hints of the existence of a further world beyond this one. We balance on a brutally swinging see saw of fear and exultation. Martin Luther King is assassinated and emotions plummet. Five days later Civil Rights become law and we rejoice. Then we spiral downward again when Andy Warhol is shot by an actress he himself hired. The final blow is received when New York Senator Bobby Kennedy is killed after accepting the nomination for president at the Ambassador Hotel in Los Angeles. It's a mixed bag, another frightening rollercoaster ride. Helen Keller dies. Billie Jean King wins her third Wimbledon title. We ride the roller coaster of the vagaries of life with equanimity, perform this delicate balancing act that is survival with careful vigilance.

I fill the vacuum of my emotional life voraciously wade through tomes of any and everything else concerning spiritualism and the world beyond, am quick to commence a discussion that might by its very existence bring to light any new fact relating to my obsession. That is how I become close to Connie Scott. During painting classes we begin tentatively discussing the latest rage, ESP, and moving quite naturally onward to Edgar Cayce. You know him, I ask feeling very honest surprise, and she answers, yes, of course, everyone does, everyone has questions they want answered. She invites me to visit her church in order to hear this new clairvoyant. A church? A bizarre thought because I have never even been inside a church, but there are important facts to be learned and I will not be deterred by anything. So begins my attendance at the spiritualist meetings that are beginning to take hold all over.

It seems the most natural thing in the world, exploring beyond my life experience; I am so full of disillusion with Judaism given all of Steve's attitudes and behavior…I have not been permitted to accompany him to shule on the

High Holy Days, leaving me at home, which is my place as a woman, with the children who are not allowed to attend, either. I have found little saving grace belonging to the temple sisterhood, and I have always been inquisitive, wondered what was out there, what to believe.

Connie's first invitation is to join her at a place to discuss and investigate matters of the occult. With much trepidation and heady anticipation I tag along, an inquisitive Eileen at my side not to be left out of the moment's entertainment. Sunday morning and Steve is at the house visiting, and if I stay there he will stay locked in the bedroom all day with his Times and the television so I have taken the day off to renew myself hoping he will spend some quality time with his children. This is not somewhere that I would like to bring them anyway; I am not yet certain what it all means. I don't know yet that these meetings are part of a church schedule; when I discover the venue I am a little disturbed, still a bit apprehensive about going to a church but I find these Sunday morning church services invigorating and soothing as well as intellectually stimulating and wish to discover more about this as yet barely uncovered strata of life. How have I lived so many years without any knowledge of this stuff? In my state of suspended animation and quivering insecurity; in my hiatus of non–marriage, non–divorce I seek mountains of answers. I yearn to learn what the blank and uncompromising future has to offer. When I first attend one of these services which include psychic readings I am enthralled and not a little shocked by the precision and accuracy achieved in the predictions. It is not so very different from the Egg Lady in whose crowded parlor heavy with expectation Louise and I waited to have our fortunes told, my initial initiation into this strange new world. It is so easy to become addicted to this innocent and esoteric mode of new wave self-realization, this new method of finding relief from the ravages of fear of the terrifyingly elusive future. I embrace my new knowledge in a schizoid world my children in one sphere my yearning search for spiritual awareness in the other.

Sometimes meetings are in the form of a church service followed by a sermon and then psychic readings. Sometimes they are in the form of a séance where a group of would-be psychics sit in a circle, palms facing upward meditating and calling to the departed to come through and make contact with those of us unlucky enough to have been left behind in this most unrelenting of worlds. Although somewhat uncomfortable I am getting into it. We are all the misfits and leftovers, all of the malcontents and rape victims; all of the uglies and losers. I never stop to question why this group who claims to have found the sacred doorway to the sacrosanct inner circle, the place of blessed oneness and revelation is so poor and unsuccessful, so odious and unloved. I never stop to think at all for my entire waking time is spent with concentrating on making the great connection. I don't mean to make light of this at such a late date, perhaps because in my heart of hearts I still believe the principle if not the flavor of that particular belief. At this time still in my early twenties I have yet to figure out that physical beauty and wealth and of course romantic love are not the highest goals of the pure of spirit.

There is no doubt at all that there exists another level of awareness, another plane of consciousness that is peopled with the dearly beloved, since departed— those who spend their eternal time trying to make contact with those of us sensitive enough to desire it, needy enough to request it. There are the beloved relatives and friends on one level the renowned and omni-knowledgeable of fame, of historical documentation. There are friendly visitors wishing to make mortal contact and the assorted spirit guides whose selfless goal is to inform and aid those of us who required outside help. It makes perfect sense in a weird sort of way and we are ready to believe anything that makes any kind of sense. It is so easy for me to believe all of this as I recall the time of Grandpa's death, of my dream of Richie's plane crash, of my own recent auto accident...

The weird part of the whole thing is the awareness now of otherworld entities, of the returning of the departed who hover everywhere throughout our very mortal days and nights...the funny thing is we all seem to go through a sort of initiation phase as novices to be sure of inability to continue with natural functions gravely self-consciousness in the face of the ever constant audience of spirits. How can I go to the bathroom or bathe properly or have sex for God's sake with my grandfather standing right there? Or my ex-husband's mother? My two smiling grandmothers and three Indians and the spirit of Edna St Vincent Millay. Oh, indeed problems are created here by the very adoption of a structure of belief that while it seems so necessary to survival there exist these concurrent problems that are super-imposed over and above everything that is happening.

Our lives become so encumbered with the pieces and parts of the elements of our beliefs that the fragments of it all float about our daily lives in an abundance that precludes access to our respective spaces of anything else. Like most infatuation of any nature but truly that of the religious, obsession becomes the only mode of operation, the only rationale for existence.

One bright and promising spring Sunday morning filled with great excitement and expectation we all join together in one car to travel up island to hear one Ken Coulter, a pastor of great renown who is ministering in guest capacity at a Universalist church in Hempstead, in mid-Long Island. We run *en masse* to receive some news of the future. Our cumulative apprehension and the collective burdens of our personal pain create an atmosphere of such emotional density that it can almost be touched. I sit in that little church for a long time entranced by the magnetic Ken Coulter and mesmerized by his words. My legs are icy with the chill of the room and stiff with discomfort from the metal folding chairs. Still, I cannot remove my attention from the face, the eyes, the mouth of this dynamic charismatic man who stands before me capturing his entire audience with his rhetoric as well as his remarkably perceptive readings. I feel goose bumps start as he *reads* me for he has names at his fingertips, and facts that no one can have known besides me. I have never repeated these particular very personal ideas or feelings to anyone. He tells me that I will find true love and that the object of this love may be identified because he will walk in a manner reminiscent of a dancer; I find this information to be pointed enough to be valid. I vow to find out where this pastor will be speaking in the future or even where his home base is. I am determined to delve as deeply as I am able into this newly discovered phenomenon called psychic power. It is the beginning of my intense and bizarre journey into matters esoteric that carries me on its strong buoyancy for years.

❧

Now I need to inquire more intensely into these demanding questions about these enticing esoteric matters; I need explanations. I need to know what the hell is going on and what I should expect from here on in. Actually I crave all manner of answers, kind of demand them. I travel to his storefront church in Brooklyn to hear Ken Coulter read in my mad desperation to know the future. I wonder if he will also know about my accident and if he will say something. Stubbornly despite reality as I have finally accepted it I wonder if there is a chance that Richie will appear in my future, maybe even Cliff, especially Cliff.

In addition to the regular weekly readings Pastor Coulter or Ken as he prefers to be called holds his own séances on Tuesday nights in the guise of a class when he sinks deeply into a trance while the group holds hands and intones The Lord's Prayer over and over again as a true medium and becomes taken over by his own personal guide, an Indian chief. Many of the guides seem to be Indians, Native Americans who were supposedly connected to the Supreme Spirituality and structure of the Native American religion. It never occurs to me to wonder about the connection between The Lord's Prayer and the American Indian culture. So Ken prances around spouting Great Truths and Supreme Prophecies with absolute and emphatic sincerity while under the control of this power. We are asked to state what we are able to see, see in a spiritual sense; some actually are seeing things, people, the other side in the murky whispering shadows of the backroom of this dreary storefront church. I never see anything or anyone, not in Ken's sessions anyway but the spirituality that is engendered here has remained with me for all of these years. It is here that I memorize the Lord's Prayer the words of which give me a new peace and strength that carries me through the many horror-filled days and years that follow. It doesn't matter where it comes from or what its connotations are, it is a powerful magical intonation with immutable authority

As a matter of fact it is here that I first become acquainted in detail with the entire Christian faith and here also that I begin to take in earnest the teachings of the Sermon on the Mount of which I have previously had no awareness at all. It seems such a natural and normal route for Judaism to have taken I think and become fond of repeating. I reiterate my earlier theory. Wasn't Jesus after all a rabbi, and a charismatic Jewish leader who was merely trying to help his people during trying times? Isn't Christianity based on Judaic teachings and the First Testament? There seems to be such a likely sequence to events in its entire evolution; I am able to cleave to Christianity with a tenacity that bears me in its strong arms and keeps me alive at a time when I am barely functioning emotionally finding no solace from my actual forbearers. Here is where I adopt the do unto others principal and that of turning the other cheek …understanding and forgiving, blessing your enemy, ignoring your adversary. What other rationale could have helped me to survive through the years that follow? It is inevitable that this becomes my newest obsession. Through the surgical removal of my children by court order; through the bludgeoning of the entire world at large, the systematic and methodical rape and battery from every corner which is how I felt in those years. Through the spiritual bankruptcy brought on by depletion of a modestly untenable account of emotional strength never fully secured. The one bad thing is that I have no one with whom to share this new facet of my life. Not my mother who would be sent into immediate cardiac arrest and certainly not my small children presumably Jewish, like their father (although he makes no effort at all to ensure this), into perpetuity, too young indeed to begin to grapple with this stuff. So I go through the motions of my life with my children keeping this side of it secret while the day-to-day business of survival continues and I do battle with my fight for independence. There is very little actual Jewish education for the children, I cannot afford either the membership at the temple or the school and Steve is absent in every way that matters from their lives even their religious education except when it becomes necessary much later for the bar mitzvahs of the boys which are compulsory and of some bizarre importance in their isolation from reality. The girls are *persona non grata* in Steve's life, even Wendi, always previously Daddy's little girl is ignored with equal opportunity neglect.

While I am struggling with my spirituality petite, dark, and pretty Diane, an Irish princess safe and secure married to an Italian prince who is in the imported Italian ceramic tile business tries to instill in me some sort of self-esteem. I failed Jewish American Princess a long time ago, I tell the girls; survival is the only mode I know. Something has to happen soon if we are going to survive; the $50 per week that Steve has agreed to send me when he left in the name of child support is grossly deficient. It is an important issue now that I have decided to follow through on the divorce thing and I am about to sign final separation papers and head soon thereafter to Mexico for the actual divorce.

Diane insists again that I am entitled to support for the children and myself, what about how awful he was to you, she says. You've forgotten already. You are too inclined to altruism. You are too generous. You need to stop insisting that you are guilty for depriving a father of his family. What kind of father and husband has he been, and what about his girlfriend, she sputters. Well, maybe he will change, when he realizes he has lost me, and I have someone too, I admit even though he has had his longer. I truly believe that since I am the one who is forcing him to leave and find a new life it is only fair to allow him enough where-with-all to find it. I am becoming a true Christian, applying Golden Rules to the decisions I am making regarding my future. Diane disagrees violently with me but her warnings and admonitions fall on deaf and stubborn ears. It appears that stubborn is what I do best. She chatters away while concentrating on applying brushstrokes to the fruit and flowers in her still life. I am framing paintings, planning what to bring to the next show.

࿋

Connie and I share a room in the old Grasmere Hotel in Westhampton Beach back in 1968 for the duration of that year's Mary T. Fritchie Annual Westhampton Beach Outdoor Art Show, part of the agenda of street shows that we are following, not wishing to commute at the ungodly hours back and forth to Northport in the crush of the summer tourist traffic. We revel in the ancient and historical building, sensing immediately the presence of many beings in a dense spirituality that has us throwing meaningful glances at each other even before we have reached our room and unpacked our belongings. It is all country, vintage, antiques and ruffles and quaint accessories. Two huge old high four poster beds complete with the requisite down comforters. We settle ourselves and go out for a bite of dinner. Then quite early we return to the quaint room to get a good night's sleep preparatory to the tedious weekend ahead to which we look forward with much intensity. We have visions of dollar signs dancing in our heads. We hope to do some business.

We each climb into her high fluffy quilted bed and proceed sanctimoniously and with high hopes to do our nightly meditations staring all the while into the intense murk of the darkened room. There is an intangible silence; there is not even the squawk of a bedspring. The room seems to be filled with a palpable presence actually a multitude of presences. I remember thinking to myself how gullible we are, how we do sell ourselves an unrealistic bill of goods when we wish to not knowing whether to believe or scorn, adopt or discard too anxious to have it be real to let go, too needy to run away. At the very moment that I am about to suggest some other form of amusement my bed begins to shake. It starts delicately, softly, almost indiscernible, and I glance at Connie still in her own bed, thinking that she is fomenting some practical joke prepared fully to disdain and condemn such feeble attempts at sacrilegious humor but before I can utter a word the shaking becomes more and more frantic, more intense, more and more wild until in a state of intense panic peripherally noticing Connie still lying in her own bed staring bug-eyed back at me, I call out to her for by this time my teeth are rattling in my head and indeed I clutch the headboard with white knuckled fists fearful that in moments I will be flung to the floor. Connie leaps out of her own bed jumps into mine and we hold onto each other repeating the Lord's Prayer in a frenzy of rote until the shaking subsides.

We dismount the now silent and innocent looking bed and dress quickly; we are too frightened to stay there any longer, we will sleep in one or the other's car. As we put on our clothing, Connie asks me tentatively if I too have seen the figure of the girl in a white dress with leg of mutton sleeves, long flowing hair, ribbons and lace, standing in the corner during our mystical ride and stunned I admit that I have but have been too doubtful of the reception that this information would receive to mention it. We stare into each other's faces for long terrified prescient moments.

We are too frightened to make inquiries, too embarrassed to delve too deeply in what might turn out to be the wrong places perhaps connected with evil rather than good. What are the right places? We have no idea. We were always afraid to even consider the obvious conclusion to our mutual experience, unable to accept it as proof of anything at all. Connie is gone now another of that group, the ones who swore that their time here would be short. All of us made a pact that we would return after our mutual passings and make certain that messages would be forthcoming from beyond for the others still left here on earth. Now, I am the only one left. I still even now await some sort of message proving that it is all true but it never comes.

෨෧

Then I meet John Segreto on the street during another show in the next show space, off white cargo pants and shirt, brown leather sandals covering filthy feet, straggling white-gray hair and beard and mustache; he helps me secure my stuff in the sudden summer rain storm, we go into the Artful Dodger to wait out the storm our displays covered with drooping plastic sheeting and we talk. I tell him how I am inspired by nature, trees and fields, flowers. His inspiration is LSD or pot; he is broadening his consciousness, investigating other worlds. Isn't that what I am doing, without the use of the drugs? We talk all night when he ends up spending that brief damp August night at my house to recover from the day's monsoon. It's the least I can do after all his help and I can't see him sleeping in that disreputable Volkswagen van before we return for Sunday's business. He gifts me a miniature copy of Khalil Gibran which I add to my collection of Edgar Cayce tomes. I develop a new habit, opening the pages at random, pointing with eyes closed at the open page to receive my message of the day, hang desperately on the official sounding esoteric and oblique words of the popular sage. Later, someone gives me a copy of I-Ching and I move on. It all comes from the same place anyway doesn't it? Somewhere in all of this are some answers to all of those eternal questions.

While my spiritual life is exploding my material life continues in endless days of tedious work and compulsive escape. I paint daily in my newly converted studio bedroom. I have closed my school successful as it is in order to be around for the children at home at least weekdays especially now that Steve is gone. I need now to concentrate on the new paintings that are on the verge of real success. Also, I don't need that extra expense, that income can better be applied to home and family. I move out of the classroom-studio-gallery next door to Azenaro's Steak Pub in Northport in the dead of night with the help of Eileen and two of her current boyfriends, Ray Somebody, the staid chunky contractor and tall lanky goofy Billy Ramonetti all hustling and hassling and jostling, bursting with good humor and willingness to help. They have a truck; Eileen and friends to the rescue.

CHAPTER 53

The sun gleams extra bright along the tedious desolate length of the Belt Parkway which seems to unroll ribbon-like before me forever and ever. I sigh; if one wanted a good description of infinity the Belt: with its flat unwinding monotonous as yet un-gentrified urban scenery would do admirably, I think. I always divide the journey into phases in my mind; it helps to avoid what is clearly obvious, a knowledge that sneers condescendingly, scathingly insisting that only a person obviously in the last stages of mental decay would be deranged enough to attempt such a long and complicated journey especially as frequently as I do. Innocently as the whole thing begins I eventually end up making this trip over and over again.

It is 1968 and the Israelis and Arabs are blowing each other's brains out with no hope in sight for peace. In Newark and Detroit blacks are rioting in rebellion over social injustices and young people all over burn draft cards and flags to protest the fighting in Nam. I am oblivious to all of this; it never touches me for at this time I exist in a no-man's-land fighting demons of indeterminate origin and unknown destination. I live in a morass of broken marriage trauma and the ever widening and frightening search for Life's Hallowed Meanings. I find Hope that first time at the Church of St. John so called, the storefront house of worship whose minister, Ken Coulter is that charming and talented master of the mystical. The church itself is a shabby and disreputable storefront on Third Avenue in Bay Ridge, a place so alien to my experience after so many years of living the good life in lovely cosmetically improved suburban Long Island that I might have arrived on the moon. I might be lost in the middle of some old movie set for the Little Rascals or Angels with Dirty Faces or another of those filmes noires from the 1940s or even earlier.

Everything though in these days is dreamlike, surreal and at the same time super real. It is the Age of Aquarius; a fine time to embrace the mystical. I am a latter day Aldous Huxley playing in alien worlds but too involved in them to realize it.

I feel this first time as though I am voyaging into another dimension and in some ways the time surely is. The whole atmosphere of this locality as opposed to that of Long Island as I know it is other worldly turn of the century; brick and concrete gingerbread apartment buildings, streets and streets of taxpayers, storefront businesses gray and dingy with age or artfully and hopefully renovated. Blocks and blocks of sprawling classic homes long ago been constructed in carefully delineated neatly planned plots, stately and pedigreed fronted by giant oaks, maples, sycamores, that reach out to cover houses and streets as well in shady security. It is much different even than the stately posh and elegant Forest Hills Gardens of my miserable adolescence and early marriage.

And the people! They seem to be scurrying all over the cracked gray concrete and oily littered patched macadam streets, antlike in their uniformly bland costume looking to my upwardly mobile slightly elitist suburban eye like full-page ads for a St. Vincent de Paul thrift shop. Eleanor Rigby is walking with Nowhere Man carrying the jar with her face under her arm, leaving a gaping space by the door. They carry their shopping bags and packages many keeping their true style and status well hidden behind the ever normal facade of tradition and walking, swarming, going about their daily business; a far cry from the malls and quiet, neat sidewalks of Huntington Township, Suffolk County, Long Island. Not a city lover, I, the warmth and homeliness and aura of a sturdier era as represented in my newly discovered sojourn in Brooklyn touch a hungry ever expanding demanding place inside my rib cage.

There is a pealing sound of metaphorical ringing bells that bring back memories of the Bronx, Grandma and Grandpa and my other Grandma in Manhattan and those early days of my childhood when I thought that I was troubled but hadn't yet truly learned the meaning of the word trouble.

By my third or fourth visit the route is second nature to me thereby losing some of its strange fearsome awesomeness and the place itself acquires that familiarity born of habit that ultimately becomes so comfortable. It becomes a sort of oasis in a strange land. I sit through several psychic readings fascinated at first, awaiting my turn never ceasing to marvel at the skills of this spiritualist minister. I wonder at this whole newly opening world that contrasts so finely with the hypocrisy of the fundraiser Las Vegas nights, bingo, and card games and sisterhood power politics of my recently quasi-discarded Jewish heritage. Awed by the world of spirits and the call of the vast unknown I magically intone my recently learned verse of the Lord's Prayer rolling the potent words around my mind like an awesome and magical incantation.

I wait and wait, for all of these people to get their readings growing more and more impatient. Patience has never been my best thing. Finally as I adjust my position in this uncomfortable chair yet again, cross and re-cross my legs for the umpteenth time, feel the pins and needles beginning in my rear end it is my turn. Ken goes through the usual, family and initials and illnesses, tells me that am going through a difficult time, tells me not to worry my art will sell well in the future, informs me tentatively that he sees a love relationship in my near future, someone who moves like a dancer dark and slim, charming and bright, from a different Mediterranean type culture. Now this is a reading I tell myself. What more could I have asked for? This is Richie to a T. All I need is patience. I am practically floating, barely able to walk out the door without skipping; a broad smile splits my face in half. Everyone joins me, arms entwined, looking good kiddo, they say. Now I am truly a convert, ready for anything.

After my first encounter at the Church of St. John my thirst for knowledge about mysticism and spiritualism and my hunger for connection to this thing that obliquely promises immortality becomes so overwhelming that it is my sole sustenance in a trying and unsatisfying world. Steve still sends me a mere $50 a week for all six children and for me. This is supposed to pay for the mortgage, electricity, heat, food, clothing, medical care, insurance, and whatever else you can imagine, assumes a steady additional income from my art. How am I supposed to accomplish this? The omnipresent wolf pounds insistently on the door. I live in a terror of not knowing where my next dollar is coming from. I am making some progress toward my goal in terms of a unique painting style and financial solvency but time is the enemy. There is an occasional sale at the gallery or an outdoor show that enables me to pay some nagging debt just as each penultimate catastrophe looms. Still, I crave some sort of promise of security that will rescue us, the children and me, from the threat of the clawing tentacles of doom. Steve watches from a distance, wishing me failure the sooner the better. He smiles when he tells me so.

He is incredibly dense and uncooperative accidentally or deliberately I am not certain. He will neither help out with any extra cash nor advance me a nickel when extreme emergency makes demands. I have a pretty good idea that he is waiting patiently for me to crash and burn. Then he will claim the prize; his children, his house.

What did you expect, asks Diane, that he would change suddenly just because you are separated?

I am floating in a vacuumous suspension of emotional and financial insecurity no solution in sight.

෧෧

I have been too mortified to show my face at Louise's house after the car accident debacle and finally determine to stop obsessing over Richie and let him go. I am sufficiently grateful that my station wagon has been repaired so that I have been able to function. I transfer my attention to a new obsession. I going all the way to Brooklyn again and again, a great strain but following an offer of optimism and faith that belies any discomfort to attend classes in spiritual development at the Church of Saint John. I hope to penetrate that barrier to the spiritual world that promises aid and sustenance beyond any available here in the real world that offensive place of materialism that defies control. I need to find a key to open the lock that conceals immortality and the answers to long unanswered questions. Meanwhile, I keep busy on the outdoor art show circuit

But after a while I become bored with prediction after prediction of endless repetition and ordinary problems and of feigning interest in the worlds of others. I feel a pain, someone, could it be the initials D.R.? This person has a pain, could it be a left leg? Is there someone in the room with a recent loss? A deceased husband; I feel a chest pain, here, and on and on. An impatient sigh escapes my lips and I rise silently sidling self-consciously towards the rear door and relief from the heavy stuffiness and odor of desperate faith and expectant fear. I stand outside the store, part of me wondering what the hell I am doing here in this alien and ugly place and the other desperate part waiting impatiently for my turn. If only I could know the future, what lay in store for me, if only there were any hope! Will I ever be happy? I feel my inside mechanisms tightly wound up as I teeter on an abyss of hopelessness and apprehension, like an ancient and weary clock whose works wince waiting to be sprung.

Several others wander out by this time and idly I sort of eavesdrop as two women chat near me. They discuss the marvels and talents of the so godlike man within and remark about this one and that one whom they have known. The smaller one is birdlike has a predatory look petty in her pre-occupation with herself; the second heavier her tent-like flowered muu–muu covers her corpulence, long thick shiny black hair wound coronet like in tight braids around her head. My attention keeps on being drawn to this second one, she seems different somehow than the usual assorted flotsam that seem to gravitate to this place of miracles and hope (hope, again)! For one thing, she wears a look of self-confidence on her sculpted classic features, of certainty that I immediately envy. For another, there is something in her face, her demeanor that pulls me closer makes me sense a great store of wisdom and a warm enveloping security.

I feel so drawn to her that it confuses me, that this stranger in her unremarkable house dress and slippers could seem so familiar, so unique. I am also listening shamelessly, attentively by now to their conversation. It appears that the small birdlike woman is wheedling and cajoling over something that she wants, some potion, would you believe, or other. I can't believe my ears and strain to hear, better. It appears that the braided one seems reluctant to part with this potion trying to shush the other, her eyes flicking and sweeping the group nervously as well as somewhat amused as if to avoid being overheard. I become even more determined not to miss anything. Finally she sighs reaching into the cavernous depths of a large brocade purse and covertly hands over the tiny bottle that she brings out oh so discreetly and then palms. I catch a glimpse of tantalizing bilious bottle green glass and the glimmer of gold. Birdy woman falls all over Mrs. Braids thanking her profusely and heaping great blessings of spiritual largesse upon her, and scampers away her style-less over-permed grey cap of hair bouncing against her pasty creped neck. I am wanting that potion; I am needing it.

Noticing a look on my face that is probably a combination of both disbelief and envy and obviously of curiosity the woman moves a little closer to me chuckling with a dismaying amusement and glee and murmurs to me. It never ceases to amaze me, she confides. No matter how vigorously I insist to someone that there are no magical love potions, that magic doesn't exist, that there's no such thing, that she is wasting her time and mine; the more I refuse, the more they insist that they must have one of these potions or another. She begins to chuckle again thinking about it and soon she is roaring with laughter and the whole tent of her is shaking with mirth. Tears roll helplessly from her eyes and down her cheeks, and as if acknowledging my existence for the first time, she says. Now you look like an intelligent girl, can you beat that, she clucks, slapping her ample thigh. Actually I am not convinced, but she has indeed piqued my interest. Imagine that! If there is such a thing I want it.

I laugh a little self-consciously, politely trying to feign ennui and amusement and agree with her. I am hoping to conceal the obvious fact that a rapacious little tumor of desperation spawned by loneliness is growing inside of me defying reason until curiosity and greed become too much for me to bear. I oh so cleverly (I believe) maneuver the conversation into the areas occult that appear to be her particular venue until I procure for myself sighing with consummate relief an invitation to her home to discuss the world of esoterica *et al.* over tea sometime. Maybe I can get my hands on one of those illusive love potions. I am thrilled and amazed by my cleverness and ability to manipulate this stranger. It had been too easy. But our connection is certainly still tenuous; I have not yet been given an invitation that is concrete enough to satisfy me. This will evidently be a waiting game. Once again, I am faced with my greatest trial in life, patience. What can I do? It is probably some scam but what if it is not, what if it really works?

☙❧

I continue my weekly pilgrimage to Ken's readings at the church each Tuesday evening, keeping an eagle eye out for Hope but the novelty is beginning to pale, nothing too new or promising ever happens, his readings are mundane and without that special sparkle and edge. Still I compulsively continue to attend the Tuesday night readings fearful of missing the Big Revelation. Surely I reason, even a most talented and spiritually connected psychic can have off days or those lacking in inspiration. I apply my newly acquired Christian values of patience, compassion, and understanding and pray for deliverance and a good message. Indeed I have no right to expect instant gratification all the time.

One hot still summer night the stale air in the darkened room becomes almost as oppressive as Ken's continued litanies over the physical distresses of these pathetic aging constituents with their seemingly petty and insignificant problems. I wander out again into the fresh and cooling night air of the street seeking both escape and refreshment. And there is the woman with the love potions again looking a bit different, appearing slighter, wearing more appropriate clothes her hair cut in a long bob! In an instant I decide for once and for all that Ken is not the authority that he purports to be, is not fulfilling my expectations and I accept her offer of a cup of tea. Rumor has it that she does an amazing job reading Tarot cards. I am not certain just what that means because I have no

334

experience with real fortune telling before this except of course the Egg Lady and Louise's games but that's different, do-it-yourself with no authority. With some luck and a tiny amount of cajolery I believe I can convince her to take out her Tarot cards, and read my fortune.

Well pleased with myself I follow her to her home finally upon her invitation; my excitement is palpable.

ॐॐ

Yes, please, I answer, a trifle self-consciously feeling like an intruder still in this strange kitchen, and wondering what I am doing here. We sit at her kitchen table and I have been given a large white mug and a tea bag and hot water has been poured. I am tingling with anticipation, titillated by the unknown. Maybe this woman can reach past the dense layers that shroud my future, that prohibit me from knowing where to turn, which decisions to make, directions to take, what to do next. Those hopeful and perfunctory sessions in Louise's dining room playing with that silly tantalizing toy the Tarot Card Tell Your Own Fortune game searching for hidden meanings and vital answers or the Ouija board seeking answers from other worlds and old departed souls assuming it is not self-propelled. Those desperate waits in that drab anteroom immersed in an effluvia of anxious sweat of the others who are also waiting for the infamous Egg Lady whose genius and precision are legendary until she beckons to someone sitting in her parlor from the doorway to her inner sanctum. Now here is Hope which is really her name.

I wait awkwardly barely containing my anxiety. My fidgeting and the sweat trickling down my side under my arm, the fever that begins to spread from my cheekbone across my forehead and into my eyes are witness to my desperation. Gently she begins to question me, draws me out. I'm such a failure, I sob into my cooling mug of tea suddenly collapsing inwardly into that usually disguised familiar despair. Everything I have ever done in my life is doomed to failure. I am the consummate klutz, the quintessential non-achiever, worthless.

No, darlin', her sharp, dark, hooded eyes burn into mine, you are not worthless, you are not a failure. She takes out a deck of strange cards with exotic pictures on them and begins shuffling. I am mesmerized by the motion of her hands and the cards, feel soothed by her compassion, drawn into her deep eyes. Her face ripples with waves of differing emotions. She watches my face, puts the cards down, and asks me more questions about my life. Encompassed by the aura of strength that seems to radiate from her I begin speaking again tentatively and soon words are pouring out of me as from a burst pipe after a freeze followed by a thaw; before I know it I have spilled everything, all the pain and disappointment and fear that have held me prisoner for so long. She listens, her eyes glued to mine, piercing the surface of my stories. She never seems to judge me not even when I relate those episodes that hold me the most in their guilty grip, that weigh so heavily upon me, cause me to accept punishment for my sins both real and imagined. When finally I cannot speak any longer exhausted from the emotional effort, the physical strain of so long a speech she takes both my hands in hers, pauses for a long, long moment and looking deeply into my heart begins to speak. Are you aware, she says slowly and softly that you are special? *You are*, she says her words drawn out in almost slow motion, *a valuable person*. Do you know this, she asks me intensely. *You are a valuable person!* Again there is a long pause, our eyes locked together in some sort of bone chilling atavistic gear and I am suddenly aware that I am in the midst of a great and life-changing revelation.

You are, she continues as my ears burn with self consciousness, embarrassment, no less than a wonderful individual, a warm, wonderful, talented, charming person. But most important, even if you never achieve many of those lofty standards and goals you have set for yourself, even if you never reach those heights that loom so tantalizingly out of reach…you are still a valuable person. She takes my hands again and looks into my eyes, deep into my core and I can feel a current of power coursing through me. In that moment I can almost believe her. Not truly accept it just know that maybe somewhere deep down inside my being I can believe that it could be true. I begin to sense that it is possible that I can begin to climb instead of plummet ever downward.

This new strength and knowledge are fragile indeed, need to confront years and eons of action and reaction, guilt and the resultant self destruction. A price will need to be exacted for the exorcism of each and every demon. The price however is not a charge by my new savior for her ministrations are guided by love not greed.

Now, she says, waving her wings of black hair away from her eyes; let me read your cards.

ॐॐ

That is how I find Hope. But I am greedy, an opportunistic little bitch and there is more that I need from her so I continue to return to her kitchen and she wonders at my determination to make this long boring voyage from Northport to Brooklyn for this purpose. We tend to disagree Hope and I about just which is the ass end of the world Eastern Long Island or Fort Hamilton, Brooklyn. Crazy as any trip of this length is in general the reason for my own original trip is even more psychotic, more manic, more desperate, and has its rationale quite simply in the fact that had I never taken it in the first place I never would have found Hope. And maybe never have survived to be writing this.

But I have become a believer. At last I have found something to believe in. I believe in the tiny green bottles that Hope refers to as potions even as she denies their efficacy insisting that they are nothing more than a scam, something to amuse herself playing with others' needs. The lady doth protest too much. The more she protests the more I believe. I believe in the mysterious prayers and chants and incantations that address themselves to the minions of the powers that be. Any and all of them. I am willing to obey even the most ridiculous of directives in the search for the changing or charming of fate. One little green bottle guaranteed to bring a man into my life which Hope gives me one day when I wear her down it shouldn't be a total loss barely containing her mirth, comes into the possession of my small daughter Wendi who consistently rummages through my belongings in her search for the accouterments of playing house that she somehow manages to overturn despite the dire warning that Hope has left with me. Whatever you do be careful of this bottle, of what is in it because it has immense powers and misuse can result in God only knows what grave disaster. So she does believe, I think. Be very careful honey, she admonishes sternly, and I imagine at a much later time what would have been the resounding raucous roaring echoing sound of Hope's eye tearing thigh-slapping mirth when I report to her the spilling of the potion and the resultant commencement of a march of multiples of would be swains to my front door which doesn't end until a tear-soaked red-faced Hope, still choking back errant laughter administers an antidote some time later.

Wendi brings the bottle to the tiny log play cabin in our rear yard. The cap comes loose and the little bottle tips over spilling its green and frothy contents over the small fingers that hold it precariously and onto the spongy moss floor of the cabin in the woods. Within hours a new home comes suddenly under construction a scant hundred feet away and in no time at all the wealthy middle-aged builder, the handsome young contractor, the bulldozer operator, the backhoe driver, and various and sundry tradesmen make their ways to my front and back doors in order to use my bathroom, my telephone, the water, the electricity, not any other neighbor but me. Soon they realize that they have discovered an attractive divorcee, the mere existence of her many children attest to her passionate tendencies and soon my driveway resembles a modern day adaptation of the Sorcerer's Apprentice with cars and trucks taking the place of brooms; the phone rings incessantly and men are taking polls, making inquiries, selling insurance and landscaping and appliances and household services, offering freebies with purchases, asking for appointments. Invitations begin to pour in for social events. Eileen with her pale blond bubble coif, her Irish maiden's face, her sky blue eyes, her killer body, her own four children whose home is as close to the new construction as mine is not included in this scene. Is it because she is still married? And it continues to rain men.

Hope, I ask, what do you suppose is happening?

It's the potion, dear heart, she says, I told you to be very careful. Her voice sounds funny as if she is choking on something.

Are you all right? I ask. My question is met with a strange silence. After a while I continue. Well I know you said it was powerful but this is something unusual, really odd.

Are you sure you didn't spill it, she asks, barely controlling her voice, or lose the bottle?

Is she laughing at me? I ask myself. *No, I answer, as far as I know, it's all right, in my jewelry box on my dresser. And I only dabbed a drop on my forehead and over my heart as you directed. I never even put any on my navel because I wasn't really ready for a romance, yet.*

Go, baby, she says sternly, *and make certain it's all right, because now, I'm worried.* I return from the bedroom in a hurry; the green bottle is nowhere to be seen.

My heart fluttering in my throat, I tell Hope, and throw the phone down and race to find the children asking them breathlessly where my green bottle is. Wendi looks down at her frayed little pink sneakers her blond ponytails bobbing and afraid to lie to me tells me the story of the demise of my potion which she believes in her innocence to be an expensive scent. For all I know that's all that it is, some scent, but certainly not expensive. Too many of these little green bottles have worked their way out of Hope's kitchen. I race back to where I have left the phone and relate the story to Hope who chokes back her laughter and somehow gets control of her voice and proceeds to tell me that of course this is what is wrong, this is what has happened, this explains my sudden popularity and good fortune, the perfect storm of men that I have been experiencing.

Now, honey, she gasps, we are going to have to remedy this, for there's no telling where it will end, otherwise.

Are you all right, I ask tremulously, hearing choking sounds from the other end of the phone.

Fine, she answers, but did you hear me? We need to fix this...

We do? I ask, a trifle dismayed and disappointed thrilled at the change of fortune that has been effected. Why of course, baby, can you imagine what could actually occur? Why, there's no telling what could happen. She leaves these dire fantasies to my own fevered imagination. It doesn't disappoint me but I am wondering just what could be bad, to be desired by many men.

I allow my overactive anyway mind to meander and soon I can see where Hope is going with this and quickly though reluctantly agree that steps will have to be taken. Tchaikovsky will have to find another place to play his magical symphony and without the help of the irrepressible mystical Hope.

Here's what you have to do. *Is that another gasp of choked laughter I hear at the other end? No. It couldn't be. It's my imagination once again playing tricks on me.*

First do you have green shoes, she asks? Why green, I ask myself? But I do have Kelly green sneakers. Put on the shoes and inscribe a large circle on a flat surface. A flat surface does she mean the floor? Okay I think, I can do that. Now hop counter clockwise around the circle five times chanting the Lord's Prayer.

By the way, in the future, she says, if you are wanting something write it down on a piece of paper, fold it twice and lay it on top of a glass half full of water which you place under your bed directly where you lay your head. I do this faithfully for a long time but I am not certain if it ever worked at all.

CHAPTER 54

But there is still that question of the future looming distantly and vaguely and frighteningly in the great unknown ahead and while Hope's mystical Tarot readings and sensitive compassionate philosophical advice are encouraging, soothing, it is insufficient to satisfy my obsessive hunger, my insatiable need for foresight, knowledge, prescience. Hope's heritage is Basque, she has been born in the Pyrenees and it is said has magic powers and she has a copy of a most esoteric hoary ancient book of magic spells. She has done research; she knows things. She whispers sacred things about Druids and spells and magical cures among other things. Her mother lives with her, a skeletal, crooked old woman with wild white hair followed everywhere by an enigmatic old white cat, who looks like *Baba Yaga,* the legendary Russian witch.

My pilgrimages to Bay Ridge have become an irresistible compulsion and whenever I am able to maneuver free time I find myself following that familiar route sometimes wondering how I got there and even why. What am I doing? This is a question that I ask myself more than once.

With no plan, no rhyme or reason I find myself en route to Bay Ridge. I arrive that bright spring morning the city sun sparkling from myriad spots of mica and pebble embedded in the cracked and uneven side walk aggregate. Hope is not home, I never thought of that. So I make my way to the dark and shrouded glass storefront door which hides answers to eons of questing and eternities of seeking. Oh God, help me, I moan; I am so desperate. Why is this? What is wrong with me?

Ken isn't there either. My first response is the hollow feeling in my chest and stomach; that elevator sinking sensation and I sit down heavily on a folding wooden chair. I have taken this long ride for nothing and it all my own fault as usual. I never thought it out. I take a deep breath and deciding that if I wait here maybe I will be surprised by his arrival; he is held up, stopped somewhere on the way, is a little tardy I tell myself. Maybe Hope will return also. In the meanwhile I cloak my intense disappointment by joining the group that is already discussing something or other esoteric, philosophical, faith oriented. I hang around not wishing to waste the time spent on the monumental effort to get here hoping that Ken will show up before too much time passes, before I have to leave. What I crave is a word from the master psychic; any thought at all that he might pick up in his meditations that might shed some light, offer some promise for the future. I hang these days, on words of prophecy with a tenacity that excludes belief in anything else in the world. I am hungry for any information that might be shed by the initiate about the hidden worlds of the other side. I am a seeker of a holy grail, answers to the immortality of life. I am unwilling, unable to question or leave this shabby and uninspiring storefront that masquerades as a place of worship, of inspiration. I never even begin to doubt what so obviously and glaringly points to the contradiction between the very shoddiness of this place and the sparkling promise of spiritual connection and salvation. If you're so smart why ain't you rich goes the age-old quip that I heard my mother mouth so many times.

Nevertheless it is the only grail that proffers itself for the grabbing; this is what I intend to do. They are speaking of spirit writing, a new and seemingly absurd idea, to me, although Cayce has done it, but that's him, but I am merely passing time waiting for Ken, my guru and savior. What is it, anyway? Cayce calls it automatic writing. I recall reading about this somewhere. So I listen halfheartedly one eye on the door but perk up my ears when discussion turns to plans for an experiment, a demonstration. Here is an opportunity to find perhaps irrefutable proof of some nature. The sad, seedy looking participant in her faded housedress hair askew, overweight and gray and wrinkled chants the Lord's Prayer as she holds a pencil loosely in one hand; great swirls of line and letter emerged on her paper. Here is a shock of huge proportions. Not what I had expected at all. Entranced and thinking that it looks so easy I try it myself but nothing happens. Hold the pencil loosely, she says trying to facilitate my efforts, close your eyes and meditate, say the Lord's Prayer in your head. I try again and again but meet with no success. Undaunted, I decide that this failure is due to my discomfort in an alien place as well as to the many distractions. I can never work anywhere but my own studio, this is a fact. I can't wait to get home to try this new and promising initiation to the world of the spiritual. It might prove the validity of the entire premise, still floating tantalizingly in my mind in an absurd realm of uncertainty.

During the entire trip my mind is working, looking for a way to validate the improbable connection of this world with the next, find proof that not even the famous and brilliant magician Houdini could discover despite vows and promises was unable to fulfill after his own untimely death. I get home and look at the children and a light bulb moment overwhelms me. Who wants to play a game, I sing out gaily. Me, me, me…here is a chorus of little voices joined together in the spirit of Mommy's invitation. Now I need to think this through. In order to prove the possibility of contact with another side I need a control. Every experiment needs a control I remember from science class in junior high school. Wendi can already read and write a little so she is disqualified and of course Bruce, too. Andrew and Kevin are too young no attention span. Caryn.

Caryn is my cuddly kitten smiling and acquiescent, always. She is five years old and cannot read or write. Take this crayon, I tell her, and this piece of paper and sit here on the floor. Hold the crayon loosely, like this, and close your eyes and dream. Don't draw just hold the crayon and dream. She follows orders and looks up tilting her pixie face smiles that beatific smile at me. She closes her eyes and places her hand holding the crayon on the paper holding it loosely as told. Think happy thoughts, I tell her, keep your eyes shut. Yes, she shakes her head eyes still closed. Happy thoughts are Caryn's specialty, then, her cherubic face is always lit up with joy except when she falls into her moods of heavy mournful self-indulgent Russian misery. We know which of our ancestors Caryn has taken after. Nothing happens at first but soon the crayon is moving all over the page. Caryn is drawing a scribbly picture, I think, and everyone laughs not knowing where I am going, what I am expecting. My mind wanders away somewhere. Mommy, Caryn says, quietly, my crayon stopped. Not sure what she means, I say, that's okay, baby, let me see the picture. She reaches up and hands me the paper and I begin to examine it. At first I see just masses of scribbles and then I look a little closer and there they are words written in script. It says, as clear as day, Hello, Ida.

What does it say, Mommy, asks Wendi, let me see. No it's nothing, I answer, afraid to even begin any kind of explanation. My hand is shaking, holding the paper; my mind is racing. Can this just be a bunch of scribbles that seem to say those two words? I look again. No. It is clearly Hello, Ida. I am petrified, frightened to death, terrified. Why? This is what I have been taught to believe, this is what I have been expecting, Maybe, not exactly this. But there is no mistake. How can I explain this? I call Connie, the rest of the girls, and they come running over. We stare at the paper, we question Caryn. Have you learned how to write, we ask her. No, she says, but I like to draw. She doesn't know Steve's mother's name, Ida, I say, we never talk about her. Her name is never mentioned; Steve has forbidden it. I don't understand.

I call Hope. She laughs, and says, have you ever heard, there are more things in heaven and earth, Horatio, than are dreamt of in your philosophy, she asks. What is she trying to tell me? I know my Shakespeare but I am still puzzled. All I want to say is something strange is happening. More things in heaven and earth, baby, says Hope, laughing again. I spend that night and all my free time thereafter holding pen to paper and meditation repeating the Lord's Prayer over and over. Nothing happens. I still don't understand.

I make up my mind to find and to read even more of those books I have been told about, by Arthur Ford and Cayce and others that describe and even validate manifestations of this type, commence an intensive search for anything that has been written on the subject. Some of these books have supposedly been entirely written by some spirit guide while they, the host-writers, remain under the influence of a trance. I have been experimenting with meditation by this time the proscribed and necessary tool of these believers even though my efforts have been futile. Although I remain skeptical unable or unwilling to give myself completely to this new faith system I am able to find at the least some small consolation in the calming effects of this technique. I decide that mere writing will be a waste of my valuable time. What do I need with more words? Suddenly it is far more natural for me, a minor decision, to sit at my easel a dripping paint brush in my hand and hope for some result. It's worth a try anyway. I am not very hopeful.

I don't expect anything to happen but again, what could be bad? I murmur the words of the Lord's Prayer over and over again as I have been taught. I let my thoughts go inward and my mind goes blank and shortly I feel a sense of heaviness in my extended arm. I am gripped by a sudden terror greater than any other I have experienced in my life, and a feeling of awe. I keep my eyes closed and feeling a tug, feeling the brush moving allow it to go wherever it wants. Trembling I allow this strange phenomenon to continue. I do not open my eyes. I am afraid to break the spell and afraid of what I might see on the canvas. I am more terrified that I will see nothing than something; knowing that there will be nothing there but scribbles. Caryn had nothing but scribbles, I think. While my eyes are shut I can believe that something remarkable and spiritual is happening.

When the brush stops moving I open my eyes tentatively expecting to see a mish–mash of jumbled lines and colors. I have been almost afraid to look. To my great surprise I discover an entire field of poppies. Each one is carefully articulated, unique, huge petals, intricately formed, with shockingly specific details. There are large ones in the foreground and smaller ones receding toward the distant ridge of trees. They are curled and folded and twisted and straight; firm and soft and rigid and flopping. This might not seem strange to anyone who is in the habit of painting flowers in fields, flowers of this type but I am stunned. This particular type of detail is not my area of expertise. When I paint flowers I must have them right in front of me, use them as models.

I continue to concentrate on this strange power that seems to possess my arm independent of my control. I allow it to guide me as I set about coloring in the flowers, tentatively but gaining courage slowly, adding great swaths of pigment with my knife and thrilled with the results begin half a dozen new canvasses in the same manner. All of them have the same quality of lovely fields receding into the distance, blossoming trees reaching up and out, and the masses of flowers, sometimes poppies of various colors, sometimes daisies or mums but always beginning large in the front, and getting gradually smaller as they recede. I am working feverishly now, a one-person band of Sorcerer's Apprentices painting, painting, painting one canvas after the other tossing the finished ones to the side. I continue to murmur the Lord's Prayer over and over, a magical incantation, and pray with deep and intense desperateness as I work reaching out to whatever power from whence this comes. Finally I fall into my bed exhausted, too exhausted to even think about what has just happened.

࿔

I pack the canvases with shims of wood between them still wet with gleaming swaths of juicy oil paint, in my station wagon and head for the Greenport wharf s art fair at the easterly end of the North Fork of Long Island and set up my work on the wharf near the dock. I am gratified by the response. Not only do I sell several of the new pieces but the reaction of the public is intensely gratifying. I meet a successful and esteemed artist, Mary Vickers at that show who is set up next to me. I find out that we are practically neighbors; she lives a few blocks away from me. Not only is she an artist of great achievement and renown in her genre she quite graciously shows me some new techniques using oils and introduces me to the world of acrylics a brand new medium that everyone is trying that plays such an important part in production in the following years because of its quality of drying quickly.

She also introduces me to some dealers who are buying huge piles of work from her on a weekly basis in order to accommodate the burgeoning art thirst that is infecting a brand new market in the United States. By the time I share the adjoining space with Mary in Westhampton Beach in August, I have all but eliminated all my earlier attempts and proceed to show a combination of the newer woodland pieces that have met with success as well as the fields of flowers. I make more money at that show than I have ever expected to see in one place at one time. I fly home each evening to replace the sold pieces with new ones

343

working feverishly again all night only to carry them back the next morning separated by chunks of wood and cardboard so that they will not touch and smear to dry in the summer beach breezes.

৵৽

Delicate shy sharp-featured small-boned Eleanor my art student and one of those attendees of our early spiritualist meetings, séances, held in shabby homes in even more shabby neighborhoods by scruffy threadbare needy lonely persons in ill health and physically and emotionally bankrupt speaks to me of deeper places, strange strata, weird happenings and bizarre directions. Oh yes, I have read of late everything I can get my hands on relating to extra sensory perception, other worlds beyond, the writings of various mediums that seemed to abound, the transcriptions of vehicles of returned souls. The promise of higher meanings for this more and more insidiously meaningless thing called life. I crave some tangible proof of worlds beyond, of higher purpose. We speak of out-of-body travel and my conscious mind rebels while my inner soul revels. What does this mean? I must try it; see if it's something real. I spend hours on my solitary bed meditating seeking messages from beyond, connection with the spirit world, all those departed taunting from afar promising answers to great and ponderous questions about life. I await the appearance of an all powerful deity who will spell out for me for once and for all the meaning of existence. I try to leave my body and fly through the atmosphere to other lives and places, wonder about parallel universes where someone just like me is living the same life but maybe making it work.

In my next spiritual experiment I float in a world of unwitting self-hypnosis spiraling ever inward to the recesses of my mind where it is at least supposed to be safe awaiting revelation. In general these experiments are unsatisfactory; while all sorts of manifestations occur, all manner of tantalizing happenstance and effluvia appear that promise imminent revelation there is never anything that I can sink my teeth into. Connie always says that when she dies which she expects will happen at a very young age she promises to return and prove to us all that our suspicions are valid, that life exists beyond the veil. At least if it does then she will return. Almost at the verge of giving up but too stubborn to admit defeat or give my detractors reason to gloat I hunker under the covers surrounded by the deep darkness of ungodly hours practicing my meditation although without my usual intense concentration finally driven by guilt to double down and concentrate even more strongly than usual.

To my surprise the room seems suddenly to be infused with some heavy black impenetrable smoke. Something unusual is happening, and I concentrate even harder sensing an icy thread of terror beginning to worm its way through my body. Still I am too close to discovering something to stop. All at once I can see figures looming in the murk, working their way toward me, indiscernible figures alien and menacing…this is not what is supposed to happen. Where is Mary, Jesus, an Indian guide, my grandmother? Enough I think and try to snap back to consciousness finished with all this meditation, done with it all, but the figures continue to advance toward me swooping down upon me with their dark swirling billowing cloaks, blending with, floating in and out of the dark smoke clouds scaring me to death. A scream is sticking in my throat and I begin reciting the Lord's Prayer in my mind over and over again faster and faster more and more desperate with each terrified moment. The closest figure leans over me clutching one of my pillows in his huge unseen hands, clamping it over my face. I am suffocating, suffocating unable to fight back, fright has taken over my senses paralyzing me and I am now screaming the Lord's Prayer, screaming it in my brain for my mouth is filled with the stuffing of that pillow and the black smoke. This is not a dream. I know this because I can feel, sense, the edges of reality all around me, my room, my furniture, my paintings, my stuff…I am fighting back now frenzied not wanting to die or to become one with these powerful evil beings that I am certain are not those spirits that I have been seeking. Suddenly the smoke begins to clear, the figures to recede, the terror in my chest to abate and I am still in my bed. I have not traveled anywhere.

When I am able to move, to speak even at this ungodly hour I reach for the telephone and call Hope. I need not have worried if I even do, Hope is not likely to castigate me for disturbing her even at this hour. She listens to my story, hears the panic and terror in my voice seriously commences direction for how to exorcise my home of these evil forces but so great is my terror that she must of necessity move on to more drastic tactics. Wisps of black smoke are still curling toward the ceiling; I know that the figures are not far away. I am in terror of their imminent return.

Do you have one of your paintings around, she asks softly, you know, the ones with the field of flowers where the deep fields recede into the horizon between where the fringes of trees meet?

Of course I do, they are stacked up by the window wall waiting to be picked up.

Well, honey, concentrate on that pinpoint of light in the distance where the trees meet, stare at it and concentrate on me and picture me travelling through space until you see me walking through that spot in between the trees. Meanwhile I will concentrate on a pinpoint of light. I will arrive in your room. You will feel my presence but you will not see me.

Oh, Hopie, I sigh, wanting to believe but hesitating at the absurdity of it all aware of my own gullibility, not wanting to play the fool. It is probably too late to worry about that. Can you do that? I ask, incredulous. Why would she do that to me considering the state of hysteria that I am presently in if it were not true? Am I not certain that other dimensions exist beyond my comprehension?

I stare at the painting as bidden and soon the last of the smoky wisps have disappeared. I can feel the soothing presence of Hope and as she has warned me I do not speak to her. I savor the sense of safety that I feel with her presence and soon feel myself drifting off into a deep dreamless sleep. I do not call her until the next morning and she is not at all surprised to know that I have indeed felt her presence in my bedroom and that everything is now all right.

Don't under any circumstances try that again, Lynnie, she admonishes me with dire sincerity, you have no idea...you are playing with forces of which you have no knowledge. I want your solemn word, she says.

I promise, I say with all sincerity. Hopie, were you really here or did you just hypnotize me so that I would not be so overcome with fear? Is it possible to travel out of body or is that a bunch of bunk?

Honey, yes, I could have hypnotized you, but I didn't. Yes, I was there. Of course I can travel out of my body but it's such a pain and it's really quite dangerous...just think! I don't do it very often but this was an emergency. Please don't go spreading it around. Disbelievers will only ridicule us.

But Hopie, I need proof. This is very important to me. Can you prove it? Could you give me information that would make it certain for me that this was true? A sense of excitement as though I am waiting to step over some brave new threshold taunts me, tantalizes me. I need to know.

I tell you what. Have I ever been to your house, before?

No.

Have I ever seen any of your paintings? Have you ever told me more than that they are fields with flowers? Well, the painting through which I came is a pale yellow with a sort of lavender overtone. The trees are that silvery lavender tone shot with blue. The flowers are a dusty pink, some of them mauve, some of them cream. The sky is a deep rosy salmon streaked with pink. The flowers are huge in the front, and become smaller as they recede into the distance. How's that?

I am stunned at how close she has come. I never say another word for this is a brand new experiment in color, one of more unique of my paintings, the others stacked behind it are more ordinary, green trees, red poppies, or yellow and orange daisies. There is no way that she could have known about this painting. I shiver. I am doing a lot of that lately.

I remember this so clearly after all these years but there is no one to reminisce with now that Hope is gone. In later times when I had grown, matured some and become her friend instead of one of her marks we used to roar and roar with laughter remembering my naïveté and the silliness of it all and I still blush when I think about it. But I have no proof either that it didn't happen just as I told it.

None of us not the dearest or the closest of us were inured to the naughty and diabolical whims of our deity for that is what Hope was to all of us. Depending upon her mood, to the state of her most current state of boredom or ennui, cumulative hostility, or just plain impatience, annoyance with someone's naïveté, bothering, or general obtuseness so did she temper her kindness, aid, nurturing and generosity with mischief or silliness. In later years we would reminisce; recall some of the stories that never lost their hilarity, their poignancy. Sometimes there was just the revelation of a moment of truth.

Filled with a great and joyous sense of ultimate discovery I rush one brisk morning to Bay Ridge to visit Hope and share my news. In the midst of my search for answers I have discovered something new and tantalizing, a group called Jews for Jesus, and there is an immediate sense of serendipity, an instantaneous sensation of destiny fulfilled. It is all falling into place; I can embrace my newly discovered Christianity without guilt or pain because it is all logical and normal. All of my syllogisms are valid. But Hope is aghast, more agitated than I have ever seen her, chain smoking and pacing around her kitchen, waving her arms as she pontificates. Oh Lynnie, don't you realize that all religions are the same? You might as well stay with the one what brought you. Just as in the rest of life, the rich and powerful corrupt all faith, Look at the Papacy, at Fundamentalism, at the rest of the fanatics; it all leads to some sort of Fascism which is accomplished with massive brainwashing techniques. She sighs. Don't you see yet that faith is a tool for control? Now it is my turn to be shocked, but I am nothing if not obstinate.

Despite her attempts to educate me about reality my intensity ultimately wears her down. In answer to the continuing barrage of my voluminous questions about matters religious and esoteric and my growing interest in Christianity and my need for something more than the Our Father that I am wearing out from overuse, Hope sighs deeply and teaches me the words to the Hail Mary and Hail Holy Queen. I scribble these onto the back of an envelope in my purse, and rapidly memorize these magical incantations, practice rolling the words around my mouth, chanting intensely my inner mind formulating desperate pleas, a new avocation while driving or attempting sleep back home in bed.

CHAPTER 55

It is the very beginning of a new year. While I struggle to feed my children absent help from their father our government is sending gifts of food to Biafra. While I attempt to figure out how to pay for heating fuel an oil well blowout threatens Santa Barbara and drilling is halted. Biafra and Santa Barbara are equally distant in my world of children and art and survival.

I am compelled to produce more and more art for my newly acquired dealer contacts. I continue to write poetry at this time but spend more and more effort in the captivating pursuit of spirit writing experiments awaiting the further revelations that I know are there.

With a sense of focused obsession, I still go to other readings and seek out new and more reputed psychics ever seeking that tantalizing glimpse into the future that eludes capture even more convinced that there is something there. If I could only see what lay in store! Who would I meet? Would there ever be anyone to share the lonely days and nights and dreams with? Will Cliff ever be free, available? Would Richie ever find himself and perhaps want me in his future? Would anyone ever want a woman who is saddled with six children? Should I go ahead with the divorce from Steve and continue in my quest for the impossible dream? Or should I cop out and place my efforts into trying to make that sick liaison well take Steve back and forget about the perfect dream of love and a real marriage?

Better to stick with the old mess, opines Eileen echoing Daddy, hanging out lately at my studio with the rest of the girls, there are no bargains out there. At least what you already know is safer than some new horror. I know that she is thinking about her own well known horror Mr. Patrick and is also well acquainted with the variety of new ones out there waiting to be found.

Oh, go for it, says Anne in a similar marriage afraid to make any move of her own, anxious to see if it will work out. After careful and agonizing thought I decide to go for broke and once again let my sins be of commission rather than omission. As a matter of fact those words are now officially my mantra, which lasts oh so conveniently and of its nature non-censurably for many years.

I don't want to be sitting in my rocking chair at ninety years of age ancient lips pulled grimacing back across empty gums and moan, Oh why didn't I do that or that sixty years ago, I am fond of remarking at this time safely embraced by the immortality of youth and the endless time stretching ahead. I like the sound of it. Let my sins be rather of commission that omission I decide anew and proclaim yet again.

I continue to make the trip to Bay Ridge to see Hope.

I was so desperate for love in those days; Love the magic cure all. How she must have roared, I remember thinking many years later at the easy capture of this new mark! Not that she ever made a financial gain from those needy, desperate creatures who ran to her enfolding warmth in numbers that approached legion. Her need was to fill the restless hours of gaping endless stretching days with people to occupy and entertain her. She was a good person I knew this instinctively and she rejoiced in helping people although she did possess a slightly wicked naughty streak that no one could ever predict. I recognized it rather quickly. Her naughty wicked instincts immediately connected to my own.

Much later I found out about her medical and psychiatric training as well as her acquaintance and personal involvement with both the entertainment world and literary circles. For many years, though, I vastly feared her omnipotence and was apprehensive and exceedingly respectful of her seemingly infinite powers. She went to great lengths to convince all of us followers of these and she did while she went to incredible lengths to help us to save us from ourselves.

CHAPTER 56

A dry hot Saturday in June, 1968, and I have spent the entire day in Brooklyn at the Church of St. John and then at Hope's kitchen table drinking tea and having my cards read over and over again seeking magical answers to my life's problems. I am overwhelmed and immersed in the sensation of being directionless without past or future no possible clarity to any sign before any path that presents itself. I feel as if I am blindfolded trying to pin the infernal tail on an unseeable donkey; unable it would seem to even locate the infernal donkey. I cannot get far enough away from any of it to make a coherent decision about anything, the least of which is my future direction. I drive home from Bay Ridge trying to sort out a mélange of thoughts, mumbling my new mantras, my prayers to Mary over and over again, trying to come to any coherent conclusion pertaining to my life. Steve and I have been separated now for six months. I have decided that I owe it to myself to make quite certain that this thing with Steve whatever it has come to is definitely going in the correct direction.

I am feeling lost, without past or future. I fear so much, the looming emptiness in which now that Steve is gone there may never be anyone else.

Today's Tarot cards have been, quite deliberately on Hope's part, ambiguous, replacing all responsibility for decisions squarely on my own very inept shoulders.

That is why I made the dinner date with him for this evening; I am going to find out and ascertain for once and for all whether there is any chance at all for this marriage, whether there is any chance at all for its salvation. I owe this to all of us. She does make certain that I am fully aware of the fact that I have a divine animal right to protect myself and my children. Haven't I told each of them at the moment of their births that I will always protect them, care for them, assure their happiness and success and best interests?

I meet Steve at his apartment in Jamaica feeling very strange and awkward. We pass each other in the hallway and I am reminded of our wedding night. And brush against each other, find ourselves in an awkward embrace, a sudden kiss that escalates into desperate all consuming passion instilled by nostalgia no doubt and soon we are in bed, on bed, immersed in our old familiar activity, our special rhythm, poignant with memory, lost hope, desperation, futility. The sex was always good, but where was all that promised *love?* Falling into a well of despair I recall the sarcasm, the condescension and lack of respect; none of this had dawned on me in earlier days. I had never really been properly loved. Silently afterward I get myself into a special dating outfit that I have brought with me and apply fresh makeup in a twilight zone of familiarity, of comfortable marital intimacy while Steve changes his own raiment and off we go to Patricia Murphy's in Manhasset on the Miracle Mile like any other happily married suburban couple. (The melancholy of it puts a strain and pressure on us that is difficult to tolerate; we have been here many times before, in a different time.)

The scene at the restaurant, thick with tension, all of the ugliness and separateness of months between us is otherwise a repeat of that first honeymoon dinner that we had partaken of in Bermuda those ten years ago and tears run down my face continually no matter my attempts to control them for it seems that there is truly no saving that which we have already put way asunder. I defiantly eat the entire basket full of bread and ultimately buy my own shrimp cocktail and dessert showing a new and sudden strength of independence that serves only to antagonize Steve. Did I do this on purpose? I eat each shrimp with clenched teeth swallowing past a lump in my throat and congestion in my chest and I am hard put to keep it all down at all. I have persevered and won a pyrrhic victory indeed.

For a few sweet moments as we dance and he holds me in his arms I think to myself, would it be so bad; for the sake of the children? Could we possibly learn to live together? But an otherworldly voice whispers in my ear that there is no way so we leave abruptly and the die is cast once again forever and all time, for the sake of the children. The dice have been thrown and I will take courage from Caesar's crossing of the Rubicon take my chances going forward.

The day of my divorce from Steve feels like the day of my actual birth. Not rebirth for that comes much, much later; first birth, sort of a reincarnation from the life of my childhood and the dead sea of my marriage. When I think of my childhood even now the whole mass of years seems to fade away mirage-like. The time with Steve is relegated into a few bittersweet moments; most of them are concerned with unfulfilled dreams and the bringing out and bringing up of babies and a monstrous hiatus of nothingness. At this late date as time begins to run out and becomes the more precious the thing I resent most about it all is the terrible waste, the loss of precious time that those years represent. Dead years swallowed up in a morass of childish romantic daydreams and escapism.

The birth pains begin years before he even leaves and grow the strongest that last New Year's Eve when he finally packs his bags and drives away. From this day I am finally free but an ugly legacy remains; this is the day that begins Steve's hellish vendetta which reaps its ever progressive ever reaching boomeranging harvest. The running, the searching, the various court battles, the private holocausts, the additional painful lost years with Eddie, and the desperate time of recovery from his desertion and betrayal; these become the rebirth. But that's getting ahead…Even now the ultimate fallout of Steve's rage is quietly wreaking the destruction of its deadly heritage. A shame that the children bear the brunt of the destruction which is of course aimed at me; I merely wear the hairy shirt of guilt and try not to let the attendant depression and fear rule my days excessively. But I am still here damaged though I am and they are the ones whose lives have been altered beyond redemption.

CHAPTER 57

They call it the Freedom Plane and its passengers are overwrought with high spirits and joy. A party atmosphere reigns and champagne flows like the proverbial water. Not of Niagara Falls; more like the River Styx. The Freedom Plane this sunny June day is wending its way to El Paso, Texas where exchanges will be made via air shuttle to the charming city of Juarez, Mexico. This will be my first exposure to Hispania.

The Freedom Plane is an affectionate euphemism for the Quickie Divorce Special. In 1967, before divorce law reforms clutching your legal separation in your hot little expectant hand, for a few dollars you can fly the Special complete with singing, swinging, and free flowing booze to luxurious Hiltonesque accommodations in a lush Juarez suburb. There you can fulfill the twenty-four-hour necessary requirement thereby establishing legal residency. There is no time to absorb the incredible surrounding antiquity, the local color. You awaken to the awesome colors of the rising desert sun, barely having a moment to breathe in the sweet morning air and wafting odors of Mexican cuisine and flora and fauna. There is barely time to explore the luxuries of the exorbitant and elegant hotel. Rapidly and expeditiously you are whisked into formation before your morning muffin has the chance to go soggy and rancid in the heavy humidity or dry out in the desert heat. The entire group is quickly and efficiently lined up and loaded onto, taken by ancient and noxious bus to stand on lengthy multiple sets of queues in varieties of decrepit and shabby quaint Juarez Civic Center buildings. You are moved from clerk's office to seedy judge's chambers line by sweating line listening to flies buzzing and dive-bombing and finding both comfort and apprehension in the alien background hum of gibbering Spanish, peppered with American slang and an occasional interpretation.

This is the sacred ritual that finalizes the ends of so many marriages originally born in heaven. To pass the time while shifting from one burning foot to another I try to calculate in my head based on the number of bodies on our plane, number of planes per day, week, month, year, etc., etc., the immense volume of divorces the sickening and putrefying corpses of unions made with huge hopes and expecting to last until forever. It is beyond depressing. Juarez has itself a burgeoning industry as long as our New York State legislature declines to reform divorce laws.

When all the papers are signed and we are returned to our hotel the festivities begin. I cannot celebrate with the joyous group as they somewhat hysterically drift out like so many sequined and perfumed Keystone Swingers to finalize the sundering of sacred bonds with alcohol and loud raucous music and gyrating dance and wild desperate anonymous orgiastic bed-flings. I am suddenly prude and proper. It's almost as though the divorce decree has returned to me my lost virginity. But the sundering of marriage vows is as sacred as the taking of them.

I sit in my gorgeous room and sob. I let the memories flow over me one by one and I feel the hot salty flood sluice down my face and hope that they will cleanse out all the pain and guilt and precious scratchy dreams fragmented like so much shattered crystal. I stifle the impulse to call Steve and share with him by habit the description of the outrageously luxurious suite. My first impulse is always to tell him something of interest. Even though he probably won't listen, never has, never will. I am the original tree that falls in the forest that no one hears. I throw myself across the huge alien bed in this huge alien room and sleep fitfully. The ghosts of all my ancient dreams flit in and out of the tomb like air-conditioned stillness. I awaken finally swollen eyed and not rested to rush helter-skelter to join the airport-bound group and face the anticlimactic five-hour trip back to New York which ultimately ends ignominiously with six additional hours of circling in air traffic waiting permission to land.

I don't come down to earth until years later.

CHAPTER 58

Finally I am free. I am free except for my responsibilities as a mother and provider for my brood. Steve is his usual soul of compassion and generosity meaning that he has neither. Being married to Steve had been a kind of hell. Being separated was merely another side of the coin; divorce will be just another level of the same old, same old. But I am now free to find another man to love, to find someone who will give my children a safe and happy home and security and love. This appears to be an important imperative in my world. What was that? Freedom's just another word for nothing left to lose...?

A woman needs a man like a fish needs a bicycle, this is the latest example of Feminist humor making the rounds. *I am one fish that needs a bicycle. Badly. The moving force of my existence is my craving for male affection which I am designating as love. Perhaps because of my father's disappearance to the netherworld of the war in Europe for my first most formative six years I have no experience of what a father's love is, what a marriage or a real loving relationship looks like; even after his return the relationship between my parents was so peculiar, so bizarre. I crave that absent paternal affection more than anything in my life. The search for this love becomes my raison d'être. All of the choices that I make in regard to men revolve around this need. Fear of losing this love is the guiding force for all of my hesitance to stand up for my rights, all of my acceptance of abuse. Fear of losing love, fear of losing someone who is important to my supposed salvation. An overwhelming sense of unworthiness is responsible for my fear that I will never find anyone other than my current abuser, my settling for the status quo instead of something better. Fear of loss, of being alone, of not having love, of being without a man. Luckily, I have the children and I love them with all that I have all that I am receiving tremendous doses of love in return. But still I need the love of a man. Sadly enough so do my children and they did not get this either. I mourn the fact that the very thing that I have been denied in my own childhood is being denied to my own children and their father isn't even away in a great war for six years. That is the greatest loss, the most awful lack in their lives. It is what I consider to be my biggest failure, depriving my children of a father's love. And this was when we were still together. He has no inclination or aptitude for fatherhood. Maybe it was because he hasn't had a father around during his own childhood. How could I have known, surmised that? It went from bad to worse as time went on. He learned though over the years to compensate for his failings, to fabricate feats of sleight of hand involving the juggling and proffering of vast amounts of money secured by profound investments during those times that he was able to avoid the paying of significant child support until he managed to create an endearing image of daddy dearest that was accepted by one and all as verity.*

Just as soon as I return from Juarez my divorce decree tightly held in my hot little hand I am off to make my first purchase as a single girl. *Woman.* Eileen and I drive to Smithtown to the dealership owned by her brother in law, Dennis, so that I can be assured to get a decent deal. I am hoping that he is different from his brother Patrick, maybe more trustworthy; I swallow hard, fighting the emergence of creeping apprehension. So what exactly are you looking for, Dennis asks, relaxed and confident, hands in his expensive trouser pockets, jazzy gold chain around his neck, a wide phony smile of deep interest and sincerity pasted on his well tanned face; he takes one hand out of its pocket, shakes his wrist and glances pointedly at a huge gold watch. A sports car, I answer with some trepidation, something jazzy, now that I am a single woman, again... He barely manages to cover his inherent disdain with patronizing condescending warmth. What color do you have in mind? Gee, I never thought about that. How about blue, he asks, and I am embarrassed to say that blue has never been my favorite color. But there it is, a baby blue Austin Healy Sprite convertible, tiny and adorable, and I am in love. I fall in love so easily. It is evident that he thinks this is all a waste of time, that it is so cute that a woman is attempting to purchase an automobile by herself, has ventured out into this protected private male world. Would you like to test drive it, asks Dennis and I answer, yes please, butterflies leaping and bounding in my stomach and chest. I get into the car and stare at the instruments blankly, wondering why there are three peddles on the floor, and Dennis asks smirking, do you drive shift, and I tell him, no, I have no idea what that is... so he gets in and teaches me about shifting and we lurch around the empty part of the car lot grinding and scraping, and pretty soon I actually get the idea. So he pats me gently on my head and he fills out the papers, takes my check, sends an employee to obtain the new plates, and I am quickly on the road home, Eileen in my car directly behind me. I glance back and see Dennis and his cohorts standing in front of the dealership, hands clasped behind collective backs, shaking their heads in wonder and derision And of course it is rush hour, and we get caught again and again in the usual commuter traffic and it seems at each and every traffic light on route 25 and I am leaping and bucking and stalling at every move; I finally arrive breathless and weary back home, ease into the driveway with pride and newly acquired aplomb, disembark before my audience of wondrous youngsters. I am not content to park my new treasure in the driveway behind the Dart, but as soon as the kids are settled down I call my sitter and prepare to take it to Brooklyn that very first night to show it to Hope. Once in her kitchen after she has made the perfunctory appreciative noises over my latest accomplishment, I am good for the evening, sipping tea and talking, and it is past midnight when I depart. I am enjoying the experience of driving a sports car, vroom, vroom, and as I negotiate the Belt Parkway with a newly acquired expertise, high on freedom and excitement don't notice at first that faint knocking sound. But now it has become more and more evident, KNOCK, KNOCK, KNOCK, getting louder and louder, **KNOCK KNOCK KNOCK** the knocks closer and closer together, until it becomes a sort of explosion and the car begins to slow down and here I am stuck in Coney Island when the engine blows. I pull over to the side, barely, as the engine expels its last gasp, and I sit there, helpless and terrified in alien surroundings in early morning. Soon, bright headlights come up behind me illuminating the entire inside of the tiny auto and way beyond and slow down, come to a stop. Two huge men in black suits dismount this immense black sedan and ask me what the trouble is. I notice their gold neck chains and heavily encrusted rings as they lean into the car window. Yeah, one says, popping the lid and checking the engine, you're out of oil, you have a major leak. Oh God, I moan, I have to get home to my kids, and I live all the way out on Long Island. I guess you have to phone for help, says one with great innocence, and he points at a brightly lit phone booth several blocks away, certainly too far for me to walk. We'll drive you, says one firmly, and noticing my reticence, or what could be called terror, says, listen, lady, we can drive you or you can walk, it makes no never mind to me, but what is it exactly that you are so afraid of? If we wished to harm you, we would have already done so. So I get into this giant car surrounded on both sides by two very solid friendly enough well turned out baboons and off we go. I am not surprised when they pass right by the phone booth, a sensation of hot lava sinking in my stomach, and as I struggle with the words to discover my fate, one of the guys says with a grave smile, don't get your bowels in an uproar, we're just going to a place we know where you can warm up and we can get some refreshment. So we pull up at the no name bar somewhere in Greenpoint, long black limousines parked up and down the street in front of this pub without signs. There is a warm vibrant smoky buzz of conversation peppered with *dese, dem, dose* and various other Brooklyn vernacular. Names are called out, Lefty, Mugs, Killer; it is a veritable Damon Runyan festival. A few women round out the group, miniskirts and black mesh stockings, elaborate beehive coiffure, burgeoning cleavage and sparkling jeweled adornment. My new friends and saviors insist on buying multiple drinks enjoying my discomfort. They go through elaborate maneuvers of treating each other to multiple libations in a show of one-upmanship and patently transparent noblesse oblige that succeeds in being completely intimidating. I am too frightened of unknowable repercussions to refuse, to their great amusement, and I swallow more Scotch sour that I would have liked. Finally tiring of this sport they allow me to use the phone, after which they graciously offer to drive me all the way home to East Northport. So I am rescued by mobsters on the Belt Parkway in Sheepshead Bay, Brooklyn that evening. *When I relate the story to Hope the following day, she laughs with a great sad gusto. I could have told you that you were safe, never in any danger; it is an inviable part of their code about protecting women, children, family. How do you know that, I ask her, and she tells me about her own experience, her marriage, her husband's family. My jaw falls so low that it almost rests on my chest. This explains a lot about Hope, and her strange lifestyle, preoccupations and avocations.*

૏‧ૐ

I alternate working round the clock with sporadic sleep and an occasional trip to some psychic or other seeking any solace in the possible foreknowledge of what the future holds looming so impossibly ahead with nothing so much as more projected agony and loneliness, and forego social life having no energy for the efforts involved in getting myself together and running around. I have precious little time to spend with the children, now that their upkeep gobbles up such huge blocks of time itself. Steve sees them as little as possible does as little as can be done for them. As far as companionship goes I have to content myself with few and sporadic relationships with various ill-chosen and undesired admirers with little saving grace except that they offer contact with another warm human in the name of love in a cold and unfeeling world where work is the only reality.

Another dingy afternoon. What season is it? No one can say but the grayness permeates everything. I struggle through the healing of my inner soul my tortured self, the search for my new direction enveloped in a morose cocoon devoid of color or season. I am struggling with bombarding fears, the chilled and chilling forces of the world and all of its material demands and disappointments. The ancient portable radio is rattling on and on in the background. I hear that an El Al jet has been hijacked to Algeria which doesn't lift my spirits. Once again I find myself seated at Hope's kitchen table. The entire scene from pink flowered wallpaper to white enameled cabinets and white subway tile backsplash and counter, diamond pattern leaded glass windows covered with organdy curtains constitute the most intense and compelling reality of my existence even though I am never able to bring it back to mind when I am absent from it, even though it seems my only valid reality when I sit here.

Read my cards Again, Hope, I plead, fearfully aware that in some perverse moment of capricious whim she could deny me possibly annoyed with my obsession.

Hope sighs and gives me that little look, indulgence, affection, combined with exaggerated annoyance. Removes the worn deck from its hiding place amongst the secret contents of that special drawer. Okay, Lynnie, she sighs again, with that feigned impatience, slight exasperation; shuffle them, mix them three times, and give me the cards. I don't know why you persist in believing all of this, she adds petulantly.

But you believe it, don't you? You do it, and it always works. I mean, you're never wrong.

Ah, Lynnie, there's more to all of this than tarot cards, maybe someday I'll explain it all to you.

You mean like in Edgar Cayce and Sybil Leek and Arthur Ford?

Well, sort of, but more like that Druid thing we've talked about, that is what comes closest to mind. But there's even more. It goes deep into the origins of mythology, the beginnings of man's spiritual realizations, the accumulations of the beliefs of ancient peoples.

You mean like astrology? Like all those ancient sciences and philosophies of antiquity?

Exactly!

I sigh. There is so much to learn, and I have wasted so much time. My entire life so far had been nothing but a waste of time. How am I to encompass all of this, get enough wisdom in time for it to solve my problems? I need guidance to take care of my children, to find my destiny. Where am I going, I muse out loud, lost in my meandering thoughts. There is a lengthy pause as Hope stares at me her own thoughts obviously going inward.

I can feel her encompassing me with her warmth and simpatico. I know an astrologist, she says, I saw his name in the *Voice*, and asked some friends and he is very well spoken of. She browses through the pages of the paper, runs her fingers down the columns, here it is, she says, Rod Chase, Astrological Charts, Readings. Why don't we make appointments and get our charts done? Hope's eyes twinkle with mischief, I can see her escaping into some other place where some insipient thirst for experience, combines with relief from the boredom of everyday life. I am thrilled that I am more to her than just a lost soul, a bothersome pest, one of the many gnats that swarm around her sacred hive seeking succor feeding on the blood of her soul. I preen myself inwardly with this sudden knowledge of my new status, bustle around making plans for our outing, acquiring dates and times for the perusal and ultimate digestion of the sage's words.

We meet one crisp winter evening in quaint picturesque Brooklyn Heights and walk with awed expectation through the embracing canyons of solid old brownstones. We pass the time until our appointment sipping wine in a tiny traditional old English country pub glowing in its manufactured antique patina.

We sweat silently in tense expectation needing for some reason to be properly on time rather than to appear to be overly anxious.

Finally we stroll the chilled street with barely held restraint to his particular brownstone, climb the clacking, echoing stairs to his room and are somewhat disarmed, dismayed to see the disarray in the midst of obvious poverty, smell the stench of the place. We had pictured something more elegant, sumptuous, traditional, But no. Antithetically Rod Chase is matinee idol handsome in that fair chunky Nordic fashion, tall and svelte. All my instincts come to attention and Hope noticing whispers, no, Lynne, he's gay and I feel myself blushing crimson, stupid, stupid. Too bad I think, he is really attractive in that fifties pretty boy movie star kind of way, long swooped blond coif shading classical tanned features, six feet of perfectly ripped buff body. On second glance I see that he is enveloped in a cloud of dissolution, decay, slowly rotting around the edges from the outside in, or is it the other way around. But soon as he brings out piles and piles of astrological charts and wanders off into tandems of explanation, refers to anecdotes of mythology and biblical text it becomes obvious to me that he is an extremely talented and ascetic man of science and philosophy, perhaps in fact another lost soul seeking the ultimate truth. We sit in the rubble of his domain in full view of the reeking scummy dishes piled in the filthy sink, the rank unmade bed, piles of discarded garments in various states of disarray, the disorder of heaps of books and papers. Although the door to escape beckons as though it has digits and arms of its own we are paralyzed to inaction by shock and embarrassment unwilling to hurt his already threatened feelings. We are reluctant to threaten this fragile creature, this ranting psychic drowning in his own pain and instability. Yet, he bears an aura of otherworldliness, has a sense of power, divinity about him that effectively forces us to wait and listen. The more he speaks the more he radiates a kind of inner beauty that soon corrects our earlier judgments.

When he begins to speak we are instantly mesmerized. I find myself holding my breath as I notice that Hope is looking at him the way I look at her. We have handed him our lists of facts and he has begun his reading. Hours later we are as full spiritually as though we have consumed an immense feast, heaps and platters of food and Hope prods him with gentle compassion into other areas esoteric. For the most part I sit silent and mute way out of my league absorbing everything that is said like a giant sponge. Arcane details of stars and ancient history, ungraspable mythologies of Greek gods and goddesses and their exploits and tragedies. Ishtar, Isis...Aphrodite, Athena, Artemus, Demeter (which translates to Hope)...Apollo, Dionysus, Zeus... Names and titles and stories of cryptic particularity roll off his tongue so quickly that I am barely able to absorb it all. He ties it all into the history and practices of the Druids and rambles on...

The great thirst that I have for esoteric knowledge and information, my hunger for awareness of the unknown rivets my attention to them as they speak. (The dimness and gloom and dinginess and overpowering sense of doom become the stage set for an otherworldly communion.) Hope nods at me, seems to be listening to some higher power that is speaking to her and bids me to be patient. I yield to my own priestess and wait silently for what I do not know.

The dynamic changes seamlessly before I am aware that it is happening. Drawn to whatever essence it is that pulls us all to cleave to, confide in Hope Rod sloughs off his cloak of sage and begins to pour his heart out into her gently cradling presence. I watch her as she changes subtly, edges and features moving and morphing into something else, a phenomenon to which I have become accustomed, as the room fills with strange moving shadows and shifting forms. She is no longer what she has recently been, the quintessence of a suburban matron out for an evening's entertainment but a powerful creature commanding focus. This is almost too much for me to take in.

Most of what they talk about goes way over my head. References to mythology and philosophy seem almost to be an exercise in speaking in tongues causing my brain to ache with trying to understand. Similarly all their veiled references to the gay world and his involvement in it which is becoming increasingly clear. My knowledge of this world is practically nonexistent at this time but I have been acquainted with enough gays at Pratt to understand that he is not at all happy or accepting of his situation.

There are quite a few references to a book that appears to be Rod's bible of sorts by Robert Graves and I soon realize that he considers himself to be a kind of prophet of Graves's *White Goddess* which is the name of the book. *She is the goddess of birth, love and death,* he explains, *inspired by the phases of the moon, based on pagan mythology. The Gaelic names of the Ogham letters of the alphabet,* he chants as if in a trance, *contain a calendar with a key to ancient liturgy involving the sacrifice of sacred kings and ancient Greek hexameter describing the goddess. It is a poetical language bound up in mythology and popular religious ceremonies dating back to the Stone Ages honoring the Muse, the Moon Goddess. How dare those critics question Grave's scholarship, the Goddess herself?* (He is pacing, wringing his hands.) *He has not deceived us,* he rants on, agitated, *we are not misled innocents, Graves does not merely deliver eloquent deceptive statements about her, the goddess is not nebulous...* I listen fascinated although most of this floats enticingly above my awareness yet strange tremors overcome me and I somehow know that I am in the presence of some great truth and power. Later I ask Hope to explain it all to me and immediately run out to procure my own copy of *The White Goddess.* I struggle to comprehend it all, find myself drowning in obscurity and contradiction. I am enchanted by the concept of Grave's Tree Calendar and Zodiac, juxtapositions of Winter Solstice, Spring Equinox, Sagittarius and Gemini; suddenly see a connection to my love of trees and forests and my landscape painting. A close relationship develops between Rod and me, mostly over the phone. He is seeking respite and salve for his tormented spirit, craves connection and understanding. I am craving entrance into this closed world of secret esoteric knowledge.

Hope teaches me about the entire cult and mythology of the Goddess, the connection to Greek Mythology, the parallels with the Kabala, Judeo-Christian philosophy, Druids and Wicca, and I feel a great expanding sense of wonder and awe, a sudden kinship with all that she says. I feel the power of this Goddess coursing through me; see Hope as her disciple and representative on this earth. Sent to me by a strange and ironic combination of circumstances that merely seems to make more concrete and certain my belief that here is the answer to my quest for understanding, power, and solace in a cold and unrelenting world. Juxtapositions of planets and stars and entire galaxies seen and interpreted in analogous traditions and language by ancient sages in parallel cultures, evolved into complex fable and rhetoric explaining that which can otherwise not be known. It is a sort of Aldous Huxley moment, Huxley in the midst of a psychotic break, everything in his world more real than real... I am experiencing an awakening to answers for ancient mysteries to questions that have plagued mankind since time immemorial. My senses soar, hope and spirit, as I embrace this new theology and draw on it for strength and direction careful to obey the orders and cautions of my prophets. I dedicate an Ode to Robert Graves; *sir, I am a slave also to your Muse, your White Goddess, led by her encompassed by her powerful force, tantalized by wisdom sought, tasted of knowledge's famous apple, tickled by faint fading glimpse of eternity...* I have a new preoccupation, talking with spirits of relatives and dead authority about either my inspirations or insecurities; denials, demands for proof, critique of my connection, technical squabbles,

I maneuver the Car over endless roadways in my daily sojourns, my mind roiling with a combination of my multitudes of monumental personal problems and new and disorganized, unclassified ungraspable knowledge. Suddenly I am praying to Ishtar, to Isis, to universalities of Goddess, but it is the sense of the pastoral, the Druid tree folklore, jackals and birds and serpents, Greek mythology, Ninefold Goddess and Threefold Muse permeate the atmosphere, lost in meditation and fervent plea. I juxtapose the names of Ishtar and Isis and the text of my extensive intonations of Hail Mary and although it seems a little weird, I am satisfied that it will work. Is it not true that God is One, doesn't that mean that all gods are the same? Shma Yisroel, I think, Adonoy, Elohenu, Adonoy echod...Here oh Israel, the Lord our God, the Lord is One. Isn't that what I was taught so many years ago? I am a mere child though, experimenting with new catechisms ignorant and naive and shallow. I seek true love and answers to matters that are no more than trivial, mundane, venal that must have left the gods rolling around on the floor with mirth much as I have imagined Hope responding to some of my ridiculous anecdotes or questions has done if metaphorically.

The reality of it is that I believe; believe again. Believe in something, anything, in a world that had gone flat, without meaning. Believe and derive power from it whether this power gains impetus from outside this world or from within my own tenuous being. I believe in this all powerful earth mother goddess whom I feel is equal at least to any other god being worshipped by my fellow humans. I can therefore believe in Mary, and in her son, Jesus, the rabbi, who became quite naturally to me the wronged Jewish prophet who developed the natural liturgical progression to Judaism. It is the natural evolution of the faith into which I have been born which I have believed in all of my life until recently when everything in my world soured. Now I am able to evolve my very own ideology custom made for my specific personal failings and needs answerable to my own private inner gods. I can reach down into the depths of my own soul, my core being, and access the strength that thus far in my life has been dissipated, flung wispily into the winds taking with it my very life force, leaving behind the mere husk of a person too enfeebled by indirection to even move.

I am never able to observe Graves' reasoning in impending versions that the God of Judaism, one male omnipotent god, and its descendants are to blame for the demise of the White Goddess and thus most of the world's woe; the possibility of such a concept never even touches my awareness.

I continue to exist, to survive, in this strange pixilated world that has become my new reality.

Back in the real world Jackie Kennedy is marrying Aristotle Onassis and Shirley Chisolm becomes the first black woman to be elected to Congress which is monumental. The cherry on the top of the sundae is when TV viewers are aghast as a ballgame is cut to allow for the screening of *Heidi*, oh horrid day. Then, in a most extraordinary move for mankind the first astronauts orbit the moon and return safely. Indeed, *the times they are a changing*.

Still I make the voyage to Bay Ridge to see Hope whenever I can fit it into my schedule. We sit at that famous kitchen table drinking tea into the wee hours of the morning, on many occasions and as usual are interrupted by the strident sound of her telephone or a knock on the back door. Hope is much in demand by her coterie and that is just how she likes it usually. Now after my long drive I am invited to Friday night dinner, consistently pasta with Progresso clam sauce. Hope is not that much of a cook despite her adeptness with esoteric chemistry and leans toward whatever can be thrown together from canned goods.

❧

Hope, I can't believe how wonderful I am feeling, bubbles the real Ken Coulter not the iconic preacher bursting through the venerable door of Hope's kitchen his face aglow his expression animated his bearing fey and effeminate. She throws me a look replete with rolling eyeballs which I field knowingly; I have known for a long while now all about Ken, his relationships, his proclivities, his carny schtick at the Church of St. John.

Why, Ken, asks the unflappable Hope tending to the boiling of water and the opening of cans continuing to prepare her dinner working at the kitchen sink, just another busy housewife.

You'll never believe what has happened. Everything is hyperbole with Ken. *Guess what? Louie is leaving on a business trip and won't be back all weekend.* Louie is Ken's wealthy *husband. I have an entire weekend for myself.* He can barely contain his joy. He either doesn't see me or dismisses my existence as totally insignificant.

That's great, Ken, she answers without much enthusiasm, *do you already have plans?* I can tell that she doesn't care much, she has long ago become accustomed to Ken's rapid mood swings, exaggeration, and hectic social life, is bored already with his typical scenario. He is much more fun when he is preaching or divining, reading futures in his church over on Third Avenue, keeps his followers enchanted and paying with that old carny scam. I have long since accepted Hope's explanation of all of this, am becoming something of a sophisticate in matters spiritual. Hope and I have become friends of a sort, sisters.

Great God Almighty! Ken clasps his hands together and stares at the pink plaid wallpaper on the kitchen ceiling. Plans? *Do I have plans, Hopie? I have something set up so sweet that you won't believe it! I'll bet*, thinks Hope rolling her eyes again. I can tell what she is thinking by looking at the expression on her face. She is thinking that he has another cheap tootsie lined up at that cheesy gay gin mill over on Fifth Avenue, another cheap pickup, a young handsome moocher; another sad encounter of brief duration and limited value that is doomed to end in tears and recriminations. Ken Coulter the sad desperate gay minister of the Spiritualist Church who does not even know his own future fakes readings of his own faithful followers with carny tricks. Poor Ken loving the things that money can buy and craving even more young nubile boys trapped as he is in a loveless farce of a convenience *marriage* of his own making to the well-to-do Louie, trapped again by his sexual needs into a series of devastating, destructive one night stands whenever logistics allow, never giving up hope for true love, or failing that, *a sweet evening*, as he is wont to describe them.

Good, Hope murmurs softly, *have a great time.* She continues her dinner chores.

Ken sits down at the kitchen table kind of side saddle on the old wooden chair, a little awkward, not wanting to seem greedy wishing to not seem needy, to be abusing taking advantage of the relationship, of this tentative friendship, guilty in his need. After a short pause, he speaks. *Hopie?* A very hesitant question in his voice.

What, Ken? She is impatient, she knows what is coming, the inevitable. This is nothing new, she has been here before. She sighs.

I was thinking, Ken answers softly, *I was wanting this to be a sweet weekend...* So you mentioned, is her caustic reply, not even turning around.

...So I was thinking...do you think you could...fix me one of those potions? He is a mixture of dismal sincerity and abject terror. We all know what Hope is capable of if pushed. She has gone to great lengths to perpetuate her reputation for capriciousness, for retribution, for knowledge of the arcane, the deadly and supernatural. What will she do now? Is he is any danger? Who knows, with Hope.

She expels a huge sigh of resignation that says, *here we go again. Come on, Ken,* she says, *you of all people, know it's all bunk, give me a break.*

Well, I guess so, but could it hurt? Just in case it works? I know it does, it always does, couldn't you just do it anyway? Please? I need this weekend to be sweet.

You drive me crazy, she snaps, *you know better. What am I going to do with you? Okay, okay,* she says, *I'll get you your damned potion,* and she stalks off angrily, not really, just mocking, a little impatient, stifling a giggle, almost stomps upstairs to her inner sanctum, her bedroom, a little bit annoyed to have her dinner ministrations, this pleasant dusk disturbed. She returns a short time later to the kitchen which is filled with the living essence of Ken's palpable tension and anxiety.

He sighs with relief as she hands him the tiny bottle filled with foaming green stuff, but remains in his seat, despite an aura surrounding Hope that says that it is time to go. He is still not certain, not content.

Go, Ken, says Hope, *meaning it. You've got your stuff, now go. Have a ball.*

Hope? She has already turned back to the stove.

What now, Ken, she answers testily without turning around.

Hopie, what do I do with it?

She responds with an evil snicker, *I'll tell you what you can do with it.*

Please Hopie, I need this to work, I need this to be a sweet weekend.

She is fighting impatience. *Listen Ken,* she says in a tightly controlled almost monotone voice, *you take the stuff in the bottle, very carefully, and you place it on your body. On your forehead if you wish cerebral satisfaction, on your heart if you are looking for true love or romance, and on your belly button if your needs are of a more carnal variety.* There is a short silence.

Are you sure that will be enough, he asks in a small querulous voice?

Trust me, it's enough. It's enough already, Ken.

I am listening to this in a place of stunned silence.

Are you sure that's all I have to do? He pauses, and asks her, his voice tiny and tentative, *could you write it down, so I don't forget, make a mistake?*

As he continues talking, Hope quickly, impatiently scribbles the instructions on a sheet of yellow paper from a legal pad and thrusts it at him. *Take it,* she says. *And go. Ken, believe me, I am sure. I am also sure that if you do not leave right now, I will put a spell on you so evil and diabolical that you will never recover.* She is glaring her most menacing leer at the cowering Ken just a little repentant to have been so short with him but if she doesn't get a few minutes to herself before the family descends on her and her kitchen she will begin gravitating rapidly through the fucking ceiling. She adores her daughters, but her husband, Carmine member of a infamous crime family is hard to take. They have had a sort of truce, lived within a carefully regulated armed camp for many years. I have shared many dinners with them over these past months and they are usually over quickly, endured civilly and with minimal small talk.

Ken grabs the paper takes his green bottle and scurries quickly out the back door clutching his treasures to his bosom.

The late afternoon grayness creeps into the kitchen and Hope turns the phone ring down to its lowest decibel so she won't be disturbed by some other needy creature. She sits down at the kitchen table, pours us another cup of tea and we relax in the deepening dusk as the minutes pass on the frowning clock.

As ye sow, she murmurs to herself as the hot liquid courses down her throat immediately beginning to soothe her insides. I am able to hear the faint tinkle of the telephone somewhere far away and I can see by Hope's expression that she hears it also, it is prodding her and she looks at me and away. She will not answer it, she knows who it is. It continues ringing, demanding, insistent. But our eyes meet again, and there is always that unspoken question, what has happened, has something happened, and instinct overcomes resistance, something could be wrong with someone someplace and she reaches for the phone in case it is important.

*Hopie...*I can hear Ken's rasping voice at the other end as she holds the receiver away from her head, grimacing...*I was thinking...*

Hope moves the entire telephone over to the table and reaches for her cooling tea. The look on her face says that she is resigned to the continuation of this conversation, there is no way to escape it, to avoid this conversation but there is a sense of bristling. I feel the short hairs on the back of my neck standing on end. Hope is not to be disputed is most usually a force to be reckoned with. No one has the nerve to challenge her, no one dares to believe that she is not capable of creating the most odious spell; no one wishes to be recipient of her fury or what it might incite. We have all seen her ancient book of arcane magical incantations, observed her countenance when she is annoyed or angry; some of us have even been. recipient of her fury, real or magical.

Ken continues unabashed unafraid of that which he can neither sense see nor comprehend, he is so involved with his own drama. *Are you certain that this is all I have to do? Are you sure that this will work? Is there nothing else I can do that will make it even better?*

Hope aims a sharp glaring look at me. *He has his damned potion, he has all the instructions written down and listed in gory detail. What more does he want from my poor life?* She takes a deep breath. *Ken darling,* she simpers, saccharine dripping from her lips, *there is actually something else that I forgot and I am going to tell you what it is. BUT WHEN I HAVE FINISHED, WHEN I HAVE HUNG UP THIS PHONE, I DO NOT WISH TO HEAR YOUR VOICE AGAIN FOR A VERY LONG TIME, AT LEAST UNTIL AFTER THIS WEEKEND, AND THEN ONLY TO HEAR WHAT A FABULOUS TIME YOU HAD AND HOW HAPPY YOU ARE. GET IT?*

We can feel Ken shrinking, becoming smaller at the other end of the phone, we can sense his abject terror; still, he holds his ground. *Yes, Hope,* he answers obediently, *so what do I do?*

You want a sweet time, right? You take some sugar. You have sugar, don't you? You rub sugar on the soles of your feet. And when you have done this, I promise you that whatever you do it will be very sweet. I am noticing a slight tremor of naughtiness, almost evil, in her voice, and there is certainly a strange barbed piercing look in her eyes. She replaces the receiver in its cradle.

It appears that Ken is unaware of Hope's state of mind, is too intent on his plans to notice. Hope is smirking at the phone struggling to restrain the laughter that threatens to bubble from her chest and not at all surprised to hear it ring once again, She is prepared to answer quickly but lets it ring for a long time, staring at me with a look combined of fury and amusement. When she finally lifts the receiver and says, *WHAT* in an annoyed tone, Ken's disembodied voice continues as though there has never even been a brief halt in the conversation.

Hopie? He is tremulous, timid, but insistent. A pause, and then, very faintly, *I'm sorry.* Another pause. I can feel his terror and know his determination. Then: *I didn't know whether I was supposed to do the sugar before or after the potion?* It is a question.

It-doesn't-matter-when-you-do-it, is her tense answer, *just do it...and Ken? Don't Call Me Again!*

The evening wears on with the same old tedium, the usual supplicants who are called Loonies by Hope's husband Carmine make their appearances. Carmine and their two daughters who have appeared for dinner disappear quickly upstairs when dinner is over and Hope and I are left to commune and share time with the others who wander in and out on whim. Hope dispenses tea and sympathy, advice and Tarot readings as warranted depending on the particular need. Again she turns off the phone tucking it deep inside a drawer in mute desperation. Later when the last visitor has left and I have gone she goes upstairs and falls into a deep and dreamless sleep of exhaustion and of course has forgotten to turn off the bedroom phone in her fatigue. She tells me about it all the next morning.

The night is dark and heavy and she sleeps in a deep murky hole grateful for the respite, sinking into the depths of oblivion where remnants of her difficult life do not exist to taunt and torment her. At first she fails to hear the persistent jangle of the telephone, it exists in some faraway place where she doesn't wish to go. She reaches out for the phone automatically, without thought unaware what to expect, annoyed, even a little angry as consciousness slowly dawns. The clock says that it is four in the morning. Who could it be at this hour?

Hope? It is the once again tremulous but now also exultant voice of Ken echoing sharply over the line. She prepares to loose the full thrust of her wrath but something in his tone intrigues her, warns her off. She continues to listen as that familiar fury rises from her toes into her chest, gathering herself, marshalling all her forces of speech and coordination planning her most vitriolic invective.

Hopie! I knew you would be angry but I just had to tell you. IT WAS SO SWEET! Yeah. The only problem was that the sugar felt really weird sloshing around in my socks all night long.

Hope pulls herself up short frozen by these words her prepared diatribe halted before ever beginning. She sits up straight in her bed, pulls the down quilt around her holds it up to her chin. *Sugar in your SOCKS?* She queries hesitantly feeling the rumble of mirth rising in her chest, forcing the querulous treble from her voice. Cavernous echoes of raucous guffaws are threatening to burst from her tightly held lips. Suddenly, she is very, very alert. At attention. What madness is this, now? She cancels her desire to slam the receiver down in its cradle after inflicting scathing and extremely painful punishment on the infidel and waits impatiently for the story. This had better be good, she thinks.

Yeah, says the always effervescent Ken, *it's about the sugar. You told me to rub a little of it on the soles of my feet and I figured what could be bad and I thought if a little was good...and I wasn't certain how much...and I was afraid to call you again so I figured what could be bad? More would only be better. So I poured the sugar into the socks before I put them on and they sloshed a little. It felt weird, actually. It's true, it was a little uncomfortable and when I took my clothes off it spilled on the floor but he didn't notice and boy, was this evening ever sweet!*

Say good night, Ken, Hope gurgles barely controlling herself.

Somehow she manages to wait for morning to call me and tell me the end of the story. *These gay guys (that's not the word she uses) and their dramas,* she expostulates as she begins.

CHAPTER 59

I speak with Rod Chase frequently now, for I yearn to tap into his connection with God Power, a place to be that promises respite from the eons of failure and guilt that drive me mercilessly. I am desperate to make contact with whatever lies beyond the hidden veil of the unknown, power that once unleashed promises to solve all of my problems into those far-reaching fearful limits of eternity. I am enthralled to have discovered this strata of life of which hither-to-fore I have never even conceived of. I develop an insatiable hunger for knowledge of the source of this power. I run to visit Rod whenever my schedule permits, hungry to converse in fields of tantalizing secrets, ever ready to uncover some marvel of awareness that could be added to my increasingly growing store of spiritual knowledge.

One icy winter morning I drive the quixotic Sprite rapidly over the ruts and cobblestones of the BQE, the Brooklyn Queens Expressway and arrive in record time at the quaint and shabby streets of Brooklyn Heights, the only problem remaining is to find parking, a grave nuisance. Cursing city congestion I round the block several times becoming more and more impatient and annoyed and it finally appears out of nowhere, the only place that seems to exist at all right in front of a Russian Orthodox Church a marvel of Rococo Ukrainian architecture and statuary. The big old building beckons to me, I glance at my watch and note that I am nearly late for my appointment but some force beyond me draws me into its mystical and glowing core. I climb the deep stone stairs and open the heavy oak door reveling in the carvings and stained glasswork and masses of iconography, wander insensible with awe, encompassed by the strange spiritual feeling that pervades the atmosphere and seems to seep into my body, my very essence transporting me beyond the realm of sensibility. I stumble over to a marvelous lifelike sculpture of the Virgin Mary and obeying a strange ineffable force kneel at the base of it and light a candle one of many that stand brightly flickering row upon row their glorious heads waving and glowing in invisible breezes. I stare at the holy figure concentrating intensely on her expression, mindlessly exploring unknown thoughts and unrealized requests, lost in the moment not surprised when the folds of her clothing, her features, her lips appear to be moving as though she speaks to me. I hear no actual words but can feel her intensely inscrutable thoughts like hot soothing comfort food, sauce drenched pasta, thickly frosted chocolate cake, kung pao chicken in the pit of my stomach as though they have been transferred into my soul. They are full of love and wisdom, all knowing, all powerful, comforting. Problems will disappear and solutions will appear. Soon I rise to my feet and wander preoccupied into the brisk winter chill puzzling at the excessive feelings and disconnected thoughts that churn ineffably in my mind.

I continue on my way toward Rod's apartment filled with a mélange of thoughts and emotions that refuse to gel impatient to convey them to someone, to Rod. I feel confused, struggle to find the words to describe what has just happened to me. A tiny shop appears down a few stairs, beneath a nearby brownstone and for no reason at all not even conscious of my actions I am descending the stairs entering the shop. I don't have any idea why I am doing this but I sense that there is something that I am supposed to do, I don't know what. Since it is a shop it would seem that I am supposed to buy something. The store is filled with junk and costume jewelry and edgy crafts and the kind of second-hand stuff that abounds in the inner city. I can see nothing here that I would even wish to receive as a gift. I feel at a loss yet I am compelled to continue looking around, helplessly turning in circles, feeling really stupid. I am certain that there is something here that I am meant to acquire. Then suddenly there is this large flat glass case filled with more jewelry and junk, religious stuff, a stunning silver cross, and it all but leaps out in front of me. There is no doubt in my mind that this is the item I am destined to purchase. I never even give it a thought never question my actions just go ahead and buy it convinced that something of great importance has just happened. The cross is heavily carved, a nativity scene on one side, the crucifixion on the other. I hold it tightly in my palm feeling power course through me. I race up the stone stairs to Rod's apartment to show him my treasure.

There is a poem called *Crossroads* that I have written about where I have come, where I am today, in my search for faith. I add this poem to the ever growing pile of my soul's outpourings of pain, desire, and blind despair. The words come to me in my various states of induced flow from a place of such dire desperation and agony, almost trancelike in their hypnotic essence. I always feel as though some stronger force that the normal or accepted was guiding both my mind and my hand. I remain under the spell of mystical forces that hold the spiritually moribund parts of me together with fragile and tenuous threads, and read and reread the weighty missiles for some modicum of mortal strength.

I live in a place gone limp from constant flagellation both of a spiritual and economic nature. I read over the results of what lies before me on the paper. Even so, I revel in the knowledge that indeed, I could not be at least that failure in life, that bankrupt nonentity, that waster of life I have believed myself to be to this date, ever intensely spiraling downward. Why, I had written this poetry that to my mind appeared to be marvelous, it had sprung from my own mind, like the daughter of Zeus, it touched the soul of the reader and might even some day stand on its own and speak to multitudes. It was only much later, years later, when my kernel had been chaffed on the threshing room floor spoken of by Khalil Gibran, and the very core of me lay exposed all of the residue and irrelevancy scraped away, that I reread the words, long stored away in a faded manila folder in the recesses of some aging file cabinet, and saw from the various point of a new and shining place that my own words were indeed universal, that they applied not only to incidences of love, true and unrequited, but to the whole image of life itself in all its most esoteric and consummate meanings.

Years later I realize what I was going through was universal, the typical confusion along the pathway of self discovery, yet it was easier to believe in another than to believe in myself. I lived in that never-never-land of bars and booze and endless searching for love, love of another of the opposite sex, love as it translated in mutual physical contact, mutual exchanges of material nature, cleaving and cloning and curing. I resided in a place of heavy guilt, weighty responsibility, burdensome obligation, made the more imponderable with each passing day, each added infraction to the great universal code as translated by all those in the facility of guidance in the years that had preceded it.

Cliff had rescued me from the stone hell of Steve's non-tactility, non-communion. Richie rescued me in turn from my own downward spiraling self-destruction in direct response to incongruous and cumbersome caches of precious guilt. Why did I suddenly respond to feelings that seemed to surface, of great tenderness, feelings of deep and untenable compassion and empathy for those whom I came across who seemed to be as spiritually bankrupt as I was myself but were too lost in the whirlpool of it all to know? Why did I feel compelled to become a saver of souls? Why indeed were all of these lost souls, from the first which was Richie himself, recently deserted and divorced in a most painful manner, down the line, through the faceless nameless persons I found draped over gin mill counters, at sidewalk art shows, littered all around the parameters of my life, waiting to be found, picked up and saved?

Indeed, by the time I trip across Rod Chase, the pattern has established itself, but being right here in the midst of it, I never see the design emerging. Well, I make the trip to Brooklyn Heights some mornings; as soon as the kids are safely on the school bus, I race out of the house. I run in answer to frantic calls, threatening suicide, I clean the festering filthy apartment and listen to the ramblings of a drunk, albeit an intensely spiritually one, about the powers of the Imperious Goddess, Ishtar, of the waving dancing speaking trees, of the glib rantings of Graves who exposes all of the above. I hold his trembling hand and put my arms around him when the delirium tremors begin, I even bring him yet another bottle, when it seems the only way to save his pitiful life. I hold his head when he vomits into the reeking pail that lives next to his putrid bed, sponge his forehead with cold rags. I mourn the fact that his brilliance, his great fight will drown with him, and be lost to the world. I plead with him to get help for his decaying body so that he may have a living vessel to contain his beautiful soul.

Ultimately, I give up, and leave him to his own devices. I lose track of Rod, in those years, for by then I have found Eddie, true to the prophecies of Ken and Rod; the readings of my astrological chart and the exactness of the description leaves me speechless...the very perspicuity of it all makes the whole thing the more reasonable, for Eddie emerges as another piece of the puzzle, merely another section of the great pattern that is yet to be revealed. I do hear in later years that Rod had somehow himself come to grips with the guilt that he carries over his sexual predilections, and has gone on to great heights and lucrative successes as an astrologer to the rich and famous. I continue however to rescue lost souls in great excesses of maternal ablution never realizing the import of it all, never seeing either the pattern or the direction or the end to it all. Finally, did I satisfy the payments of some ancient or not so ancient karmic debt? Did I come to the end of the coupons in the booklet, and reach my own crossroad where now I could choose to move ahead with a free heart, a burden-free soul?

Oh, I am so smug and complacent in my new knowledge so painfully obtained from Hope and Rod that explains the secrets of life and prescience, newly aware that I am now holding the key to the universe in my own palm. I jump up and catch this new knowledge like a punted football on the opposition one-yard line, and clutching it to my heaving bosom, run with it down the field, avoiding alike all interception, all blockers, all obstacles. With the same intensity that comes only with redemption and true intellectual conceit, I invent my own rules and interpretations, racing excitedly, seeking the ultimate realization of the finish line. I make up my own prayers heady with new power, with the need to make some dreams at least come true, to create at least some minor viability in the struggle to survive.

I bless Hope and Rod and Robert Graves with grave intensity, and lie in my lumpy bed in a room grown crowded with my works in progress and a world of spirits, and pray. Meditate, and pray. Pray with careful detail, custom tailoring the words to information tediously gleaned from Hope and Rod, shrewdly mindful of pitfalls and precipices, smug, oh so smug in my newly acquired knowledge and wisdom. Be careful what you ask for, warns Hope, for you will inevitably get it. You may even get more that you bargained for. I am so clever. And then...Don't you realize that what you ask for always comes with a price tag? Oh my dear, for every request received, there will be a price to pay. So, be very careful, darlin'.

Oh please, Holy Goddess, oh all powerful Ishtar...I must, absolutely must achieve success as an artist. This is my life. Cross out *life*. We don't wish that word to be taken literally. Change it to, this means everything to me. I'm still not sure...*everything*? Oh, well, leave it, you know what I mean. Ishtar, please bring me success. At least, please help me to make a living at my work so that

I can provide for my children. Please find me someone to share my life so that I will not be alone. I cannot face life all alone. I promise you, I will pledge you a portion of my work, I will do work in your name, please, help me now to pull myself out of this pit that is claiming me as its own.

As is usual, in no time at all, not only have I immediately found new themes and methods but the phone is ringing off the hook with sudden unexpected and lucrative orders. The multi-limbed octopus of my economic structure is fed, and once again satiated. Tension is reduced, and I am able to relax, because of this modicum of success. I relate this grand news to Hope with awed conceit, still in a state of wonder, and tell her of course of my ardent pleas, that had to my shock and surprise been answered in full.

You asked for success and love. Okay. And you promised WHAT demands Hope in a tone expressing growing horror.

My art, I answer, wondering at her chagrin, a sensation of fear creeping icily across my neck. Why?

My God, darlin', don't you know what you are saying? How could you be so careless?

But Hopie, I answer, as her meaning begins to dawn, I chose the words very carefully. I promised, I pledged a piece of my art, what could be wrong with that? A faint memory tinkles across my mind, of a silent plea some time ago when I was so anxious to connect with Cliff, when I offered to give half my life. Terror grips me in its icy talons, suddenly. I am speechless, a tight claw gripping my throat. I fear to tell Hope the rest.

Honey, honey, you have to be so careful. Words are not always what they seem to be. Did I not tell you that you will have to pay for prayers answered? Do you not realize that when you promise your art you may be made to pay with an arm, or an eye? *God forbid!* Don't you see what a dangerous game you are playing?

But Hope, I never thought...

That is true. You never think, she snaps. *(I have noticed that she is losing patience with us all, these days).* What am I going to do with you? Maybe, just maybe, we can mitigate the damage. I'll see what I can do. In the meanwhile, promise me that you will not play around with stuff that is beyond your knowledge and comprehension, alone.

I promise, and frightened half to death, wondering about that half of my life that I pledged, and I am very careful in the coming days in the way I word my pleas. The thought crosses my mind, quickly sent away that there is a possibility that Hope is playing some game of her own with me. I dismiss this thought summarily believing it to be unworthy.

But there are more things in heaven or hell than are obvious to me. All of this exists in a bubble outside of my real life, which is caring for the children and earning enough money to do so. And the inevitable loneliness.

CHAPTER 60

1969

The week stretches out in incessant continual toil, no end in sight. The days run into one another barely separated the dark inexorable nights filled with tedious long hours of steady unrelenting work. Canvasses in multiples of sizes are piled on every available surface, organized by color, and sometimes subject; hints of blue and green, red, violet, purple, blue vibrating, peeking out from in between in effervescent streaks and stripes of pulsating hue. I take few tentative breaks when, too exhausted to accomplish another stroke I lay my brush down for a while, collapse fully clothed onto the welcoming embracing bed.

I am working now in the master bedroom wing which has become my studio, rarely leave it, eat, sleep, and work in the same spot. The Baby Grand piano that I have purchased in a moment of madness at the Northport Salvation Army Thrift Shop now lives in the area that previously housed Steve's desk; I am determined to revive my piano skills as a part of my personal restoration. I can sense a difference to the days as the week's end morphs into weekend; Helen the housekeeper leaves, the children arrive, meander in one by one as they return from school, cluster, coalesce around me as I work telling me stories, listing gripes and complaints, presenting their never ending questions. My friends, Eileen, Diane, Dorothy mostly come by and sit for a while watching me work and meander off to other occupations. I sense a gradual leaching of spinal starch, feel myself begin to wilt; will myself to remain strong and upright, smile and hug and offer loving and cogent responses I do not truly feel, prepare dinner, return robot like to my work.

Ultimately Steve appears for his famous obligatory Sunday visit. He arrives exactly as my kitchen clock reaches 9:00 o'clock a.m., punctual as ever, He rarely if ever takes them anywhere, remains at the house all day. His routine still never varies. He turns up bearing one dozen Dunkin Donuts which would total thirteen with the predictable freebee. Have no fear, he shouts out with exuberance, Daddy's here. He plops the Sunday *New York Times* on the double bed in the former master bedroom, tunes in the TV for the sports programs, and ignoring me settles himself on the bed, closing the door so that the children will not disturb him.

Sometimes we brush inadvertently past each other barely touching, but there is that old electrical current pulsing in that spot that was touched. Or we find ourselves face to face and there is a momentary connection between us, initiated perhaps by habit and loneliness. So we fall together onto the old marriage bed consumed by a brief moment of passion and are married again for a few fleeting poignant moments, followed by heartfelt tears at the inexorable ways of Fate and our own foibles. Soon, whatever closeness has been engendered turns again to rancor and sarcasm and I leave him to his Times and sports programs remembering the times of trauma and his neglect when Andrew was small and when Tracy was born, and hearing the door snap shut behind me, find some other diversion to pass the time. How can I work when he is in the room? Promptly at 5:00 p.m., Steve reappears and announces that he is going for dinner (I visualize the rolling out of red velvet carpets and the trumpeting of brass instruments in accompaniment) as he predictably disappears returning in one half hour with a bag containing six MacDonald hamburgers and six small bags of fries, sometimes a one liter bottle of Pepsi. No more, no less, no change. And then he leaves, disappearing into the great unknown of Steve-world to be neither seen nor heard from until the next Sunday morning. That is the extent and degree of his involvement with his children, those precious beings whose custody he is willing and ready to go to any lengths to acquire; that plus the twenty more or less dollars per week, per child, that he is required to pay by legal contract.

He rarely brings anything, save for those few aforementioned items of fast food; maybe a box of Goobers, his special gift of love, to me, back in the fifties, in the old halcyon days. His stinginess has always been a family joke, everyone laughs at Steve's adorable penury; it is a huge joke. In the old days, on one occasion he gave me a set of steak knives collected weekly as part of a promotion at a local Exxon station where he purchased gasoline, and another time a chipped serving bowl won by raffle at a monthly Kiwanis dinner. I never, ever was given either pocket money or had a request for some small amount for a minor luxury item answered, or for that matter even one of necessity, granted; if it was not for my mother and surprisingly enough, Aaron, I could not have managed to survive in those days. Aaron had been the originator of the grand entrance announcement, arriving Sunday mornings to imaginary trumpets on unfurled red carpets with giant bags of bagels and doughnuts; have no fear, Grampy's here. His son obviously believes that by adopting the same mantra, he automatically wears the cloak of generosity and caring which in turn makes it real.

Being married to Steve had been a kind of Hell. Being divorced is merely another side of that coin; Hell, that is. He had tried to own me, get me to give up pieces of myself. He took great pains to convince me that I was inadequate, mentally ill, even. Now my reality is that spread thin by my responsibilities I am made worthless by my exhaustion and loneliness. In addition to all my other jobs and responsibilities I am now charged with the task of putting myself back together again like Humpty Dumpty, one fragment of delicate shell at a time. Yesterdays... all my troubles seem so far away, now it looks as though they're here to stay... Oh I believe in yesterdays...

The entire bedroom, converted into a workshop cum studio, is piled with canvasses of different sizes, arranged according to color and subject and state of completion; I am a veritable factory of art, turning out quantities that would make anyone's head reel. One can barely move around the room, for large pieces that are drying or are stacked like so many giant playing cards or dominoes out of the deck, arranged all over the room so that every inch of space is taken. Eileen insists gravely that she can see what I cannot, and that if I don't get away from all of this rather soon for at least a short time, I am in danger of a breakdown that Steve will not only relish but use to his own advantage. As a matter of fact, that is what he has hoped and prayed for; this, I have come to believe. This is his strategy. Just because you're paranoid doesn't mean they're not out to get you.

I alternate working round the clock with sporadic sleep interrupted only by an occasional trip to some psychic or other, seeking any solace available in any available specifics of what the future holds, that future that looms so impossibly ahead with no promise but projected agony and loneliness. I abstain from social life having no energy for the efforts involved in putting myself together or the simple sounding act of going out.. Visiting Hope is my only social life. I have precious little time to spend with the children, now that the efforts involved in working at my art to pay for their upkeep gobbles up such huge blocks of time itself. On occasion I drive over to Louise's house for quick dinner. Sometimes I connect with Richie when he drops by the house after work. Bruce and Wendi, in separate reconnoiters, curious, peek in my bedroom windows at night when I have company. In odd moments I have completed an awesome oil portrait of Richie, his glowing face is surrounded by a black velvety background utilizing everything I learned from Paul Puzinis incorporated in this labor of love which sits on my easel for company. I arrive home from a rare evening out, and discover that Bruce has destroyed it, slashed it into ribbons in a fit of jealousy. Bruce is accustomed to being the man of the house, in his father's absence, even when his father lived with us, now, he is claiming me as his own, resenting the competition, letting it be known that he will not share me with anyone. Oedipus is at work, and I am helpless to deal with this pattern.

In general, I have to content myself with minimal and sporadic male companionship most of which has little value except that they are contact with another warm human in the name of companionship in a cold and unfeeling world where work is the only reality. And Worry. As a matter of fact, I am working so hard that all of my friends begin to be concerned.

Yasser Arafat, I hear, is the new leader of Palestine forces, and then the news reports that a bomb has ripped the largest market in Jerusalem. My head is whirling with extraneous stuff, nameless fear, compassion, anxiety, and regret. My friends have their own ideas. They are pushing for me to find a rich man and marry again, so that all my problems will be solved. I hear echoes of my mother's admonitions over the years, it's just as easy to fall in love with a rich man as a poor man…but something is not registering.

I am so weary that I am easily convinced for my thoughts have been a jumbled mess of late, bordering rather closely on the suicidal, and so much of my time is spent in tears. The pressure is beginning to tell! This is a heavy burden for one person. What you need, says Eileen, is a week or two in the Caribbean and definitely not Jamaica; I've been there, luxury and sun and surf and music and new people. I allow Eileen to propel me limp and mute and obedient to George's Travel Service for plans and reservations, and before I know what has happened, we have arrived in Puerto Rico.

Today, 2009
So I have come to the end of the first part of this saga; it is the end of innocence. I send off the manuscript and move on to the next momentous chapter in my life which begins with my hopeful vacation to Puerto Rico, Rich Port, in search of rest, relaxation and destiny. If I had only known then what I know now, that I would lose my children as a direct result of this trip…

End

Preview of Book II

Unintended Circumstances

The present day 2009

Spring is morphing into summer. Rain pelts everything in sight, torrents wash across car and road enveloping the entire world in the middle of a steady determined late summer afternoon storm; windshield wipers scrape and whine their rhythmic moaning complaint. It has become a matter of rote, driving nearly mindlessly here and there, signaling automatically for approaching turns, taking one curve after another, curling and swirling down Swamp Road avoiding those ever present puddles that impersonate lagoons, hence Swamp Road…seeing the familiar sight of Merchant's Path disappearing into its masses of tall oaks directly across Route 114 connecting Sag Harbor to East Hampton while waiting for an opening between the steady flow of cars and trucks. It is five thirty, the height of commuter traffic, and even here at the end of the world, the tip of Long Island, the falling off place, there is a certain heightening of movement, an accelerating of activity and mass. Every place I pass is a conduit of memory, a button to be pushed that triggers words and sentences and sound and smell, a rapid fire fluttering and flickering of fleeting movie frames. It is almost too much, a cacophony of recollection, a true world without end.

I meet Eileen, a new Eileen on the way to our writing workshop nearly fifty years after those East Northport Arleigh Court days and my first marriage; she is Eileen Moskowitz, which tickles me, a fortuitous mystical supernatural combination of my two old early sixties buddies Shelley Moskowitz and Eileen Corby that cannot merely be a random act of happenstance, must have some metaphysical meaning in the greater picture; we meet in the parking area outside Pierson High, in Sag Harbor, on the Jermaine Avenue side, rolling spacious green lawns reaching up to the classic brick building, and I am on my mark ready get set go across town to pick up the Sag Harbor-Bridgehampton Turnpike, and commence the route, that well honed path, that famous short cut through the back roads to Southampton. Scuttle Hole to Deerfield to Lower Seven Ponds; Tinkers to Evers to Chance, whispers Mom in my ear, her pet baseball reference. I can not only see but hear her impish satisfied grin. The country roadways once framed by rampant masses of lacy white Queen Anne's Lace, wild lavender blue Chicory, brilliant orange Day Lily and staring golden

Black Eyed Susan are now edged by neatly manicured tasteful suburban lawns, and I am assaulted by a sense of loss, of nostalgia for times long gone.

Both Eileen and I are revved; we are titillated by the assurance of companionship, sisterhood, the promise of an audience for our creation of this week, the Tantalus of unpredictable gastronomical delights. We have grown close because we come from such similar backgrounds, although she is from Brooklyn and have reveled in comparing nostalgic mid twentieth century Jewish mores, family and food. For me, this gathering usually means the rapid fire clashing of synopses, the hastening of sorcerers' apprentices in my mind, the mad accumulation of words and ideas racing each other for supremacy on the page, the creation of pages and pages of thought and feeling. There is also that tricky element of critique that throws itself *in flagrante delecto* on top of all of the input offered by various instructors both solicited and uninvited alike. I am most excited on this particular day because I have almost solved a vital problem of formatting, the division of my lengthy memoir into sections, actually separate books, although I still need to discover the glue that will hold it all together.

But today, I am crushed by the weight of guilt, fighting valiantly and without success the worst of memories that cascade around me. I have been editing hundreds of pages, reading and re-reading, putting myself back out there in the horrendous past, dredging up details, seeking answers. The evidence is overwhelming. I have sought the villain in my story and it is me. Eileen, I say, sadly, I am afraid that the reason my kids despise me is that I am the one who is responsible for everything that went wrong. It is all about my bad decisions and flawed choices.

What are you talking about, she asks me with a wail of horror, running her long dark hair through her fingers, reminding me so much of a Jewish version of Hope. Eileen has just been reading the first book of my story in what it appears is going to be a trilogy; she feels it, she says, patting her chest.

I never should have divorced Steve in spite of everything. I should have made it work, kept the family together. Everything I have done in my life has resulted in harm and destruction. That's why I have lost my children. It is all my fault. I am responsible for the unintended circumstances.

But she reads me a riot act, haven't you been writing about all of this, reading your story out loud to us for all these months, didn't you tell all about how he treated you? How could you have stayed with him, under any circumstances? And, you made your choices and decisions after very careful thought and analysis, didn't you? That's what I thought, anyway. You did what you could. It certainly isn't your fault.

But there's more, I tell her, that you haven't heard yet...

I don't care, she says, I'm sure your reasons were good...

I am soothed, though not really convinced.

We arrive at the cultural center; find the group already sitting around the table, setting out the cuisine offering of the moment, chatting about their week. What are you reading tonight, asks Linda taking charge of the itinerary?

I am bombarded by a rush of thoughts, chapters and pages, momentous incidents and breathtaking emotions. A familiar sensation rolls over me...

It is the result of the continuing thoughts about my children, when they were small, old memories of untenable circumstances and uncontrollable pain; sadness and unnamed recrimination clutching at my heart. My weaknesses and flaws as an individual are directly responsible for my situation. Eileen's comforting words have not eliminated my craving for absolution, for affirmation of some sort; this goes back even further than more recent history.

࿐

February, 1969; Condado, Puerto Rico

The automobile moves raucously down the Avenida Ashford, spewing laughter and wild pulsating salsa, its occupants filled with that ebullient fiesta fever that permeates the entire island. It tears along, a sort of large finned Keystone Comedy Bus Latino Style of nondescript color sporting shag carpeting on both dashboard and rear window, an assortment of decorative and mystical trinkets dangling from the rear view mirror; baby shoes and great foam dice, elaborate crosses and plastic flowers. The great joy and gusto that fills its confined spaces, pours, no rolls out of the windows, anxious to be shared with great enthusiasm and generosity with the world at large. A woman walking along the street is immediate recipient, willing or not, of a magnanimous largess of spirit, tinted perhaps by a slight salacious intent that endorses that ever present *viaquera* ... horniness ... that seems to be one with the culture as well as the people.

I walk along the sidewalk, feeling an inexpressible effervescent joy of life. I don't know whether to credit this to the fact that this is my first vacation away from the children and weighty responsibility in many years, the pains, guilt, pressures, stresses and strains of my multifaceted and over complicated life, or the sensation of eeriness that persists after my visit to the Cathedral. It is true that I have been divorced now for less than a year, after nine years of internment in a hopeless marriage. Perhaps that sense of life moving along at full blast at an hour of the night (or does four a.m. designate morning?) that in a normal setting might have been silent and somnambulant and still. I feel strangely enough, safe, to be strolling along a twinkling concrete walk past boutiques displaying exotic wares, evening wear, negligees and bikinis of every imaginable variety, and hotels advertising gala entertainment. Cars and taxis zoom along, in and out of parking lots and circular driveways, meters clicking, spewing forth their resplendent and celebrating occupants only to pick up others in a moment to whisk them back to the place from which they had just left with their last load of celebrants; musical casinos. There is something in the air, something different that I cannot put my finger on, an aura, perhaps, of fantasy; a secret never never land not responsible to the world at large. Perhaps it is that unaccustomed tropical sibilance, that steamy air redolent with the odors of blossoming and rotting vegetation, the sensation of a black and sparkling unseeing sky twinkling protectively overhead and the cumulative reflecting street and store lights throughout that makes the night seem like day.

When the winged auto passes by as I walk along, half a dozen dark faces, framed by slick black coif or tumbling black curls, teeth flashing and eyes sparkling, are suddenly at the car window, one on top of the other, fighting to gain window space. The car bounces and jolts with the movement within. *Ave Maria, Venca, cheeeeca...Mira Pa Ya, Hombre* and that sibilant invitation theme song of the land, SSSSSSSSSSSSSSS, a kind of staccato whistling between the teeth to denote the presence of a female. I smile and allow myself to feel flattered, and stand a little straighter, mincing along on my high 1960's Cuban heels. I am aware that I make quite an attractive picture but I am unaware yet of the inherent nature of the Latino Male, and the hidden depths and complexity of the customs and mores of these people; I didn't know that all you had to be was female.

I have lost Eileen Corby somewhere. She is undoubtedly off with one of the mighty string of willing swains that she manages to accumulate with such ease. Back home, her dresser drawers continue to fill with hand stitched lingerie and gold earrings and bracelets and strings of pearls, which appear miraculously as her entourage of *friends* grows. I have no such luck, nor do I wish for it, for the men that she captures for her fun and games, including shopping and drinking sprees to be paid for later with favors, I find to be boring. Try as I might, the mere thought of such relationships annoys and disgusts me. True love, is what I seek. I am SO fine and pure, and SO lonely. Eileen thinks I am a laugh riot.

Eileen and I have spent the first few evenings bouncing from one lounge to another, sampling the exotic Caribbean drinks and becoming one with the dizzying strobe lights, flashing and pulsating, and the strident combination of salsa beat and sixties rock. I am getting into the mood, rising above my recriminations. I have been transported into another world, a separate plain of existence apart in time as well as geography from my real life which has apparently disappeared completely. We do our own successful Long Island shtick at bars too numerous to mention, thereby attracting a list of admirers so lengthy that if we stay a month instead of the planned for week, we will never begin to enjoy them all. This is a fact that makes us heady with success and glee, as well as just plain joy of freedom that captivates us with its infectiousness. The thing is, for me, the feat of attracting them is exciting, but on closer examination, they are all a bunch of gross and boring clods. Or married. What are they doing here alone? The answer to this question is beyond my pay scale. I am not interested in them. I try my luck at the casino, as per my instructions from the travel agent who with a great leer has suggested that this is the very best place to find some action and/or a wealthy husband, whichever thrills my fancy. The trick is to check the craps tables, he says, and to find a well dressed gentleman without a wedding band and with a large pile of chips at his elbow. Then, it's easy, turn on all the charm, work the same spiel that seems so successful at the bar, and move in for the kill. The idea is to capture a worthy, by our predetermined standards, opponent, and then move on to a life of uninterrupted ease and luxury. I am so worn out and hopeless. I have decided to try it, it shouldn't be a total loss, but my heart is not in this exercise. But one thing is apparent, the picture frame of this movie has jammed, and time is standing still...

June, 1970

Here I am once again, a cringing child, in my old familiar seat behind my father. The musty smell of old upholstery, tobacco smoke, and discarded food wrappers makes me gag. My stomach is clenched as I fight back the familiar nausea. I have automatically closed my window, even though my father no longer mouths, chews, sucks, those awful rolls of dried tobacco called cigars; he has rediscovered, instead, his old pipe collection, and now sucks on one of these. Now I do not need to fear the advent of explosive spittle carried from the driver's open window to mine; I will not need to mop slimy gobs of it from my cheek. In the background, my father's favorite radio station mews plaintively, *A cigarette that bears a lipstick's traces...* the melancholy melody, the words of the song hit me like barbed steel darts...

We must have crossed the borough of Queens in record time, Daddy's well worn Oldsmobile weaving and ducking the Kennedy airport traffic, threats and curses shouted and returned, the usual... son of a bitch, what the fuck do you think you're doing? Fuck you, anyway...BEEEEEEP... but I am so numb, so petrified, I register nothing. Trickles of sweat travel downward from my armpits, and yet I feel a chill that goes beyond weather. I am feeling adrift without Eddie, who has been unable to be here to support me today. There is an empty space in my world where his dark, svelte, striking Latino presence should be. I am forced to face this travesty alone, feeling as though yet another of my limbs is missing. I have my hastily scribbled notes clutched in my hand, along with the Blueback covered Order to Show Cause…a demand for me to appear before a court to explain why I am not unfit to care for my six children. Legalese tends to parse its venom in the negative. I am being charged with abandonment. Now my six *abandoned* children packed like sardines in a can, sit silently beside me, except for Tracy, now three, who is nestled in a nest of my arms, on my lap. There is no squirming today, no whining or quibbling. *…An airline ticket to romantic places…*

A shiver skitters through me. Daddy maneuvers the moribund Olds through varieties of side streets, between a motley assortment of wide craters and deep looming crevices, over weather and rutted wear ruined Queens's streets, and into Nassau County, whose roads are just barely better. He knows his way around. He also knows his way around the law, although he hasn't practiced law since his graduation with honors way back in the Great Depression. But he sports his usual confident, arrogant façade. He will know what to do, I have faith. Not so sure if my faith runs to the high powered attorney that we have retained to defend me.

Are we here yet? Kevin, five, true to form, asks the inevitable question, breaking the unbearable silence, and we all chuckle. I murmur the inevitable answer, yes, Kevin, we are right **here**. More rapid laughter, that fades quickly, breaks off in an instant. This is a most serious and threatening time.

A pregnant silence… *Oh how the thought of you clings…* We move silently through a canyon of ancient buildings, taxpayers and storefronts with businesses that have existed for eons. Auto parts, Chinese take-out, Family Deli, Laundromat, Real Estate, Insurance… These establishments are labeled in an assortment of languages. The Hispanic ones catch my eye first, touch deep buttons leading to nostalgic sensations. Flashes race across my mind of another place, if I squint I can believe that I am there, and then quickly I am back in Queens. An effluvium of litter, garbage, is met by indifference. Faded brick, windows clouded with years of exhaust fumes that have solidified into a uniform gray muck. Some of them are boarded up, or show *for rent* signs. I barely notice, as I barely notice the throngs of humanity moving *en masse*, bobbing and weaving along the route, people going about their daily business on a bright June morning in the year 1970. Sad, preoccupied people, concerned with the business of surviving. None of them I muse, my thoughts centered on myself and my predicament has ever had to face a day such as this. I am encased in my personal horror; no one exists outside of it.

*These simple things, remind me of you…*Eddie, I whisper inside my head. Where are you today, what are you doing that is so important that you have been unable to be here with me on this earth shattering day to support me?

White letters on the archetypal green sign at the side of the street declare that we are approaching the Mineola Courthouse, bile rises in my throat, bitter tasting, acidic, burning my throat and mouth. What am I doing here? How has this happened? What if Steve really takes the children away from me? Phrases flit through my mind, they never take children away from the mother, and then another, it's not what you know, it's who you know…Step right up, place your bet. Pick a winner, Ladies and Gentlemen, choose your poison. Who will take the prize? Prizes; six children are the grand prize.

How did this happen? What am I doing here?

I do not recall Daddy parking the car, but that long walk up stone stairs bordered by vast lawns and elaborate shrubbery and early multi-hewed summer flower borders, perennial and annual, stands out in my memory; I glimpse peripherally masses of violets hugging the edges with their characteristic abandon, in obdurate stillness. It is my last mile; I sense the inevitability of some manner of capital punishment awaiting me at the end. I feel numb, flanked by Mom and Dad, who have each put an arm through one of mine, and they all but carry me into the huge building. I sense their concern, their support, but I am not comforted. An image flashes somewhere in the tangled wiring in my mind of the day of my wedding to Steve, when they escorted me down the aisle in similar fashion, my feet barely touching the ground. They cavalierly feign certainty, confidence they do not feel. But they never take children away from the mother. I hang onto the mantra, mindlessly.

I see a massive, dark, carved wood door open, and we are propelled inside as if by some unseen force. I feel my insides shrivel, my mind go blank; blanker that it already is but for the occasional memory flash. Now I have to pee. Why do I always need to pee? Incongruously, I hear daddy's voice in the far distant past, I want you to eat every carrot and *pea* on your plate, wrinkle my nose with the unsettling memory. Can I make it to a restroom, and back again without crumpling into a pile of useless refuse, dissolving into fragments? How will I get through this, I ask silently? My mother glances at me, sideways. She is about to cry, at any moment. Daddy is grim-faced, resolute. I don't remember how I manage to make it happen, but somehow I maneuver myself inside the courtroom. Massive walls, uncountable juxtapositions of polished mahogany paneling and elaborate crown molding, sturdy deeply stained wooden conference tables buffed to a mirror-like finish, a higher than high podium for his Honor, the Judge. In God We Trust, engraved in huge larger than life gold Roman capitals shouts its message from above the podium, just beneath the ceiling. Surreal; I am overwhelmed by the impact of icy cold pomp and circumstance, completely intimidated by architecture, massive and austere. Where am I going on this next voyage, a small voice asks deep inside me? Don't worry, says the oily voice of my well paid attorney as if responding to my internal query, they don't take children away from the mother.

I glance over at Steve, and his attorney, tightlipped and confident, smug and righteous. I am gripped by a sense of terror greater than any sensation I have ever felt before, many times greater than that first crushing labor contraction that signaled incredible pain yet to come. At least that pain was finite, was precursor to getting a baby; this is the signal for interminable loss, for the beginning of the end, the access to a dark place of perpetual ever downward spiraling loss. Eddie's absence is a glaring neon sign, creates a visible vacuum. Steve's sister Elaine, and his father Aaron, are sitting behind Steve, as my parents sit behind me. They, however, are fat cats, and their smug faces tell me that they have already swallowed the canary. I imagine them licking cream from their whiskers, or canary feathers. I am the canary, drowning in cream. Steve learned an immutable lesson at his father's knee. It's not what you know, it's who you know. How many conversations have I overheard at Bar Association meetings held at my home, where I was the caterer, the scullery maid, and the waitress, invisible to the membership at large? Who would have ever known that this would be the final proving point of Aaron's grand theory, to be validated on the head of the mother of his grandchildren and at their expense? Steve's attorney glances over, and winks at mine, a wink, so slight and delicate as to barely be visible. I have served him drinks in my own living room. I have been sitting across the table from him at Kiwanis dinners. Ice rather than blood is racing through my veins.

Oyez, oyez, this session of the Supreme Court in and of the Town of Mineola, in the County of Nassau, in the State of New York, is now in session. A case like this one should be about to be heard according to protocol and statute in Family Court in Suffolk County, where we all live, instead it is being heard in Mineola Supreme, where Steve has his very carefully nurtured business contacts. You would think this would instigate immediate red flags, would be an obvious enough ploy to contest, but it is a classic Catch 22, impossible to fight this issue in this particular venue. I slide down in my seat, a crumpled bundle of defeat. His Honor, the judge, is a member of the same Bar Association of which Steve has been vice president. I have shaken his hand, in the day, at one or the other Knights of something dinner: Columbus, Pythias? This is a show. There is no way I can win this battle. Maybe, hopes an inveterate Pollyanna, I am imagining all this. Maybe everything will be all right. Maybe Steve will realize...

He is a good person, an honorable man, whispers Pollyanna in my ear, he would never do that to his beloved children, or to me, not even to me. Take my babies away. He would never separate children from their mother. He once represented a streetwalker in one of his rare court appearances, who was being sued for custody by her child's father, fought with devout intensity and morally indignant certainty, and won for the mother. Imagine that. They never take children away from the mother, he said almost piously, at the time. The Steve I fell in love with so many years ago could not commit an act like that. I attempt to convince myself, but my own words fall on hollow ears. That is the reason we are here, indeed. My nerves are strung so tightly that I fear their imminent strained splitting. Steve takes the stand.

Mr. Heffner, are you the petitioner in this proceeding? His attorney, Gabe Kohn, his solid presence enhanced by gray silk suiting, crisp button down shirt and elegant sky blue tie, his large florid coarse featured face framed by masses of thick gray tipped bronze hair begins questioning his client. The atmosphere in this immense hall is so tense and fraught with emotion that Gabe's skillfully framed words echo like gunshot in the icy silence, echo threateningly in the large court room....

I am.

Are you an attorney?

Yes.

Admitted to practice in the State of New York?

Yes.

Where do you maintain your office?

Jamaica Avenue, New York.

Were you and the respondent married on June 15, 1958?

Yes.

Where did the marriage take place? Kew Gardens Hills, New York.

Did you have children of that marriage? Yes. Are they the subject of this proceeding?

Bibliography

Twentieth Century American Art – Erika Doss, Oxford Press
The Twentieth Century Artbook – Phaedon Press Limited
Chronicle of the Twentieth Century – Chronicle Publications
The Millennium Year by Year – D.K. Publishing, Inc.
The Chronicle of World History – Konechy and Konechy

In the recreation of my memories, upon occasion I do take some poetic license, but to the best of my information and belief everything that I present as fact is indeed true, and as for everything else, I believe it to be true.

About the Author...

Lynne Heffner Ferrante has been a painter, sculptor, printmaker, writer, poet for most of her life. She has shown her work internationally, and in several of her own galleries on Long Island, New York. She has taught art, presided over art organizations, and studied law. Her life has been a long journey filled with happenstance, joyful and sad; she is the mother of seven children. She has been writing this story for over forty years and is currently completing both books II and III and a color anthology of her art which will follow soon. Lynne and her husband, who have been together for thirty five years, live in East Hampton, New York, accompanied by their three dogs, a Bichon Frise and two Maltese.

Made in the USA
Charleston, SC
24 August 2012